Communications
in Computer and Information Science 367

T0212840

Ivan I. Ivanov   Marten van Sinderen
Frank Leymann   Tony Shan (Eds.)

Cloud Computing and Services Science

Second International Conference, CLOSER 2012
Porto, Portugal, April 18-21, 2012
Revised Selected Papers

 Springer

Volume Editors

Ivan I. Ivanov
State University of New York
Empire State College
Long Island Center, NY, USA
E-mail: ivan.ivanov@esc.edu

Marten van Sinderen
University of Twente
Enschede, The Netherlands
E-mail: m.j.vansinderen@utwente.nl

Frank Leymann
University of Stuttgart
Institute of Architecture of Application Systems
Stuttgart, Germany
E-mail: leymann@iaas.uni-stuttgart.de

Tony Shan
CTS, Charlotte, NC, USA
E-mail: tonyshan@live.com

ISSN 1865-0929   e-ISSN 1865-0937
ISBN 978-3-319-04518-4   e-ISBN 978-3-319-04519-1
DOI 10.1007/978-3-319-04519-1
Springer Cham Heidelberg New York Dordrecht London

Library of Congress Control Number: 2013957788

CR Subject Classification (1998): D.2, K.6, C.2, H.2, H.4

Typesetting: Camera-ready by author, data conversion by Scientific Publishing Services, Chennai, India

Printed on acid-free paper

Springer is part of Springer Science+Business Media (www.springer.com)

Preface

This book includes extended and revised versions of a set of selected papers from CLOSER 2012 (the Second International Conference on Cloud Computing and Services Science), held in Porto, Portugal, in 2012, and organized by the Institute for Systems and Technologies of Information, Control and Communication (INSTICC), in cooperation with the ACM Special Interest Group on Management Information Systems (ACM SIGMIS), EuroCloud, and Euro-Cloud Portugal. The conference was also technically co-sponsored by SINTEF and mOSAIC.

The purpose of the CLOSER series of conferences is to bring together researchers, engineers, and practitioners interested in the emerging area of cloud computing. The conference has four main tracks, namely, "Cloud Computing Fundamentals," "Services Science Foundation for Cloud Computing," "Cloud Computing Platforms and Applications," and "Cloud Computing Enabling Technology."

In the last few years, cloud computing has expanded steadily, both horizontally across industries and vertically in organizations' information technology stack, for raw computing and storage, databases and system's utilities, e-collaborative tools, and enterprise applications. Certainly cloud computing is a phenomenon grasping businesses and professional communities' attentiveness in various important dimensions. Cloud computing development likewise creates exciting challenges and opportunities for scholars, developers, and IT experts. It is a thrilling journey driven by many agendas such as: cost cutbacks; better utilization of existing IT infrastructures and systems; and designing, developing, and delivering dynamic mobile and interactive computational services based on advanced provisional models. The immense economic demands in the last several years, in conjunction with the immediate reduction of upfront capital and operational costs when cloud-based services are employed, increase the speed and the scale of cloud computing creations and adoptions.

While information and communication technology developments have enabled the shift from manufacturing to service industries, this did not coincide with the emerging of an academic discipline that provided training and conducted research into the management and engineering of services from an integrated perspective. Only a few years ago, the need for such a discipline was identified, and services science was established as a blending of, among others, computer science, engineering, management, and social science. Today the services sector already accounts for up to 80% of the economic activity in many developed countries. Services science can ground the development of "moving to the cloud" with a solid understanding of new cloud-based services, leading to knowledge on how they should be designed, deployed, and managed, and how they affect economy and society. With this linking, problems of diverse nature can be identified and addressed in early stages, and opportunities can be more effectively exploited.

CLOSER 2012 received 145 paper submissions from all continents. From these, 27 papers were published and presented as full papers, 44 were accepted for short presentation, and another 20 for poster presentation. These numbers, leading to a full-paper acceptance ratio of 19% and an oral paper acceptance ratio of 49%, show the intention of preserving a high-quality forum for this and next editions of the conference.

The papers included in this book were selected from those with the best reviews taking also into account the quality of their presentation at the conference, as assessed by the session chairs. We hope that you find these papers interesting, and we trust they represent a helpful reference for all those who need to address any of the research areas mentioned above.

We wish to thank all those who supported and helped to organize the conference. On behalf of the conference Organizing Committee, we would like to thank the authors, whose work mostly contributed to a very successful conference, and to the members of the Program Committee, whose expertise and diligence were instrumental in ensuring the quality of final contributions.

Last but not least, we would like to thank Springer for their collaboration in getting this book to print.

September 2013

Ivan Ivanov
Marten van Sinderen
Frank Leymann
Tony Shan

Organization

Conference Chair

Tony Shan   Keane Inc., USA

Program Co-chairs

Frank Leymann   University of Stuttgart, Germany
Ivan Ivanov   SUNY Empire State College, USA
Marten van Sinderen   University of Twente, The Netherlands

Organizing Committee

Marina Carvalho   INSTICC, Portugal
Helder Coelhas   INSTICC, Portugal
Patrícia Duarte   INSTICC, Portugal
Bruno Encarnação   INSTICC, Portugal
Liliana Medina   INSTICC, Portugal
Carla Mota   INSTICC, Portugal
Raquel Pedrosa   INSTICC, Portugal
Vitor Pedrosa   INSTICC, Portugal
Cláudia Pinto   INSTICC, Portugal
Susana Ribeiro   INSTICC, Portugal
José Varela   INSTICC, Portugal
Pedro Varela   INSTICC, Portugal

Program Committee

Marco Aiello, The Netherlands
Jörn Altmann, Korea, Republic of
Cosimo Anglano, Italy
Joseph Antony, Australia
Claudio Ardagna, Italy
Liliana Ardissono, Italy
Steven Van Assche, Belgium
Muhammad Atif, Australia
Benjamin Aziz, UK
Amelia Badica, Romania
Remi Badonnel, France
Janaka Balasooriya, USA

Simona Bernardi, Spain
Karin Bernsmed, Norway
Nik Bessis, UK
Sami Bhiri, Ireland
Stefano Bocconi, The Netherlands
Ivona Brandic, Austria
Francisco Brasileiro, Brazil
Iris Braun, Germany
Andrey Brito, Brazil
Ralf Bruns, Germany
Anna Brunstrom, Sweden
Rebecca Bulander, Germany

Moreno Marzolla, Italy
Ioannis Mavridis, Greece
Michele Mazzucco, Estonia
Richard McClatchey, UK
Alba Melo, Brazil
Jose Ramon Gonzalez de Mendivil,
  Spain
José Merseguer, Spain
Barton P. Miller, USA
Raffaela Mirandola, Italy
Owen Molloy, Ireland
Rubén Santiago Montero, Spain
Reagan Moore, USA
Kamran Munir, UK
Víctor Méndez Muñoz, Spain
Wolfgang E. Nagel, Germany
Hidemoto Nakada, Japan
Philippe Navaux, Brazil
Lee Newcombe, UK
Hamid Reza Motahari Nezhad, USA
Jean-Marc Nicod, France
Mara Nikolaidou, Greece
Karsten Oberle, Germany
Enn Ounapuu, Estonia
Alexander Paar, Germany
Federica Paganelli, Italy
Sara Paiva, Portugal
Dhabaleswar K. Panda, USA
Fabio Panzieri, Italy
David Paul, Australia
Siani Pearson, UK
Jih-Kwon Peir, USA
Dana Petcu, Romania
Dorina Petriu, Canada
Giovanna Petrone, Italy
Maria Chiara Pettenati, Italy
Agostino Poggi, Italy
Wolfgang Prinz, Germany
Juha Puustjärvi, Finland
Li Qi, China
Judy Qiu, USA
Rajendra Raj, USA
Arkalgud Ramaprasad, USA
Manuel Ramos-Cabrer, Spain
Andrew Rau-Chaplin, Canada

Norbert Ritter, Germany
Tarcísio da Rocha, Brazil
Luis Rodero-Merino, Spain
Chunming Rong, Norway
Pedro Frosi Rosa, Brazil
Jonathan Rouzaud-Cornabas, France
Marek Rusinkiewicz, USA
Elena Sanchez-Nielsen, Spain
Alexander Schill, Germany
Lutz Schubert, Germany
Giovanni Semeraro, Italy
Carlos Serrao, Portugal
Marten van Sinderen, The Netherlands
Cosmin Stoica Spahiu, Romania
Josef Spillner, Germany
Ralf Steinmetz, Germany
Heinz Stockinger, Switzerland
Philipp Strube, Germany
Yasuyuki Tahara, Japan
Yehia Taher, The Netherlands
Domenico Talia, Italy
Samir Tata, France
Cedric Tedeschi, France
Joe Tekli, Lebanon
Maria Beatriz Toledo, Brazil
Orazio Tomarchio, Italy
Johan Tordsson, Sweden
Paolo Trunfio, Italy
Hong-Linh Truong, Austria
Eddy Truyen, Belgium
Konstantinos Tserpes, Greece
Francesco Tusa, Italy
Astrid Undheim, Norway
Athina Vakali, Greece
Luis M. Vaquero, UK
Fabio Luciano Verdi, Brazil
Massimo Villari, Italy
Sabrina de Capitani Di Vimercati,
  Italy
Bruno Volckaert, Belgium
Hiroshi Wada, Australia
Chen Wang, Australia
Martijn Warnier, The Netherlands
Dennis Wegener, Germany
Erik Wilde, USA

Marco Winckler, France
Jan-Jan Wu, Taiwan
George Yee, Canada

Ustun Yildiz, USA
Zhifeng Yun, USA

Auxiliary Reviewers

Suhair Alshehri, USA
Viktoriya Degeler, The Netherlands
Ando Emerencia, The Netherlands
Daniel Espling, Sweden
Elena Gómez-Martínez, Spain
Juan S. Gonzalez, Spain
Christophe Gravier, France
Leo Iaquinta, Italy
Wubin Li, Sweden
Therese Libourel, France
Toni Mastelic, Austria

Giuseppe Di Modica, Italy
Giuliano Andrea Pagani,
    The Netherlands
Tommaso Pecorella, Italy
Pasqualina Potena, Italy
Aurora Pozo, Brazil
Ismael Bouassida Rodriguez, France
Ricardo J. Rodríguez, Spain
Johann Stan, France
Sylvain Vauttier, France
Shuying Wang, Canada

Invited Speakers

Arlindo Dias
Helen Karatza
Frédéric Desprez

Fabrizio Gagliardi

IBM, Portugal
Aristotle University of Thessaloniki, Greece
Laboratoire de L'Informatique du Parallélisme
    - LIP/Institut National de Recherche en
    Informatique et en Automatique – Inria,
    France
Microsoft Research Switzerland

Table of Contents

Invited Paper

Adding Virtualization Capabilities to the Grid'5000 Testbed*

Daniel Balouek[1], Alexandra Carpen Amarie[1], Ghislain Charrier[1], Frédéric Desprez[1], Emmanuel Jeannot[1], Emmanuel Jeanvoine[1], Adrien Lèbre[2], David Margery[1], Nicolas Niclausse[1], Lucas Nussbaum[3], Olivier Richard[4], Christian Perez[1], Flavien Quesnel[2], Cyril Rohr[1], and Luc Sarzyniec[3]

[1] INRIA, France
[2] Ecole des Mines de Nantes, France
[3] Université de Lorraine, France
[4] Université de Grenoble, France
FirstName.LastName@inria.fr, FirstName.LastName@mines-nantes.fr,
FirstName.LastName@univ-lorraine.fr, FirstName.LastName@imag.fr

Abstract. Almost ten years after its premises, the Grid'5000 testbed has become one of the most complete testbed for designing or evaluating large-scale distributed systems. Initially dedicated to the study of High Performance Computing, the infrastructure has evolved to address wider concerns related to Desktop Computing, the Internet of Services and more recently the Cloud Computing paradigm. This paper present recent improvements of the Grid'5000 software and services stack to support large-scale experiments using virtualization technologies as building blocks. Such contributions include the deployment of customized software environments, the reservation of dedicated network domain and the possibility to isolate them from the others, and the automation of experiments with a REST API. We illustrate the interest of these contributions by describing three different use-cases of large-scale experiments on the Grid'5000 testbed. The first one leverages virtual machines to conduct larger experiments spread over 4000 peers. The second one describes the deployment of 10000 KVM instances over 4 Grid'5000 sites. Finally, the last use case introduces a *one-click* deployment tool to easily deploy major IaaS solutions. The conclusion highlights some important challenges of Grid'5000 related to the use of OpenFlow and to the management of applications dealing with tremendous amount of data.

Keywords: Distributed Systems, Large-Scale Testbed, Virtualization, Cloud Computing, Experiments.

1 Introduction

The evolution of technology allows larger and highly distributed systems to be built, which provide new capabilities, in terms of applications as well as in terms of

---

* The Grid'5000 experimental testbed and all development actions are supervised and financed by the INRIA ALADDIN framework with support from CNRS, RENATER, and several Universities as well as other funding bodies (see https://www.grid5000.fr). Grid'5000 experiments are partially supported by the INRIA large scale initiative Hemera. The IaaS deployment utility is a particular action developed with the support of the EIT ICT Labs.

I. Ivanov et al. (Eds.): CLOSER 2012, CCIS 367, pp. 3–20, 2013.

infrastructures like peer-to-peer systems, Grids, and more recently (federations of) Cloud platforms. Such large scale distributed and parallel systems raise specific research issues and computer science, as other sciences, needs instruments to validate theoretical research results as well as software developments. Although simulation and emulation are generally used to get a glance of the behavior of new algorithms, they use over-simplified models in order to reduce their execution time and thus cannot be accurate enough. Leveraging a scientific instrument to perform actual experiments is a undeniable advantage. However conducting experiments on real environments is still too often a challenge for researchers, students, and practitioners: first, because of the unavailability of dedicated resources but second also because of the inability to create controlled experimental conditions, and to deal with the so large variability of software requirements. Started in 2003 under the initiative of the French ministry of Research, the Grid'5000 testbed is a scientific instrument for the study of large scale parallel and distributed systems. With the aim of providing a highly reconfigurable, controllable and monitorable experimental platform [14], Grid'5000 was solid enough to attract more than 600 users and led to a large number of research results and publications. Nowadays, Grid'5000 is internationally recognized and serves as a foundation for new scale platforms, e.g. FutureGrid [17] in the USA. With almost ten years of background, several members of its scientific or technical board are invited take part to different working groups, events focusing on the design and the building of new experimental testbeds [16,27] with the ultimate objective of improving the quality of experiments.

The Grid'5000 instrument is continuously evolving toward providing more flexibility, more control of both the electronic devices composing the infrastructure as well as of the experiments running over. The scientific and technical boards carefully follow the major trends and the latest innovations of distributed and parallel systems from both hardware and software point of views. This enables to renew the infrastructure while ensuring the delivering of a testbed that meets user-expectations. As an example, one of the most important change of the last decade is the renewal of interest of virtualization technologies. The virtual machine concept that enables to run any system over any other one has radically changed the use of distributed systems, leading to new large-scale platforms built upon shared data-centres and usually classified into the new cloud-computing IaaS (Infrastructure-as-a-Service) paradigm. Indeed, in addition to abstract the complexity of IT systems, the use of virtualization is motivated by the fact that physical resources are usually under-used and that virtualization technologies enable to consolidate them and thus improve the productivity of the whole platforms.

Considering that the current trend consists of "virtualizing" all physical resources, adding virtualization capabilities to Grid'5000 is obviously expected. From the end-users point of view, the objective is twofold: first, it will enable to leverage virtualization technologies to improve the quality of the experiments at a larger scale. Second, it will enable to investigate new concerns related to the management of virtualized infrastructures. Indeed, despite of the tremendous progress in the virtualization area and the large number of companies providing virtualized platforms for various users, several important issues remain to be solved. Among them, Quality of Service (QoS), fault-tolerance, energy management, and scalability are major ones. Extending the Grid'5000 software and services stack to investigate such concerns is important for the community. The key progress, beyond the state of the art, is to provide the user with an infrastructure where each component can be virtualized. In addition to the system virtualization capabilities provided by modern computers, Grid'5000 targets the virtualization of active network equipments as well as storage facilities.

In this paper, we describe the latest contributions of the Grid'5000 software and services stack to make large-scale experiments involving low level virtual technologies up to full IaaS software stacks. Grid'5000 is one the very few platforms that allows to conduct such experiments between multi-sites and in an isolated and reproductible manner.

The reminder of this paper is structured as follows. In Section 2, we give an overview of the Grid'5000 instrument. Section 3 describes the latest contributions of the Grid'5000 software and service stack while Section 4 illustrates the use of such contributions through discussing three use-cases. Other experimental testbeds are introduced in Section 5. Finally, we discuss perspectives and conclude this article in Section 6.

2 Grid'5000 Overview

In 2003, several teams working around parallel and distributed systems designed a platform to support experiment-driven research in parallel and distributed systems. This platform, called Grid'5000 [14] and opened to users since 2005, was solid enough to attract a large number of users. It has led to a large number of research results: 575 users per year, more than 700 research papers, 600 different experiments, 24 ANR projects and 10 European projects, 50 PhD, and the creation of startup companies as well.

Grid'5000 is located mainly in France (see Figure 1), with one operational site in Luxembourg and a second site, not implementing the complete stack, in Porto Alegre, Brazil. Grid'5000 provides a testbed supporting experiments on various types of distributed systems (high-performance computing, grids, peer-to-peer systems, cloud computing, and others), on all layers of the software stack. The core testbed currently comprises 10 sites. Grid'5000 is composed of 26 clusters, 1,700 nodes, and 7,400 CPU cores, with various generations of technology (Intel (60%), AMD (40%), CPUs from one to 12 cores, Myrinet, Infiniband {S, D, Q}DR and 2 GPU clusters). A dedicated 10 Gbps backbone network is provided by RENATER (the French National Research and Education Network). In order to prevent Grid'5000 machines from being the source of a distributed denial of service, connections from Grid'5000 to the Internet are strictly limited to a list of whitelisted data and software sources, updated on demand.

From the user point of view, Grid'5000 is a set of sites with the exact same software environment. The driving idea is that users willing to face software heterogeneity should add controlled heterogeneity themselves during their experiments. Three basic workflows are supported when staging an experiment on Grid'5000: a web interface-based workflow, an API-based workflow, and a shell-based workflow. These differ not only in the interfaces used but also in the process they support.

The core steps identified to run an experiment are (1) finding and booking suitable resources for the experiment and (2) deploying the experiment apparatus on the resources. Finding suitable resources can be approached in two ways: either users browse a description of the available resources and then make a booking, or they describe their

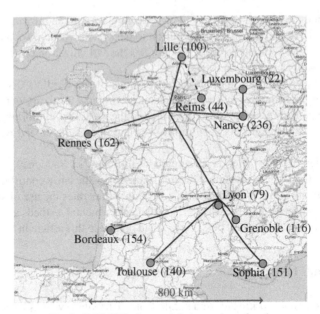

Fig. 1. Grid'5000 sites and their number of nodes

needs to the system that will locate appropriate resources. We believe both approaches should be supported, and therefore a machine-readable description of Grid'5000 is available through the reference API. It can be browsed by using a web interface or by running a program over the API. At the same time, the resource scheduler on each site is fed with the resource properties so that a user can ask for resources describing the required properties (e.g., 25 nodes connected to the same switch with at least 8 cores and 32 GB of memory). Once matching resources are found, they can be reserved either for exclusive access at a given time or for exclusive access when they become available. In the latter case, a script is given at reservation time, as in classical batch scheduling.

Several tools are provided to facilitate experiments. Most of them were originally developed specifically for Grid'5000. Grid'5000 users select and reserve resources with the OAR batch scheduler [13,30]. Users can install their own system image on the nodes (without any virtualization layer) using Kadeploy [18]. Experiments requiring network isolation can use KaVLAN to reconfigure switches and isolate nodes from the test of the testbed. Several monitoring tools (resource usage on nodes with Ganglia, energy consumption) are also available. All tools can be accessed by a REST API to ease the automation of experiments using scripts. The tools used to support the experiments over Grid'5000 will be described in Section 3.

Different approaches to deploying the experimental apparatus are also supported. At the infrastructure level users either use the preconfigured environment on nodes, called the production environment, or they install their own environment. An environment consists of a disk image to be copied on the node and of the path in the disk image of the kernel to boot. This environment can be prepared in advance by modifying and saving reference environments made available to users, or a reference environment can be dynamically customized after it is deployed on the resources. The approach chosen can affect the repeatability of the results. Therefore, choices concerning the experiment testbed environment are left to the experimenters.

Whatever approach used for the first two steps described here, access to resources (sites and nodes) is done through SSH. Each site has its own NFS server. This design decision was taken to ensure that resources of a particular site can be used even when the link to other sites is undergoing maintenance. In other words, the infrastructure does not depend on a single site to stay operational—an important consideration because maintenance events become frequent when 10 sites are operated.

3   A Software Stack to Support Experiments

This section describes four key Grid'5000 services that contribute to support virtualization and Cloud experiments on Grid'5000. *Kadeploy* (Section 3.1) enables users to deploy their software stacks of choice on the nodes. *g5k-subnets* (Section 3.2) and *KaVLAN* (Section 3.3) provide two different ways to configure the network (respectively by reserving IP address ranges, and by isolating an experiment from the rest of the testbed using on-the-fly switches reconfiguration). Finally, the Grid'5000 REST API (Section 3.4) uniformizes the access to those services that facilitate the automated execution of experiments.

3.1   Providing Custom Experimental Environments with *Kadeploy*

On most clusters, users do not have the option of changing the operating system installed on nodes. This is a severe problem for experimentation, since experimenters often need to perform experiments in many different contexts in order to extend the scope of an experimental result by verifying that it is not limited to specific experimental conditions (specific kernel, library or compiler version, configuration, etc.).

Grid'5000 enables the deployment of custom software stacks (including the operating system) on bare hardware[1]. This allows users to perform experiments without being bound to one particular Linux distribution or version, or even operating system. Users could use their own modified Linux kernels to work on live migration or memory deduplication techniques, or even install FreeBSD or Solaris to evaluate the interest of process containers available on those operating systems (such as FreeBSD Jails or OpenSolaris Zones) for Cloud computing.

While it is common for Cloud infrastructures to provide the ability to deploy custom OS images in virtual machines, Grid'5000 provides this feature on physical machines, which brings two advantages. First, it avoids the overhead of the virtualization layer, which can be a problem when doing experiments involving performance measurements. While the overhead is extremely low for CPU-intensive workload, it can be much higher for IO-intensive workloads. Second, it allows deployed environments to contain virtual machines themselves, without requiring the use of *nested* virtualization (hypervisor inside a virtual machine), which is not supported very well by today's hypervisors.

On Grid'5000, the installation of custom OS images on nodes is implemented using

---

[1] This has been recently named as Hardware-as-a-Service.

the *Kadeploy* [18] cluster provisioning system, which has been developed in the context of the Grid'5000 project. *Kadeploy* achieves efficient and scalable installation of system images using advanced mechanisms (adaptative tree-based command execution thanks to TakTuk [15]; chain-based image broadcast [18]). The deployment process is controlled by an automata to handle the unavoidable errors (due to unreliable protocols and hardware), and the corresponding retry policies. Thanks to those features, the installation of a 1.5 GB image on 130 nodes takes less than 10 minutes. Additionally, instead of restricting deployments to the system administrator, *Kadeploy* provides flexible permissions management to allow users to start deployments on their own. This is used on Grid'5000 to enable users to deploy their own deployment environments.

Grid'5000 users can provide their own deployment images, and install them on nodes with no prior validation from the technical team. While minor problems have been encountered (e.g. a FreeBSD network driver that was disabling – until the next reboot – the IPMI implementation sharing the Ethernet port with the operating system), no major problem has been encountered due to this policy. This is also an example of the security policy that is deployed throughout Grid'5000. We focus on mitigating normal user errors, and on checking users before giving them access to the testbed, but we do not try much to fight malicious actions from users since this would often limit the experimental capabilities of the testbed at an unacceptable level.

3.2 Network Reservation with *g5k-subnets*

Virtual machines used during experiments must be accommodated on the testbed's network. While it is sometimes possible to limit experiments to purely virtual networks (inside one physical machine, or spanning several physical machines using e.g. Open vSwitch), this would be a severe limitation. Additionally, Grid'5000 is composed of several sites with routing between sites (Figure 1), and different users can run concurrent experiments on the same Grid'5000 site.

Therefore, techniques to reserve address ranges or to isolate an experiment from the rest of the testbed are needed. Grid'5000 provides two such solutions: *g5k-subnets* (described in this section) extends Grid'5000 resource reservation mechanism to allow users to reserve IP ranges for their virtual machines; *KaVLAN* (presented in the next section) reconfigures network switches so that an experiment is isolated from the rest of the testbed.

The whole $10/8$ subnet ($10.0.0.0 - 10.255.255.255$) is dedicated to user virtual machines on Grid'5000. The first half ($10.0 - 10.127$) is used for KaVLAN, while the second half ($10.128 - 10.255$) is used by *g5k-subnets*. Since Grid'5000 sites are interconnected via L3 routing, the $10.128/9$ network is divided into one $/14$ network per site ($2^{18} = 262144$ IP addresses per site). This $/14$ network per site is again divided, with the last $/16$ network ($2^{16} = 65536$ IP addresses) dedicated to attributing IP addresses over DHCP for machines in the $00:16:3E:XX:XX:XX$ MAC range (which is the Xen reserved MAC range).

The last $3 * 2^{16} = 196608$ IP addresses are allocated through reservation with *g5k-subnets*. *g5k-subnets* is integrated in the *Resource Management System* used on Grid'5000, OAR [30]. Users can reserve a set of network IP addresses (from $/22$ to a

/16) at the same time as nodes: the following command reserves two /22 ranges and 8 nodes:

```
oarsub -l slash_22=2+nodes=8 -I
```

Once a specific IP range has been allocated, users can retrieve it using a command-line tool. Additional information, such as DNS servers, default gateway, broadcast address, etc. is made available through this tool.

It is worth noting that *g5k-subnets* only manages the reservation of IP address ranges, not of MAC addresses. Since the available MAC address range (47 bits, since one is used to indicate multicast frames) is much larger than the available IP range (18 bits), choosing MAC addresses at random does not result in significant chances of collision. This strategy is also used by several Cloud software stacks.

Finally, *g5k-subnets* does not enforce the reservation. A malicious user could *steal* IP addresses from a concurrent user. If a user requires stronger protection, the use of KaVLAN is recommended.

3.3   Network Isolation with *KaVLAN*

In some cases, the reservation of IP ranges, as provided by *g5k-subnets*, is not sufficient to satisfy the experimenters' needs. Some experiments are either too sensitive to external noise (coming from broadcasts, or from unsolicited connections), or too disruptive (e.g. when using network discovery protocols that rely on network broadcast). A typical example in experiments involving virtualization is the installation of a DHCP server to serve IP addresses to virtual machines. If not properly configured, it could start answering DHCP requests from other nodes on the testbed. Such experiments cannot be performed on the same network as other experiments, as they could compromise the testbed's infrastructure or other experiments, or be compromised themselves.

KaVLAN is a tool developed inside the Grid'5000 project that provides controlled isolation of user experiments at the network level. *KaVLAN* isolates experiments in their own 801.1q VLAN by reconfiguring the testbed's switches for the duration of the experiment. It can connect to switches using SNMP, SSH and telnet, supports a number of different routers and switches (from Cisco, HP, 3com, Extreme Networks and Brocade), and can easily be extended to support other products.

Several different types of VLANs are provided by *KaVLAN* to meet different user needs (Figure 2):

- **Local VLAN** provides users with a fully isolated network that is only accessible by connecting (generally using SSH) from a machine connected to both the VLAN and the testbed's network;
- **Routed VLAN** also provides users with a separate L2 network, but that network can be reached from any node of the testbed since the network is routed by the site's router. It can typically be used to deploy a complex infrastructure including a DHCP server (e.g. a Cloud middleware) inside the VLAN.
- Instead of providing isolation limited to one site (as with local and routed VLAN), a **Global VLAN** provides a separate L2 network at the scale of the testbed, using 802.1ad (Q-in-Q) on the testbed's backbone network. It is accessible from the default testbed's network using routing.

VLAN type	Ethernet isolation	IP isolation	Multi-site	# of VLAN
local	yes	no	no	3 per site
routed	yes	no	no	3+3 per site
global	yes	no	yes	1 per site

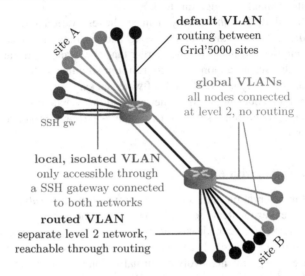

Fig. 2. Types of VLAN provided by *KaVLAN*

KaVLAN is also used on Grid'5000 in order to provide temporary interconnections with other testbeds. For example, nodes can be removed from Grid'5000, and integrated in another testbed, for the duration of an experiment.

3.4   Providing a Unified Interface with a REST API

Some Grid'5000 services are traditionally used through command-line interfaces. While this a good step towards enabling the automation of experiments through scripting, it still has a few limitations:

- Developing user-friendly command-line interfaces is hard and time-consuming.
- Ensuring consistency between several tools on the naming of parameters or the formatting of outputs is hard, and even harder if backward compatibility must be supported.
- Several tools output large volumes of structured data. In that case, parsing the output of a command in a script is inconvenient, as there is often a need to handle error conditions at the same time.
- Running external commands from scripts is inconvenient, since those commands often need to be executed on specific machines over SSH.

In order to overcome those limitations in Grid'5000, the focus has been put in providing a consistent REST API that provides access to the various Grid'5000 services. The Grid'5000 API is composed of several more focused APIs:

Reference API. This API gives access to a detailed description of most elements of the testbed, such as nodes (with their hardware description) and network equipments and links. This API can be used by users to find resources with specific character-istics (e.g. node with Intel Nehalem architecture, and at least 24 GB or RAM), or to ensure that nodes are still conforming to their description – a tool implementing this verification runs on nodes at each boot.

Monitoring API. This API provides the state of node (available for reservation, used by a job currently running on the testbed, etc.). It can be used by users, in combi-nation with the Reference API, to find available resources matching their needs.

Metrology API. This API provides a common interface to various sensors, either soft-ware (e.g. Ganglia) or hardware (e.g. energy consumption). Custom metrics can also be added. It is aimed at providing users with the performance status of their nodes during their experiments.

Jobs API. While the OAR resource management system is traditionally used through a command-line interface, this API provides a REST interface to submit and manage jobs.

Deployments API. Similarly to the Jobs API, the Deployments API provides a higher-level interface to Kadeploy.

Several interfaces have been developed on top of the Grid'5000 API. First, a web interface enables users to perform most actions, including resource selection (using the Reference API) and reservation (using the Jobs API). Command-line tools have also been developed. For example, *g5k-campaign* aims at orchestrating experiments startup. It is featured in Section 4.3 where it is used–with custom engines–to deploy Cloud frameworks.

4   Grid'5000 and Virtualization Capabilities: Use-cases

This section presents three use-cases that leverage latest contributions and system vir-tualization as building blocks. In the first one, virtualization is used as a mean to tem-porary emulate a larger testbed composed of 4000 peers. In the second one, a set of scripts that enables the deployment of a significant number of VMs upon Grid'5000 is presented. Thanks to these scripts, end-users may investigate particular concerns related to the management of large-scale virtualized infrastructures at low-level. The last one deals with the automation of IaaS deployment. Lot of Grid'5000 users want to inves-tigate the impact of the virtualization layer on a particular workload. Delivering a tool that relieves end-users with the burden of deploying and configuring an IaaS system is a real advantage. In such scenarios, Grid'5000 is seen as an IaaS platform where end-users may provision VMs according to the needs of the applications. Although adding virtualization capabilities to Grid'5000 is an on-going task targeting the virtualization of all devices, we believe that these three use-cases are already representative of a wide scope of experiments.

4.1   Testing the Scalability of Kadeploy by Deploying 4000 Virtual Machines

Large-scale testbeds are a rare resource. With its 1300+ nodes, Grid'5000 is already one of the largest experimental testbeds. However, its size can still be a limiting factor for some experiments. One example of such experiments is the evaluation of the suitability of *Kadeploy* (presented in Section 3.1) to manage Exascale clusters, which can be composed of thousands of compute nodes. On Grid'5000, Kadeploy is installed using one separate installation per site, rather than one global installation, which does not reflect the configuration expected on Exascale clusters, with only one installation managing all the nodes.

We therefore performed a set of experiments on Grid'5000 to evaluate the performance of Kadeploy when used to manage a 4000-nodes cluster [26]. In order to create a level-2 network to accomodate all the virtual machines, we used a global KaVLAN network spanning four sites with a diameter of 1000 km. 668 nodes where used during that experiment (out of 783 available with the required capabilities). 635 were used to accomodate 3999 KVM virtual machines (managed using custom-made scripts), while the remaining 33 nodes where used to host the Kadeploy server, a DNS server, a DHCP server, and HTTP servers used to serve the minimal system image used during the Kadeploy deployment.

The automated configuration of our 4000-nodes Kadeploy testbed took 40 minutes, decomposed in: 20 minutes to reserve and deploy 668 Grid'5000 nodes; 5 minutes to prepare all physical nodes; 15 minutes to instantiate the 4000 virtual machines. At this point, it was possible to perform Kadeploy deployments over all the virtual machines. We performed a successful deployment of 3838 virtual machines using a 430 MB-environment in 57 minutes.

While the success of this experiment demonstrates the ability of Kadeploy to manage clusters of 4000 nodes as well as the adequacy of Grid'5000 to perform large-scale experiments in virtualized environments, it also allowed us to identify some bottlenecks in Kadeploy, which opened the path for future works.

4.2   Playing with VMs at Large-Scale

Live-migration of virtual machines is one of the key-point of virtualization technologies. Besides simplifying maintenance operations, it provides an undeniable advantage to implement fine-grained scheduling policies such as consolidation or load-balancing strategies.

However, manipulating VMs throughout a large-scale and highly-distributed infrastructure as easy as traditional OSes handle processes on local nodes is still facing several issues. Among the major ones, we can notice the implementation of suited mechanisms to efficiently schedule VMs and to ensure the access to the VM images through different locations. Such mechanisms should assume to be able to control, monitor, and communicate with both the host OSes and the guest instances spread across the infrastructure at any time. If several works have addressed these concerns, the real experiments are in most cases limited to few nodes and there is a clear need to study such concerns at higher scales. With this objective in mind, a set of scripts[12] have been designed over the Grid'5000 software stack. They allow us to easily start a significant number of KVM instances upon several sites of the testbed. These instances can then be used at user convenience in order to investigate particular concerns such as, for instance, the impact of migrating a large amount of VMs simultaneously or the study of new proposals dealing with VM images management. Through the use of a global VLAN (Section 3.3), the

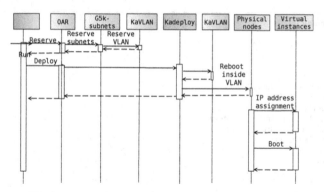

Fig. 3. Sequence diagram of the infrastructure installation

user may choose to virtualize all sites as a unique one or not. This enables to avoid network domain issues when a VM is migrated from one network to another one.

To deliver such a setup, the script goes through 3 logical steps:

Booking Resources. Using the *disco* tool that provides multi-criteria and multi-site search for available Grid'5000 resources, the first script is in charge of finding the available nodes that support hardware virtualization, booking them and requesting network resources (i.e. a /18 subnet for the IPs and a global VLAN if need be). These resources are mandatory to deal with IP assignment and routing within the infrastructure.

Deploying and Configuring Physical Machines. This task consists of deploying bare-metal hypervisors and installing the packages related to the virtualization on the host machines. It is worth noting that during the deployment phase, an additional option of *Kadeploy* enables to reboot each physical machine inside a particular VLAN. The script is leveraging this argument if the experiment involves several sites and a global VLAN has been booked. At the end of the deployment, the global routing is configured on each node and the network is isolated from the usual routing policy (cf Section. 3.3).

Starting the Virtual Machines. The virtual instances are started simultaneously, using a hierarchical structure among the physical nodes. Each virtual machine receives an IP address and a name leveraging *g5k-subnets* and a round robin assignment policy. The correlation between name and IP is stored in a dedicated file propagated on each physical node. This allows us to identify and communicate with all the virtual machines. Finally, the name and the IP of each VM are configured by customizing the related copy-on-write image before booting it.

The sequence diagram in Figure 3 illustrates these different steps.

Deploying such a large number of VM instances led to several concerns and the use of additional scripts has been required. Leveraging Taktuk [15], these scripts are used to propagate virtual machines images on each bare metal, to communicate with all the virtual instances to check whether the VMs are up or not and to control the state of the whole system during the execution of experiments.

```
1   deployment:
2     engine:
3       name: opennebula
4     sites:
5       rennes:
6         nodes: 5
7         subnet: slash_22=1
8     walltime: 2:00:00
9   opennebula:
10    controller_user: "oneadmin"
11    controller_group: "cloud"
12    hypervisor: kvm
13    datastore:
14      ONstore:
15        filesystem: hdfs
16    vmimage:
17      ttylinux:
18        path: /tmp/openNebulaImages/ttylinux.img
19        datastore: "ONstore"
```

Fig. 4. Configuration file for the OpenNebula g5k-campaign engine

Considering that physical machines must support hardware virtualization to start KVM instances, the largest experiment that has been conducted up to now involved 10240 KVM instances upon 512 nodes through 4 sites and 10 clusters. The whole setup is performed in less than 30 minutes with about 10 minutes spent on the deployment of the nodes, 5 minutes for the installation and configuration of the required packages on the physical hosts, while 15 minutes are dedicated to the booting of the virtual machines. The result of that work opens doors to the manipulation of virtual machines over a distributed infrastructure like traditional operating systems handle processes on a local node. This new functionality is currently used to validate large scale algorithms in charge of managing virtualized infrastructures such as [24].

4.3 Delivering Cloud Platforms in *One-Click*

Although Cloud Computing is gaining consensus from both scientific and industrial communities, its usage still faces some concerns that limit its adoption. The impact of the virtualization technologies, the reliability of virtualized environments and the lack of advanced provisioning technics are some examples of such concerns.

They are at the core of a new research direction targeted by the Grid'5000 community, aiming at enabling experimental research at all levels of the Cloud Computing stack. The first step towards investigating Infrastructure-as-a-Service concerns within Grid'5000 was achieved through a set of "sky computing" tools [25]. Such tools enabled large-scale experiments that spanned across Grid'5000 and FutureGrid [17], harnessing over 1500 cores for a federation of several Nimbus Clouds [19]. These experiments showed that testbeds such as Grid'5000 may play an essential role in providing researchers with configurable Cloud platforms similar to commercially available Clouds.

However, the complexity of managing the deployment and tuning of large-scale private Clouds emerged as a major drawback. Typically, users study specific Cloud components or carry out experiments involving applications running in Cloud environments. A key requirement in this context is seamless access to ready-to-use Cloud platforms, as well as full control of the deployment settings. To address these needs, a *one-click* deployment tool for Infrastructure-as-a-Service environments has been developed [21].

One-click IaaS Clouds with g5k-Campaign. The deployment utility is designed to install and configure fully-functional Cloud platforms over Grid'5000 in a fast and reliable manner. The current version of the system supports two open-source IaaS Clouds, namely OpenNebula [20,22] and Nimbus [19,29].

The deployment tool is built on top of *g5k-campaign*, a framework devised for coordinating experiment workflows and launching repeatable experiments on Grid'5000. *G5k-campaign* relies on extensible *engines* to describe experiments. Such engines define the stages of an experiment: physical node reservations in Grid'5000, environment deployment, configuration, and experiment execution.

To simplify user interaction with the Cloud deployment tools, the *g5k-campaign* framework has been enhanced with a simple, yet powerful mechanism to customize experiments. It relies on configuration files to specify user requirements in terms of reserved nodes and Cloud environment settings, which are then transparently configured during the execution of the deployment engine.

A configuration file example is provided in Figure 4. It consists of several YAML indented blocks that account for the various steps of the deployment process. The *deployment* block includes Grid'5000 node reservation details, such as the sites to be reserved and the number of nodes for each of them. The *opennebula* block comprises configuration options for OpenNebula, ranging from user information to VM storage mechanisms and APIs. Note that users can also describe virtual machine images in the *vmimage* sub-block, to automate image uploading into the OpenNebula system.

A wide range of Cloud-specific parameters can thus be managed by the deployment tools, including hypervisor and virtualization settings, host nodes configuration, installation of external packages, authentication settings, virtual networks creation, configuration of the various storage mechanisms for VM images and of the Cloud user interfaces.

The implementation of the Cloud deployment tools heavily relies on the latest version of the Grid'5000 software stack introduced in Section 3. First, to provide support for virtualization and full control over the environment, the Cloud platforms are installed on standard environments deployed on the physical machines through *Kadeploy*. The interaction with the Grid'5000 services is implemented on top of the *Grid'5000 API*, which is in charge of managing the node reservations and deployments, as well as of retrieving the available nodes and reporting errors. Another essential building block is represented by the *g5k-subnets* tool. It provides the virtual networks needed by the Cloud services to equip VMs with appropriate IP addresses on each site.

Zoom on the OpenNebula Deployment Engine. The engine is responsible for handling the installation process of the OpenNebula environment, either from Debian packages or from specific source code archives. It automatically carries out the deployment and configuration, with a particular focus on storage mechanisms for virtual machines. Currently, the OpenNebula engine supports ssh-based image propagation and shared storage based on NFS (for single-site deployments) or HDFS [28] (for multi-site deployments), to enable live migration and enhance scalability.

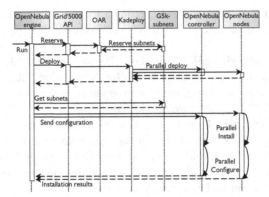

Fig. 5. Sequence diagram of an OpenNebula engine execution

The OpenNebula engine can be executed by passing a configuration file, such as the one given in Figure 4, to the *g5k-campaign* tool, which is in charge of interpreting it and delivering the ready-to-use Cloud platform, as in the following command:

```
g5k-campaign -C opennebulaMultisite.yml
```

The sequence diagram in Figure 5 describes the execution workflow of the OpenNebula engine. First a node reservation is made for each site specified in the configuration file through the *Grid'5000 API*. Along with the nodes, the *OAR* system also reserves a range of virtual IPs corresponding to each site. The next step is the parallel deployment of one or more environments on the reserved nodes enabled by *Kadeploy*. Once the nodes are operational, the OpenNebula engine retrieves the reserved IP ranges from each site and then creates specific configuration settings for each node, according to their role (e.g., the OpenNebula controller is assigned the list of host nodes). Finally, OpenNebula is installed and configured on each node in parallel and the outcome of these processes is returned to the engine. When the execution of the engine is successfully completed, the user can access and perform experiments on the deployed Cloud platform, for the duration of the Grid'5000 reservation defined in the configuration file. These execution stages apply to both multi-site and mono-site deployments, as their outcome is similar: a single Cloud comprising one controller and a set of host nodes. The specificity of a multi-site Cloud is that it will have access to several virtual networks, each of them corresponding to a group of host nodes belonging to the same site.

The OpenNebula deployment engine is written in Ruby and the installation and configuration are done on each physical node by using the Chef [23] configuration management framework. The Chef recipes are designed in a modular manner, to allow Cloud users to add or extend the current OpenNebula configuration options. This tool was validated by installing OpenNebula on 80 physical nodes belonging to 3 Grid'5000 sites, on which we deployed 350 virtual machines. The average time to deploy such a ready-to-use OpenNebula Cloud is less than 20 minutes, with about 6 minutes spent on infrastructure installation and configuration, while the rest is taken up by nodes reservation and deployment. Moreover, subsequent re-deployments take only 5 minutes, as the environments are already running and required packages are installed.

5   Related Work

Several experimental platforms exist over the world for different target sciences.

Around network and system research, Emulab [4] is a network testbed made available to the international academic community since 2001. The original motivation is to provide a single site where users can deploy and execute replayable networked experiments on dedicated hardware. The platform provides customizable network and servers but it is not designed nor sized to host numerous and large experiments related to virtualization, storage or power management. Protogeni [10] is an USA national project that extends the concepts of Emulab. The key concept is to build a federation of geographically distributed testbeds to provide users with a strongly heterogeneous infrastructure that will be suitable to a larger variety of networked experiments on dedicated hardware. PlanetLab [9] is a global research network that supports the development of new network services (overlay networks) using virtualization. The topology of PlanetLab is based on a large number (500) sites with 2 or 3 nodes on each site. While it provides a very interesting testbed from the point of view of the distribution of the resources at a global scale for network-based experiments, experiments running at the same time compete for machine-time and network links. Therefore, experiences' reproducibility is not guaranteed, and experiments involving clusters or data centers are not possible. OneLab [6] provides an open federated laboratory, built on PlanetLab Europe, which supports network research for the Future Internet. Finally, FIT [5] from the 2010 French EQUIPEX call targets the Future Internet of Things. It gathers three infrastructures, a cognitive radio testbed, a set of embedded communicating object (ECO) testbeds, and a set of wireless OneLab testbeds mostly designed for various network experiments.

Several Grid targeted platforms also exist along with Grid'5000. DAS-4 [3] is an experimental grid built in the Netherlands. It allows reproducible results but the software stack cannot be configured. FutureGrid [17], which is part of the NSFs TeraGrid high-performance cyber infrastructure in the USA, provides an architecture taking its inspiration from to the one developed in Grid'5000. It targets researches on Grids and Clouds. It increases the capability of the XSEDE to support innovative computer science research requiring access to lower levels of the grid software stack, the networking software stack, and to virtualization and workflow orchestration tools. There is also a large number of production platforms (such as the GENCI supercomputers in France) that are used for different areas of research. They are not mentioned here because the software stack of their clusters cannot be adapted for low- level research experiments or experiments using specific software stacks.

Finally, some platforms allow experiments on Clouds. Amazon EC2/S3 [1] is a commercial Cloud (IaaS platform). While this platform is mainly made for commercial and production applications, several computer science experiments have recently performed on this platform. Google/IBM provided until October 2011 a Cloud running the Hadoop implementation of the MapReduce programming interface. It could be used to test large-scale data application under this protocol. BonFIRE [2] is a FP7 European project supported by the FIRE unit (Future Internet Research and Experimentation) to build a testbed for Internet of Services Experimentation. INRIA is a member of the BonFIRE consortium and one of its 5 testbed providers, thus taking part in the construction of a European-wide facility for experiment-driven research in Future Internet technologies. Finally, Open Cirrus [7,11] targets experiments around Clouds on bare hardware using distributed clusters available over the world. Led by private companies, it allows multiple experiments using different services (physical resource allocation service, virtual machine resource allocation service, distributed storage service, distributed computing frameworks). VLANs are used to isolate experiments between each others.

6   Conclusions and Future Work

The ability to design and support experiments of large scale distributed algorithms and software is now a mandatory aspect of computer science. When it was started in 2003, the objective of the Grid'5000 project was to ensure the availability of a scientific instrument for experiment-driven research in the fields of large-scale parallel and distributed systems. It has since demonstrated that its fundamental concepts and tools to support experiment-driven research in parallel and distributed systems are solid enough attract a large number of users and to stay pertinent even though the focus of research in these areas has evolved in the past nine years. In the last years, Grid'5000 has had a structuring effect on research in parallel and distributed computing in France. Many French ANR projects have been submitted by Grid'5000 users targeting this platform as their validation instrument. Bridges have been set with production grids. Several collaborations will also be set up with scientists of other disciplines to help them port their applications at a higher scale, exploring new algorithms and parallelization approaches, before using production grids or HPC platforms. Moreover, this platform has been internationally recognized and it serves as a foundation for new scale platforms such as FutureGrid in the US. Hence, Grid'5000 has contributed to solve many challenges in the parallel and distributed computing.

Through our experience in building a large scale and reconfigurable platform and the evolution of researches towards virtualized infrastructures and Clouds, we worked on new features and tools that allow such experiments to be deployed over multiple sites. In this paper, we gave an overview of these tools and the way they can be used for different use cases. However the story is not over and some work remains to be done around new functionnalities.

Whereas abstraction in programming languages enables to design and implement complex IT systems through distributed infrastructures, system virtualization has been mainly limited to one physical machine. With respect to the current utilization of IT through networks in general and Internet in particular, as well as the large amount of available data, the next steps consist in extending virtualization concepts to network and storage facilities. The OpenFlow [8] standard that allows researchers to deploy routing and switching protocols over networks will certainly ease the deployment of large scale network-based experiments. Big Data is also a major research issues for several sciences as well as business applications. Allowing the design of new middleware frameworks for such applications will also require at least new hardware for our experimental platforms (including large number of SSD drives). Finally, we learned that the tools used for the deployment of large scale experiments involving several different software stacks need to be as simple as possible. Simplifying the use of our platform for users is thus also one of our major tasks in the near future.

References

1. Amazon ec2, http://aws.amazon.com/fr/ec2/
2. Bonfire, http://www.bonfire-project.eu/
3. Das-4, http://www.cs.vu.nl/das4/
4. Emulab, http://www.emulab.net/
5. Fit, http://fit-equipex.fr/
6. Onelab, http://www.onelab.eu/
7. Open cirrus, https://opencirrus.org/
8. Openflow, http://www.openflow.org
9. Planetlab, http://www.planet-lab.org/
10. protogeni, http://www.protogeni.net/
11. Avetisyan, A., Campbell, R., Gupta, I., Heath, M., Ko, S., Ganger, G., Kozuch, M., O'Hallaron, D., Kunze, M., Kwan, T., Lai, K., Lyons, M., Milojicic, D., Lee, H.Y., Soh, Y.C., Ming, N.K., Luke, J.Y., Namgoong, H.: Open Cirrus: A Global Cloud Computing Testbed. IEEE Computer 43(4), 42–50 (2010)
12. Booting and using virtual machines on Grid'5000, https://www.grid5000.fr/mediawiki/index.php/Booting_and_Using_Virtual_Machines_on_Grid'5000/
13. Capit, N., Da Costa, G., Georgiou, Y., Huard, G., Martin, C., Mounié, G., Neyron, P., Richard, O.: A batch scheduler with high level components. In: Cluster Computing and Grid 2005 (CCGrid 2005), Cardiff. Royaume-Uni. (2005), http://hal.archives-ouvertes.fr/hal-00005106
14. Cappello, F., Caron, E., Dayde, M., Desprez, F., Jegou, Y., Primet, P., Jeannot, E., Lanteri, S., Leduc, J., Melab, N., Mornet, G., Namyst, R., Quetier, B., Richard, O.: Grid'5000: A large scale and highly reconfigurable grid experimental testbed. In: Proceedings of the 6th IEEE/ACM International Workshop on Grid Computing, GRID 2005, pp. 99–106. IEEE Computer Society, Washington, DC (2005), http://dx.doi.org/10.1109/GRID.2005.1542730
15. Claudel, B., Huard, G., Richard, O.: Taktuk, adaptive deployment of remote executions. In: Proceedings of the International Symposium on High Performance Distributed Computing, HPDC (May 2009)
16. Desprez, F., Fox, G., Jeannot, E., Keahey, K., Kozuch, M., Margery, D., Neyron, P., Nussbaum, L., Perez, C., Richard, O., Smith, W., von Laszewski, G., Voeckler, J.: Supporting Experimental Computer Science. Report, Argonne National Laboratory, Argonne (March 2012), http://www.nimbusproject.org/downloads/Supporting_Experimental_Computer_Science_final_draft.pdf
17. FutureGrid, https://portal.futuregrid.org/
18. Jeanvoine, E., Sarzyniec, L., Nussbaum, L.: Kadeploy3: Efficient and Scalable Operating System Provisioning for HPC Clusters. Rapport de recherche RR-8002, INRIA (June 2012), http://hal.inria.fr/hal-00710638
19. Keahey, K., Freeman, T.: Science Clouds: Early Experiences in Cloud Computing for Scientific Applications. In: Proceedings of the 2008 Conference on Cloud Computing and Its Applications (CCA), Chicago, IL, USA (2008)
20. Moreno-Vozmediano, R., Montero, R.S., Llorente, I.M.: Elastic management of cluster-based services in the cloud. In: Proceedings of the 1st Workshop on Automated Control for Datacenters and Clouds (ACDC), pp. 19–24. ACM, New York (2009)
21. One-click Cloud deployment tools, https://www.grid5000.fr/mediawiki/index.php/Deployment_Scripts_for_IaaS_Clouds_on_Grid%275000
22. OpenNebula, http://opennebula.org/

23. Opscode. Chef, http://www.opscode.com/chef/
24. Quesnel, F., Lèbre, A., Südholt, M.: Cooperative and Reactive Scheduling in Large-Scale Virtualized Platforms with DVMS. Concurrency and Computation: Practice and Experience, p. XX (December 2012), http://hal.archives-ouvertes.fr/hal-00675315
25. Riteau, P., Tsugawa, M., Matsunaga, A., Fortes, J., Keahey, K.: Large-Scale Cloud Computing Research: Sky Computing on FutureGrid and Grid'5000. ERCIM News (83), 41–42 (2010)
26. Sarzyniec, L., Badia, S., Jeanvoine, E., Nussbaum, L.: Scalability Testing of the Kadeploy Cluster Deployment System using Virtual Machines on Grid'5000. In: SCALE Challenge 2012, Held in Conjunction with CCGrid 2012, Ottawa, Canada (May 2012), http://hal.inria.fr/hal-00700962
27. SC11 Support for Experimental Computer Science Worskhop, http://graal.ens-lyon.fr/~desprez/SC11workshop.htm
28. Shvachko, K., Huang, H., Radia, S., Chansler, R.: The Hadoop distributed file system. In: MSST 2010: Proceedings of the 26th IEEE Symposium on Massive Storage Systems and Technologies, Incline Village, NV, USA, pp. 1–10 (May 2010)
29. The Nimbus Project, http://www.nimbusproject.org/
30. The OAR Project, http://oar.imag.fr/

Papers

Improving Cost-Efficiency through Failure-Aware Server Management and Scheduling in Cloud⋆

Laiping Zhao[1] and Kouichi Sakurai[2]

[1] School of Computer Software, Tianjin University, China
[2] Department of Informatics, Kyushu University, Japan
zhaolaiping@gmail.com, sakurai@csce.kyushu-u.ac.jp

Abstract. We examine the problem of managing a server farm in a cost-efficient way that reduces the cost caused by server failures, according to an Infrastructure-as-a-Service model in cloud. Specifically, failures in cloud systems are so frequent that severely affect the normal operation of job requests and incurring high penalty cost. It is possible to increase the net revenue through reducing the energy cost and penalty by leveraging failure predictiors. First, we incorporate the malfunction and recovery states into the server management process, and improve the cost-efficiency of each server using failure predictor-based proactive recovery. Second, we present a revenue-driven cloud scheduling algorithm, which further increases net revenue in collaboration with server management algorithm. The formal and experimental analysis manifests our expected net revenue improvement.

Keywords: Net Revenue, Server Management, Scheduling, Failure Prediction.

1 Introduction

With the infrastructure-as-a-service (IaaS) model in cloud computing, a business is enabled to run jobs on virtual machine (VM) instances rented from the infrastructure service providers in a pay-as-you-go manner. As shown in Figure 1, multiple applications are consolidated to share the same physical server through virtualization technologies. VM instances are offered from a diversified catalog with various configurations. Jobs are encapsulated into VMs, and customers can start new VMs or stop unused ones to meet the increasing or decreasing workload, respectively, and pay for what they use thereafter. In this process, customers do not have full control over the physical infrastructure. Instead, the provider sets a resource management policy determining the physical servers for starting VMs. VM instances are commonly provided under a Service Level Agreement (SLA), which gurantees the service quality, and a penalty is punished on the provider if SLA is violated. For example, Amazon EC2 claims that the customer is eligible to receive a service credit equal to 10% of their bill, if the annual uptime percentage is less than 99.95% during a service year. During the job execution, a VM may migrate from one server to another according to the policy.

⋆ This work is based on "On Revenue Driven Server Management in Cloud", by L. Zhao and K. Sakurai, which appeared in Proc. of 2nd International Conference on Cloud Computing and Service Science, Portugal, April 2012.

I. Ivanov et al. (Eds.): CLOSER 2012, CCIS 367, pp. 23–38, 2013.
© Springer International Publishing Switzerland 2013

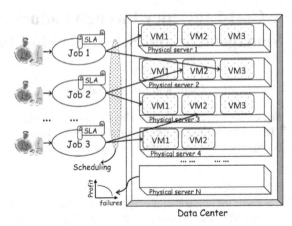

Fig. 1. The cloud IaaS model

SLA violation, that is failing to meet the availability level, is generally caused by in-adequate resources or server failures. Managing SLA violations caused by inadequate resources has been studied in [1]. However, few of them consider reducing the SLA vi-olation cost caused by server failures. As the system scale continues to increase, prob-lems caused by failures are becoming more severe than before ([2], or [3, chap.7]). For example, according to the failure data from Los Alamos National Laboratory (LANL), more than 1,000 failures occur annually at their system No.7, which consists of 2014 nodes in total [2], and Google reports 5 average worker deaths per MapReduce job in March 2006 [4].

The frequent failures as well as the resulting SLA violation costs lead to a practi-cal question: *how to improve the cost efficiency of service providing?* In this paper, we aim to explore a new cost-efficient way to manage the cloud servers by leveraging the existed failure prediction methods. The basic idea is that, a failure-prone server should reject a new arrived job, or move a running job to another healthy server, then proac-tively accept manual repairs or rejuvenate itself to a healthy state. Our contributions mainly fall into three parts:

– We analyze the cost for job execution and SLA violation, and propose a novel server management model by combining the failure prediction together with proactive recovery into server state transitions.
– We design an adaptive net revenue-based decision making policy that dynamically decides whether accepting a new job request or not, and whether moving the run-ning job to another healthy server or not while achieving high cost efficiency.
– We further increase the cost-efficiency through a collaboration of server manage-ment algorithm and scheduling algorithm, i.e., *MaxReliability*. The experimental results manifest the revenue improvement.

2   Related Work

Feasibility of our approach depends on the ability to anticipate the occurrence of fail-ures. Fortunately, a large number of published works have considered thecharacteristics of failures and their impact on performance across a wide variety of computer systems. These works include either the fitting of failure data to specific distributions or have demonstrated that the failures tend to occur in bursts [5],[6]. Availability data from BONIC is modeled with probability distributions [7], and their availabilities are restricted by not only site failures but also the usage patterns of users. Fu and Xu [8] propose a failure prediction framework to explore correlations among failures and forecast the time-between-failure of future instances. Their experimental results on LANL traces show that the system achieves more than 76% accuracy. In addition to processor failures, failure prediction is also studied on hard disk drives [9]. As a survey, Salfner et al. [10] present a comprehensive study on the online failure prediction approaches, which can be split into four major branches of the type of input data used, namely, data from failure tracking, symptom monitoring, detected error reporting, and undetected error auditing. In each branch, various methodologies are applied, for instance, bayesian network, machine learning, time series analysis, fuzzy logic, markov chain, and pattern recognition.

Economic cost for constructing a data center has been studied in [11], [12], [3], which provide us with a deep understanding of cloud system cost. The revenue maximization problems discussed in the literature[13][14][15], are quite close to our work. Mazzucco et al. [15] measure the energy consumed by active servers, and maximize the revenue by optimizing the number of servers to run. Macías et al. [14] present an economically enhanced resource manager for resource provisioning based on economic models, which supports the revenue maximization across multiple service level agreements. Maximizing of the quality of users' experiences while minimizing the cost for the provider is studied in [16]. And Fitó et al. [13] model the economic cost and SLA for moving a web application to cloud computing. The proposed *Cloud Hosting Provider* (CHP) could make use of the outsourcing technique for providing scalability and high availability capabilities, and maximize the providers' revenue. In contrast to their proposals, our goal is to improve the cost efficiency of servers by leveraging the failure prediction methods.

3 Policy for Server Management

3.1 Cloud Server Management

A physical server is described with five states as follows:

IDLE: There are no VMs executing on the server.

RUNNING: The server is executing some VM(s).

TERMINATED: The server successfully finishes jobs, then recycles the memory and clears the disk.

MALFUNCTION: A failure occurs, and the server breaks down.

RECOVERY: Troubleshooting, which could be a simple reboot or repair by a skilled staff.

Figure 2 illustrates the above states and their state transitions for a physical server. We incorporate both the MALFUNCTION and RECOVERY into the states due to the common failures. Although failures may occur at anytime, the probability of failure

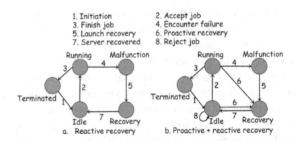

Fig. 2. The state transitions of (a) Reactive recovery and (b) Proactive-Reactive recovery

occurrence in the TERMINATED or IDLE state is far less than in the RUNNING state. Therefore, a single in-degree to the MALFUNCTION state is exploited.

Initially, when a new physical server joins a server farm, or an existing server has finished all deployed VMs and refreshed his status, the server enters the IDLE state and becomes ready for serving a next job.

Reactive Recovery. When a job arrives, the server starts a required VM and accepts the job without hesitation, then comes into the RUNNING state. In case of a successful execution, the job is completed, and the server enters the TERMINATED state. After clearing the memory and disk, the server returns to the IDLE state. If a failure occurs, the server comes into the MALFUNCTION state. Certain recovery methods, e.g., repair, rebooting, would be activated to fix the malfunction, then the server returns to the IDLE state. Note that the recovery could be launched by a skilled staff or automatically activated by a tool like watchdog.

Proactive-Reactive Recovery. Proactive recovery is a useful tool for improving the system efficiency and reducing the economic cost. However, the effects of proactive recovery heavily depend on the failure prediction accuracy, which is still in the rough primary stage currently. Therefore, we employ a hybrid approach based on both proactive recovery and reactive recovery here. An architectural blueprint for managing server system dependability in a proactive fashion is introduced in Polze, Troger, and Salfner (2011).

When a job arrives, the server can: 1. accept the job and change to RUNNING (step 2 in Figure 2(b)); 2. reject the job and stay in IDLE (step 8); 3. reject the job and activate a proactive recovery operation if a failure is predicted (step 6). To assure a positive net revenue, we devise a utility function to handle such decision making problems.

In the first case, if the server comes into the RUNNING state, there are three further possible transitions coming out from the RUNNING state: 1a. if a failure is anticipated during RUNNING, move all running VMs and proactively launch the recovery (step 6); 1b. if a failure occurs without warning, the server reactively comes into the MAL-FUNCTION state (step 4); 1c. if there are no failures, complete the job successfully (step 3). A similar utility based function is also employed here for the proactive recovery operation. In the second and third cases, the server needs to decide whether to stay in IDLE state, or activate a proactive recovery after a job rejection. This is reasonable

Table 1. List of notations

Notations	Definition
Prc_i	Price of the VM instance i ($/hour).
Prc_{egy}	Price of energy consumption. ($/kw.h)
U_{SIO_i}	Fixed cost of a VM i.
P_i	Energy consumption per time unit for VM i.
$Ucoe_i$	Task execution cost per time unit. $Ucoe_i = U_{SIO_i} + Prc_{egy}P_i$
T_{vm}	Job execution time, or contract life.
Coe_i	Total task execution cost of VM i. $Coe_i = Ucoe_i T_{vm}$
Pen	Penalty for SLA violations.
T_M	Time spent on MALFUNCTION state.
T_R	Time spent on RECOVERY state.
P_{SLA}	The percentage of total bill that the provider has to refund.
P_{fail}	Probability of failures.
$Cmig$	VM migration cost.
T_{vm}^{rmn}	VM's remaining lifetime.
P_{fail}^{mig}	Probability of failures for a migrated VM.

because a negative net revenue may be expected from a long-running job, whereas a positive net revenue is expected from a short-running job. If the rejected job is a normal or small size one, then the server activates a proactive recovery, otherwise stays in the IDLE state.

3.2 Net Revenue

Our net revenue model is similar to those used in the literature [14] [13] except that we do not consider the situation of outsourcing a application to a third-party and hence there is no outsourcing cost [13]. Notations are listed in Table 1.

Price (Prc): is the amount of money that a customer has to pay if a cloud provider finishes his job successfully. It usually takes the time piece as the unit. For instance, Amazon EC2 standard small instance charges 0.085$ per hour. *Cost of execution* (Coe): is the amount of money that a cloud provider has to spend on maintaining a healthy VM as well as a physical server for providing service. As the service providing is the major source of profit, any cost for maintaining such service providing will be considered as the part of the total costs, which typically includes fixed costs (e.g., site infrastructure capital costs, IT capital costs) and variable costs (e.g., energy costs, operating expenses). *Penalty* (Pen): is the amount of money that a provider has to pay if the SLA is violated. Denote by T_{vm} the working time (i.e., contract life or job execution time), the net revenue obtained from deploying VM i is computed as below,

$$Rvu_i = Prc_i \cdot T_{vm} - Coe_i - Pen_i \tag{1}$$

The prices of different VM instances have been clearly announced by the providers, and can be publicly accessed. For the cost of execution, we have $Coe_i = Ucoe_i \cdot T_{vm} = (U_{SIO_i} + Prc_{egy} \cdot P_i) \cdot T_{vm}$, where U_{SIO_i} comprises site infrastructure capital costs (Sic), IT capital costs (Icc) and operating expenses (Ope). Prc_{egy} denotes the hourly energy cost (Enc), and P_i denotes the consumed energy [3][11][12]. For the penalty,

	Run	Idle	Termi.	Malfunc.	Reco.
Running	0/0	0/0	P'_{02}/P_{02}	P'_{03}/P_{03}	$0/P_{04}$
Idle	$1/P_{10}$	$0/P_{11}$	0/0	0/0	$0/P_{14}$
Terminated	0/0	1/1	0/0	0/0	0/0
Malfunction	0/0	0/0	0/0	0/0	1/1
Recovery	0/0	1/1	0/0	0/0	0/0

Fig. 3. The state transition probability for Reactive/Proactive-reactive recovery

Reactive recovery	Revenue
Path 1	IDLE - RUNNING - TERMINATE - IDLE	A_R
Path 2	IDLE - RUNNING - MALFUNCTION - RECOVERY - IDLE	$-B_R$
Proactive-Reactive recovery	
Path 1	IDLE - RUNNING - TERMINATE - IDLE	A_{PR}
Path 2	IDLE - RUNNING - MALFUNCTION - RECOVERY - IDLE	$-B_{PR}$
Path 3	IDLE - RUNNING - RECOVERY - IDLE	C_{PR}
Path 4	IDLE - IDLE	0
Path 5	IDLE - RECOVERY - IDLE	$-D_{PR}$

Fig. 4. The server running paths and their corresponding net revenues

we have $Pen_i = Prc_i \cdot T_{vm} \cdot P_{SLA}$, where P_{SLA} denotes the fraction of total bill that the provider has to refund.

3.3 Expected Net Revenue

Next we compute the expected net revenue from providing service or possible losses from server failures. Figure 3 shows the probabilities of state transitions for both the reactive recovery and proactive-reactive (Figure 2). Figure 4 shows all the state transition paths and the corresponding revenues for both of them.

In reactive recovery, the cloud server could obtain positive net revenue from job execution in path 1 (denoted as $A_R = (Prc - Ucoe) \cdot T_{vm}$). While in path 2, the cloud server not only obtains nothing due to the failure, but also has to pay the penalty and losses the execution cost. Let T_M and T_R be the time spent on MALFUNCTION and RECOVERY state respectively, then $B_R = U_{SIO}(T_{vm} + T_M + T_R) + Prc_{egy} \cdot P \cdot T_{vm} + Prc \cdot T_{vm} \cdot P_{SLA}$.

In the proactive-reactive recovery, the cloud server shows a similar situation in path 1 and path 2, that is $A_{PR} = A_R$ and $B_{PR} = B_R$, but with different probabilities. In path 3, a proactive recovery is activated during the running process. The running VMs are interrupted and moved to other healthy servers, where they subsequently proceed until finish. During this process, the cloud provider eventually gets the revenue from these jobs. The revenue generated in terms of the old server is computed based on the finished fraction of the total workload, denoted by P_{fnd}, therefore, we have $C_{PR} = P_{fnd}(Prc - Ucoe)T_{vm} - U_{SIO}T_R$. In path 4 and 5, a job rejection operation only implies a local server's decision, and the rejected job is eventually accepted by another healthy server from the perspective of cloud provider. Thus, there are no losses caused from the job rejection. And the recovery cost spent on the proactive recovery operation in path 5 is: $D_{PR} = U_{SIO}T_R$.

According to Figure 3 and Figure 4, the expected net revenue generated by reactive recovery is:

$$Rvu_R = A_R P'_{02} - B_R P'_{03} \qquad (2)$$

The expected net revenue generated by proactive-reactive recovery is:

$$Rvu_{PR} = A_{PR} P_{10} P_{02} - B_{PR} P_{10} P_{03} + C_{PR} P_{10} P_{04} - D_{PR} P_{14} \qquad (3)$$

Theorem 1. $Rvu_{PR} > Rvu_R$.

Proof.

$$Rvu_{PR} - Rvu_R = PrcT_{vm} \times$$
$$[P_{SLA}(P'_{03} - P_{10}P_{03}) + (P_{10}P_{02} - P'_{02}) + P_{fnd}P_{10}P_{04}] +$$
$$U_{SIO}[T_{vm}(P'_{03} - P_{10}P_{03} - P_{fnd}P_{10}P_{04} + P'_{02} - P_{10}P_{02}) + \qquad (4)$$
$$T_M(P'_{03} - P_{10}P_{03}) + T_R(P'_{03} - P_{10}(P_{03} + P_{04}) - P_{14})] +$$
$$Prc_{egy}PT_{vm}[P'_{02} - P_{10}P_{02} + P'_{03} - P_{10}P_{03} - P_{fnd}P_{10}P_{04}]$$

With the two prerequisites, $P_{10}P_{02} = P'_{02}$ and $P_{10} \cdot (P_{03} + P_{04}) + P_{11} + P_{14} = P'_{03}$, we have,

- $P_{SLA}(P'_{03} - P_{10}P_{03}) + (P_{10}P_{02} - P'_{02}) + P_{fnd}P_{10}P_{04} > 0$
- $T_{vm}(P'_{03} - P_{10}P_{03} - P_{fnd}P_{10}P_{04} + P'_{02} - P_{10}P_{02}) + T_M(P'_{03} - P_{10}P_{03}) + T_R$
  $(P'_{03} - P_{10}(P_{03} + P_{04}) - P_{14}) > 0$
- $P'_{02} - P_{10}P_{02} + P'_{03} - P_{10}P_{03} - P_{fnd}P_{10}P_{04} > 0$

Hence, the theorem is established. □

3.4 Decision Making

The server state transitions contain three decision making points. The first one is to decide whether to accept or reject a new arriving job, and followed by a further decision is on whether or not to activate proactive recovery if the job is rejected. The third one is to decide whether to activate a proactive recovery or continue the job execution when the job is under the RUNNING state. In our proposal, these decisions are made on behalf of physical servers based on the expected net revenue.

Accept or Reject a Job. A job arriving at a cloud server could be a new or rejected or failed or migrated job. After its lifetime (i.e., T_{vm}) is determined by user's specification or estimates, we can predict the probability of failures (i.e., P_{fail}) in this interval using associated stressors [17]. The possible net revenue obtained from accepting a job by server i can be computed as,

$$\overline{Rvu_i} = A^i_{PR} \cdot (1 - P_{fail}) \qquad (5)$$

Accounting of malfunction losses during the middle of job execution consists of direct economic loss and indirect economic loss. A cloud provider would directly get a penalty from the SLA agreement, and he also has to afford the cost for recovery operation. The possible losses can be computed as,

$$\overline{Los_i} = B^i_{PR} \cdot P_{fail} \qquad (6)$$

If $\overline{Rvu_i} > \overline{Los_i}$, the VM i will be deployed for execution, and if not, the VM i will be rejected. In other words, the VM i is accepted when the following condition is held,

$$P_{fail} < \frac{A^i_{PR}}{A^i_{PR} + B^i_{PR}} \qquad (7)$$

In case of a migrated VM, additional cost is spent on VM migration. Let $Cmig$ be the cost for moving the VM from an old physical server to a new one, and T_{vm}^{rmn} be the remaining lifetime. We have, $\overline{Rvu_i^{mig}} = (A_{PR}^{i,rmn} - Cmig) \cdot (1 - P_{fail}^{mig}) = ((Prc_i - Ucoe_i) \cdot T_{vm}^{rmn} - Cmig) \cdot (1 - P_{fail}^{mig})$ and $\overline{Los_i^{mig}} = (B_{PR}^{i,rmn} + Cmig) \cdot P_{fail}^{mig} = (Pen_i + U_{SIO}(T_{vm}^{rmn} + T_M + T_R) + Prc_{egy} \cdot P \cdot T_{vm}^{rmn} + Cmig) P_{fail}^{mig}$

Let $\overline{Rvu_i^{mig}} > \overline{Los_i^{mig}}$, then the condition 7 is changed into,

$$P_{fail}^{mig} < \frac{A_{PR}^{i,rmn} - Cmig}{A_{PR}^{i,rmn} + B_{PR}^{i,rmn}} \qquad (8)$$

Proactive Recovery or Not. Once a job is rejected, a cloud server further has two options of launching the proactive recovery or doing nothing. Denote by $\overline{T_{vm}}$ the average lifetime of all history VMs successfully completed on a server, and $P_{fail}^{\overline{T_{vm}}}$ the predicted probability of failures within next $\overline{T_{vm}}$ time. Then if $P_{fail}^{\overline{T_{vm}}} < P_{fail}$ (The right side of Inequality 7), the cloud server does nothing but waits for the next job. Otherwise, the server activates the proactive recovery. This is because failure probability increases over time. A next normal size job still can be accepted if $P_{fail}^{\overline{T_{vm}}} < P_{fail}$ is held. Note that it is possible that the server stays in a starvation state for a long time, if no short-running VM is dispatched to the server. In such case, activate the proactive recovery if the leisure time exceeds a pre-defined threshold.

Activate VM Migaration or Not. For a long-running VM, it is difficult to have an accurate prediction on the failure probability during that long time. Moreover, certain types of failures always come with some pathognomonic harbingers. It is a difficult to predict such failures without particular harbingers. Therefore, we also activate the failure prediction during the running process. And proactive recovery is launched when inequality 7 (inequality 8 if it is a migrated job) is violated for all the local VMs.

The VM migrates from a server i to a server j only because j can yield a greater net revenue. The expected revenue obtained from no migration is the same as $\overline{Rvu_i}$ (Equation 5), except that the failure probability (P_{fail}^{rmn}) is for the remaining lifetime (i.e., T_{vm}^{rmn}): $\overline{Rvu_i^{rmn}} = A_{PR}^{i,rmn} \cdot (1 - P_{fail}^{rmn}) = (Prc_i - Ucoe_i) \cdot T_{vm}^{rmn} \cdot (1 - P_{fail}^{rmn})$. The expect net revenue obtained from a migration has been described as $\overline{Rvu_j^{mig}}$. Let $\overline{Rvu_j^{mig}} > \overline{Rvu_i^{rmn}}$, we have,

$$P_{fail}^{mig} < \frac{A_{PR}^{i,rmn} \cdot P_{fail}^{rmn} - Cmig}{A_{PR}^{i,rmn} - Cmig} \qquad (9)$$

Therefore, a new server j whose failure probability (i.e., P_{fail}^{Mig}) follows both Inequality 8 and 9 will be selected to execute the migrated VM. In case of more than one server meets this condition, the VM migrates to the one with maximum reliability to proceed. If no appropriate processors are found, maintain the VM at the original server until finish or failure.

Algorithm 1. Algorithm for server management.

---

1 [Parameters]
2 **double** f_p {*the predicted failure probability*}
3 **double** P_{fail} {*the probability that ensures the job acceptance*}
4 **double** P_{fail}^{Mig} {*the probability that ensures condition 9*}
5 **double** $\overline{P_{fail}^{rmn}}$ {*the failure probability in the remaining time*}
6 **integer** $\overline{T}$ {*the average job execution time*}
7 **STATE** *state = IDLE* {*server state, initialized with IDLE*}

8 **upon** *receive(job)*
9 **if** *state = IDLE* **then**   *job_submit(job)*;

10 **upon** *receive(job, P_{fail}^{Mig})*   /* received a migrated job */
11 f_p = *fail_predict(T_{job}^{rmn})*; P_{fail} = *fail_expect(T_{job})*   /* ensure condition 8 */
12 **if** $f_p < P_{fail}^{Mig}$ **and** $f_p < P_{fail}$ **and** *state = IDLE* **then return** *true*;
13 **else return** *false*;

14 **procedure** *job_submit(job)*
15 T_{job} = *time_estimate()*; f_p = *fail_predict(T_{job})*; P_{fail} = *fail_expect(T_{job})*;
16 **if** $f_p < P_{fail}$ **then**   /* ensure positive revenue */
17 | *job_execute(job)*; *state = RUNNING*;
18 **else if** $T_{job} \leq \overline{T}$ **then**   /* proactive recovery */
19 | *proactive_recovery(job)*; *state = RECOVERY* ;
20 **else**   /* wait next job */
21 | *state = IDLE* ;

22 **procedure** *job_execute(job)*
23 **if** *failed = true* **then**   /* reactive recovery */
24 | *state = MALFUNCTION*; **return**;
25 P_{fail}^{rmn} = *fail_predict(T_{rmn})*;
26 **if** $P_{fail}^{rmn} \geq P_{fail}$ **then**   /* negative revenue */
27 | compute P_{fail}^{Mig} using 9; *reschedule(job, P_{fail}^{Mig})*;
28 | **wait until** *find another processor*
29 | *migrate(job)*; *proactive_recovery(job)*;   *state = RECOVERY*;

30 **procedure** *fail_expect(T_{job})*
31   **return** P_{fail} using 7;

3.5 Algorithm Description

Algorithm 1 presents the detail description for server management. The migrated job and other job requests are handled by *receive(job, P)* and *receive(job)* respectively. If it is a migrated job, the server will reply with an affirmative answer if its predicted failure probability follows both inequality 8 and 9, otherwise with a negative answer (line 10-13).

We use the function *job_submit()* to decide whether to accept or reject the job. If the job is rejected and its execution time is less than the average level of job execution time, activate a recovery operation directly (line 18-19). Otherwise, do nothing but wait for the next job request (line 21). Function *job_execute()* activates the proactive recovery after all VMs migrated to other servers because of a sudden higher failure probability ($P_{fail}^{rmn} \geq P_{fail}$).

4 Revenue-Driven Scheduling

Since proactive recovery contributes to avoid the possible penalties caused by server failures, the server management algorithm is able to increase the revenue for cloud

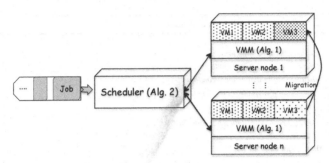

Fig. 5. The scheduling framework

provider. In fact, the revenue could be further increased through collaborative use of server management and cloud scheduling algorithm. Figure 5 shows the framework. Algorithm 1 is implemented at the Virtual Machine Monitor (VMM), which takes in charge of failure estimation, VM migration and proactive recovery. Below, we discuss how to schedule the VMs for increasing cloud provider's revenue.

4.1 MaxReliability

As physical servers perform high heterogeneity in failure probability, the probability of state transition from *RUNNING* to *MALFUNCTION* would be different for different servers (i.e., P_{03} in Figure 3).

Theorem 2. *Suppose server i is more reliable than server j. For performing the same VM, the expected net revenue yielded by i is greater than j: $Rvu^i_{PR} > Rvu^j_{PR}$.*

Proof. Because server i is more reliable than j, it means the probability of state transition from *IDLE* to *RUNNING*, then to *TERMINATED* for server i is greater than j. Thus, according to Figure 3, we have $P^i_{10} > P^j_{10}$, $P^i_{10}P^i_{02} > P^j_{10}P^j_{02}$, $P^i_{14} < P^j_{14}$, and $P^i_{03} + P^i_{04} < P^j_{03} + P^j_{04}$. Note that, for the predicted failure probability: $f^i_p = P^i_{03} + P^i_{04}$ and $f^j_p = P^j_{03} + P^j_{04}$.

Suppose the failure detection accurancy is: $\alpha = No.of detected failures/ No.of failures$, then $P^i_{03} = (1 - \alpha)f_p$ and $P^i_{04} = \alpha f_p$. As $P^i_{02} + P^i_{03} + P^i_{04} = 1$, and regrading Equation 3, we have,

$$Rvu^i_{PR} = A_{PR}P^i_{10}P^i_{02} - B_{PR}P^i_{10}P^i_{03} + C_{PR}P^i_{10}P^i_{04} - D_{PR}P^i_{14}$$
$$= P^i_{10}[A_{PR}(1 - f^i_p) - f^i_p(B_{PR}(1 - \alpha) - C_{PR}\alpha)] - D_{PR}P^i_{14}$$
$$= P^i_{10}[A_{PR} - f^i_p(A_{PR} + B_{PR}(1 - \alpha) - C_{PR}\alpha)] - D_{PR}P^i_{14}$$

Because $f^i_p < f^j_p$, $A_{PR} + B_{PR}(1 - \alpha) - C_{PR}\alpha > 0$, then $A_{PR} - f^i_p(A_{PR} + B_{PR}(1 - \alpha) - C_{PR}\alpha) > A_{PR} - f^j_p(A_{PR} + B_{PR}(1 - \alpha) - C_{PR}\alpha)$. Likewise, because $P^i_{14} < P^j_{14}$, then $D_{PR}P^i_{14} < D_{PR}P^j_{14}$. Hence, we have $Rvu^i_{PR} > Rvu^j_{PR}$. □

Theorem 2 suggests that scheduling VMs on reliable servers could increase cloud provider's revenue. Therefore, a natural way of cloud scheduling is always dispatching an incoming VM to the most reliable server. We call the rule as *MaxReliability*. Algorithm 2 shows the details: Upon receiving a job by the scheduler, either a new job or a migrated job, iterate over all servers and predict the probability of failure. Then dispatch the job to the server with maximum reliability (Line 1-5). Whenever a VM is completed, because capacity is freed on the host server (e.g., s_k), VMs located on less reliable servers could migrate to s_k for increasing revenue. Iterating over all busy servers (Line 7), we find the job j with least reliability, and j's capacity requirement is able to be satisfied by s_k available capacity. Then, move j to s_k (Line 13). The process is repeated until s_k is full. Note that the migration comes with overhead (i.e., C_{mig}), hence a VM is migrated only when the difference on failure probability, i.e., $f_p^{s,j_{min}} - f_p^{s_k,j_{min}}$, is greater than a threshold ϵ (Line 13-14).

Algorithm 2. Algorithm for cloud scheduler: *MaxReliability*.

---

    input   : S {*the servers set*}
    output   : schedule for jobs

1 **upon** *receive(job)*   /* Either a new or a migrated job */
2 **for** $s \in S$ **do**
3      $f_p^s = fail\_predict(T_{job})$;

4 $s_{max} = max\{(1 - f_p^s)\}$;
5 *send(job,s_{max})*;   /* Send the job to the server with max reliability */

6 **upon** *free(s_k)*   /* Part capacity of s_k is freed due to completion of jobs */
7 *flag = 1.0* ;
8 **for** $s \in S$ *&&* $s.state == RUNNING$, *except s_k* **do**
9   **for** *job j running on s* **do**
10          $f_p^{s,rmn_j} = fail\_predict(T_j^{rmn})$;
11   **if** $flag > f_p^{s,rmn_j}$ *&&* $j.capacity < s_k.availablecapacity$ **then**
12              $flag = f_p^{s,rmn_j}$; $j_{min} = j$;   /* Find the most fragile job j_{min} */

13 **if** $f_p^{s,j_{min}} - f_p^{s_k,j_{min}} > \epsilon$ **then**
14   *move j_{min} to s_k*; /* Move the job with least reliability to s_k */

4.2 Combined with Energy-Saving

Let us revisit the equation for computing revenue: $Rvu_i = Prc_i \cdot T_{vm} - Coe_i - Pen_i$. To increase the revenue, there are several possible ways regarding the equation. For example, cloud provider could increase Rvu_i through providing flexible pricing functions (i.e., Prc_i), reducing execution cost Coe_i or reducing Pen_i. Flexible pricing function has been discussed in the literature [18], [19], [20], and also employed in practice (e.g., the spot instance at Amazon). In fact, pricing functions is based on long-term service providing. For a single VM, after it is submitted, the price is fixed no matter which pricing functions is applied. Therefore, we do not address the pricing function here, but tend to increase the Rvu by reducing Coe_i and Pen_i.

According to equation $Coe_i = (U_{SIO_i} + Prc_{egy} \cdot P_i) \cdot T_{vm}$, reducing energy cost (i.e., P_i) is the most likely way to reduce Coe_i, because U_{SIO} belongs to fixed-asset investment. Thus, we explore to increase cloud provider's revenue through reducing energy cost and penalty simultaneously. Fortunately, reducing energy cost does not conflict with reducing penalty. Scheduling VMs to reliable servers could avoid penalty, and consolidating several VMs on a server could reducing the energy cost. A natural combination of them would be, consolidating VMs on the least number of reliabile servers. That is, a high reliable server could contribute to reduce the penalty, while consolidation is able to reduce energy cost. For example, Mastroianni et al. [21] present a decentralized solution for VM consolidation. That is, if the CPU utilization of a server is below certain threshold, VMs on other servers could be migrated to it. While if the CPU utilization of a server is above certain threshold, VMs on it can be migrated to other underloaded servers. The improved version with considering penalty cost could be: if the CPU utilization of a server is below certain threshold, VMs on the least reliable and overloaded server could be migrated to it. While if the CPU utilization of a server is above certain threshold, VMs on it can be migrated to the first available server with maximum reliabily.

5 Experiments

5.1 Simulation Environment

Server Farm. We simulate a server farm with 20 physical servers, which can provide seven different types of VM instances, corresponding to the seven types of instances from Rackspace Cloud Servers [22]. The processing speed of each server is supposed to be the same, and is initialized with eight cores, with each is of $2.4GHz$.

Job. We simulate a large number of jobs ranging from 1000 to 6000, for maximizing the utilization of all servers. Through this way, the cost for maintaining a server could be fairly shared among all the VMs deployed on it, and leading to a positive net revenue. This is also reasonable in practice because cloud providers commonly design policies to optimize the minimum number of active servers for reducing the energy cost, thereby resulting in a high utilization at each active server (Mastroianni, Meo, and Papuzzo, 2011; Mazzucco et al., 2010b).

Allowing two instructions in one cycle, the workload of each job is evenly generated from the range: $[1, 6] \times 204,800 \times 2^i$ million instructions, where $0 \le i \le 6$ and $i \in Z$, represents the type of VM instance this job requires.

Scheduling. Jobs are placed on cloud servers using a First-Come-First-Served (FCFS) algorithm. Scheduling priority is supported, and follows the sequence: *migrated job > failed job > rejected job > unsubmitted job*. The rejected or failed jobs will not be scheduled on the same server at the second time, because it is probably rejected or failed again.

Failures. Failures are considered from two dimensions. The first dimension concerns the time when failures occur. In our experiments, failures are injected to servers following a Poisson distribution process with $\lambda = [1,4]/\theta \times 10^{-6}$, where $\theta \in [0.1,2]$. According to the Poisson distribution, the lengths of the inter-arrival times between failures follow the exponential distribution, which is inconsistent with the observations that the time between failures is well modeled by a Weibull or lognormal distribution [2]. The deviations arise because an attempt to repair a computer is not always successful and failures recur a relatively short time later [23]. Implementing a real failure predictor is out of the range of this paper, and we alternatively consider different failure prediction accuracy in evaluations.

The second dimension concerns the repair times. If an unexpected failure occurs, the server turns into a MALFUNCTION state immediately, and followed by recovery operations. As discussed in [2], the time spent on recovery follows a Lognormal distribution process, which is defined with a mean value equaling to 90 minutes, and $\sigma = 1$.

Price and Server Cost. The prices for all seven types of VM instances are set exactly the same as the ones from Rackspace Cloud Servers [22], that is $Prc = 0.015\$ \times 2^i$, where $0 \le i \le 6$ and $i \in Z$.

The capital cost is roughly set at 8000\$ per physical server, which is estimated based on the market price of *System x 71451RU server* by IBM [24]. The price of electricity is set at 0.06\$ per kilowatt hour. We suppose that the power consumption of an active server without any running VMs is 140 Watts. Additional power ranging from 10 Watts to 70 Watts is consumed by VMs corresponding to seven types of VM instances [16]. Suppose a server's lifetime is five years, and as the IT capital cost takes up 33% to the total management cost, we roughly spend 4300\$ on a physical server per year with additional energy cost.

As modeling of migration costs is highly non-trivial due to second order effects migrations might have on the migrated service and other running services, we simplify migration costs as an additional 20% of the unexecuted workload without profit (i.e., 10% for the original server, and another 10% for the target server). A preliminary attempt on modeling migration cost is given in Breitgand, Kutiel, and Raz (2010).

Penalty. If a SLA is breached due to the provider's failing to complete jobs, the customer gets compensation by a rather high ratio of fine, which ranges from 10% to 500% of the user bill in the experiments (i.e., $P_{SLA} \in [0.1,5]$). This is because SLA violations cause not only direct losses on revenue but also indirect losses, which might be much more significant (e.g., in terms of provider reputation).

5.2 Results

We choose the evaluation approach by comparing our proposed proactive-reactive model with the original reactive model. Experiments are conducted across a range of operating conditions: number of jobs, failure frequency (θ), P_{SLA}, and the accuracy of failure prediction. Accuracy implies the ability of the failure prediction methods, and is presented by both the false-negative (fn) and false positive (fp) ratio. Denote by

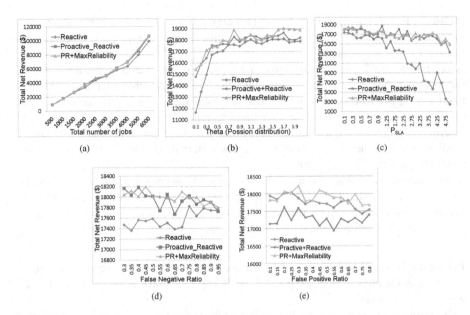

Fig. 6. The total net revenue: (a) under different No. of jobs; (b) under different qs (failure frequency); (c) under different SLA penalty percentages; (d) under different levels of false-negative ratio; (e) under different levels of false-positive ratio

$No(FN)$ the number of false-negative errors, $No(TP)$ the number of true-positive predictions, and $No(FP)$ the number of false-positive errors, then we have $fn = \frac{No(FN)}{No(FN)+No(TP)}$ and $fp = \frac{No(FP)}{No(FP)+No(TP)}$. Unless otherwise stated, the parameters are set with $jobnumber = 1000$, $\theta = 1$, $P_{SLA} = 0.1$, $fn = 0.25$ and $fp = 0.2$. Each experiment is repeated five times and the results represent the corresponding average values.

Figure 6 shows the total net revenue obtained by the reactive recovery, proactive-reactive recovery (PR) and PR+MaxReliability (PRM) from executing jobs under different operating conditions. Note that random selection is employed in both reactive recovery and proactive-reactive recovery (PR) for dispatching VMs to servers, while PRM uses *MaxReliability* for scheduling. Generally, net revenue yielded by the proactive-reactive model is greater than the reactive model, which is consistent with our analysis in Theorem 1. However, compared with random selection, *MaxReliability* does not yield much improvement on revenue. This is because, we have submitted so many VMs that nearly all servers are fully occupied. Thus the difference on revenue between them is not apparent. In particular, Figure 6(a) shows the net revenue as a function of the number of jobs. The difference on net revenue is increasing over the number of jobs, which is reasonable because more jobs come with more revenue.

Figure 6(b) shows the net revenue as a function of failure frequency. By the definition of λ, we know failure frequency decreases as θ increases. As shown in the figure, the PR and PRM model could yield more net revenue than the reactive model when the failure frequency is high. In particular, the proactive-reactive model yields 26.8% net revenue improvement over the reactive model when setting $\theta = 0.1$. And an average improvement of 11.5% is achieved when $\theta \leq 0.5$. This suggests that the proactive-reactive model makes more sense in unreliable systems. Furthermore, the proactive-reactive model also outperforms the reactive model in rather reliable systems where $\theta > 0.5$.

Figure 6(c) shows that the PR and PRM model yields a greater net revenue than the reactive model under different P_{SLA} values. Net revenue yielded by the proactive-reactive model does not decline much because most penalty costs are avoided by possible proactive recovery and VM migrations. Whereas the reactive model has to pay the penalty when failure occurs, and penalty cost increases as P_{SLA} increases.

Figure 6(d) shows the net revenue under different levels of false-negative ratio ranging from 0.05 to 0.7. With the increase of false-negative error, there is a slight decrease on the net revenue by the PR and PRM model, whereas the reactive model fluctuates around a certain level because the reactive model does not employ failure prediction and the fluctuation is due to the random values used in the experiments. Our proactive-reactive model averagely yields 3.2% improvement on the net revenue over the reactive model, and performs similarly with reactive model when $fn \geq 0.7$.

Figure 6(e) shows the impact on net revenue from the false-positive ratio under a fixed $fn = 0.25$. Net revenue obtained from PR and PRM model decreases gradually over the false positive ratio. Moreover, the differences on revenue between proactive-reactive and reactive model decreases as the false-positive ratio increases. This is because a high false-positive ratio results in a large number of meaningless migrations, which come with migration costs. Figure 6(d) and Figure 6(e) suggest that our algorithm still performs well with even modest prediction accuracy (i.e., $fn \geq 0.5$ or $fp \geq 0.5$).

6 Conclusions

In this paper, we address the problem of cost-efficient fault management, and present revenue driven server management and scheduling algorithm for cloud systems. Using the algorithms, cloud providers could obtain a significant improvement on net revenue when serving the same jobs. In particular, our proposal could yield at most 26.8%, on average 11.5% net revenue improvement when the failure frequency is high. In the future, we will study more scheduling algorithms working together with the proposed server management model. Our goal is to maximize the net revenue for cloud providers without affecting the performance.

References

1. Bobroff, N., Kochut, A., Beaty, K.: Dynamic Placement of Virtual Machines for Managing SLA Violations. In: 10th IFIP/IEEE International Symposium on Integrated Network Management, pp. 119–128 (2007)
2. Schroeder, B., Gibson, G.A.: A large-scale study of failures in high-performance computing systems. In: DSN 2006, pp. 249–258 (2006)
3. Hoelzle, U., Barroso, L.A.: The Datacenter as a Computer: An Introduction to the Design of Warehouse-Scale Machines, 1st edn. Morgan and Claypool Publishers (2009)
4. Dean, J.: Experiences with mapreduce, an abstraction for large-scale computation. In: PACT 2006, pp. 1–6. ACM (2006)

5. Vishwanath, K.V., Nagappan, N.: Characterizing cloud computing hardware reliability. In: SoCC 2010, pp. 193–204 (2010)
6. Nightingale, E.B., Douceur, J.R., Orgovan, V.: Cycles, cells and platters: an empirical analysisof hardware failures on a million consumer pcs. In: EuroSys 2011, pp. 343–356. ACM (2011)
7. Javadi, B., Kondo, D., Vincent, J.M., Anderson, D.P.: Discovering statistical models of availability in large distributed systems: An empirical study of seti@home. IEEE Transactions on Parallel and Distributed Systems 22, 1896–1903 (2011)
8. Fu, S., Xu, C.Z.: Exploring event correlation for failure prediction in coalitions of clusters. In: SC 2007, pp. 41:1–41:12. ACM (2007)
9. Pinheiro, E., Weber, W.D., Barroso, L.A.: Failure trends in a large disk drive population. In: FAST 2007, pp. 17–28 (2007)
10. Salfner, F., Lenk, M., Malek, M.: A survey of online failure prediction methods. ACM Comput. Surv. 42, 10:1–10:42 (2010)
11. Koomey, J., Brill, K., Turner, P., et al.: A simple model for determining true total cost of ownership for data centers. Uptime institute white paper (2007)
12. Patel, C.D., Shah, A.J.: A simple model for determining true total cost of ownership for data centers. Hewlett-Packard Development Company report HPL-2005-107 (2005)
13. Fitó, J.O., Presa, I.G., Guitart, J.: Sla-driven elastic cloud hosting provider. In: PDP 2010, pp. 111–118 (2010)
14. Macías, M., Rana, O., Smith, G., Guitart, J., Torres, J.: Maximizing revenue in grid markets using an economically enhanced resource manager. Concurrency and Computation Practice and Experience 22, 1990–2011 (2010)
15. Mazzucco, M., Dyachuk, D., Deters, R.: Maximizing cloud providers' revenues via energy aware allocation policies. In: IEEE CLOUD 2010, pp. 131–138 (2010)
16. Mazzucco, M., Dyachuk, D., Dikaiakos, M.: Profit-aware server allocation for green internet services. In: MASCOTS 2010, pp. 277–284 (2010)
17. Abraham, A., Grosan, C.: Genetic programming approach for fault modeling of electronic hardware. In: The 2005 IEEE Congress on Evolutionary Computation, vol. 2, pp. 1563–1569 (2005)
18. Marbukh, V., Mills, K.: Demand pricing & resource allocation in market-based compute grids: A model and initial results. In: ICN 2008, pp. 752–757 (2008)
19. Zheng, Q., Veeravalli, B.: Utilization-based pricing for power management and profit optimization in data centers. JPDC 72, 27–34 (2012)
20. Macías, M., Guitart, J.: A genetic model for pricing in cloud computing markets. In: SAC 2011, pp. 113–118. ACM, New York (2011)
21. Mastroianni, C., Meo, M., Papuzzo, G.: Self-economy in cloud data centers: statistical assignment and migration of vms. In: Jeannot, E., Namyst, R., Roman, J. (eds.) Euro-Par 2011, Part I. LNCS, vol. 6852, pp. 407–418. Springer, Heidelberg (2011)
22. Rackspace (2012), http://www.rackspace.com (Online; accessed January 31, 2012)
23. Lewis, P.A.: A branching poisson process model for the analysis of computer failure patterns. Journal of the Royal Statistical Society, Series B 26, 398–456 (1964)
24. IBM: Ibm system x 71451ru entry-level server (2012), http://www.amazon.com/System-71451RU-Entry-level-Server-E7520/dp/B003U772W4

Designing an IPv6-Oriented Datacenter with IPv4-IPv6 Translation Technology for Future Datacenter Operation

Keiichi Shima[1], Wataru Ishida[2], and Yuji Sekiya[2]

[1] IIJ Innovation Institute Inc.
[2] The University of Tokyo

Abstract. Many big network operators have already deployed IPv6. Most of the popular client operating systems are ready to use IPv6. The last part is the service providers. It is a kind of a chicken-and-egg problem. If services are not provided over IPv6, then users will not shift to IPv6, and if users do not use IPv6, then the service providers do not deploy IPv6. However, considering the global trend of shifting to IPv4/IPv6 dual-stack world, it is mandatory for service providers to accept all three types of users, 1) IPv4-only users who will remain in the Internet for long time, 2) IPv4/IPv6 dual-stack users who will be a dominant users in near future, and 3) IPv6-only users who will appear in the future as IPv6 deployment progresses. In this paper, we propose a recommended operation model for IaaS operators to soft-land from IPv4-only operation to IPv6-only operation without losing existing IPv4 users. The proposed operation utilizes a wide area L2 network and IPv4-IPv6 translation software for backward compatibility. With our proposal, we can reduce the use of IPv4 addresses in the cloud backend network by shifting to IPv6-only operation, and provide high-performance, scalable, and redundant address translation software suitable for the IPv6-only IaaS system that can be one of the reference operation models of future datacenters.

Keywords: Cloud Middleware Frameworks, IaaS, Scalability, Redundancy, Cost Reduction: IPv6, IPv4 Compatibility.

1   Introduction

The computing power of computers is growing every year. However, many studies show that there is an obvious limitation of computing power if we stick one single processor system. Because of this reason, cloud computing technologies are getting attention of many people. Researchers are now investigating its usage, application model, and operation techniques to utilize the limited resources more effectively. At the same time, virtualization technologies that enable us to slice one physical computer into several virtual computer resources to suppress idle resources as much as possible. With the virtualization technologies, it is expected that we will have a huge computer network that includes far larger number of virtual computers than the physical computers.

The network protocol used to interconnect computers has been the IPv4 protocol for long time. However, because of recent depletion of IPv4 addresses, the successor protocol, IPv6, is now being deployed. Since we can still use IPv4 addresses and its

I. Ivanov et al. (Eds.): CLOSER 2012, CCIS 367, pp. 39–53, 2013.

network even though we do not have new IPv4 addresses, the future network will be a mixed network of IPv4 and IPv6 for many years until IPv4 disappears completely.

Service providers must support both IPv4 and IPv6, because service users will be mixed users of IPv4-only users, IPv4/IPv6 dual-stack users, and IPv6-only users in the future. Although IPv4 and IPv6 are technically quite similar except the size of their address space, however, these protocols do not have interoperability because their protocol header formats are completely different. The operators have to manage two similar networks. That is a duplicated effort.

If we can manage and operate a single stack network for the service backend nodes and place dual-stack nodes only as the entry points to the services, then we can reduce the operation cost to manage two duplicated networks. We can also quickly follow the technology advance of the network by focusing on only one single protocol stack. In this paper, we focus on a virtual computer resource management environment (IaaS, Infrastructure As A Service) and propose a system whose backend network is operated by IPv6-only with dual-stack public nodes as service entry points using IPv4-IPv6 protocol translator software. This kind of IPv4-IPv6 protocol translator is not a new technology. It was proposed almost as same time as IPv6 was proposed. However, such a translator is basically assuming to map one IPv4 address to multiple IPv6 addresses, because its main usage is to provide IPv4 connectivity to IPv6 only nodes originally. This means the software tends to become complicated because it has to keep track on the address mapping status and session status among multiple IPv6 addresses. It also has a scalability and redundancy problem because it needs to manage many mapping information and session status and this status information is hard to share and synchronize among multiple translator nodes. Our proposed system particularly insists on one-to-one address mapping which doesn't have problems addressed above, with the assumption that the translator is used as a part of an IaaS system. With this compromise, we can design a realistic IaaS system without having problems of existing IPv4-IPv6 translation system as described before and realize IPv6-only backend service operation.

2   Related Works

2.1   IaaS Model

Needless to say, most of the current service providers are using IPv4 as their base IP protocol to build services. As IPv6 is getting popular, some of them are now considering to supporting dual-stack service using translators. Although there are several transition scenarios to move from IPv4 to IPv6 [1], they basically use IPv4 for server nodes and provide IPv6 connectivity to IPv6 clients using translator technology. This is the biggest difference from our approach. We use IPv6 addresses for server nodes and provide dual stack connectivity to client nodes. Considering that the IPv6 clients are going to grow in the future, focusing on IPv6 and providing IPv4 as an additional service seems the right choice.

The traditional translation operation is shown in section 2.1 of Chen's paper [2]. We think that the model has several drawbacks. First, since it uses IPv4 for their backend service networks, it may face the IPv4 depletion problem. Second, if they use private IPv4 address space to avoid the IPv4 depletion issue, they may face IPv4 NAT traversal issues for servers they are operating in their private networks. Third, if they use NAT for their servers, they have to operate two NAT services, one for IPv4 private addresses, and the other for IPv6-IPv4 addresses. In our proposed model, IPv6 services are provided natively, and IPv4 services are provided using translation. Detailed discussion is provided in section 3.1.

2.2 Translators

Discussion to develop technologies to bridge IPv4 and IPv6 was started as early as when IPv6 protocol designers decided not to provide IPv4 backward compatibility in IPv6. Waddington and Chang summarized IPv4-IPv6 transition mechanisms in their paper [3]. From the viewpoint of translation mechanisms, we can classify these transition technologies into three approaches. The first approach is providing interoperability in the application layer, the second approach is relaying data in the transport layer, and the last is converting an IP header in the IP layer.

The first approach, the application layer approach is performed by proxy server software designed for each application protocol that needs interoperability between IPv4 and IPv6. The proxy server will be located at the boundary of IPv4 and IPv6 networks and accept specific application requests (e.g. web requests) from client nodes. The proxy server interprets the request contents, build a new request for the destination server, and send it using a proper IP protocol. The response from the server node is intercepted and resent by the proxy server as well. Since the proxy server understands the application protocol completely, this approach can be most flexible compared to the other approaches. On the other hand, development per application protocol is required which will increase development and operation cost. This approach is mostly used when we only need complex context processing in between IPv4 and IPv6 networks, since many services can be interoperable using the rest of the approaches.

In the second approach, the transport layer approach, the relay server located in between the IPv4 and IPv6 networks terminates incoming connections from clients at the socket level, and starts new transport connections to the destination server on the other side of the network. The well-known mechanisms of this approach are, for example, SOCKS64 [4,5] and Transport Relay Translator [6]. In SOCKS64, the client side SOCKS64 library replaces the DNS name resolution and socket I/O functions to intercept all the client traffic and forward to a SOCKS64 server. This mechanism requires client applications to be updated to use the SOCKS64 library, however, once the library is replaced, applications do not need to pay any attention to IPv4-IPv6 translation issues. The Transport Relay Translator does not require any update to client applications. Instead, the mechanism assumes that clients use specially crafted IPv6 addresses in which IPv4 address of the server is embedded, when IPv6 clients are going to connect to IPv4 servers. The relay server terminates the incoming IPv6 connections from client nodes and starts new connections to the destination servers using the server address extracted from the special IPv6 address. Such special IPv6 addresses are usually provided by the site level special DNS server in the client site that supports DNS64 [7].

The third approach, the IP layer header translation is similar to the NAT technology used in IPv4. Examples of this approach are NAT-PT [8] and NAT64 [9]. In this approach, the translation server does not need to terminate connections between clients and servers. The address fields and other header fields of packets reached to the translator node will be translated based on the predefined header transformation rules between IPv4 and IPv6.

These related technologies were originally designed for the situation that there are IPv4 server nodes in the Internet, and IPv6 client nodes are going to connect to those IPv4 servers. It is assumed that one or a few IPv4 addresses are allocated to the translation server, and many IPv6 client nodes share the IPv4 addresses. However, the system discussed in this paper assumes the opposite case, that is, there are IPv6 server nodes in a cloud system, and existing IPv4 or IPv6 client nodes are going to connect to the IPv6 servers. In this case, we cannot share IPv4 addresses between many IPv6 servers without any modification to the IPv4 client side. Because of this nature, we have to map one IPv4 address to one IPv6 server eventually. Of course, the previous works and proposed mechanisms can do the same scenario in theory, however, there are few implementations that can support the case we are assuming.

There are some evaluation studies in these translation technologies [10,11]. However, since the performance of the mechanisms highly depends on how the mechanisms are implemented, we need to compare whenever we design a new translation software.

There are several commercial devices providing IPv4-IPv6 translation function. Most of them are targeting a translation service of internal IPv6 client connection requests generated inside the customer's network, to global IPv4 servers. Different from the existing translation products, our approach targets on service provider side and provides a function for IPv4 legacy clients to connect servers running with IPv6 only.

Our approach runs without keeping any state information of connections, while most of translator products are stateful to share IPv4 addresses among IPv6 clients. Our proposal does not share IPv4 addresses but have one to one mapping between an IPv4 address and an IPv6 address. Because of this difference, our approach is implemented as stateless service. That makes it easier to place multiple translators at several network exit points and distribute traffic load.

In this paper, we propose a new IaaS system design and IPv4-IPv6 translator design and implementation that only use IPv6 as its service backend network, providing dual-stack service to both IPv4 and IPv6 clients. We also give the performance measurement results of the system.

3 Design and Implementation of the IaaS System and the Translation Software

In this section, we describe the overview of the proposed IaaS system and design of the IPv4-IPv6 header translation software.

3.1 Design and Implementation of the IaaS System

The system we are targeting is an IaaS system that provides virtual computers as a unit of resources using virtualization technology. Service integrators can use virtual computers as their service components by requesting the IaaS system to slice physical computers to make virtual computers whenever needed. The actual configuration of a service varies in each service, however, one service usually composed of several computers, such as a web frontend node, load balancers, a database node, and so on. Services such as a distributed storage may need larger number of virtual computers as a backend system. When we consider providing a dual-stack service to users, one possible implementation is building the IaaS system as a complete dual-stack system. However, as we discussed in section 1, we will have a duplicated effort to maintain two different network stacks, which they have almost same functions. Since the service users usually only see the frontend nodes, it will be sufficient if we can make those frontend nodes dual-stack. The communication between the frontend nodes and backend nodes do not necessarily be dual-stack. By focusing only one protocol stack inside the IaaS system, the network design will be simpler that will benefit the IaaS service provider, and the service development cost and testing cost can also be reduced that will benefit service providers.

In this proposed system, we assume an IPv4 address and an IPv6 address are mapped one to one. Because the proposed system discussed in this paper is for IaaS providers providing server resources to their users, who are PaaS providers, SaaS providers, and/or ASPs, we cannot design the system to share one IPv4 address by several IPv6 server nodes. We also don't consider implementing this requirement using application level proxy solution, since service providers have different requirements for their services, we cannot limit the communication layer function to application layers. This may be a problem considering that the IPv4 address is scarce resource. However, we need to use IPv4 addresses anyway if we want to support IPv4 clients. And also we need to map addresses one to one if we want to provide services without any modification on the client side. Our best effort to handle this issue is that we do not allocate IPv4 addresses to backend nodes to avoid non-necessary IPv4 use.

The version of an IP protocol used in the backend network can be either IPv4 or IPv6. In the implementation shown in this paper, we use IPv6 as an internal protocol for the backend network considering the trend of IPv6 transition of the whole Internet.

Fig. 1 depicts the overview of the proposed system. We said that the frontend nodes provide dual-stack services to the client before, however precisely speaking, these frontend nodes do not have any IPv4 addresses. The mapping information between IPv4 and IPv6 addresses are registered to each IPv4-IPv6 translator node and shared by all the translator nodes. Since the mapping is done in the one to one manner, no translator nodes need to keep session information of ongoing communication. They can just translate IP packets one by one. This makes it possible to place multiple translator nodes easily to scale out the translation service when the amount of the traffic grows. This feature also contributes robustness of the translation system. When one of the translator nodes fails, we can just remove the failed node from the system. Since there is no shared session information among translator nodes, the service is kept by the rest of the translator nodes without any recovery operation.

Fig. 2 shows the overview of the actual system we are operating. The virtual machine resource management system located at the bottom of the figure is the WIDE Cloud Controller (WCC) [12] developed by the WIDE project. The two network operation centers (NOC) located at Tokyo and Osaka are connected by a wide area layer 2 network technology. The layer 2 network is a 10Gbps fiber line dedicated to the WIDE project

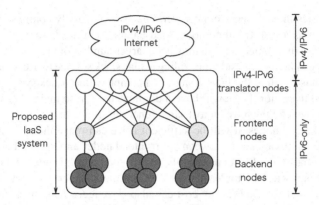

Fig. 1. The overview of the proposed IaaS system

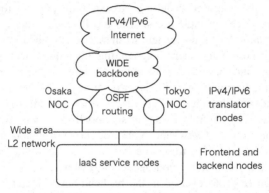

Fig. 2. The actual network configuration of the proposed IaaS system implemented and operated in the WIDE project operation network

network operation. There are two network segments in Tokyo and Osaka NOC whose network address spaces are same. These two layer 3 networks are connected by the layer 2 link using VLAN technology. The translator nodes are placed at each location. The routing information of the IPv4 addresses used to provide IPv4 connectivity to IPv4 clients is managed using the OSPFv3 routing protocol in the WIDE project backbone network. Since all the translator nodes advertise the same IPv4 address information using the equal cost strategy, incoming traffic is distributed based on the entry points of the incoming connections. The aggregated IPv4 routing information is advertised to the Internet using the BGP routing protocol. Any incoming IPv4 connection requests from the Internet are routed to the WIDE backbone based on the BGP information, routed to one of the translator nodes based on the OSPFv3 routing information, and finally routed to the corresponding virtual machine based on the static mapping table information stored in the translator nodes. The translation mechanism is described in section 3.2. Failure of either Osaka or Tokyo NOC will result in failure of the OSPFv3 routing information advertisement from the failed NOC, however, thanks to the nature of a routing protocol, and one to one stateless IPv4-IPv6 mapping mechanism, the other NOC and translator will continue serving the same address space to the Internet.

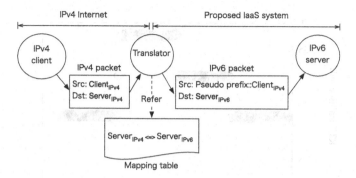

Fig. 3. IPv4-IPv6 header translation procedure

3.2 Design and Implementation of the Translator Software

The server nodes in the IaaS backend system will see all the communication from their clients as IPv6 connections, since the backend system is operated in IPv6 only. All the IPv4 traffic from clients are intercepted by the translator nodes and converted to IPv6 traffic. Fig. 3 shows the translation procedure used in the translator software.

IPv4 address information bound to IPv6 addresses of servers is stored in the mapping table. Based on the table, the destination address of the IPv4 packet from client nodes is converted to the proper IPv6 server address. The source address of the IPv6 packet is converted to a pseudo IPv6 address by embedding the IPv4 address of the client node to the lower 32-bit of the pseudo IPv6 address. The pseudo IPv6 address is routed to the translator node inside the backend network. The reply traffic from the server side is also converted with the similar but opposite procedures.

The mechanism has been implemented using the tun pseudo network interface device that is now provided as a part of the basic function of Linux and BSD operating systems, originally developed by Maxim Krasnyansky[1]. The tun network interface can capture incoming IP packets and redirect them to a user space program. The user space program can also send IP packets directly to the network by writing the raw data of the IP packets to the tun interface. The translator nodes advertise the routing information of the IPv4 addresses in the mapping table to receive all the traffic sent to those IPv4 addresses. The incoming packets are received via the tun network interface and passed to the user space translator application. The translator performs the procedure described in Fig. 3 to translate the IPv4 packet to IPv6 packet. The converted IPv6 packet is sent back to the tun network interface and forwarded to the real server that is running with IPv6 address only.

For the reverse direction, the similar procedure is applied. Since the translator nodes advertise the routing information of the pseudo IPv6 address that includes the IPv4 address of the client node is advertised to the IaaS backend network, the translator nodes receive all the reverse traffic. The nodes convert those IPv6 packets into IPv4 packets using the embedded IPv4 client address and mapping table information, and forward to the original IPv4 client.

---

[1] http://vtun.sourceforge.net/tun/

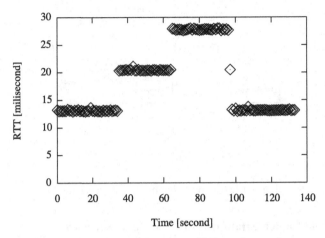

Fig. 4. RTT measurement in case of failure of a translator

This translator software *map646* is published as open source software [13], and any-
one can use it freely.

4   System Evaluation

We implemented the proposed IaaS system as a part of the WIDE project service network as shown in Fig. 2. By focusing on IPv6-only operation, we could be free from
IPv4 network management.

For the redundancy, we located two translator nodes in different locations of the
WIDE project core network. We sometimes stop one of them for maintenance. In that
case, the other running node is working as a backup node. We confirmed that the redundancy mechanism is working automatically in a real operation.

The incoming traffic to IPv4 addresses are load-balanced based on the BGP and
OSPFv3 information. For the outgoing traffic, currently a simple router preference
mechanism is used to choose an upstream router from IPv6 servers. We are considering using more advanced traffic engineering methods, such as destination prefix based
routing in near future.

Fig. 4 shows the RTT measurement result from an IPv4 client to an IPv6 server.
Initially, both translator nodes are running. At time 35, we stopped the router advertisement function of translator in Tokyo. The traffic from outside to the cloud network still
goes to Tokyo node, but the returning traffic will be routed to Osaka. At around time
65, we stopped routing function of the Tokyo node. After this point, all the traffic goes
to Osaka and returns from Osaka. We restarted the routing function of Tokyo node, and
restarted router advertisement at Tokyo node at around time 90. Finally, all the traffic
came back to go through Tokyo node.

5   Performance Evaluation

The obvious bottleneck of the system is the translator nodes where all the traffic must go
through with them. This section shows the evaluation result of the translation software.

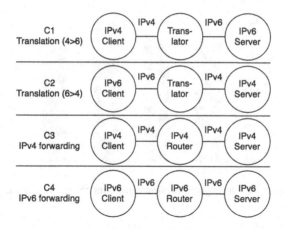

Fig. 5. The four configurations used in performance evaluation

Table 1. Specification of nodes

	Client/Server	Translator/Router
CPU	Core2 Duo 3.16GHz	Xeon L5630 2.13GHz $\times$ 2
Memory	4GB	24GB
OS	Linux 3.0.0-12-server	Linux 3.0.0-12-server
NIC	Intel 82573L	Intel 82574L

5.1   Translation Performance

The performance evaluation is done with the four different configurations shown in Fig. 5. The configuration 1 and 2 (C1 and C2) are the translation cases using our translator software. Configuration 2 (C2) and 3 (C3) use normal IPv4 and IPv6 forwarding mechanisms to compare the translation performance with no translation cases.

Evaluation is done using two methods, one is the *ping* program to measure RTT, and the other is the *iperf* program to measure throughput. All the results in this experiment show the average value of 5 measurement tries[2]. The computer nodes used in this performance test are shown in Table 1, and all the tests were performed locally by directly connecting 3 computers as shown in Fig. 5.

Table 2. RTT measurement result using the ping program

Case	C1	C2	C3	C4
RTT (ms)	0.45	0.43	0.36	0.36

Table 2 and Fig. 6 show the result of the RTT measurement result and the TCP throughput measurement result respectively. The throughput values were 923.8Mbps in C1, 922.8Mbps in C2, 938.0Mbps in C3, and 925.8Mbps in C4.

---

[2] We didn't record standard deviation of these tries, since the results were stable.

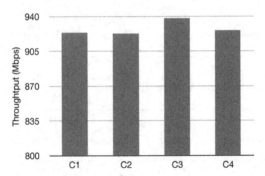

Fig. 6. TCP throughput measurement using the iperf program

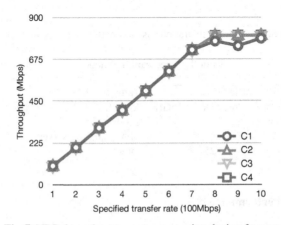

Fig. 7. UDP throughput measurement using the iperf program

Fig. 7 shows the result of the UDP throughput measurement test. We changed the transmission rate of the sender side from 100Mbps to 1000Mbps with 100Mbps step, and measured how much throughput was achieved at the receiver side. The maximum throughput values were 786.0Mbps in C1, 802.0Mbps in C2, 802.0Mbps in C3, and 802.0Mbps in C4.

5.2   Comparison with Related Methods

In this section, we compare the translation performance of map646 to *linuxnat64* [14] which is one of the NAT64 implementations. The main usage of NAT64 is to provide access to IPv4 servers from IPv6-only nodes. Because of the difference of the usage scenario, we located a server in the IPv4 network side, and located a client in the IPv6 network side in this test (the C2 case). This is opposite to our proposed IaaS usage, however we think the test can give us meaningful result in the sense of performance comparison. In this test, we used Linux 2.6.32 instead of 3.0.0-12-server because linuxnat64 did not support Linux version 3 when we performed this test. There is no big difference of IPv4/IPv6 forwarding performance between Linux version 2 and 3. Unfortunately, the development of linuxnat64 is discontinued, we cannot compare them in

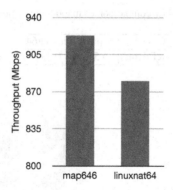

Fig. 8. TCP throughput comparison of map646 and linuxnat64

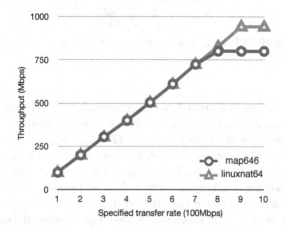

Fig. 9. UDP throughput comparison of map646 and linuxnat64

Linux version 3 environment. We are planning to try different kernel-based translators in the future.

Table 3 and Fig. 8 show the RTT measurement result and the TCP throughput measurement result respectively. The throughput values were 903.2Mbps in the map646 case, and 879.8Mbps in the linuxnat64 case. Fig. 9 is the result of the UDP throughput measurement. The maximum throughput values were 943.0Mbps in the map646 case, and 943.0Mbps in the linuxnat64 case.

5.3   Throughput in 10Gbps Environment

10Gbps network interface is now being more popular and popular. It is worth knowing how the proposed user space translation mechanism behave in such a high speed network environment. Fig. 10 is the result of TCP throughput measurement using Intel Ethernet Converged Network Adapter X520-SR2. We observed the map646 could only achieve 1.32Gbps in C1 and 1.96Gbps in C2 case, while IPv4 and IPv6 native forwarding could achieve 8.96Gbps and 9.26Gbps respectively.

Table 3. RTT comparison of map646 and linuxnat64

Case	map646	linuxnat64
RTT (ms)	0.55	0.39

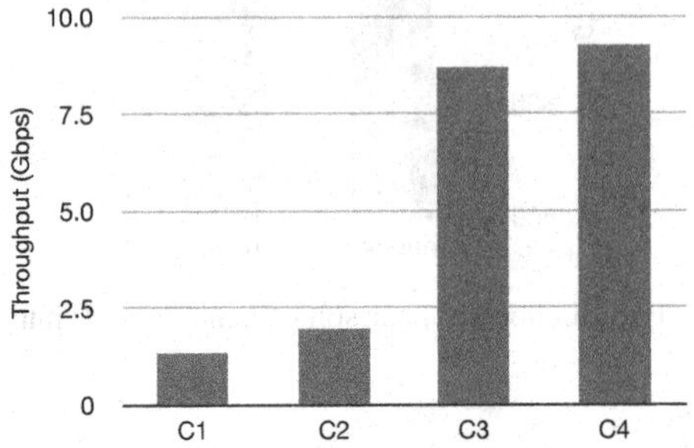

Fig. 10. TCP throughput comparison over 10Gbps network

6   Discussion

Based on the observation in section 4, we could consider the proposed IaaS system could reduce the maintenance cost, achieve redundancy and scalability.

For the performance, as shown in Fig. 2, the RTT degradation is around 0.07ms to 0.09ms. This is reasonable because map646 is implemented as a user space program while IPv4 and IPv6 forwarding are implemented inside kernel. The other potential reason of the degradation is a mapping entry lookup overhead. In this experiment, we only defined two mapping entries in map646. To evaluate the scalability of the mapping entry lookup mechanism, we performed a simulation. Fig. 11 shows the simulated result of the lookup and address conversion overhead for different number of mapping entries. In our implementation, the lookup mechanism uses a hash table and the size of the table is 1009. From the magnified part in Fig. 11, we can see the table lookup and address conversion is done in almost constant time when the size of the mapping entries is less than 10000. When the size of the table grows, the lookup and conversion time grows linearly as can see in the entire figure in Fig. 11. The lookup and conversion overhead of one entry is around 2 μs when there are 128 thousands of mapping entries. This value is enough small that can be ignored compared to the RTT degradation value. However we agree that the real measurement of the performance degradation with many mapping entries is an important topic, and it is one of our future works.

The forwarding performance of map646 is 1.5% to 1.6% worse than the normal forwarding case in the TCP case, and 2.0% in the UDP case. We actually did not see a big degradation in both TCP and UDP cases in the 1Gbps network environment. This means that the translation itself is enough fast to process all the incoming packets. We can conclude that the performance of the map646 translator software is acceptable for the real operation.

From Fig. 8 and 9, we can see almost no degradation compared to linuxnat64 implementation. Map646 achieved even better performance than linuxnat64 in the TCP case. We expected a slight degradation in the map646 case, since linuxnat64 is implemented

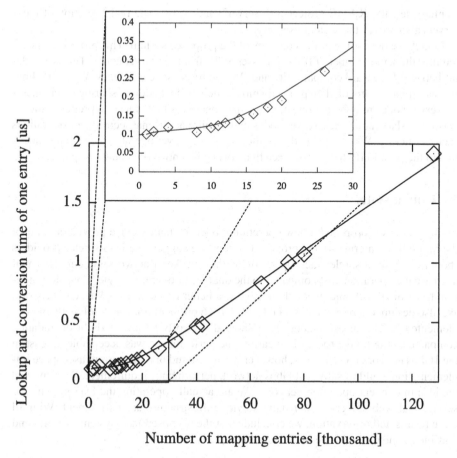

Fig. 11. Simulated result of mapping table lookup and address conversion overhead

as a kernel module while map646 is a user space program, but the result did not show any big difference. This result shows that the performance highly depends on how the software is implemented.

We then measured the throughput using 10Gbps network environment, which is not popular at this moment but is believed to be deployed in near future. As shown in Fig. 10, the throughput of map646 was capped around 1.8Gbps. The bottleneck is packet coping part between the kernel and user space, implemented using the tun network interface. Two possibles solutions are, 1) designing a high performance packet read/write mechanism for user space, or 2) implementing the translation part in the kernel.

We are actually operating several web servers as a part of our daily operation. The examples of those servers are the WIDE project web server[3], the web server of the Graduate School of Information Science and Technology at the University of Tokyo Japan[4], the DNS server for the wide.ad.jp domain, the web server for the Internet

---

[3] http://www.wide.ad.jp/
[4] http://www.i.u-tokyo.ac.jp/

Conference[5], the KAME project web server[6], and so on. The real operation of these servers also proves the system usability.

Finally we note some of the concerns of the proposed system. This proposed system requires the same number of IPv4 addresses as the frontend server nodes. This is a trade-off between backward compatibility and IPv4 address usage efficiency. When IPv4 becomes a minor protocol, then probably more efficient IPv4 address sharing mechanisms for server nodes may be deployed. The other concern is that since the proposed mechanism translates addresses, server nodes may require additional security considerations such as filtering. When writing down filter rules, the server operators need to pay attention to the pseudo IPv6 address space that covers the entire IPv4 address space.

7   Conclusions

In this paper, we proposed a new operation model for IaaS service providers to adapt the future IPv6 Internet. In the proposed system, we suggest the IaaS service providers should focus on a single stack operation as their backend network system. That will decrease the operation cost compared to the dual-stack operation style. Considering recent trend of IP technology, we think IPv6 is a better choice for the backend network. We also designed a robust and scalable IPv4-IPv6 protocol translator software and implemented it. The measurement result showed the software has a slight degradation compared to the native forwarding cases. The performance was acceptable at least in the 1Gbps network environment, however we also found that the current user space implementation couldn't satisfy 10Gbps network performance requirement. We deployed the idea in our real operation network. We are actually operating the IaaS system and several real web servers as our daily service infrastructure at this moment. With all these results and observation, we conclude that the proposed IaaS system is useful and feasible as one of the future IaaS operation models.

References

1. Mackay, M., Edwards, C., Dunmore, M.: A Scenario-Based Review of IPv6 Transition Tools. IEEE Internet Computing 7(3), 27–35 (2003)
2. Chen, G.: NAT64 Operational Considerations. IETF (October 2011); draft-chen-v6ops-nat64-cpe-03
3. Waddington, D.G., Chang, F.: Realizing the transition to ipv6. IEEE Communications Magazine 40(6), 138–147 (2002)
4. Kitamura, H.: Entering the IPv6 Communication World by the SOCKS-Based IPv6/IPv4 Translator. In: INET 1999 (June 1999)
5. Kitamura, H.: SOCKS-based IPv6/IPv4 Gateway Mechanism. IETF, RFC3089 (April 2001)
6. Itojun Hagino, J., Yamamoto, K.: An IPv6-to-IPv4 Transport Relay Translator. IETF, RFC3142 (June 2001)
7. Bagnulo, M., Sullivan, A., Matthews, P., van Beijnum, I.: DNS64: DNS Extensions for Network Address Translation from IPv6 Clients to IPv4 Servers. IETF, RFC6147 (April 2011)

---

[5] http://www.internetconference.org/
[6] http://www.kame.net/

8. Tsirtsis, G., Srisuresh, P.: Network Address Translation - Protocol Translation (NAT-PT). IETF, RFC2766 (February 2000)
9. Bagnulo, M., Matthews, P., van Beijnum, I.: Stateful NAT64: Network Address and Protocol Translation from IPv6 Clients to IPv4 Servers. IETF, RFC6146 (April 2011)
10. Mackay, M., Edwards, C.: A Comparative Performance Study of IPv6 Transitioning Mechanisms NAT-PT vs. TRT vs. DSTM. In: Boavida, F., Plagemann, T., Stiller, B., Westphal, C., Monteiro, E. (eds.) NETWORKING 2006. LNCS, vol. 3976, pp. 1125–1131. Springer, Heidelberg (2006)
11. Škoberne, N., Ciglarič, M.: Practical Evaluation of Stateful NAT64/DNS64 Transition. Advances in Electrical and Computer Engineering 11(3), 49–54 (2011)
12. WIDE project: WIDE Cloud Controller (August 2011), http://wcc.wide.ad.jp/
13. Shima, K., Ishida, W.: Map646: Mapping between IPv6 and IPv4 and vice versa (August 2011), https://github.com/keiichishima/map646/
14. Kriukas, J.: Linux NAT64 implementation (February 2012), http://sourceforge.net/projects/linuxnat64/

Realization of a Functional Domain within a Cloud

Jonathan Eccles[1] and George Loizou[1,2]

[1] Department of Computer Science and Information Systems, Birkbeck, University of London,
London WC1E 7HX, U.K.
[2] Department of Computer Science, University of Cyprus, 1678 Nicosia, Cyprus
Jonathan.eccles@hp.com, george@dcs.bbk.ac.uk

Abstract. This paper describes a specific aspect of the work that has been done to virtualize the IT server estate of a company with a modern business architecture of about three to four hundred servers. This yields a practical server environment with the same architecture and servers and integrated networking in an abstracted form by using sets of HP c7000 chassis units. It has been achieved by applying hypervisor-based virtualization technologies to clusters implemented across constituent blades between sets of chassis units. The working system is enhanced by enabling specific HP c7000 operational capabilities together with separate virtualization technologies, which are consolidated in a single coherent design model enabled as a virtualized system implemented within one to three chassis units on a single site. Furthermore, the system is enhanced by enabling virtual L3 Ethernet via specific HP c7000 chassis operational capabilities which are consolidated in a single coherent design mode. The system is now enhanced so as to operate on a multiple site basis and also to use physical as well as virtual systems (e.g. servers, appliances, applications, networks, storage) in the same functional domain.

Keywords: Cloud Architecture, Profiles, Policy Management, Virtualization, Abstraction Classes, Service Control.

1   Introduction

There are many projects now underway which involve producing virtualized environments to support large-scale systems. Some of these are created as the result of physical-to-virtual (P-to-V) transformation programs where, in the first instance, virtual servers may replace the equivalent physical servers. In many cases, this may not involve any improvement in design other than the consolidation of server processes inherent in the virtual model. However, the virtualization paradigm may yield many improvements in systems architecture and design at many levels [6], some of which are discussed in an upcoming paper [8].

It is often the case that the system designer requires a method in order to be able to model and simulate part of the target system using the infrastructure intended to support it. In this case the target system constitutes a virtualized environment and the infrastructure that complements it is also made up of virtualized components. These virtualized components are derived from the orchestration policy which is in turn part

I. Ivanov et al. (Eds.): CLOSER 2012, CCIS 367, pp. 54–70, 2013.
© Springer International Publishing Switzerland 2013

of the modelling system as shown in Fig. 2. The target area for the Functional Domain (FD) is given as the specific layer in the model that is derived via the orchestration system whose function is to take not just the Virtual Machine (VM) object references, but also the Virtual Appliance (VA) object references and construct the equivalent virtual objects in the designated FD, subject to the policy of that specific FD. Additionally, the target system is fabricated as part of the overall virtualized environment and essentially can be said to be an FD [7]. This FD is separated from the main parent virtualized environment by a construct which we have called a Functional Domain Nexus Interface (FDNI). (See Fig. 1, where NAS, RDP, SAN and VDI stand for Network Accessed Storage, Remote Desktop Protocol, Storage Area Network and Virtual Desktop Interface, respectively). The FDNI provides a secure point of entry to the designated FD such that neither TCP/IP-based traffic nor files may traverse the construct in either direction except by using a specific transit process. Thus the FD is a secure area within the Virtualized Environment, or within the cloud as a whole. This paper describes how the FDNI and the FD are hosted within a totally virtualized environment created by using one or more HP chassis units and a set of blades with X86 hypervisors (VMware ESXi v4.1 [26]). This concept has been referred to as 'super-hosting', since in essence it consists of the hosting of a virtualized distributed system by a totally virtualized environment. Distributed systems may be implemented within this environment and tested according to requirements. Alternatively, this method of virtualized systems engineering can be regarded as a method by which specific areas, within a dynamic cloud structure, can be defined to exist within certain policy constraints pertinent to the specific FD.

This paper introduces the FDNI and will illustrate the practical development of the associated FD based on the use of a chassis, blades, and the chassis-based On-Board Administrator / VC system together with sets of hypervisors to host sets of VMs in conjunction with Virtual Ethernets. The detailed construction of the FDNI in conjunction with its role in integrated FDs is a key part of another upcoming paper [9].

One of the key additional areas of practical development that is shown hereafter is how to enable the practical extension of the FD across more than one site within a Wide-Area Network (WAN). The corollary of this is that the Functional Design object gains the properties of being able to integrate with physical servers or appliances as well virtual ones. This leads to highly flexible designs for FDs within the business environment context of a cloud.

This paper also discusses how the classes and inter-connectivity of the constituent VMs is based on modelling structures [2] and paradigms for the virtualized cloud that are the focus of an upcoming paper [8]. The latter modelling structures are initially based on those used for distributed systems and are modified in order to produce networks of VMs, VAs and Virtual Storage in the context of an FD. Therefore, this paper presents a new way of formulating a solution to the problem of producing a practical model for a (virtualized) subsystem of a distributed application. This can be used in the assessment of the performance and the behaviour of the latter by direct access and measurement of the relative performance and capabilities of the sub-components with reference to the system as a whole [17].

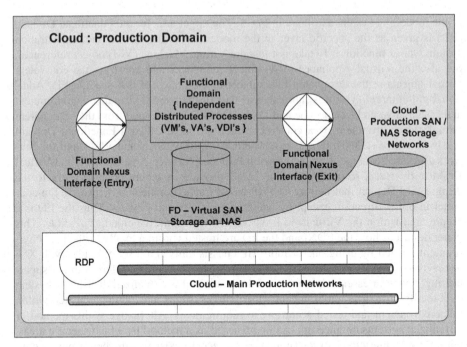

Fig. 1. The basic overview of the FD concept within a Cloud

2   Preliminaries

2.1   Current Paradigms

The initial purpose of this work was to meet the challenge of delivering the same functional solution at the application level to the business problems faced by a customer, but at a much lower level of delivery cost (say 30%), and also at a much lower level of cost with respect to future expansion and implementation. This requires that the solution be at least an order of magnitude more flexible and able to add more value. In order to achieve this, it is required that the new system be modelled [21] at every level, and also ideally virtualized at every level in a fully networked abstracted environment.

This solution becomes important not only because of the implicit reduction in costs but also because the mapping of the business perspective to the technological areas used in the abstracted environment allows for transparent integration of systems to improve performance, and also to extend the lifetime of most classes of legacy systems. Therefore, the solution extends the natural lifetime of a legacy system, as it becomes virtualized and therefore no longer dependent on the functioning of its hosting hardware. Additionally, it enables the evolution of proven software programs to become more powerful by becoming part of larger-scale integrated systems, which in turn may become a part of a virtualized enterprise. Over time, this virtualized environment provides a vehicle to enable service-based implementations, eventually

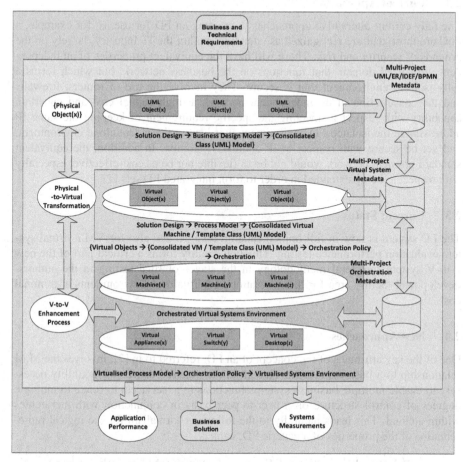

Fig. 2. Derivation of the practical Virtualized Environment from the Process Model of the VMs created from the P-to-V Process Model

enabling the deployment of SOA (Service Oriented Architecture) in a virtualized environment.

A more immediate purpose of this work was to enable the delivery of a virtualized FD that mimics the Production Domain but also has the capability of independent policy-based control. This must simulate the business problems faced by the customer and must enable system testing within an effective Proof-of-Concept (PoC) virtualized environment. Within this requirement the capital cost of the interface to the virtualized FD (PoC) must equate to zero. In order to achieve this, it is required that the new system be modelled and virtualized at every level in a fully abstracted networked environment. The natural extension to this scenario is how to enable the virtualized FD to operate in a transparent manner across a WAN. This requires the production of an effective FD that may serve as a PoC operating amongst operational domains or network sites. Such a system must be able to include physical as well as virtual servers in the PoC operational server set.

2.2   Current Approaches

The only current alternative approaches to creating an FD for use as, for example, a PoC are those that are recognized as 'standard' within the IT industry, largely on the grounds of security and risk. These will have the equivalent properties of an independent virtualized domain that functions on the business network, but which forms a fully isolated environment that is secure. They involve the use of routers, firewalls and the construction of an independent network at high capital cost and uncertain capability with respect to meeting the specific requirement of keeping the same IP addressing in the isolated FD environment as is kept in the parent cloud environment, and yet be secure with respect to IP address separation. In addition, the equivalent standard physical network would not be as flexible nor be as cost-effective, especially with respect to being extended in order to form integrated FD sets [1].

2.3   Current Status

The FD system is now in full implementation for PoC and also for VM / virtual system evaluation performance testing. This PoC facility forms a critical part of the new P-to-V system transferal methodology in the stages of final testing in the authors' development facility area for the generation of Virtualized Environments at minimal cost.

2.4   New Approaches

One of the key attributes of the concept of an FD, referred to in [7], involves the M:M relationship to a business system. This gives the required degree of flexibility necessary to enable multiple business systems functions (e.g. services) to relate to multiple degrees of control structure on a peer-to-peer basis in conjunction with hierarchies within a cloud. This leads naturally to the following formalism for the logical representation of the properties of a generic FD; namely,

$$\forall \ \text{Network\_Node}(x_i) \ \exists \ \big\{ \ \text{Functional\_Domain}(y) \mid \text{Network\_Node}(x_i)$$
$$\in \{\text{Functional\_Domain}(y)\}$$
$$\wedge \big((1 \leq y \leq \text{Max}(\text{Functional\_Domain}(y)))$$
$$\wedge \ (1 \leq \ x_i \leq \ \text{Max}(\text{Network\_Node}(x_i)))\big)$$
$$\wedge \big((\text{Network\_Node}(x_i) \in \{\text{Business\_System.Node}(a_i)\})$$
$$\wedge \ (1 \leq a_i \leq \ \text{Max}(\text{Business\_System.Node}(a_i)))\big)$$
$$\wedge \big((\text{Business\_System.Node}(a_i) \ \in \ \{\text{Functional\_Domain}(y).\text{BusSys}(z)\})$$
$$\wedge \ (1 \leq \ z \ \leq \text{Max}(\text{Functional\_Domain}(y).\text{BusSys}(z)))\big) \ \big\}$$

which is in [7].

The concept of FD, as it is herein presented, enables the requirement that a node may belong either to different domains within an operational session, depending on the set of abstracted processes being invoked; or alternatively, it may be a member of more than one domain simultaneously. By abstracting the concept of the network

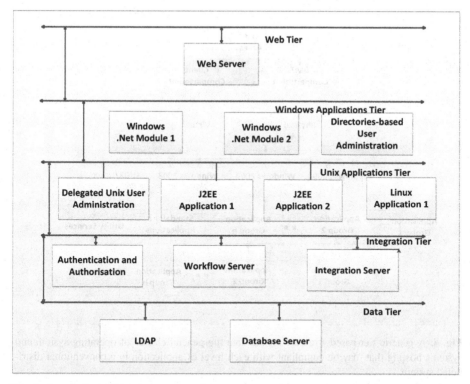

Fig. 3. A generic tier-based structure to illustrate the major classes and subclasses of an application that may exist within a conventional distributed systems environment

node within a cloud, each Network_Node object can be associated with different subclasses of abstracted cloud classes, e.g. those of users, user groups or workstations.

2.5   Server Process Abstraction

There is a great degree of overlap in the structure and the basic design of a cloud when compared to a large-scale open enterprise system. There is an ever-increasing tendency to formulate applications as distributed systems for a variety of reasons. Amongst these is the requirement for source code to become more agile in the sense that it can become more re-usable. When dealing with conventional physical systems this essentially means that modules that are constructed and compiled using such code (e.g. ActiveX, .NET [4], CORBA [19,22], JMS [10] modules) are copied between different physical servers. In such cases their degree of separation within a single project tends to be governed by their relative degrees of utilization within that self-same environment. Thus this pattern tends to follow the relatively restricted pattern of the distribution of server class shown in Fig. 3.

Hence it becomes essential to add value to the process of virtualization, and from there to the formation of a cloud through the use of processes that are currently being developed to consolidate the distribution of VMs in conjunction with their relative

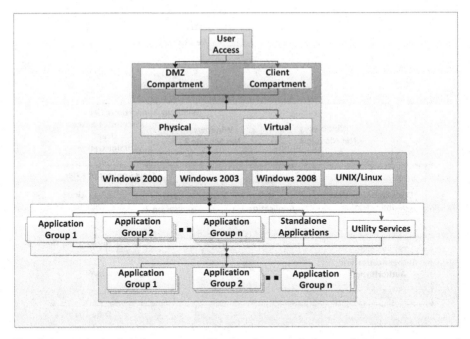

Fig. 4. A generic tier-based structure to illustrate the general classes of operating system and systems hosting that may be compliant with each level of application in a conventional distributed system

degrees of utilization [24]. This enhancement of virtualization is presently being modelled [8], so as to achieve a greater level of consolidation of application modules on the basis of their function with respect to their access functions. If the access functions are distributed and yet owned by separate projects, then the ownership paradigm must not be a determinant for which application modules become associated by threads to the required software modules. This indicates that many projects can therefore have temporary 'ownership' through the use of associated threads of one or more virtualized processes.

If this policy is implemented, then the result tends toward a distributed software environment that is more in line with that shown in Fig. 4. This illustrates the basis of a distributed environment that is, whilst ideally virtualized, also shared such that multiple projects within a business may have access to the same resource sets (VMs, VAs et al.) that exist within each level [16,13]. This concept leads to the formulation of a generic tier-based structure to illustrate the general classes of operating system and systems hosting that may be compliant with each level of application in a conventional distributed system. The essential concept to convey is that each instance of such a structure can be configured to occupy a single FD, where it may be examined in detail. The natural extension to this paradigm is that multiple areas of such shared resources may be deployed within one or more FDs in the same superhost.

Each such tier contains many VMs, VDIs and VAs that may be accessed by multiple access modules from multiple projects. The security level issues are not addressed in this paper but are the result of different policies from different FDs resulting in different software module access profilers being generated in accordance with different system requirements.

2.6   Hardware Environment

The Virtualization Environment was developed using blade technology on an HP c7000 chassis which has 16 internal device bays. A chassis is able to host up to 16 half-height blades or up to 8 full-height blades or any combination of the two depending on the class of blade. The chassis operational system was configured using an HP c7000 Operational Administrator (OA) module and an HP c7000 Virtual Connect (VC) bay module. All external interface modules (power, network, Host Bus Adapter (HBA) for Fibre-Channel (FC) storage access) were implemented in duplicate for seamless failover. The virtualized environment selected involved the use of X86 processor architecture to implement the VMware ESXi v4.1 hypervisor.

This was done through the use of the HP BL490c blade (2 * 4 core @2.56GHz, 96GB RAM, 2 * 1 Gbps NIC). The external HBA interface consists of 4 * 4Gbps FC interfaces to the SAN controller for direct access to the SAN-based hard drives through an HP XP24000 storage chassis. The network consisted of dual 3 * 10Gbps Ethernet from the VC bay (port 3X, 4X, 5X) implemented as a shared system connected to the dual Cisco 6509 L3 switches. This is complemented by a dual link to the NAS storage drive via a NetApp VFiler which is accessed through port 6X of the VC bay using IP at 10Gbps. This hardware setup is duplicated on both sites and is illustrated in Fig.10. The HP XP24000 SAN is simulated through the use of a VM in the FD that accesses the NAS whilst running a software emulator for the HP XP24000 SAN.

2.7   Proof-of-Concept / Subsystem Abstraction

The concept of the virtualization of distributed subsystems has been utilized in order to test complex distributed applications, some of which have been produced by P-to-V operations and some through more conventional UML modelling (Muller, 1997). These VMs are required to be integrated in a duplicate environment to that of main production using equivalent software design but in a situation that was secure and where the relative performance criteria could be assessed. This system is now in full implementation for PoC testing and also for VM Factory testing.

3   Design of a Generic Approach

The initial approach was to undertake an analysis of the extant physical environment, producing the required landscape and cost of the basic business solution. This was followed by a projection based on the model of future operations with available compute technology for high level processing, yielding the initial levels of %CPU utilization based on physical server hosting. This solution concept was re-worked using the 'superhosting' concepts described within this paper. A 'superhost' is a computing system capable of running a very large number, in our case more than 200,

COTS-based subserver operating systems. These systems are normally extended applications that are implemented as distributed systems and have the property of being able to be interconnected at the level of a routable protocol (e.g. DCOM, COM+, ODBC, .NET [5]).

The latter sets of systems also have the requirement to be interconnected at a routing (L3) level and are thus able to be implemented within flexible environments produced by different FDs. This re-working was followed by process analysis of the extant physical system as a whole. This is in order to evaluate the optimum processing capability of the proposed classes of Target Host server with reference to the measured utilization of the threads of the extant physical server processes. From this, the VM-to-target Host Server mappings are computed in order to evaluate the theoretical P-to-V consolidation ratios of the VMs to the Target Hosts. This can create a number of alternative mapping scenarios, depending upon the sets of VMs and target classes selected.

The initial approach involved an automated analysis of the current customer physical environment, producing the required system and P-to-V model and cost of the basic VM-to-target mapping solution. This was followed by a projection based on the model of future operations and costs with available compute technology for high level processing, yielding the initial levels of %CPU utilization based on the best projected set of VM-to-target mappings. For each functional sub-domain within the derived host model, this solution concept as a whole was re-worked using 'superhosting' by employing blades within chassis architectures.

The next step in the Transition Mode of Operation (TMO) was to create an FD in the HP c7000 chassis, separated by an FDNI, so as to be able to create VMs from the current Production area and test the basic functionality of each generated VM. This was done by creating sets of Virtual Ethernets using the VC functions on the HP c7000 chassis. The critical point of the architecture is where the separation of the independent FD for the superhost is achieved using the FDNI. The separation of the Production network into two or more networks with the same IP subnet domain is achieved by the FDNI, effectively acting as a network diode, so as to achieve a unidirectional dataflow between them, where the event of passing an object through the diode is only able to be achieved through a deliberate action using a transfer facility within the FDNI. This degree of separation is achieved as a consequence of the FDNI implementing the following criteria: No IP Forwarding between the two physical NIC's of the blade server; Virtual Ethernet Separation via nested VMs hosting nested firewalls and via Protocol Separation through a VM hosting a dual-point of access created to a SAN datavolume, which is addressed using both the NFS and the CIFS protocols. This results in no capital cost overhead.

The range of this solution was extended by evaluating the internetworking of each physical server with respect to the hosted application's dataflow(s), and adding this information to the model of the current TMO environment. The next step in the TMO was to create a restricted area in the HP c7000 chassis in order to be able to create VMs from the current Production area. This was complemented by the creation of a TMO 'proving area' to test the basic functionality of each generated VM. The FD in the proving area enables the validation and tuning of the VM in conjunction with final confirmation on the functionality of the VM.

This was followed by the creation of the Virtualized Ethernets and their inter-connection using both L2 networking through sets of inter-connecting VMs. The virtual networks which are defined within the model are implemented using HP Virtual Network technology which utilizes OSI Level 2. We have extended this through the use of both VAs and VMs. In our case a set of Linux-based VAs were created to enable OSI Layer 3 routing between different subnets as well as firewalls to separate different virtual Ethernet environments, such as DMZ architectures, within the Virtualized 'SuperHost' (cf. Fig. 8, 9). This is the most basic overview utilizing approved modelling techniques. A full model is multi-layered and too complex to be included in this short paper. We utilized the IEEE standard RFC1918 which allowed the building of controlled networks such that L3 routing was required to enable their inter-connection.

The initial area of innovation presented here is the derivation of a full virtualized system from a complex physical model. This level of complexity must be retained as systems management will be integrated with the full multi-layered model. The main area presented extends the L2 Virtualized Ethernet to L3 using specific sets of L3 routers implemented as VAs, which enables the integration of sets of disparate COTS-based technologies, so that they may inter-operate transparently in the same HP c7000 device. This involves using sets of specific VAs to enhance the functional capabilities of the Virtualization Management software controlling the HP Smart Chassis and Blade Solution. The next area of innovation is to use the described extensions to enable a VDI layer virtual Ethernet to give a layer of secure access from the Cisco-based production network in a transparent manner through an uplink (Fig. 10).

3.1   Functional Domain Nexus Interface Mk II

Nexus Mk II Zones for the PILOT Environment Design: the design essentially becomes similar to a 'Jump Box' using IEEE RFC1918 networks and Microsoft Terminal Services technology. A Microsoft Firewall is active on the Nexus VM. IP forwarding is NOT permitted on this VM. Shared FC SAN is still used in the datacentre implementation allowing the implementation of a 'Reverse Nexus'. The virtualized equivalents of the physical environment are consolidated into Virtualized Ethernets (Vnets) for Vmotion and for Virtual Business networks that are within a defined virtual site which hosts the virtualized datacentre. The VLAN principles for the FD pilot area are that the VLAN configurations from the Cisco 6509 L3 switch to the HP c7000 chassis are standard for each production chassis. The term Vnet is used to describe an HP VC internal chassis network. Internally, the HP VC module software and VMWare ESXi hypervisor will be configured to provide intra-chassis variance. The pilot intra-chassis variance (Fig. 5) will be as per FDNI Mk II design, where a Vnet connected to production is present; a Vnet 'Transit' NOT connected to production is present and Vnets 'Pilot-V-Production1' and 'Pilot-V-Production2' NOT connected to 'Production' are present. 'Transit' Vnet is a 172 IP; 'V-Datacentre1' and 'V-Datacentre2' are similar in structure to those in the Production area, but are segregated by 'Transit' and the FDNI VM from main production.

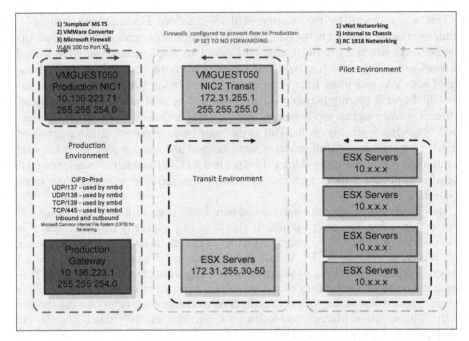

Fig. 5. A summary illustration of the FDNI that shows the basic parameters that are involved in the interfacing between the Production, the Transit and the FD (Pilot) environments

3.2   Functional Domain: Creation of the Basic 'Superhost'

This section illustrates the more detailed construction of the FD by increasing the complexity, and thereby the corresponding degree of functionality, of the superhost. Initially, as shown in Fig. 6, the production network of the cloud is linked through a VC port (3x, 4x, 5x) of the HP c7000 chassis to the FDNI entry port via the production NIC (NIC-1) of the HP BL490c blade upon which the FDNI / FDNI VM has been installed.

The FDNI is connected to the exit port via NIC-2 of the blade, which is in turn connected to the 'Transit' virtual Ethernet. As the name implies, all constituent HP BL490c blades in their respective clusters (Fig. 7) within the FD have one of their two NIC's connected to the 'Transit' virtual Ethernet. This gives a method of L2 TCP/IP connection for all VMs/VAs that are installed in the FD. However, not all installed VMs require direct connectivity to the 'Transit' virtual Ethernet. It is only important that there is a route that can be taken by L2 to 'Transit' at this point. The next level of development is to use the latter L2 connectivity to facilitate the addition of further virtual Ethernets (e.g. Virtual_Datacentre2, Pilot_V_Production1 in Fig. 7) using HP c7000 VC software.

This is now complemented by the addition of an extra virtual Ethernet for the hosting of a set of VDIs. The VDIs are communicated with via the FDNI using the RDP (Microsoft). When activated the user has access to a remote desktop window which operates inside the FD/PoC, and with this the user may operate safely without

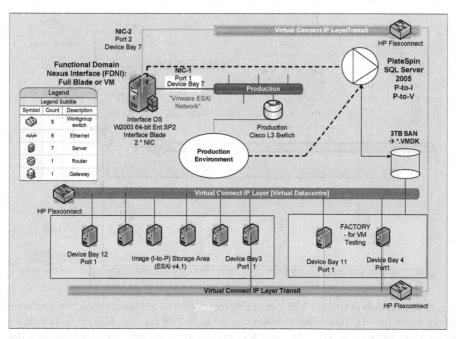

Fig. 6. View of the initial 'Superhost' structure showing the interface between the Production, the Transit and the FD (in this case the Virtual Datacentre) environments

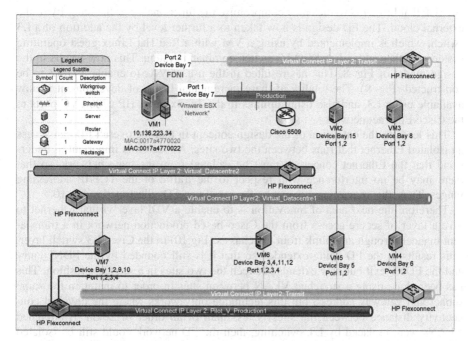

Fig. 7. The addition of more Virtual Ethernets to the FD. These can only be accessed from the 'Transit' Virtual Ethernet employing TCP/IP L2 using the 4 vNIC ports in any of the local VMs

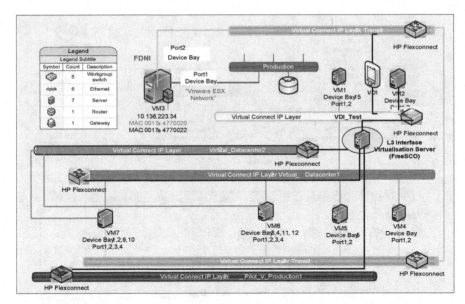

Fig. 8. The addition of an extra VDI virtual Ethernet as well as additional production emulation layers within the FD. These inter-communicate using TCP/IP L2. The addition of TCP/IP L3 switching capability to this set of virtual Ethernets is done by creating a VA-based on Red Hat Linux using the FreeSCO L3 switch software.

any risk that his/her activities may compromise the functionality or the integrity of the external cloud. The FD design is now taken to a further level by the addition of a L3 switch, which is implemented by using a VM with a Red Hat Linux guest operating system together with a FreeSCO L3 switch command system. This now results in the design model of Fig. 8. This has resulted in the use of VAs to enable a DMZ to be constructed (Fig. 9). The totality of these incremental layers of development is now available using L3, and also using uplinks to the 3x, 4x or 5x HP c7000 VC ports to the Cisco Ethernet networks.

This leads to the extension of the design concept in that the overall FD can access an isolated Ethernet that runs between the two sites. As such it is important to understand that the Ethernet concerned must be isolated from the main network, so that there may be no interference with respect to the traffic or the TCP/IP addressing ranges. Thus, this requirement is met by the set of two FDs illustrated in Fig.10.

Therefore the next area of innovation is to enable a VDI layer virtual Ethernet to give a layer of secure access from the Cisco-based production network in a transparent manner through an uplink from the chassis (Fig.10) to the Cisco L3 switch layer. This results in the FD being extended so that it is still bounded by the FDNI_entry and the FDNI_exit but now extends between the two sites in a seamless fashion. This has been done using a stretched VLAN between sites in order to maintain the same subnet and gateway address, but this technique only works where the physical connectivity distance between the sites is less than of an order of 20km. If stretched VLANs were replaced by L3 switching, then the FD network could still be isolated but the IP addresses of the constituent FD elements will be different on each of the

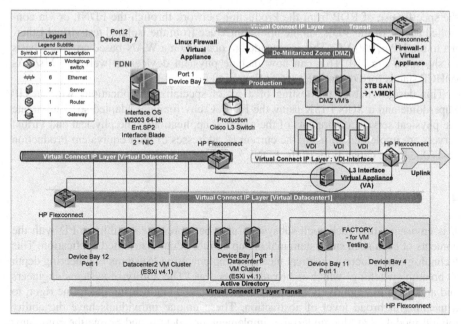

Fig. 9. The addition of a De-Militarised Zone (DMZ) made up of Linux-based VA Firewall units on a separate DMZ virtual Ethernet, and a L3 switch to link all of the FD virtual Ethernets

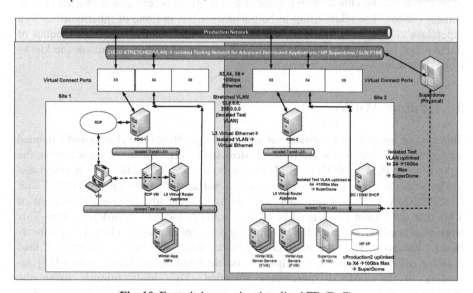

Fig. 10. Extended cross-site virtualized FD (PoC)

respective sites. This does not mean that this design no longer works, but rather that the mapping models in Fig. 2, 3 and 4 must be accurately detailed so that the IP addressing of each VM on each site is categorized and implemented through the use of DHCP/DNS. This design enables users to use the VMs/VAs either directly through the specific use of RDP from the Production network through the FDNI, or via controlled access of the VDIs via the uplink interface from the isolated test virtual Ethernet to the HP c7000 VC. This is extended to operate on a WAN-based cross-site basis as shown in Fig. 10. This can now include physical devices as well as VMs/VAs (DHCP stands for Dynamic Host Configuration Protocol.).

This design enables the testing of a set of specialized applications with an HP Superdome and a SUN F15K using the FD/PoC environment adapted so as to isolate the physical server components of the required applications. The physical and virtual servers are implemented using the current IP addresses of their equivalent Production hosts due to the capabilities of the FDNI.

4   Discussion

It is envisaged that each such subsystem may be represented within an FD with the contents of each such subsystem making up an individual distributed application. This technology introduces a practical means of implementing 'Systems Engineering depth to breadth switching' which is broadly defined as "The ability of systems engineers and architects to cognitively alternate, from a detailed engineering discipline rigor, to a meaningful broad level of abstraction. These unique individuals have the ability tobuild models that hide underlying implementation details and bridge the communication gaps between multiple disciplines." [25]. Each such subsystem modelled within an FD should be able to be represented as a single class composed of a set of constituent classes. The relationship to be pursued here is not one of inheritance as in a superclass to a set of subclasses [20,23] but rather one employing the techniques of frame-based modelling [18,14] to produce a framework class to represent the knowledge of how the system is constructed.

5   Future Work

This area of integration is carried out within a single HP c7000 chassis and extended across multiple chassis units to form a distributed centre capable of supporting in the order of more than 1000 VMs. Further work is required in building a fully integrated model with distributed sets of chassis units that are linked using L3 TCP/IP with DHCP/DNS/X.500-based directory services to facilitate the dynamic movement of VMs that are within the same FD, but are actually located on different sites. This work also needs to be extended in applying different classes of QMS Requirement-based Clustering [3] to the multi-cluster blade model within the 'SuperHost', thus enabling different 'SuperHost' entities to be clustered in different manners [15] according to the QMS Requirements specified. This leads towards using the 'SuperHost' system as a key component in a practical solution to cloud computing. The principle here is that an FD could be used to enable a set of pattern-based design tools to create a practical means of designing and modelling systems [12,23], from the simple to the very complex indeed. Such systems, through the use of associated metadata, could also have the capability of interfacing to complex simulation systems based on describing systems in terms of specific class-based connectivity, such as

Hyperformix. Creating multiple sets of overlapping FDs for accelerated policy simulation and system modelling is another area that is being currently pursued. This can be done through the use of mathematics followed by the creation of VMs as simulated application servers. This will create overlapping models where the resultant effect on the net policies can be virtualized.

6   Conclusions

This paper presents the basis for advancing the concept of the metamodel by moving from a set of modelling methods within a framework methodology [11] to an equivalent model that is virtual and can participate in positive testing and evaluation before the main product is finally constructed, thereby lowering the overall cost and risk involved in a development project.

References

1. Caetano, A., Pombinho, J., Tribolet, J.: Representing Organizational Competencies. In: ACM Symposium on Applied Computing (SAC 2007), pp. 1257–1262 (2007)
2. Carman, C.: Applying UML and Patterns, 2nd edn. Prentice Hall (2001)
3. Codina, J.M., Sanchez, J., Gonzalez, A.: Virtual Cluster Scheduling Through the Scheduling Graph. In: IEEE International Symposium on Code Generation and Optimization (CGO 2007), pp. 89–101 (2007)
4. Conrad, J., Dengler, P.: Introducing .NET. WROX Pub. (2000)
5. Corn, C., Mayfield, V.: COM/DCOM Primer Plus. SAMS (1998)
6. Daniels, J.: Server Virtualization Architecture and Implementation. ACM Crossroads 16(1), 8–12 (2009)
7. Eccles, J., Loizou, G.: Functional Domain Concepts in the Modelling of Cloud Structures and the Behaviour of Integrated Policy-Based Systems Through the use of Abstraction Classes. In: 1st International Conference on Cloud Computing and Services Science (CLOSER 2011), Noordwijerhout, The Netherlands, May 7-9, pp. 86–97 (2011)
8. Eccles, J., Loizou, G.: A Methodology to Control the Production of a Practical Virtual Environment for a Cloud in an Optimal Manner from a Complex Physical Environment (in preparation_a)
9. Eccles, J., Loizou, G.: An Extended Methodology to Integrate Multiple Functional Domains within a Virtualized Environment by Enhancing the Functional Model-ling of the Nexus Interface units (in preparation_b)
10. Farley, J.: Java Distributed Computing. O'Reilly (1998)
11. Fayed, M.E., Johnson, R.E.: Domain-Specific Application Frameworks. Wiley (2000)
12. Hohpe, G., Woolf, B.: Enterprise Integration Patterns. Addison-Wesley (2004)
13. Traore, I., Aredo, D.B., Ye, H.: An Integrated Framework for Formal Development of Open Distributed Systems. In: ACM Symposium on Applied Computing (SAC 2003), pp. 1078–1085 (2003)
14. Karp, P.D.: The Design Space of Frame Knowledge Representation Systems, SRI International Technical Note No 520, Artificial Intelligence Centre, Computing and Engineering Sciences Division (1992)

15. Kim, G.-J., Han, J.-S.: The clustering algorithm of design pattern using object-oriented relationship. In: Gervasi, O., Gavrilova, M.L. (eds.) ICCSA 2007, Part III. LNCS, vol. 4707, pp. 997–1006. Springer, Heidelberg (2007)
16. Loy, I., Galan, F., Sampaio, A., Gill, V., Rodero-Merino, L.: Service Specification in Cloud Environments Based on Extensions to Open Standards. In: ACM Communication System Software and Middleware (COMSWARE 2009), Dublin, Ireland (2009)
17. Menasce, D.A., Almeisida, V.A.: Performance by Design. Prentice Hall (2004)
18. Minsky, M.: A Framework for Representing Knowledge. MIT-AI Laboratory Memo 306 (1974)
19. Mowbry, T.J., Malveau, R.C.: Corba Design Patterns. Wiley Computer Publishing (1997)
20. Muller, P.-A.: Instant UML. Wrox Press (1997)
21. Niculescu, V., Moldovan, G.: Building an Object Oriented Computational Algebra System Based on Design Patterns. In: Proceedings of the Seventh International Symposium on Symbolic and Numeric Algorithms for Scientific Computing (SYNASC 2005), p. 8. IEEE Computer Society, Washington, DC (2005)
22. Otte, R., Patrick, P., Roj, M.: Understanding Corba (Common Object Request Broker Architecture). Prentice Hall (1996)
23. Shannon, B., Hapner, M.: Java 2 Platform Enterprise Edition – Platform and Component Specification. Addison Wesley (2000)
24. Solomon, B., Ionescu, D.: Real-Time Adaptive Control of Autonomic Computing Environments. IBM Centre for Advanced Studies, Toronto, pp. 1-13 (2007)
25. Trowbridge, D., Mancini, D., Quick, D.: Thoughtworks Inc.: Enterprise Solution Patterns using Microsoft .NET, Version 2.0. Microsoft Press (2003)
26. VMware Corporation: VMware Server Administration Guide 1.0 VMware Inc. (2006), http://www.vmware.com/support/pubs

Mining Facebook Activity to Discover Social Ties: Towards a Social-Sensitive Ecosystem*

Sandra Servia-Rodríguez, Rebeca P. Díaz-Redondo,
Ana Fernández-Vilas, and José J. Pazos-Arias

Department of Telematics Engineering, Escuela de Ingeniería de Telecomunicación,
University of Vigo, Spain
{sandra,rebeca,avilas,jose}@det.uvigo.es

Abstract. Clearly there is a growing omnipresence of social networking sites in particular and social services in general. Given this translation of social relations into the cloud, services are facing the problem of deciding, for every user, what are the really relevant links to provide a social-sensitive response. To this end, this paper provides a model for calculating the strength of social ties based on interaction information collected from various social APIs in the cloud. We apply this general model over users' data gathered from the Facebook API and preprocess this data to extract representative stereotypes. Apart from evaluating the tie strength according to the observed behaviour of the stereotyped users, we describe the utility of our model to deploy a social-sensitive ecosystem. We envision a ecosystem where services functionality is enhanced by the knowledge about users' social ties; services in the scope of social marketing, attention management and contacts management are included to clarify our vision.

1 Introduction

Social networks have become increasingly popular, turning into an important mean of communication among people of all ages. Although they do not expect to supply traditional communication, they are an important complement to it, allowing users to keep their contact list, share information and interact with others through cross-posting, messaging, games, social events and applications. Recently, several researches on online social networks have came up as consequence of their importance among Internet users. A plentiful number of them have focused on improving users' social experience by means of socially-enhanced applications using, for this purpose, information from their profiles and links in these networks, as in Wilson et al. [1] and in Chen and Fong [2]. The former suggests improving a white-listing system for email using social ties strength that allows emails between friends to bypass standard spam filters or detecting Sybil identities[1] in an online community to protect distributed applications.

---

* Work funded by the Ministerio de Educación y Ciencia (Gobierno de España) research project TIN2010-20797 (partly financed with FEDER funds), and by the Consellería de Educación e Ordenación Universitaria (Xunta de Galicia) incentives file CN 2011/023 (partly financed with FEDER funds).

[1] Sybil attacks happens when a malicious user pretends to have multiple identities -Sybil identities- to get to control a peer-to-peer system.

I. Ivanov et al. (Eds.): CLOSER 2012, CCIS 367, pp. 71–85, 2013.
© Springer International Publishing Switzerland 2013

The latter, in turn, proposes a framework of collaborative filtering on social networks, for which study the contribution of trust, similarity between profiles, relation between users and reputation.

These applications, as others recently developed, assume that social ties between users and their friends have not the same strength, i.e. the more interaction they have, the more relevant their tie will be. So, improving the effectiveness of these applications requires distinguishing strong ties from weak ties in social networks. With this aim, we have developed an approach to infer social ties between users from their interactions on Facebook. We have selected Facebook to put into practice our approach of gathering users' interaction activity because it is the largest social network with over 800 million active users [3]. Besides considering different tie signs (which denote interaction) on Facebook, we take into account aspects such as that relationships change over time and that they are more intense when less people are involved in them.

This paper is organised as follows. The following section provides a selection of works related to our proposal. Before detailing our method to infer ties strength indexes from Facebook in Section 4, in next section (Section 3) Facebook signs that imply interaction between users are indicated. Experimental evaluation that shows how our application works properly are provided in Section 5. Section 6 describes the context in which our application is included and shows examples of services to socially-enhance. Finally, in Section 7, a discussion in this field is provided.

2   Related Work

The concept of tie strength was introduced by Granovetter [4], who defines it as a function of duration, emotional intensity, intimacy and exchange of services from which ties are split into 'strong' and 'weak' ties. Although this work, as well as many others about this subject, are included in the field of social science, there are also several studies related to the same topic in computer science. For example, Mutton [5] describes a method of inferring a social network by monitoring an IRC channel in which, to obtain the network, an IRC bot observes the messages exchanged between users in the channel and, from this information, infers the social network in which they are involved. Other example is the case of Tyler et al. [6], who propose a method for identifying communities using e-mail data.

In the case of online social networks, they already provide users' social graphs, which are made of links between users and their contacts in these networks. However, initial studies on interaction networks (networks made up of ties among users who often interact through social networks) have brought great insights into how an interaction network is structurally different from a social network. Examples of these works are Wilson et al. [1], Viswanath et al. [7] or Backstrom et al. [8], which study users' activity on Facebook to built on the interaction network, taking into account different interaction signs. In Wilson et al. [1], for each user, these signs are links in the social graph (they only consider interactions between Facebook friends), wall-posts and photo comments, whereas Viswanath et al. [7] only take into account wall-posts to study the varying patterns of interaction over time affect the overall structure of the interaction network. Finally, Backstrom et al. [8] study how Facebook users allocate attention across friends, taking into account, as well as messages, comments and wall-posts, information about how many times one user views another's profile page or photos posted by another user. Both Wilson et al. [1] and Viswanath et al. [7] use Facebook data obtained using crawlers otherwise, Backstrom et al. [8] retrieve data directly from Facebook, since information about users' passive interactions such as browsing updates, photos or profiles from their friends through homepage, is not available.

Other studies to deduce the interaction network, as in Gilbert and Karahalios [9], are supported by the information kept in users' profiles: age, political ideals or distance between hometowns, for instance. However, Kahanda and Neville [10] study how to infer the nature and strength of relationships among Facebook's members using attribute-based features (gender, relationship-status,...), topological features (connectivity of the users in the friendship graph), transactional features (Wall postings, picture posting and groups) and network-transactional features (Wall posting in another users Wall,...) to obtain users' "top-friends". They have concluded that the most outstanding features to predict tie strength are network-transactional features, followed by transactional ones.

In this paper, we propose an approach to infer social ties between users from their interactions on Facebook. Although studies like Gilbert and Karahalios [9] consider information kept in users's profiles (age, political ideals,...), from our point of view, they are not as reliable as other signs left by users in the network, mainly different modes of interaction which we consider in our application. Apart from other features of interaction, we consider wall-posts, tagged photos or membership of a group as in the case of Kahanda and Neville [10]. However, in our proposal, as well as using these features, we take into account aspects such as that relationships change over time and that they are more intense when less people are involved in them.

Finally, aforementioned works get Facebook data using crawlers or directly from Facebook servers. However, as our approach is part of a large project to provide personalized services in the cloud, we are interested in using information obtained through social network APIs. In this paper, we propose getting the most out Facebook API and taking into account all users' information available having their suitable permissions, which is relevant from the view of interaction. Anyway, the procedure can be easily generalized to any social networking site with a public API.

3   Tie Signs: The Facebook Case

Facebook provides users with the typical interpersonal communication features, although its highlight is the *wall*. Subscribers use the wall to post photos, videos, links and messages that may be enriched with any friends' comment. Besides, *mini-feeds* provide detailed logs of each subscriber's actions, so any friend may see at a glance how has been his evolution in Facebook over time. As in any social network, security is a key factor and Facebook allows their subscribers to personalize the privacy settings to restrict access to the profile information, mini-feed, wall posts, photos, comments, etc. only to friends, friends-of-friends, lists of friends, no one or all.

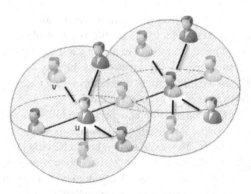

Fig. 1. User's social sphere

On the premise *the more interaction between two users, the more tie strength*, we have developed a Facebook application[2] that extracts user's activity in Facebook and infers the closeness between a target user, u, and one of this friends, v (Figure 1). Since u probably takes advantage from the Facebook facilities to communicate with v (private messages, wall-posts, photos and videos uploads, etc.), we use all this interactions as signs to build a model that calculates the tie strength between u and v, from the u's perspective: $TS_u(v)$. Please, note that this subjective point of view surely cause that the tie strength from the v's perspective, $TS_v(u)$, is different.

After a detailed analysis of Facebook features and how users interact and communicate, we have identified the interaction signs whose mathematical notation is as follows:

Wall-Posts. Let $P(x, y) = \{p_1(x, y), p_2(x, y), \ldots\}$ be the set of wall-posts user x has written on y's wall. Thus, $P_s(x) = \bigcup_{\forall y} \{P(x, y)\}$ is the set of x's posts over his friends' wall and $P_r(x) = \bigcup_{\forall y} \{P(y, x)\}$ is the set of wall-posts that x has received.

Private Messages. The set of private messages that user x has sent to user y is denoted by $PM(x, y) = \{pm_1(x, y), pm_2(x, y), \ldots\}$. Consequently, $PM_s(x) = \bigcup_{\forall y} \{PM(x, y)\}$ is the set of private messages x has sent and $PM_r(x) = \bigcup_{\forall y} \{PM(y, x)\}$ is the set of private messages x has received.

Comments. Let $C(x, y) = \{c_1(x, y), c_2(x, y), \ldots\}$ be the set of comments done by x about y's entries (photos, wall-posts, etc.). Then, $C_s(x) = \bigcup_{\forall y} \{C(x, y)\}$ is the set of comments done by x about any Facebook user's entries and $C_r(x) = \bigcup_{\forall y} \{C(y, x)\}$ is the set of comments that the x's entries have received.

Likes. Let $L(x, y) = \{l_1(x, y), l_2(x, y), \ldots\}$ be the set of likes done by x over y's entries. Then, $L_s(x) = \bigcup_{\forall y} \{L(x, y)\}$ is the set of likes done by x and $L_r(x) = \bigcup_{\forall y} \{L(y, x)\}$ is the set of likes that x's entries have received.

---

[2] Using the OAth2.0 protocol, our application requires the target user grants a set of privileges that are explicitly required when joining the application (see Section 5).

Photos and Videos. The set of x's photos where user y has been tagged is defined as $PH(x, y) = \{ph_1(x, y), ph_2(x, y), \ldots\}$. Analogously, the set of x's videos where user y has been tagged is defined as $VD(x, y) = \{vd_1(x, y), vd_2(x, y), \ldots\}$. Then, $PH(x) = \bigcup_{\forall y} \{PH(x, y)\}$ ($VD(x) = \bigcup_{\forall y} \{VD(x, y)\}$) is the set of x's photos (videos) where any of his friends is tagged.

Belonging to the Same Groups. $G_p(x) = \{g_{p_1}(x), g_{p_2}(x), \ldots\}$ denotes the set of the public groups to which x belongs and $G_s(x) = \{g_{s_1}(x), g_{s_2}(x), \ldots\}$ denotes the set of the private or secret groups to which x belongs.

Event Attendance. $EV_p(x) = \{ev_{p_1}(x), ev_{p_2}(x), \ldots\}$ denotes the set of public events to which x has shown intention to participate and $EV_p(x) = \{ev_{p_1}(x), ev_{p_2}(x), \ldots\}$ denotes the set of secret or private events to which x has intention to go.

4   Tie Strength Inference

This paper focuses on inferring tie strength indexes between Facebook friends, so we analyze how to assess the closeness u perceives about his relationship with v: $TS_u(v) \in [0, 1]$. In order to obtain the index value, we propose the following logarithmic function:

$$f(x) = \begin{cases} 0 & \text{if } 0 \le x \le \dfrac{\bar{x}^2}{x_{max}} \\[2ex] \dfrac{\ln(\dfrac{x_{max}}{\bar{x}^2} x)}{\ln(\dfrac{x_{max}^2}{\bar{x}^2})} & \text{if } \dfrac{\bar{x}^2}{x_{max}} < x \end{cases} \tag{1}$$

being $\bar{x}$ and x_{max} the mean and maximum value, respectively. So, $f(x)$ is close to 1 if $x > \bar{x}$, close to 0 if $x < \bar{x}$ and, finally, close to 0.5 if $x \sim \bar{x}$; exactly the behavior we are looking for. With this function as base, Section 4.1 shows our approach to calculate the tie strength index. However, as life itself, tie strength should be a dynamic index reflecting that old interactions are progressively less important and, so, should have less influence in the index calculation. Additionally, some signs' influence vanishes as the number of participants increase, so we have also added the concept of *relevance*. Section 4.2 shows as time and relevance are taken into account in the index calculation.

4.1   Tie Strength Calculation

We propose obtaining the strength index of the tie between u and v, from the u's perspective, as a weighted addition of three kind of interactions: (1) *on-line*, $TS_u|_o(v)$; (2) *face-to-face*, $TS_u|_p(v)$; and (3) *interest-based*, $TS_u|_i(v)$:

$$TS_u(v) = \beta \cdot TS_u|_o(v) + \gamma \cdot TS_u|_f(v) + (1 - \beta - \gamma) \cdot TS_u|_i(v) \tag{2}$$

On-Line Interactions ($TS_u|_o(v)$)**.** Under this name we include those signs that happen exclusively in the Facebook world and do not require a previous face-to-face contact:

wall-posts, comments, likes and private messages. We define two subsets: addressed-signs and open-signs. The former draw together the interactions that v explicitly sends to u –a private message, for instance; whereas the latter are those interactions without an explicit receiver –any like, for example. Therefore, $TS_u|_o(v)$ is obtained as follows:

$$TS_u|_o(v) = \alpha \cdot f(x_d(v, u)) + (1 - \alpha) \cdot f(x_o(v, u)) \tag{3}$$

where

$$x_d(v, u) = |P(v, u)| + |P(u, v)| + |PM(v, u)| + |PM(u, v)|$$
$$x_o(v, u) = |C(v, u)| + |C(u, v)| + |L(v, u)| + |L(u, v)|$$

are the number of addressed-signs and the number of open-sings, respectively and $f(x)$ is the logarithmic function in Equation 1. Since α reflects the importance of addressed-signs, that we consider is significantly more relevant than open-signs, it should be higher than 0.5.

Face-to-Face Interactions $(TS_u|_f(v))$. This contribution reflects any interactions showing a previous physical contact between u and v. It is obtained as follows:

$$TS_u|_f(v) = f(x(u, v)) \tag{4}$$

where

$$x(u, v) = |PH(u, v)| + |VD(u, v)|$$

denotes the number of u's photos and videos where v is tagged and $f(x)$ is the logarithmic function in Equation 1.

Interest-based Interactions $(TS_u|_i(v))$. This contribution assesses the common interests that u and v have explicitly shown. In the Facebook universe this may be done by subscribing to a group as well as accepting an event invitation. Thus, it is obtained as follows:

$$TS_u|_i(v) = \alpha \cdot f(y_d(v, u)) + (1 - \alpha) \cdot f(y_o(v, u)) \tag{5}$$

where

$$y_d(v, u) = |G_s(u) \cap G_s(v)| + |EV_s(u) \cap EV_s(v)|$$
$$y_o(v, u) = |G_p(u) \cap G_p(v)| + |EV_p(u) \cap EV_p(v)|$$

are the number of addressed sings (private and secret groups and events), and the number of open-sings (public groups and events), respectively and $f(x)$ is the logarithmic function in Equation 1; α, since has the same meaning than in Equation 3, should have the same value and be always over 0.5.

4.2   Impact of Time and Relevance

Not all Facebook signs, even belonging to the same kind, should have the same relevance in the index calculation. For instance, being tagged together in a five-people photo it is clearly more relevant than being tagged together in a twenty-people photo; at least, it may be assumed that in the first case the situation entails more closeness. So, some signs' relevance vanishes as the number of participants increase. For time we adopt the same pattern: relevance vanishes as time goes by. Thus, we propose modifying the previous equations by using the following decreasing function:

$$d(x) = e^{-\mu \cdot x} \tag{6}$$

where μ represent the strength of the slope, i.e. the velocity to *vanish* signs' importance: μ_r for relevance and μ_t for time.

Relevance Impact. This aspect only affects to face-to-face and interest-based contributions in Equation 2 (photos, videos, events and groups). Face-to-face contribution is obtained by:

$$TS_u|_f(v) = f(x(v,u))$$

where

$$x(v,u) = \sum_{\forall j \in PH(u,v)} d(|tags_j|) + \sum_{\forall j \in VD(u,v)} d(|tags_j|)$$

being $|tags_j|$ de number of tags in the j-picture (or video) and $d(|tags_j|)$ the result of applying Equation 6. To obtain interest-based index, Equation 5, we use the following contributions:

$$y_d(v,u) = \sum_{\forall j \in (G_s(u) \cap G_s(v))} d(|users_j|) + \sum_{\forall j \in (EV_s(u) \cap EV_s(v))} d(|users_j|)$$

$$y_o(v,u) = \sum_{\forall j \in (G_p(u) \cap G_p(v))} d(|users_j|) + \sum_{\forall j \in (EV_p(u) \cap EV_p(v))} d(|users_j|)$$

being $|users_j|$ the number of users that are expected to attend j-event or are subscribed in j-group, and $d(|users_j|)$ the result of applying Equation 6.

Gradual Forgetting. Time, however, affects all Facebook signs: the older an interaction is, the lower its weight should be. Thus, applying the decreasing function, the contributions to Equation 3 to calculate $TS_u|_o(v)$ are as follows, being $d(t_j)$ the result of applying Equation 6 to the time of the latest updated of j-Facebook sign:

$$x_d(v,u) = \sum_{\forall j \in P(u,v)} d(t_j) + \sum_{\forall j \in P(v,u)} d(t_j) + \sum_{\forall j \in PM(u,v)} d(t_j) + \sum_{\forall j \in PM(v,u)} d(t_j)$$

$$x_o(v,u) = \sum_{\forall j \in C(u,v)} d(t_j) + \sum_{\forall j \in C(v,u)} d(t_j) + \sum_{\forall j \in L(u,v)} d(t_j) + \sum_{\forall j \in L(v,u)} d(t_j)$$

In the case of calculating $TS_u|_f(v)$, the new contribution to Equation 4 is:

$$x(v,u) = \sum_{\forall j \in PH(u,v)} d(|tags_j|) \cdot d(t_j) + \sum_{\forall j \in VD(u,v)} d(|tags_j|) \cdot d(t_j)$$

Finally, the new contributions to Equation 5 are as follow:

$$y_d(v,u) = \sum_{\forall j \in (G_s(u) \cap G_s(v))} d(|users_j|) \cdot d(t_j) + \sum_{\forall j \in (EV_s(u) \cap EV_s(v))} d(|users_j|) \cdot d(t_j)$$

$$y_o(v,u) = \sum_{\forall j \in (G_p(u) \cap G_p(v))} d(|users_j|) \cdot d(t_j) + \sum_{\forall j \in (EV_p(u) \cap EV_p(v))} d(|users_j|) \cdot d(t_j)$$

5   Experimental Evaluation

Our evaluation is focused on three stereotyped Facebook users: (1) users having many friends that usually interacts with only a few of them (our instance is user A, which has 130 friends as the average Facebook user [3]); (2) users having only a few close friends and interacting with all of them (our instance is user B having 11 friends); and (3) users having a few friends with whom hardly interact (our instance is user C having 62 friends). With the objective of assessing the goodness of the previous formulation, we have developed a Facebook application that uses its API to access the available information the subscribers have upload in their Facebook profile. OAth 2.0 is the protocol Facebook uses for authentication (users and applications) and authorization (applications). OAuth provides a method for clients to access server resources on behalf of a resource owner (such as a different client or an end-user). It also provides a process for end-users to authorize third-party applications to access to their server resources without sharing their credentials (typically, a username and password pair), using user-agent redirections. Facebook implementation of the OAuth 2.0 involves three different steps: user authentication (users are prompted to enter their credentials), application authorization (users are asked to authorize the application to access some of their information through permissions) and application authentication (using the application secret, available from the Developer Application).

Since our objective is to retrieve information about subscribers' activity in Facebook, our application requires the following permissions (which are explicitly asked to subscribers whenever they run our application): (i) *basic information permission* (to access name, gender, profile picture, list of friends, networks and any other information the subscriber have shared with everyone), (ii) *offline permission* (to access the previous information anytime), (iii) permissions to access the subscriber's mailbox (*read_mailbox*), wall-posts (*read_stream*), photos (*user_photo*), videos (*user_videos*), events (*user_events*) and groups (*user_groups*). Using this information, we are able to obtain the tie strength index and all the data needed to this experimental evaluation.

5.1   Index Calculation

After several analysis, we have decided that the importance of the directed addressed-signs (α) is 5 times greater than the opened ones, as well as 60% is the weight for

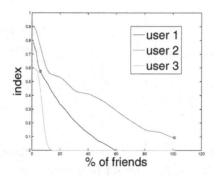

Fig. 2. $TS_A(x)$, $TS_B(x)$ and $TS_C(x)$

online interactions, 25% for physical interactions and 15% for interest-based interactions. Concretely, we have fixed $\alpha = 0.8$, $\beta = 0.6$, $\gamma = 0.25$, $\mu_r = 0.035$ y $\mu_t = 0.01$. We established these values because most of the users do not have many photos or, if they have many, they are not tagged. Also, they attended events and were members of groups with a lot of attendees (members), which indicated that this type of interaction would not be very relevant for them. Also, we observed that online interaction was their main type of interaction. Moreover, we consider that the importance of the event of interaction loses half of its value when there are about 20 users tagged in a photo (video) or members of a group (attendees an event) or when the event of interaction happened approximately two months before the moment in which indexes are calculated.

Under these conditions, Figure 2 shows the results for each stereotyped user, A, B and C. These results show that the value of the index is greater than 0.5 in, at most, the 23% of the considerate cases. It is in keeping with Wilson's article [1], which indicates that for most of the Facebook users, the large majority of interactions occur only across a small subset of their social links.

Besides, the more spread the allocation attention across friends (or not friends) is, the more difference exists among their indexes. For example, users B and C, who spread their interactions among their friends more uniformly than A, have a lower slope. For example, X is a very active user and has the same interaction signs with A and B, however $TS_A(C) = 0.58$ and $TS_B(C) = 0.009$, as expected. Thus, the tie strength index depends on how the allocation attention across friends is: high for A (A does not pay attention to many of his or her contacts), whereas for C is much lower, since C spreads his or her attention more uniformly among them.

5.2   Relevance and Gradual Forgetting

Now, we consider a user whose Facebook social graph is formed by 130 friends. We study how the index varies using different values for the params that control relevance and time (μ_r and μ_t). We chose this user because is similar than the average Facebook user, who has 130 friends [3].

We consider interaction sign's relevance and each kind of interaction separately. Figures 3(a) and 3(b) show how the index varies among the user's friends, taking into account only face-to-face and interest-based interactions, respectively.

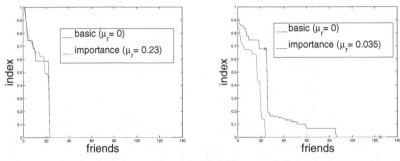

(a) Tie strength index (only face-to-face inter- (b) Tie strength index (only interest-based in-
actions)   teractions)

Fig. 3. Relevance influence in tie strength index

In graphic 3(a) we used $\mu_r = 0.23$, which means that the importance of the interaction sign loses half of its value when there are 3 users tagged in a photo (video). In
this case, the index is similar when we take into account or not the relevance of the
interaction. The reason is that the user's photos has hardly more than 3 people tagged
in them. To interest-based interaction (figure 3(b)) we fixed $\mu_r = 0.035$, which means
that the importance of the interaction sign loses half of its value when there are about
20 attendees an event (or members of a group). In this case we observe differences if we
consider or not the relevance. When we do not consider it, for the 35% of the contacts
their index is zero, while if we consider it, this percentage rises to the 80% of the users.
The main reason is because most of the groups (events) have about 5000 members (attendees), which means that the fact that the user belong to the group is irrelevant. For
example, the user B has a basic index of 0.68, while this value drops to 0 when the
relevance is considered.

Finally, we consider the importance of the time in each contribution to the index
(online, face-to-face and interest-based). In figures 4(a), 4(b) and 4(c), index variation
over the user's friends is shown. We fixed $\mu_t = 0.01$, $\mu_t = 0.002$ and $\mu_t = 0$, which
means that the event of interaction loses half of its value when it happened two months
or a year before the moment in which the index is calculated. The value $\mu_t = 0$ happens
when time factor is not considered. We used the same value for the rest of the parameters
that in previous section.

Results of this study are shown in the figures 4(a), 4(b) and 4(c). We obtain that the
number of friends with index value is equal to zero is greater when we consider the
time factor in the interaction. Also, the lower μ_t is, the more friends have index 0. It is
keeping with Wilson's article [1], which indicates that the lower the size of the temporal
window in which the interactions happened is, the lower the number of friends with the
user interacts is. Also It makes sense that a friend who is only tagged in some photos
uploaded 2 or 3 years ago has an index 0 when we consider the importance of the time
in the interaction. On the other hand, a friend that is tagged in few photos may have a
greater index than another friend tagged in many older photos when we consider the
importance of the time in interactions.

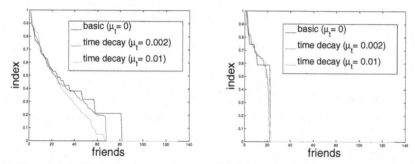

(a) Tie strength index (only online interac-   (b) Tie strength index (only face-to-face inter-
tions)   actions)

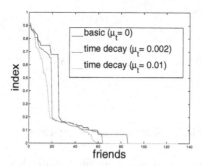

(c) Tie strength index (only interest-based interactions)

Fig. 4. Time influence in tie strength index

6   Application Context

Our application to infer tie strength from Facebook interactions is part of the project
CLOUDIA[3], which has the goal of defining a social-sensitive ecosystem to assist the
users in finding existing services in the cloud to satisfy their specific needs, and also to
detect and cater for new business opportunities in the form of services demanded but
not existing as a unique whole. To this aim, it will use information stored in the different
social networks in which the users may participate.

In CLOUDIA, to find suitable services, the assistance has to be personalized to
each user, i.e. depending on user's interests and needs, different services will be recommended. Last years, several collaborative filtering recommender systems have been
developed. All of them are based on the premise that users who have historically had
similar interests will probably continue having it into the present. An important issue
in these systems is finding a set of users, known as neighbors, that have a history of
agreeing with the target user (having rated different services similarly, tending to use
similar set of services,...). Moreover, several authors, like O'Donovan and Smith [11],

---

[3] http://gssi.det.uvigo.es/index.php?option=com_content&view=
article&id=210&Itemid=439&lang=en

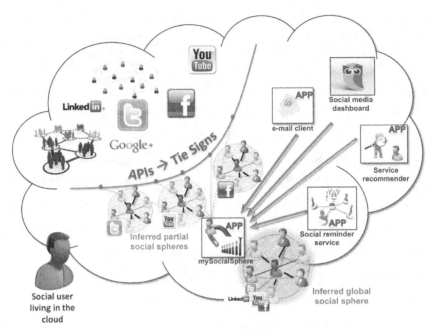

Fig. 5. Inferring social ties application

have improved neighborhood formation taking into account, besides similarity between profiles, social influence or trust between users. As in real life, when we look for an advice for a service (health, commerce, learning,...) we will often turn to our friends, on the basis that we have similar service preferences overall. In the case of applications, it is necessary knowing who are user's friends, i.e. users in which target user trusts when looks for a recommendation. Likewise, intensity of social relationships often varies, and recommender should be up on these changes. Since it is not feasible that users report to the application, we may get users' ties from social networks sites in which they have subscribed. However, as Wilson et al. [1] show, social network users usually tend to interact with a few of their friends (they applied it to Facebook, but it can be generalized to the rest social networks). That is, a friendship relation on Facebook does not necessarily indicate a real relationship between them. So, knowing which are the real ties between a user and his friends is essential in social networks.

At this point, our application would come into play, taking care of monitoring users' social networks activity and extracting, from this activity, users' ties strength. From them, the application will be able to build the users' social spheres and, ultimately, find the suitable services to them. Even though in this paper we focus on Facebook social network, our goal is to extend the application to any social network.

In Figure 5 our proposal is shown: a social service, *mySocialSphere*, which lives in the cloud and is in charge of monitoring and processing evidences of relationships to build up the user's social sphere. It builds up user's partial social spheres using user's information obtained from automated queries to different social networks APIs, which are combined to form the inferred global social sphere, which be used in CLOUDIA to find suitable services to users. Apart from the functionality of services discovery, existing services in the cloud may be socially-enhanced by the knowledge of users' social ties. Examples of these services are indicated below.

Social Marketing. The integration of web publicity and social media is emerging as a new trend in marketing. The idea behind it is that, by targeting the most influential users in the network, we can activate a chain-reaction of influence driven by word-of-mouth, in such a way that, with a very small marketing cost, a very large portion of the network can be actually reached. An outstanding example in this scope is *Groupon* ([12]), a deal-of-the-day website which offers discount coupons usable at several companies. In order to increase its customers, *Groupon* allows users to refer friends to the site and, in return for friends buying their first coupon, getting credits to spend in future coupons purchases. In this case, the knowledge of users' ties may help user to propagate coupons inside his contacts with strong ties increasing, on this way, the coupons redemption and, thereby, also the user's credit.

Attention Management. Some e-mail readers, like *Mail* of *Mac OS X*, allow users to define smart mailboxes, sorting mail into different folders depending on their content, header, sender, etc. However, defining and updating mailboxes are tedious tasks. As many received messages are from users' contacts on social sites, knowing the strength of their ties would help to suitably define smart mailboxes parameters and, even, to prioritise incoming messages. Similarly to e-mail readers, social media dashboards, as for instance HootSuite[4] and TweetDeck[5], are examples of tools in charge of managing users' attention organising users' updates in different social networks. They allow users to inspect their contacts activity and post new content without connecting to social networks sites. If social media dashboards were aware of users' social environment, they could show only the updates from contacts with strong ties, avoiding to overwhelm users with the updates. Finally, in the line of Shannon et al. [13], an interesting service in the Ambient Intelligence scope would be one which take advantage of social spheres to alert users to contact soon with certain friends to keep their social network in a healthy state.

Contacts Management. Facebook allows users to create lists of contacts (*Friendslists*) to share specific content with. Creating *FriendsLists* entails the user to assess their contacts (friends) to include them in one *Friendslists* or another. Moreover, Facebook relationships change over time and, consequently, the contacts to include in the lists could change too. For this reason, Facebook automatically creates smart lists whose members are filtered according to profiles similarity. At this respect, combining similarity with tie strength may be useful to improve these smart lists, so that they are composed of contacts who share profile characteristics and, at the same time, they usually interact (even in other social sites). The same idea may be applied to the Twitter case to organise users' followees in lists.

---

[4] http://hootsuite.com/ Last accessed on 10/05/12.
[5] http://www.tweetdeck.com/ Last accessed on 10/05/12.

7 Discussion

This paper describes an approach to infer social ties from Facebook through its public API, which is included in a large project to infer social ties from any social network in the cloud. The solution goes one step further to integrate the various links maintained by users in all their social networks sites, the ones in which they are registered. We are interested in separating the sheep from the goats, i.e. separating the relevant ties from these other ties which are almost figurative. For instance, despite maintaining Facebook a contact network, users are allowed to interact with people outside their contact network (send a private message, tag a photo with, etc.). In the same way Twitter users can retweet any post, even if they are not following the original poster. So, users may interact frequently with users with who have not direct link in any social network. Reversely, a user may have never interacted with another user with who shares a direct link in any social network. So, considering the users' activity and not only the figurative relation is a more effective approach.

Our proposal is oriented to the construction of the user's social sphere in the cloud taking into account two different-nature contributions. Firstly, the interaction network can be computed from the formulation in this paper by extending the online, face-to-face and interest-based interactions to other social network sites. Secondly, the topological networks, i.e. the real links which the user maintains (and implicitly accepts) in a plethora of social services. We make out the topological network as a surface where social tie strength is deployed. So, to obtain the social influence between two users we consider (1) the tie strength inferred from their interaction and (2) the accumulate tie strengths of paths through, at most, one intermediate user (in Facebook it would be between friends and friends of friends).

Although, in this paper, the tie strength is only based on Facebook interactions between friends, the proposed formulation may also be used to obtain the tie strength between any two Facebook users, not necessarily friends[6]. Despite of the fact that at first sight it is expected for two Facebook friends to have a stronger tie than two non-friends, statistics show Facebook users only regularly relate with a small subset of their 130 friends, on average [3]. Thus, it is perfectly possible for them to have more interaction with a non-friend than with one of their friends, which must not be ignored to obtain the users' social sphere.

Besides, and as aforementioned, users' social sphere should be obtained not only with the Facebook data, but also taking into account their interactions in other social networks. Along this line, we are currently working on extending this approach to other social sites having a public API and adapting the interactions in each social network accordingly to our classification (online, face-to-face and interest-based interactions). For instance, in Twitter, retweets, replies or private messages would be included into the online category, as well as private messages or photo comments in Flickr, private messages in LinkedIn or Wall-posts, comments or +1 in Google+. However, tags in photos or videos in Google+, Picasa or Flickr would belong to the face-to-face category; whereas interactions among users in the same group in Google+, Flickr, LinkedIn, etc.

---

[6] Please, note that some of the signs, like wall-post are only available for friends, so the absence of these contributions entails a reduction in the tie strength.

would be categorized as interest-based. Finally, interactions among users occur in any Web 2.0 application, even if it does not have a declarative network as, for example, in the case of blogs or wikis. Consequently, we bear in mind extending our proposal to cover all the range of Web 2.0 application.

References

1. Wilson, C., Boe, B., Sala, A., Puttaswamy, K.P., Zhao, B.Y.: User interactions in social networks and their implications. In: Proceedings of the 4th ACM European Conference on Computer Systems, Nuremberg, Germany (2009)
2. Chen, W., Fong, S.: Social network collaborative filtering framework and online trust factors: a case study on facebook. In: The 5th International Conference on Digital Information Management (ICDIM 2010), Thunder Bay, Canada, pp. 266–273 (2010)
3. Facebook: Facebook statistics (2011)
4. Granovetter, M.: The strength of weak ties. American Journal of Sociology, 1360–1380 (1973)
5. Mutton, P.: Inferring and visualizing social networks on internet relay chat. In: Proceedings of the Eighth International Conference on Information Visualisation, IV 2004, pp. 35–43. IEEE (2004)
6. Tyler, J., Wilkinson, D., Huberman, B.: E-mail as spectroscopy: Automated discovery of community structure within organizations. The Information Society 21, 143–153 (2005)
7. Viswanath, B., Mislove, A., Cha, M., Gummadi, K.: On the evolution of user interaction in facebook. In: Proceedings of the 2nd Workshop on Online Social Networks, Barcelona, pp. 37–42 (2009)
8. Backstrom, L., Bakshy, E., Kleinberg, J., Lenton, T., Rosenn, I.: Center of attention: How facebook users allocate attention across friends. In: Proceedings of the 5th International AAAI Conference on Weblogs and Social Media (2011)
9. Gilbert, E., Karahalios, K.: Predicting tie strength with social media. In: Proceedings of the 27th International Conference on Human Factors in Computing Systems, pp. 211–220. ACM (2009)
10. Kahanda, I., Neville, J.: Using transactional information to predict link strength in online social networks. In: International AAAI Conference on Weblogs and Social Media, ICWSM (2009)
11. O'Donovan, J., Smith, B.: Trust in recommender systems. In: IUI 2005: Proceedings of the 10th International Conference on Intelligent User Interfaces, pp. 167–174. ACM Press, New York (2005)
12. Byers, J., Mitzenmacher, M., Potamias, M., Zervas, G.: A month in the life of groupon. Arxiv preprint arXiv:1105.0903 (2011)
13. Shannon, R., Kenny, E., Quigley, A.: Using ambient social reminders to stay in touch with friends. International Journal of Ambient Computing and Intelligence (IJACI) 1, 70–78 (2009)

Secure Biometric-Based Authentication for Cloud Computing

Kok-Seng Wong* and Myung Ho Kim

School of Computer Science and Engineering, Soongsil University,
Sangdo-Dong Dongjak-Gu, 156-743 Seoul Korea
{kswong,kmh}@ssu.ac.kr

Abstract. Over the past several years, many companies have gained benefits from the implementation of cloud solutions within the organization. Due to the advantages such as flexibility, mobility, and costs saving, the number of cloud users is expected to grow rapidly. Consequently, organizations need a secure way to authenticate its users in order to ensure the functionality of their services and data stored in the cloud storages are managed in a private environment. In the current approaches, the user authentication in cloud computing is based on the credentials submitted by the user such as password, token and digital certificate. Unfortunately, these credentials can often be stolen, accidentally revealed or hard to remember. In view of this, we propose a biometric-based authentication protocol to support the user authentication for the cloud environment. Our solution can be used as the second factor for the cloud users to send their authentication requests. In our design, we incorporate several players (client, service agent and service provider) to collaborate together to perform the matching operation between the query feature vector and the biometric template of the user. In particular, we consider a distributed scenario where the biometric templates are stored in the cloud storage while the user authentication is performed without the leakage of any sensitive information.

Keywords: Biometric-based Authentication, Cloud Authentication System, Privacy Preserving Squared Euclidean Distance, Data Protection.

1   Introduction

Cloud computing is an emerging technology which allows users to request for services and resources from their service providers in an on-demand environment. It is a complex yet resource saving infrastructure for today's modern business needs, providing the means through which services are delivered to the end users via Internet access. In the cloud environment, users can access services based on their needs without knowing how the services are delivered and where the service are hosted.

The US National Institute of Standards and Technology (NIST) has defined cloud computing as follows [1]: Cloud computing is a model for enabling ubiquitous, convenient, on-demand network access to a shared pool of configurable computing

---

* This work was supported by the Soongsil University Research Fund.

I. Ivanov et al. (Eds.): CLOSER 2012, CCIS 367, pp. 86–101, 2013.

resources (e.g., networks, servers, storage, applications, and services) that can be rapidly provisioned and released with minimal management effort or service provider interaction.

Hardware devices, software, storage and network infrastructure are made available to user through Internet access. Rather than purchasing expensive but powerful resources, users lease these resources from the service providers. With cloud computing, user can access the services via Internet access regardless of time and location. They also get rid of software installation in their local machine and able to enjoy high availability of services. Furthermore, high efficiency and fast deployment benefits are also the attractions for company and individual who moves to cloud services. Due to the advantages such as flexibility, mobility, and costs saving, the number of cloud user has increased tremendously. Industry analysts have made projections that entire computing industry will be transformed into Cloud environment [2].

In this Cloud-driven era, security and privacy concerns are becoming growing problems for the user and the service provider. User authentication is often the key issue in the Cloud environment. It is an important operation for the service provider to verify who can access their services and to identify the group of each user. Some commonly used authentication services include Kerberos [3] and OpenID [4]. The service provider authenticates its users based on the credential submitted such as password, token and digital certificate. Unfortunately, these credentials can often be stolen, accidentally revealed or hard to remember. In view of this, we propose a biometric-based authentication protocol that can be used as the second factor for the cloud users to send their authentication requests. Biometric authentication can improve the quality of authentication (QoA) in cloud environment. Our solution ensures both security in the authentication and the privacy protection for all sensitive information.

1.1 Problem Statement

Cloud computing is becoming an emerging technology in many organizations especially those who require extra resources (i.e., processing power and storage) with a lower cost. Recently, the adoption of cloud services within the organization raises a significant security concerns among data owners when the data stored in the cloud are sensitive data to the public or shared environment. For example, the customer details are considered as sensitive data to the company and the data owner. The leakage of sensitive information will compromise the individual privacy and allows the competitors to gain the competitive advantages. Therefore, user authentication for cloud computing is becoming important and need to be addressed when considering sensitive data.

In this paper, we consider the user authentication for cloud computing in a distributed environment where the biometric templates of the users are stored in the cloud storage. To verify a user, several players will collaborate together to compare the query feature vector of the user and the template stored in the cloud storage.

Biometric templates are uniquely representing strong identity information of its owner. Although it provides a higher degree of security as compared with password or security token, it could be stolen or exchanged. Hence, we must be careful when dealing with the biometric data. There are several concerns should be addressed such as which party the biometric data can be revealed and whether the biometric matching operation is performed by the authentication server or the external trusted party. It is therefore clear that designing a privacy preserved protocol to support the biometric matching operation would have a great impact on the template protection and preventing the leakage of biometric feature vector.

1.2 Organization

The rest of this paper is organized as follows: The background for this research is in Section 2 and the technical preliminaries are described in Section 3. We present our proposed solution in Section 4 followed by the analysis in Section 5. Our conclusion is in Section 6.

2   Background

2.1 Cloud Computing Models

Cloud services are delivered in three fundamental models [5]: Infrastructure as a Service (IaaS), Platform as a Service (PaaS), and Software as a Service (SaaS). IaaS is the lowest level which is closest to the hardware devices whereas, SaaS is the highest level that provides services to the end-users. The Amazon web service is one type of IaaS which has been widely used since 2006 while the Salesforce.com CRM system is an example of SaaS.

PaaS level provides an application platform in the cloud. Windows Azure platform is one example of PaaS which enable the developers to build, host and scale their applications in the Microsoft data centers. Recently, a new concept called "Everything as a Service (XaaS)" has been adopted as the new trend in cloud computing. Several vendors such as Microsoft and Hewlett Packard [6] have been associated with it.

Biometric Authentication as a Service (BioAaaS) has been defined as an approach for strong authentication in web environments based on the SaaS model [7].

2.2 User Authentication

When performing authentication over the Internet, credential will be submitted by the principal (the user, machine, or service requesting access) [8]. If the credentials match, the user is allowed to access the services it subscribed from the service providers. In this paper, we only consider user as the principal who submits its credential for authentication over the cloud.

There are several types of credential the users can submit as proof of their identity. Shared-key is typically password used protocols such as Password Authentication Protocol (PAP) [9] and Challenge Handshake Authentication Protocol (CHAP) [10].

Enrolment Process

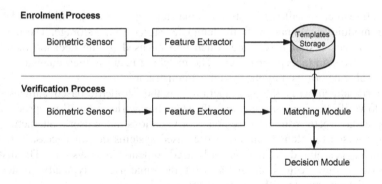

Fig. 1. General design for biometric-based authentication systems

Digital certificate is second type of credential which can provide strong authentication in the cloud environment. It is an electronic document which uses a trusted Certificate Authority (CA) to blind the encryption key with an identity [11]. Decryption key is the only way to validate the signed certificate.

Another type of credential is the commonly used one-time-password (OTP) [12, 13]. The end-user obtains the OTP from the token (hardware or software) during the login time. The token can generate a randomized password string based on a complex algorithm in real time. Since the password generated is unique and can only be used once, OTP is possible to be used in the Cloud environment. For example, Amazon Web Services (AMW) has already started to use its OTP token for use with individual AWS accounts [14].

Recently, a German company BioID proposes the world's first biometric authentication service for cloud computing [15]. In their solution, biometric authentication as a service (BaaS) has been proposed to provide single sign-on for user authentication.

2.3   Biometric-Based Authentication

Biometric characteristics such as iris patterns, face, fingerprints, palm prints and voice will be submitted by the user as the credential for authentication over the cloud. Biometric-based authentication systems provide a higher degree of security as compared with conventional authentication systems. Furthermore, it allows the system to keep track of the user's activities because individual biometric characteristics cannot be shared with others.

Generally, biometric authentication systems consist of five modules, namely, the biometric sensor, feature extractor, template storage, matching module, and the decision module. Fig. 1 illustrates the general design for the biometric-based authentication systems.

During the enrolment process, the biometric sensor scans the biometric traits of the user while the feature extractor extracts the feature vector from the scanned biometric data. The feature vector is then stored in the template storage.

At the verification stage, the biometric sensor and the feature extractor perform the same tasks as in the enrolment process. However, the extracted feature vector (query feature vector) will not be stored in the storage. Instead, it will be used by the matching module to compare with the templates stored in the storage. The matching operation outputs a similarity score which will be used by the decision module in making the decision (accept or reject). The matching result is then compares with a threshold value determined by the system administrator.

Biometric matching is the key operation in the biometric-based authentication systems to verify the users. In practical, the same biometric trait will not produce two identical feature vectors due to some noises or variations in the user's interaction with the biometric sensor. Hence, the biometric-based systems do not necessary to have perfect match as required in the password-based authentication systems. The distance between two feature vectors originating from the same user is typically greater than zero (zero distance means both feature vectors are identical).

3   Technical Preliminaries

In this section, we describe some technical preliminaries for our protocol design.

3.1   Definition

Security Definition. In a generic sense, security is the prevention of unauthorized party from gaining access to confidential information and system resources. A secure authentication system needs to ensure only the authorized users can access to the system. Therefore, we must prevent any adversary party from impersonate as an enrolled user in our solution.

Our protocol is secure if no adversary party can gain access to the sensitive information. Hereafter in this section, we refer sensitive information as the biometric feature vectors (i.e., template and query feature vector), the verification code, and the shuffle protocol.

During the authentication process, the protocol must prevents the adversary party from reconstructing the original feature vector of the user based on the verification code and the template stored in the cloud. Also, the network intruder who watches the traffic on the network must not learn any sensitive information.

Privacy Definition. Information or data privacy is referring to the ability of an individual or system to prevent the leakage of any sensitive information to any unauthorized party. A privacy-preserved system should ensure that unauthorized party does not improperly access confidential information.

In this paper, we particularly consider the privacy issues on the biometric template and the verification code protections. The intermediate result during the authentication process should not leak any sensitive information and the decision module should not be able to distinguish whether two authentication requests belong to the same user.

3.2 Homomorphic Cryptosystem

In this paper, we will utilize the additive property of the homomorphic cryptosystem (i.e., Paillier [16]) in our protocol.

Let $E_a(m_1)$ denote the encryption of message m_1 with encryption key, E_a. The scheme supports the following operations in an encrypted form:

- *Addition*: Given two ciphertexts $E_a(m_1)$ and $E_a(m_2)$, there exists an efficient algorithm $+_h$ to compute $E_a(m_1 + m_2)$.
- *Scalar multiplication*: Given a constant c and a ciphertext $E_a(m_1)$, there exists an efficient algorithm $\cdot_h$ to compute $E_a(c \cdot m_1)$.

Note that when a scheme supports the additive operation, it also supports scalar multiplication because $E_a(c \cdot m_1)$ can be achieved by summing $E_a(m_1)$ successively c times. By using the homomorphic cryptosystem, we can compute the additive operation directly on the encrypted data without the decryption. This is a useful feature because the biometric template stored in the server does not require decryption during the matching operation.

3.3 Notations Used

In Table 1, we summarize all the notations used hereafter in this paper.

Table 1. Common notations used

X	original feature vector extracted from the user during the enrolment process
Y	original feature vector extracted from the user during the verification process
X'	transformed vector during the enrolment process
Y'	transformed vector during the verification process
X''	shuffled vector during the enrolment process
Y''	shuffled vector during the verification process
π_u	shuffle protocol for the user U
x_i'	i-th element of X'
y_i'	i-th element of Y'
s	squared Euclidean distance
n	length of the original feature vector
m	length of the verification code
k	length of the transformed vector where, $k = n + m + 4$
TID	template identification number
VID	verification code identification number
E_u	encryption key from the user U

Table 1. Common notations used (cont.)

D_u	decryption key from the user U
E_p	encryption key from the service provider
D_p	decryption key from the service provider
$E_{pk}(\cdot)$	encryption operation by using the E_{pk}
$D_{pk}(\cdot)$	decryption operation by using the D_{pk}
ω	random non-zero number

4   Proposed Solution

In our solution, the authentication process is based on two credential information: (1) user's biometric feature vector and (2) the verification code. Both parts must be combined, transformed, and shuffled correctly in order for the user to successful authenticate.

Like most existing biometric-based authentication systems, our solution requires matching between the query feature vector (Q) and the biometric template (T). As shown in Fig. 2, the matching operation is supported by the service provider and the service agent over the cloud environment.

The similarity measure function used in biometric matching is based on the characteristics of the biometric feature vector. For example, Hamming distance is used for iris-based comparison while the squared Euclidean distance has been used in finger codes matching. We consider the latter as our measurement metric in this paper.

4.1   Components

We now formally describe the players in our proposed solution as follow: (as illustrated in Fig. 2):

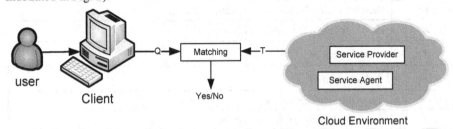

Fig. 2. Overview of our proposed solution

— *User*: individual who sends the authentication request.
— *Client*: computer or workstation with Internet access.
— *Service provider*: company or organization who provides cloud services (SaaS, PaaS or IaaS) to the user.

— *Service agent*: separate entity which helps to transform the biometric feature vector.

Unlike the conventional biometric systems, the template is the transformed feature vector and will be stored in the cloud storage. The query feature vector is a transformed feature vector. Like most existing biometric-based authentication systems, our solution consists of both the enrolment and the verification processes. In the following sections, we will describe in details the components and the authentication workflows of our solution.

The Client has the Following Components:

- *Biometric sensor*: scans the biometric traits of the user.
- *Feature extractor*: extracts the feature vector from the scanned biometric data.
- *Encryption module*: encrypts the transformed and shuffled feature vector with the correct encryption key (i.e., encrypts with the user's key during the enrolment process).
- *Decryption module*: decrypts the computation output.

The Service Agent Requires the Following Components:

- *Transformation module*: transforms the original feature vector and shuffles the transformed feature vector.
- *Verification code generator*: generates unique verification code for the user.
- *Verification code retrieval*: retrieves the verification code for the user.
- *Verification codes storage*: stores the verification code for each user.

The Service Provider Requires the Following Components:

- *Computation module*: performs the squared Euclidean distance (s) computation between the query feature vector and the template.
- *Decision module*: making the final decision by comparing the s with the given threshold τ.
- *Templates storage*: stores the template of each user.

4.2   Enrolment

The objective of the enrolment process is to process the scanned biometric data and extract a set of feature vector to be stored as the template for the user. The enrolment process is required for the new user who wants to join the cloud. A successful enrolment process enables the user to receive the *TID* and the *VID*.

4.2.1   Transformation

Let $X = \{x_1, x_2, ..., x_n\}$, $n > 0$ and $V = \{v_1, v_2, ..., v_m\}$, $m > 0$ be the feature vector of the user and the verification code generated, respectively. We transform X into

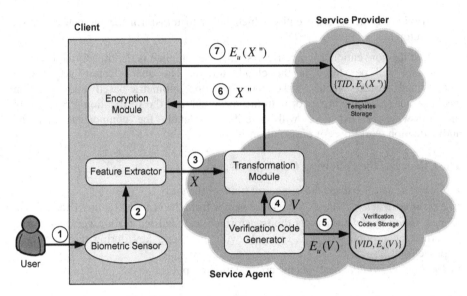

Fig. 3. The overview of the enrolment process

$$X' = \left\{ x_i' \mid i = 1, 2, \ldots, n+m+4 \right\} \quad \text{such that} \quad x_i' = x_i \quad \text{for} \quad 1 \le i \le n \ , \quad x_{n+j}' = v_j \quad \text{for}$$

$$1 \le j \le m \ , x_{n+m+1}' = x_{n+m+2}' = 1 \ , \ x_{n+m+3}' = \sum_{i=1}^{n} x_i^2 \quad \text{and} \quad x_{n+m+4}' = \sum_{j=1}^{m} v_j^2 \ .$$

4.2.2   Shuffle Protocol

We require a shuffle protocol (π_u) to permute the order of elements in the transformed vector X'. We use the same shuffle protocol during the verification process for the same user.

4.2.3   Overview of the Enrolment Process

We illustrate the overview of the enrolment process in Fig. 3 and the workflow as follow:

1. The biometric sensor scans the biometric trait of the user.
2. The feature extractor processes the scanned biometric data to extract the feature vector of the user, $X = \{x_1, x_2, \ldots, x_n\}$.
3. The feature extractor sends X to the transformation module of the service agent.
4. The verification code generator of the service agent generates a unique verification code $V = \{v_1, v_2, \ldots, v_m\}$ for the user.
5. The service agent computes $V' = -2V$ and encrypts it by using the encryption key of the user. The encrypted data will be stored at the verification codes storage.
6. Next, the transformation module transforms X into X' . It shuffles the transformed vector X' i.e., $X'' = \pi_u(X')$ before sending it to the encryption module.

7. The encryption module encrypts $X"$ by using the user's encryption key. Finally, the client sends $E_u(X")$ to the service provider. The service provider stores $E_u(X")$ as the user's template in the templates storage.

4.3   Verification

When the user wants to access data stored in the cloud storages or uses the cloud services, the user must be authenticated first. The verification process is responsible to verify the users who they claim to be.

4.3.1   Transformation

Let $Y = \{y_1, y_2, ..., y_n\}$, $n > 0$ and $V = \{v_1, v_2, ..., v_m\}$, $m > 0$ be the feature vector extracted from the user and the verification code, respectively. The verification code used must be the same in both enrolment and verification processes. We transform Y into $Y' = \{y_i' \mid i = 1, 2, ..., n+m+4\}$ such that $y_i' = -2y_i$ for $1 \le i \le n$, $y_{n+j}' = -2v_j$ for $1 \le j \le m$, $y_{n+m+1}' = \sum_{i=1}^{n} y_i^2$, $y_{n+m+2}' = \sum_{j=1}^{m} v_j^2$, $y_{n+m+3}' = y_{n+m+4}' = 1$. The length for Y' must be same as X' which is $k = n+m+4$.

4.3.2   Shuffle Protocol

We require the same shuffle protocol used in the enrolment process during the verification process. The transformed feature vector Y' needs to be shuffled in the same order as X'.

4.3.3   Overview of the Verification Process

The workflow for the verification process is as follow (as illustrated in Fig. 4):

1. The biometric sensor scans the biometric trait of the user.
2. The feature extractor processes the scanned biometric data to extract the feature vector of the user, $Y = \{y_1, y_2, ..., y_n\}$.
3. The feature extractor sends Y to the transformation module of the service agent.
4. Next, the service agent retrieves the verification code of the user based on the user's VID.
5. The verification code retrieval retrieves $E_u(V')$ of the user from the storage.
6. The transformation module computes $D_u(E_u(V'))$ and transforms Y into vector Y'. Next, it shuffles Y' i.e., $Y" = \pi_u(Y')$ and sends $Y"$ to the encryption module of the client.
7. The encryption module encrypts $Y"$ with the service provider's encryption key E_p. Next, the $E_p(Y")$ is sent together with the TID to the computation module.
8. The computation module of the service provider retrieves $E_u(X")$ from the templates storage which is associated with the TID.

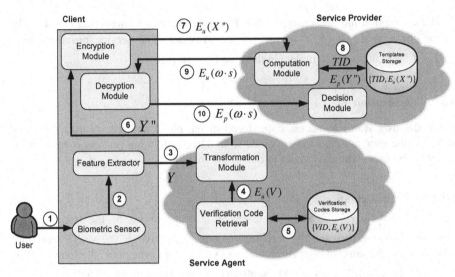

Fig. 4. The overview of the verification process

9. If both $E_u(X'')$ and $E_p(Y'')$ have the same size, the computation module computes:

    i.   Decryption: $D_p\left(E_p(Y'')\right) = Y''$

    ii.   Scalar multiplication: $Y'' \cdot E_u(X'') = E_u(X'' \cdot Y'')$

    iii. Homomorphic additive operation: $E_u(s) = E_u\left(\sum_{i=1}^{n+m+4}\left(x_i'' \cdot y_i''\right)\right)$

    iv. Add noise: $\omega \cdot E_u(s) = E_u(\omega \cdot s)$, where ω is a random non-zero number.

The computation module sends $E_u(\omega \cdot s)$ to the client.

10. The decryption module of the client decrypts $E_u(\omega \cdot s)$ and then encrypts $\omega \cdot s$ with E_p. Then, the decryption module sends $E_p(\omega \cdot s)$ back to the decision module of the service provider for making the decision. The decision module decrypts $E_p(\omega \cdot s)$ and makes the decision as follows (τ is the threshold determined by the service provider):

$$decision = \begin{cases} Accept, if\ s < \tau \\ Reject, if\ s > \tau \end{cases}$$

Note that for different authentication requests, we may require different security levels. Hence, our system can assign different threshold values for different users.

5   Analysis

In this section, we present the correctness, security, privacy and efficiency analysis for our proposed solution.

5.1   Correctness Analysis

Our protocol correctly computes the squared Euclidean distance between the query feature vector and the biometric template if all the players follow the protocol faithfully. Let $X = \{x_1, x_2, ..., x_n\}$ be the extracted feature vector of user A during the enrolment process. It will be transformed into X ' as follows:

$$X' = \begin{cases} x_1, ..., x_n, v_1, ..., v_m, 1, 1, \\ \left(\sum_{i=1}^{n} x_i^2 \right), \left(\sum_{j=1}^{m} v_j^2 \right) \end{cases} \tag{1}$$

Then, we randomly shuffle the order of elements in X '. Let $X" = \pi_A(X')$ be the shuffled vector by using the shuffle protocol π_A. Next, we encrypt $X"$ by using the encryption key E_A and store the following result as the template of the user in the templates storage:

$$E_A(X") = \begin{cases} E_A(x_1), ..., E_A(x_n), \\ E_A(v_1), ..., E_A(v_m), \\ E_A(1), E_A(1), \\ E_A\left(\sum_{i=1}^{n} x_i^2 \right), E_A\left(\sum_{i=1}^{m} v_j^2 \right) \end{cases} \tag{2}$$

Note that for ease of explanation, we do not change the order of elements in Eq. (2).

Assume that $Y = \{y_1, y_2, ..., y_n\}$ is the query feature vector during the verification process. The client retrieves the verification code from the service provider and transforms Y into Y ' as follows:

$$Y' = \begin{cases} -2y_1, ..., -2y_n, -2v_1, ..., -2v_m, \\ \left(\sum_{i=1}^{n} y_i^2 \right), \left(\sum_{j=1}^{m} v_j^2 \right), 1, 1 \end{cases} \tag{3}$$

By using the same shuffle protocol π_A (if the user is A), the client computes $Y" = \pi_A(Y')$ and encrypts $Y"$ with the encryption key E_P to produce:

$$E_P(Y") = \begin{cases} E_P(-2y_1), ..., E_P(-2y_n), \\ E_P(-2v_1), ..., E_P(-2v_m), \\ E_P\left(\sum_{i=1}^{n} x_i^2 \right), E_P\left(\sum_{i=1}^{m} v_j^2 \right), \\ E_P(1), E_P(1) \end{cases} \tag{4}$$

For ease of explanation, we do not change the order of elements in Eq. (4).

The squared Euclidean distance is computed as follow: The service provider first decrypts $E_P(Y")$ to obtain $Y"$ and computes the scalar multiplication for each i-th element in $Y"$ and $E_A(X")$ according to their index position:

$$Y'' \cdot E_A(X'') = E_A(X'' \cdot Y'')$$

$$= \left\{ \begin{array}{l} \left(-2y_1 \cdot E_A(x_1)\right), \dots, \left(-2y_n \cdot E_A(x_n)\right), \\ \left(-2v_1 \cdot E_A(v_1)\right), \dots, \left(-2v_m \cdot E_A(v_m)\right), \\ \left(\sum_{i=1}^{n} y_i^2 \cdot E_A(1)\right), \left(\sum_{j=1}^{m} v_j^2 \cdot E_A(1)\right), \\ \left(1 \cdot E_A\left(\sum_{i=1}^{n} x_i^2\right)\right), \left(1 \cdot E_A\left(\sum_{i=1}^{m} v_i^2\right)\right) \end{array} \right\}$$

$$= \left\{ \begin{array}{l} E_A(-2x_1 y_1), \dots, E_A(-2x_n y_n), \\ E_A(-2v_1^2), \dots, E_A(-2v_m^2), \\ E_A\left(\sum_{i=1}^{n} y_i^2\right), E_A\left(\sum_{j=1}^{m} v_j^2\right), \\ E_A\left(\sum_{i=1}^{n} x_i^2\right), E_A\left(\sum_{i=1}^{m} v_j^2\right) \end{array} \right\} \tag{5}$$

Next, the service provider computes homomorphic additive operation for each $\left(x_i'' \cdot y_i''\right) \in (X'' \cdot Y'')$ in Eq. (5):

$$E_A(s) = E_A\left(\sum_{i=1}^{n} -2x_i y_i\right) +_h E_A\left(\sum_{j=1}^{m} -2v_j^2\right) +_h E_A\left(\sum_{i=1}^{n} y_i^2\right) +_h E_A\left(\sum_{j=1}^{m} v_j^2\right)$$

$$+_h E_A\left(\sum_{i=1}^{n} x_i^2\right) +_h E_A\left(\sum_{i=1}^{m} v_j^2\right)$$

$$= E_A\left(\sum_{i=1}^{n} x_i^2\right) +_h E_A\left(\sum_{i=1}^{n} -2x_i y_i\right)$$

$$+_h E_A\left(\sum_{i=1}^{n} y_i^2\right) \tag{6}$$

$$= E_A\left(\sum_{i=1}^{n} \left(x_i^2 - 2x_i y_i + y_i^2\right)\right)$$

$$= E_A\left(\sum_{i=1}^{n} \left(x_i - y_i\right)^2\right)$$

After we decipher the result in Eq. (6), we can obtain the squared Euclidean distance $s = \sum_{i=1}^{n}(x_i - y_i)^2$. Note that in Eq. (6), we eliminate the verification code and all additional features. Hence, if the service provider retrieves the correct verification code and the client computes Y'' correctly, our protocol outputs the correct squared Euclidean distance for X and Y.

If one of the parties (either the client or the service provider) is not following the protocol, the final output will not reflect the squared Euclidean distance for the two vectors (X and Y). Subsequently, the verification process will fail and the user cannot access the system. The client or the service provider who is not following the protocol is considering as the malicious party in our protocol. The proof of this theorem is same as the proof in Theorem 3 and Theorem 4 under the security analysis.

5.2   Security Analysis

In this section, we will analyse two possible attacks: internal and external attack. Internal attack involves malicious party such as employee at client who attempts to gain access into the cloud. External attack involves external parties (intruders or network attackers) who watch the traffic on the network. They are interested in learning some knowledge from the computation protocol or intercept the data in the network. Note that internal attack is more serious as compared to the external attack because attackers are having more knowledge about the protocol.

Our protocol is secure against malicious user who tries to gain access to the cloud. Without the knowledge of sensitive information and the decryption key, the authentication is not possible for attacker at the client side. During the enrolment process, the system generates the biometric template for each user. Only the user who enrolled into the cloud has its template and the verification code stored in the cloud storages. In the absence of the template, the system cannot authenticate the user.

In our protocol, any malicious user who wants to pose as an enrolled user must gain access to three sensitive information: (1) the verification code, (2) the original feature vector and (3) the shuffle protocol. Since the verification codes and the biometric templates are stored in an encrypted form, the attacker will not be able to access them without the knowledge of the decryption key. If the attacker gains access to the original feature vector of the user, he is not able to use it directly for the verification process because the verification code and the shuffle protocol are not accessible. In the worst scenario, if the attacker obtains the decryption key of any user, the security for the user is still can be guaranteed. Hence, our protocol is secure against attacker who tries to gain access to the cloud system.

Our protocol is secure against malicious service provider who tries to gain access to the biometric templates stored in the cloud storages. The malicious service provider is not able to reconstruct the original feature vector of any user in the absent of the verification code. Furthermore, the templates are encrypted by using the encryption key of each respective user. The service provider has no knowledge about the decryption key. Gaining access to these encrypted vector is as difficult as attacking the encryption algorithm. Brute-force attack is also impossible since all the templates are different (after the encryption operation). Hence, our protocol is able to prevent the malicious service provider from reconstruct the original feature vector of the user.

Network attacker who listens to the traffic is not able to learn any sensitive information. In our protocol, all the data transmit over the network (between the client and the service provider) are in an encrypted form (either encrypts with the user's encryption key or with the service provider's key). When the network attacker watches the network, he cannot learn any information because he has no knowledge about the decryption key. During the verification process, network attacker is not possible to be authenticated by the cloud because he has no knowledge about any sensitive information. Hence, our protocol is secure against the network attacker.

5.3   Privacy Analysis

The privacy concern in our solution is the amount of information revealed during the authentication process. Our protocol should ensure the confidentiality of all sensitive information such that the intermediate results and the authentication result will not compromise the privacy of the user.

In our solution, both the verification codes and the biometric templates are stored in an encrypted form. The service provider is not able to learn anything because it has no knowledge about the decryption key from the user. In the worst scenario, if the decryption key of the user has been compromised, the service provider also not able to identify the original feature vector of the user because the template has been transformed with the verification code and being shuffled during the enrolment process.

During the verification process, the service provider decrypts $E_p(Y'')$ before performing the scalar multiplication operation. After the decryption, the service provider is not able to distinguish between the original feature vector and verification code. Hence, our protocol protects both the verification code and the template stored in the cloud storages.

The service provider is not able to distinguish whether two authentication requests belong to the same user. In our protocol, the verification code and the template are stored separately by the service agent and the service provider, respectively. This design prevents the malicious party from knowing which verification code is associated with which template in the case when both storages are compromised. The decision module makes the verification decision based on the similarity score (squared Euclidean distance) and the threshold value determined by the system. If the similarity score is lower than the threshold, it can reject the user. Otherwise, the system verifies the user and the authentication process is successful. With only the similarity score, the decision module is not able to distinguish whether two authentication requests belong to the same user.

5.4   Efficiency Analysis

The total communication costs depend on the amount of data transferred during the authentication process. During the enrolment process, the main computation cost incurs is the generation of biometric template which requires $k = (n + m + 4)$ encryption. The enrolment process only requires 1 round of communication in order for the service provider to store the biometric template of the user. During the verification process, the computation cost is dominated by the computation of the squared Euclidean distance. The communication complexity incurred by the protocol is $O(k)$.

In terms of complexity, our protocol requires $O(k)$ encryptions, $O(k)$ scalar multiplications and $O(k)$ homomorphic additive operations.

6   Discussion and Conclusions

The biometric-based authentication offers many advantages over other existing authentication methods. However, the processing time during the verification process is a main concern in any biometric-based system. The integration of biometric-based authentication into the cloud environment can benefit from the advantages of the cloud computing such as extra resources and processing power.

In this paper, we proposed a biometric-based authentication protocol for cloud computing. Our target is to achieve secure authentication while protecting the sensitive information of users. We incorporate the homomorphic encryption scheme into our matching protocol to compare both the query feature vector and the template in an encrypted form. The measurement metric used in our protocol is the Squared

Euclidean distance. Our solution preserves the privacy of the sensitive information and securely performs the authentication process in the cloud environment.

References

1. Mell, P., Grance, T.: The NIST Definition of Cloud Computing. National Instituite of Standards and Technology (2009)
2. Buyya, R., Yeo, C.S., Venugopal, S., Broberg, J., Brandic, I.: Cloud computing and emerging IT platforms: Vision, hype, and reality for delivering computing as the 5th utility. Future Gener. Comput. Syst. 25, 599–616 (2009)
3. Neuman, B.C., Ts'o, T.: Kerberos: An Authentication Service for Open Network Systems. IEEE Communications 32, 33–38 (1994)
4. Recordon, D., Reed, D.: OpenID 2.0: a platform for user-centric identity management. In: Proceedings of the Second ACM Workshop on Digital Identity Management, pp. 11–16. ACM, Alexandria (2006)
5. Lenk, A., Klems, M., Nimis, J., Tai, S., Sandholm, T.: What's inside the Cloud? An architectural map of the Cloud landscape. In: Proceedings of the 2009 ICSE Workshop on Software Engineering Challenges of Cloud Computing, pp. 23–31. IEEE Computer Society (2009)
6. Fiveash, K.: HP sells cloud vision amidst economic downpour. Will customers get soaked on transformation journeys? King's College London (2008)
7. Senk, C., Dotzler, F.: Biometric Authentication as a Service for Enterprise Identity Management Deployment: A Data Protection Perspective. In: Sixth International Conference on Availability, Reliability and Security, Vienna Austria, pp. 43–50 (2011)
8. Convery, S.: Network Authentication, Authorization, and Accounting Part One: Concepts, Elements, and Approaches. The Internet Protocol Journal 10, 2–11 (2007)
9. Lloyd, B., Simpson, W.: PPP Authentication Protocols. RFC Editor (1992)
10. Simpson, W.: PPP Challenge Handshake Authentication Protocol (CHAP). RFC Editor (1996)
11. Canetti, R.: Universally Composable Signature, Certification, and Authentication. In: Proceedings of the 17th IEEE Workshop on Computer Security Foundations, p. 219. IEEE Computer Society (2004)
12. Haller, N.: The S/KEY One-Time Password System. In: Internet Society Symposium on Network and Distributed Systems, pp. 151–157 (1994)
13. Rubin, A.D.: Independent one-time passwords. In: Proceedings of the 5th Conference on USENIX UNIX Security Symposium, vol. 5, p. 15. USENIX Association, Salt Lake City (1995)
14. Brooks, C.: Amazon adds onetime password token to entice the wary. SearchCloudComputing (2009)
15. http://silicontrust.wordpress.com/2011/03/04/bioid-announces-worlds-first-biometric-authentication-as-a-service-baas/
16. Paillier, P.: Public-key cryptosystems based on composite degree residuosity classes. In: Stern, J. (ed.) EUROCRYPT 1999. LNCS, vol. 1592, pp. 223–238. Springer, Heidelberg (1999)

An Efficient and Performance-Aware Big Data Storage System

Yang Li, Li Guo, and Yike Guo

Department of Computing, Imperial College London, U.K.
{yl4709,liguo,yg}@doc.ic.ac.uk

Abstract. Recent escalations in Internet development and volume of data have created a growing demand for large-capacity storage solutions. Although Cloud storage has yielded new ways of storing, accessing and managing data, there is still a need for an inexpensive, effective and efficient storage solution especially suited to big data management and analysis. In this paper, we take our previous work one step further and present an in-depth analysis of the key features of future big data storage services for both unstructured and semi-structured data, and discuss how such services should be constructed and deployed. We also explain how different technologies can be combined to provide a single, highly scalable, efficient and performance-aware big data storage system. We especially focus on the issues of data de-duplication for enterprises and private organisations. This research is particularly valuable for inexperienced solution providers like universities and research organisations, and will allow them to swiftly set up their own big data storage services.

Keywords: Big Data Storage, Cloud Computing, Cloud Storage, Amazon S3, CACSS.

1   Introduction

The truth is that data growth is rapidly outpacing our ability to store, process and analyse the data we are collecting. Cloud storage relieves end users of the task of constantly upgrading their storage devices. Cloud storage services offer inexpensive, secure, fast, reliable and highly scalable data storage solutions over the internet. Many enterprises and personal users with limited budgets and IT resources are now outsourcing storage to cloud storage service providers, in an attempt to leverage the manifold benefits associated with cloud services. Leading cloud storage vendors, such as Amazon S3 [1] and Google Cloud Storage [2] , provide clients with highly available, low cost and pay-as-you-go based cloud storage services with no upfront cost. A variety of companies have outsourced at least a portion of their storage infrastructure to Amazon AWS, including SmugMug [3], ElephantDrive [4], Jungle Disk [5] and 37signals [3]. Recently, Amazon announced that as of June 2012 it currently holds more than a trillion objects, and the service has so far been growing exponentially [6]. Even so, many enterprises and scientists are still unable to shift into the cloud environment due to privacy, data protection and vendor lock-in issues. An Amazon S3

I. Ivanov et al. (Eds.): CLOSER 2012, CCIS 367, pp. 102–116, 2013.

storage service outage in 2008 left many businesses that rely on the service offline for several hours and resulted in the permanent loss of customer data, [7, 8], an incident that led many to question the S3's "secret" architecture.

Enterprises and scientists use cloud storage services for various purposes, and files are in different sizes and formats. Some use cloud storage for large video and audio files, and some use it for storing large quantities of relatively small files; the variety and range is vast. The different purposes of using cloud storage services give rise to a significant diversity of patterns of access to stored files. The nature of these stored files, in terms of features such as size and format, and the way in which these files are accessed, are the main factors that influence the quality of cloud storage services that are eventually delivered to the end users. Another challenge to the data storage community is how to effectively store data without taking the exact same data and storing it again and again in different locations and storage devices. Data de-duplication and other methods of reducing storage consumption play a vital role in affordably managing today's explosive growth of data. However, no much research has been done on how to efficiently apply these methods to big data services.

These reasons provide an incentive for organisations to set up or build their own storage solutions, which are independent of commercially available services and meet their individual requirements. However, knowledge of how to provide efficient big data storage service with regards to system architecture, resource management mechanisms, data reliability and durability, as well as how to utilise all the resources, reduce storage consumption, costs of backup and improve the quality of the services remains untapped.

Taking one step beyond our previous work [9] to target large-scale data de-duplication for enterprises and private organisations, we present the new CACSS, an efficient and performance-aware big data storage system offering not only mainstream cloud storage features, but global object data de-duplication and data caching services specifically suited to big data management and analysis. A thorough demonstration of CACSS can offer full details on how to construct a proper big data storage service, including design rationale, system architecture and implementation. This paper demonstrates how different technologies can be combined in order to provide a single and highly superior generic solution.

2   Related Work and Problem Analysis

Amazon Simple Storage Service (Amazon S3) is an online storage service that aims to provide reliable and excellent performance at a low cost. However, neither its architecture nor its implementation has yet been made public. As such, it is not available for extension in order to develop the capability of creating private clouds of any size. Amazon S3 is the leading de facto standard of bucket-object oriented storage services. Successive cloud storage vendors, such as Rackspace [11] and Google Cloud Storage [2] all adopt s3's style of bucket-object oriented interface. This style hides all the complexities of using distributed file systems, and it has proven to be a success [12]. It simply allows users to use the storage service from a higher level: an object contains file content and file metadata, and it is associated with a client assigned key;

a bucket, a basic container for holding objects, plus a key to uniquely identify an object.

The cloud provides a new way of storing and analysing Big Data because it is both elastic and cost-efficient. Additional computational resources can be allocated on the fly to handle increased demand and organizations only pay for the resource that they need. However, companies that work with big data have been unable to realize the full potential of the cloud due to the Internet connections used to move big data in, out and across cloud infrastructures are not quite as elastic. In addition, the high read/write bandwidths that are demanded by I/O intensive operations, which occur in many different Big Data scenarios, cannot be satisfied by current internet connections [13, 14].

Besides Amazon S3, there have been quite a few efforts in cloud storage services, including the following.

The Openstack [15] project has an object storage component called Swift, which is an open source storage system for redundant and scalable object storage. However, it does not support object versioning at present. The metadata of each file is stored in the file's extended attributes in the underlying file system. This could potentially create performance issues with a large number of metadata accesses.

Walrus [16] is a storage service included with Eucalyptus that is interface-compatible with Amazon S3. The open source version of Walrus does not support data replication services. It also does not fully address how file metadata is managed and stored.

pWalrus [17] is a storage service layer that integrates parallel file systems into cloud storage and enables data to be accessed through an S3 interface. pWalrus stores most object metadata information as the file's attributes. Access control lists, object content hashes (MD5) and other object metadata are kept in .walrus files. If a huge number of objects are stored under the same bucket, pWalrus may be inefficient in searching files based on certain metadata criteria; this factor can cause bottlenecks in metadata access.

Cumulus [18] is an open source cloud storage system that implements the S3 interface. It adapts existing storage implementations to provide efficient data access interfaces that are compatible with S3. However, details of metadata organisation and versioning support are not fully addressed.

Hadoop Distributed File System (HDFS) [19] is a distributed, reliable, scalable and open source file system, written in Java. HDFS achieves reliability by replicating data blocks and distributing them across multiple machines.

HBase [20] is an open source, non-relational, versioned, column-oriented distributed database that runs on top of HDFS. It is designed to provide fast real time read/write data access. Some research has already been done to evaluate the performance of HBase [21] [22].

For the past four decades, disk-based storage system performance has not improved as quickly as its capacity. As a result, many large-scale web applications are keeping a lot of their data in RAMs, and the role of RAM in storage systems has steadily increased over recent years. For example, as of 2008 Facebook used over 28 terabytes of memory[23], and major Web search engines such as Google and Yahoo keep their search indexes entirely in memory[24]. Google's Bigtable storage system [25] allows entire column families to be loaded into memory where they can be read without disk accesses. RAMCloud[26] is a DRAM-based storage system that provides inexpensive durability and availability by recovering quickly after crashes.

Data de-duplication is a data compression technique for eliminating duplicate copies of redundant data. The de-duplication technology has been widely applied in disk-based secondary storage systems to improve cost-effectiveness via space efficiency. It is most effective in storage systems where many duplicates of very similar or identical data are stored. Many studies on block-level and file-level data de-duplication have been carried out. One of the challenges facing large-scale de-duplication enabled storage systems is duplicate-lookup created bottlenecks due to metadata and actual file data which is stored separately and the large size of the data index, which limits the de-duplication throughput and performance[27-33].

CACSS is currently deployed on top of the IC-Cloud[34] infrastructure and is being used by over 200 internal students, especially those enrolled in the "Distributed Systems and Cloud Computing" course. Several assignments, individual and group projects rely heavily on the CACSS API to manage their data. Some other external collaborators are also using CACSS as their data backup space. By monitoring the data access patterns and analysing the actual data stored in our system, we discovered two important characteristics that might help improve our system's efficiency and performance. We discovered that while some files were used intensively over a very short period, much other data were hardly accessed. We also found over 20% duplicated objects with the same checksums stored in our system. This issue of redundancy is common and exists in many enterprises: a survey by AFCOM found that over 63% of IT managers surveyed have seen a significant increase in their storage costs. One of the main reasons for that dramatic increase is file sharing across different endpoint devices and collaboration tools creating large amounts of data duplication.

These discoveries have motivated us to determine how we can improve performance and make CACSS more efficient. Increasing the efficiency and effectiveness of storage environments helps organizations improve their competitiveness by removing constraints on data growth, improving their service levels, and maintaining better leverage over the increasing quantity and variety of data. While much research has been done on data de-duplication and data caching in traditional file storage systems, there is still a lack of research and evaluation for the big data environment in which security, performance and reliability are becoming more crucial. Therefore we decided to add in-line file-level de-duplication and object caching features to our cloud storage system and evaluate them from the real environment.

3   System Design

The architecture of CACSS is shown in **Fig. 1**. From a conceptive level, it consists of the following components:

— Access interface: provides a unique entry point to the whole storage system
— Metadata management service: manages the object metadata and permission controls.
— Metadata storage space: stores all of the object metadata and other related data.

— Object operation management service: handles a wide range of object operation requests.
— De-duplication controller: manages global inline data de-duplication.

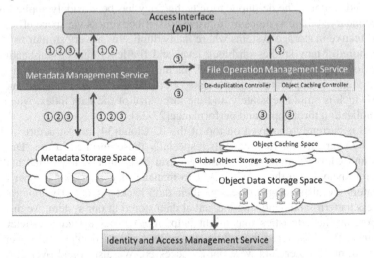

①: Put Bucket, Get Bucket, Put/Get Bucket acl, Put/Get Bucket website, List Multipart Uploads, Put/Get Bucket logging
②: Head Object, Put/Get Object acl, List Parts, Initiate Multipart Upload
③: Put/Post Object, Get Object, Delete Object, Upload Part, Abort Multipart Upload

Fig. 1. CACSS Architecture

— Object caching controller: provides data caching as a service.
— Object data storage space, global object storage space and object caching space,: store all of the object content data in different circumstances.

3.1   Access Interface

CACSS offers a web-based interface for managing storage space and searching for objects. The current implementation supports Amazon's S3 REST API, the prevailing standard commercial storage cloud interface.

3.2   Identity and Access Management Service

IAM is a separated service that provides authorization and access control of various resources. It offers sub user, group management and precise permission control of which operations a user can perform and under what conditions such operations can be carried out.

3.3   Metadata Management

To achieve high performance in metadata access and operation, CACSS's object metadata and content are completely separated. Each object's metadata—including its system metadata such as size, last date modified and object format, together with user defined metadata—are all stored as a collection of blocks addressed by an index in CACSS's Metadata Storage Space (MSS). MSS keeps all of the collections' data sorted lexicographically by index. Each block is akin to a matrix which has exactly two columns and unlimited rows. The values of the elements in the first and second columns are block quantifiers and block targets, respectively. All of the block quantifiers have unique values in each block:

$$\text{Block}_A = [a_{i,j}] \ 1 \leq i \leq m, \ 1 \leq j \leq 2, \text{ for any } k,s \in m, \text{ where } k \neq s, a_{k,1} \neq a_{s,1}$$

E.g. an index of W maps to a collection:

$$\left(\begin{bmatrix} a_{1,1} & a_{1,2} \\ a_{2,1} & a_{2,2} \\ \vdots & \vdots \end{bmatrix} \begin{bmatrix} b_{1,1} & b_{1,2} \\ b_{2,1} & b_{2,2} \\ b_{3,1} & b_{3,2} \\ \vdots & \vdots \end{bmatrix} \ \dots \ \begin{bmatrix} d_{1,1} & d_{1,2} \\ d_{2,1} & d_{2,2} \end{bmatrix} \right)$$

3.4   Metadata Management Service

MMS manages the way in which an object's metadata is stored. In such a system a client will consult the CACSS MMS, which is responsible for maintaining the storage system namespace, and they will then receive the information specifying the location of the file contents. This allows multiple versions of an object to exist.

MMS handles requests as follows. First, it checks if a request contains an access key and a signed secret key. CACSS consults AIM and MSS to verify whether the user has the permission to perform the operation. If they do have permission, the request is authorized to continue. If they don't, error information is returned. If a request does not contain an access key or a signed secret key, MMS is looked up to verify if the request to the bucket or object is set as publicly available to everyone. If it is set as public, then the request continues to the next step. All the requests are logged, both successful and failed. The logging data can be used by both the service provider and storage users for billing, analysis and diagnostic purposes.

Differing from traditional storage systems that limit the file metadata which can be stored and accessed, MMS makes metadata more adaptive and comprehensive. Additional data regarding file and user-defined metadata can be added to the metadata storage, and these data can be accessed and adopted on demand by users or computational works at any time. Searching via metadata is another key feature of CACSS.

Buckets. To reduce interoperability issues, CACSS adopts the de facto industry standard of buckets as basic containers for holding objects.

Unlike some traditional file systems, in which a limited number of objects can be stored in a directory, a CACSS bucket has no limit. CACSS has a global namespace—bucket names are unique and each individual bucket's name is used as the index in the MSS. We use various block quantifiers and block targets to store a variety of information, such as properties of a bucket or an object, permissions and access lists for a particular user, and other user defined metadata.

For example, for a bucket named "bucket1", an index "bucket1" should exist, which maps to a collection of data such as:

$$
\left(
\begin{array}{l}
\left[
\begin{array}{ll}
pp{:}key & bucket1 \\
pp{:}owner & userid1 \\
pp{:}region & uk1 \\
pp{:}web & page.html \\
pp{:}type & bucket \\
pp{:}deduplicationLevel & global
\end{array}
\right] \\
[pm{:}userid2 \quad READ;\ READ\_ACP;] \\
[um{:}info \quad this\ is\ a\ bucket]
\end{array}
\right)
$$

Objects. The index of each object is comprised of a string, which has the format of the bucket name together with the assigned object key. As a result of this nomenclature, objects of the same bucket are naturally very close together in MSS; this improves the performance of concurrent metadata access to objects in the same bucket.

For example, for an object with the user-assigned key "object/key.pdf" in bucket "bucket1", an index of "bucket1- object/key.pdf" should exist, which maps to the following collection of data:

$$
\left(
\begin{array}{l}
\left[
\begin{array}{ll}
pp{:}key & object/key.pdf \\
pp{:}owner & userid1 \\
pp{:}loc & hdfs{:}//cluster1/bucket1/uuid... \\
pp{:}type & object \\
pp{:}bucket & bucket1 \\
pp{:}sha2 & 3c20dc4a766c6df7d20\ ... \\
pp{:}md5 & 20ad802b8df7c9fc\ ....
\end{array}
\right] \\
[pm{:}userid1 \quad FULL\_CONTROL;] \\
\left[
\begin{array}{ll}
um{:}author & some\ author \\
um{:}year & 2011
\end{array}
\right]
\end{array}
\right)
$$

Object Versioning. When versioning setting is enabled for a bucket, each object key is mapped to a core object record. Each core object record holds a list of version IDs that map to individual versions of that object.

For example, for an object with a predefined key "object/paper.pdf" in bucket "versionbucket", an index of "versionbucket − object/paper. pdf" should exist, which maps to the collection data:

$$
\left(
\begin{array}{l}
\left[
\begin{array}{ll}
pp{:}key & object/paper.pdf \\
pp{:}owner & userid1 \\
pp{:}type & object
\end{array}
\right] \\
\left[
\begin{array}{ll}
ver{:}lastest & uuid1 \\
ver{:}(versionbucket)uuid1 & \\
ver{:}(versionbucket)uuid2 &
\end{array}
\right]
\end{array}
\right)
$$

Similarly, the object's version record with row key "versionbucket-object/paper.pdf-uuid1" maps to the collection data:

$$
\left(
\begin{array}{l}
\left[
\begin{array}{ll}
pp{:}loc & hdfs{:}//cluster1/versionbucket/uuid... \\
pp{:}type & version \\
pp{:}replicas & 2
\end{array}
\right] \\
[pm{:}userid2 \quad READ;]
\end{array}
\right)
$$

3.5   Object Data Management

CACCS stores all the unstructured data, such as file content, in the Object Data Storage Space (ODSS). ODSS is intentionally designed to provide an adaptive storage infrastructure that can store unlimited amounts of data and that does not depend on underlying storage devices or file systems. Storage service vendors are able to compose one or multiple types of storage devices or systems together to create their own featured cloud storage system based on their expertise and requirements in terms of level of availability, performance, complexity, durability and reliability. Such implementation could be as simple as NFS [35], or as sophisticated as HDFS [19], PVFS [36] and Lustre [37].

CACSS's File Operation Management Service (FOMS) implements all ODSS's underlying file systems' API, so that it can handle a wide range of file operation requests to the ODSS. FOMS works like an adapter that handles the architectural differences between various storage devices and file systems. It works closely with MMS to maintain the whole namespace of CACSS.

File Level Data De-Duplication. To enable data storage efficiency, CACSS has introduced a De-duplication Controller (DDC) and a Global Object Storage Space (GOSS) into the design. Currently, the DDC is only implemented to use a global file-level de-duplication method, which manages how and where duplicated objects should be stored in the GOSS. If a bucket is configured to enable data de-duplication, all the objects in this bucket will be stored in the GOSS. It is extremely unlikely to have a collision between two files with different content but the same SHA-256 checksum [38]. Therefore, CACSS uses SHA-256 hash function to calculate the checksum of each incoming storing object, and if the checksum does not exist in the MSS, a new de-duplication object metadata record with $ddes and the hash value as the key will be inserted. The physical file content will be saved into the GOSS as a new file. If the checksum already exists in the MSS, the record will be updated to attach this object's bucket name, object key and the user id (**Fig. 2**).

e. g. Row key "$ddes − D3F4D74F814D55EE80 ... " maps to records:

$$\left(\left|\begin{array}{l} pp: < bucket1 >< user1 > key1 \\ pp: < bucket2 >< user1 > key2 \\ pp: < bucket3 >< user2 > key3 \\ \\ \quad\quad pp: filesize \quad\quad\quad\quad 19751324 \end{array}\right|\right)$$

Object Data Caching Facility. The ODCF contains the Object Caching Controller (OCC) and Object Caching Space (OCS). With CACSS's OCDF, it is possible to cache certain frequently-accessed objects into the OCS. Such space provides multi-level cache capability, accelerating data access. It can be implemented by a mix of RAM, SSD and other high speed storage devices. The OCC keeps records of all object data accesses, and manages a global object access ranking table. Depending on the total spaces available on the OCS, the OCC intelligently decides which top accessed object data should be cached and where it should be cached. For example, the most accessed object data will be copied into RAM, while medium accessed object

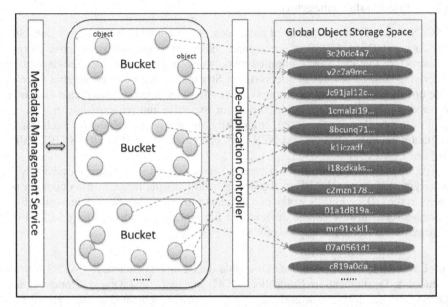

Fig. 2. Bucket-Object to Global Object Storage Space mapping

data or frequently accessed large files that cannot fit in to the RAM will reside in the SSD. When an object access request is received, the OCC first checks to determine if the latest object data are located in the OCS; if not, data will be returned from the ODSS or the GOSS. We have also enabled the "Caching on Demand" service feature, which allows users to specify exactly which object data should be cached.

4   Implementation

After considerable research and experimentation, we chose HBase as the foundational MSS storage for all object metadata. HBase is highly scalable and delivers fast random data retrieval. Its column-orientation design confers exceptional flexibility in the storing of data.

We chose Hadoop DFS (HDFS) as the foundational storage technology for storing object data in the ODSS. Hadoop also supports MapReduce framework [39] that can be used for executing computation tasks within the storage infrastructure. Although there is a single point of failure at the NameNode in HDFS's original design, many research studies have been carried out in order to build a highly available version of HDFS NameNode, such as AvatarNode [40]. Every file and block in HDFS is represented as an object in the NameNode's memory, each of which occupies about 150 bytes. Therefore the total memory available on NameNode dictates the limitation of the number of files that can be stored in the HDFS cluster. By separating object metadata and object data, CACSS is able to construct an adaptive storage infrastructure that can store unlimited amounts of data using multiple HDFS clusters, whilst still exposing a single logical data store to the users (**Fig. 4**). Using Linux Ram Disk

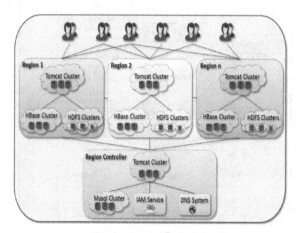

Fig. 3. Implementation of CACSS

technique, we employ server RAMs in Tomcat Clusters to serve as the Object Caching Space.

4.1   Multi-region Support

The design and architecture of CACSS are based on the principles of scalability, performance, data durability and reliability. Scalability is considered in various aspects including the overall capacity of multi-region file metadata and file storage, as well as throughput of the system. Taking another perspective, the implementation of CACSS consists of a region controller and multiple regions (**Fig. 3**).

A Tomcat cluster is used as the application server layer in each region. It is easy to achieve high scalability, load balancing and high availability by using a Tomcat cluster and configuring with other technologies such as HAProxy and Nginx [41, 42]. The region controller has a MySQL cluster for storing various data such as user account information and billing and invoice details.A bucket can be created in one of the regions, and at the same time, a DNS A record is inserted into the DNS server. This mapping ensures that clients will send a hosted-style access request of the bucket and the object to the correct region. Each region is consistent with a Tomcat cluster, an HBase cluster and a set of HDFS clusters. The object data is stored in one of the HDFS clusters in the region. The object key and metadata are stored in the region's HBase cluster. It is always important to consider that any access to a bucket or object requires access rights to be checked. In CACSS, each request goes through its region first; if the requested bucket or object is set to be public, there is no need to communicate with the region controller. If it is not set as public, it consults the region controller to perform the permission check before making a response. The region controller, which includes a MySQL cluster, keeps records of all the requests and maintains user accounts and billing information. A DNS system (such as Amazon Route 53 [43]) serves to map the bucket name to its corresponding region's Tomcat cluster IP. The region controller can also connect to the existing IAM service to provide more sophisticated user and group management.

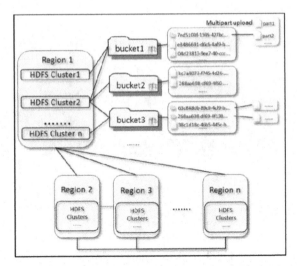

Fig. 4. Implementation multi-region HDFS clusters for storing buckets and contents of objects

CACSS also adopts other useful features of HDFS such as no explicit limitation on a single file size and no limitation on the number of files in a directory. In CACSS, most of the objects are stored in a flat structure in HDFS. Each object's file name under HDFS is a generated UUID to ensure uniqueness.

The implementation of CACSS does not need to rely solely on HDFS. The complete separation of file metadata from file content enables CACSS to adapt to one or even multiple file systems, such as GPFS or Lustre. It is now deployed as a service under the IC-Cloud platform, and is expected to work with a variety of distributed file systems through POSIX or their APIs without much effort.

5   Experiments

We have done two sets of experiments so far. The first set was performed on top of Amazon EC2 instances, to enable the comparison of CACSS and Amazon S3 under similar hardware and network environments. We used JetS3t [44], an open source Java S3 library, configuring it with our experiment code to evaluate the performance of CACSS.

We used one m2.xlarge instance, with 17.1GB of memory and 6.5 EC2 Compute Units, to run MySQL, HDFS NameNode, HBase Hmaster and Tomcat with the CACSS application. Three m1.large instances, each with 7.5GB memory and 4 EC2 Compute units ran HDFS DataNodes and HBase Regionservers. Each of these instances was attached with 100GB volumes of storage space. Another two m1.large instances were configured with the same experiment code but different S3 end points. We refer to these two instances as "S3 test node" and "CACSS test node."

To evaluate the performance of CACSS, we ran a series of experiments on both Amazon S3 and CACSS. The evaluation of the performance of Amazon EC2 and S3 has been carried out previously by [10]. A similar method was adopted here to evaluate the overall throughput of CACSS.

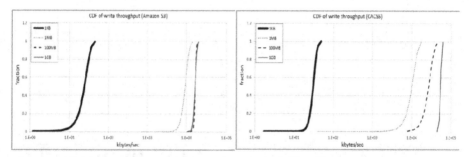

Fig. 5. Cumulative Distribution Function (CDF) plots for writing transactions from EC2 to Amazon S3 and CACSS of various sizes

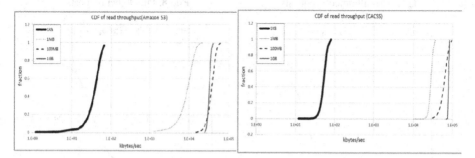

Fig. 6. CDF plots for reading transactions from EC2 to Amazon S3 and CACSS of various sizes

Fig. 5 and **Fig. 6** illustrate respectively the write and read throughputs of Amazon EC2 to Amazon S3, and of EC2 to CACSS, based on our experiments. Each graph contains traces of observed bandwidths for transactions of 1KB, 1MB, 100MB and 1GB. Both Amazon S3 and CACSS perform better with larger transaction sizes, because smaller size files would require more transaction overhead. For files larger than 1MB, the average speed of transaction of CACSS is higher than Amazon S3; this is probably due to underlying hardware differences between Amazon EC2 and Amazon S3, such as hard drive RPM and RAID levels.

Amazon S3's List Objects operation only supports a maximum of 1000 objects to be returned at a time, so we could not properly evaluate its object metadata service performance. However, we were able to run some tests to evaluate CACSS's metadata management. We ran a List All Objects operation after every 1000 Put Object operations. All of the operations were targeted to the same bucket. Each Put Object utilised using an empty file, because for this experiment we were only interested in the performance of the metadata access. **Fig. 8** shows a scatter graph of the response time of each Put Object, with respect to the total number of objects in the bucket. The result shows an average response time of 0.007875s and a variance of 0.000157s for each Put Object operation. This indicates that the response time is pretty much constant no matter how many objects are stored in the bucket. **Fig. 7** illustrates the response time of each List All Objects operation with respect to the total number of objects contained in the bucket. There are several peaks in the graph marked with

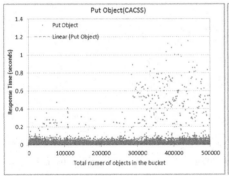
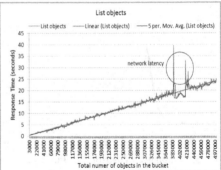

Fig. 7. List all objects requests   **Fig. 8.** Put Object requests

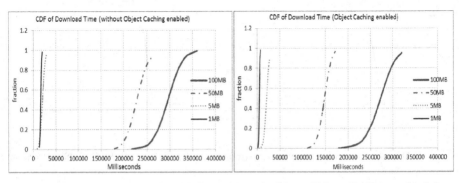

Fig. 9. CDF plots for object downloading with and without Object Caching enabled from CACSS of various sizes

red circle. These peaks are caused by sudden network latency between Amazon EC2 instances during that time. Otherwise, the overall result shows a linear relation between the response time and the total number of objects.

The second set of experiments was performed on top of the IC-Cloud in order to compare the effectiveness of the object caching mechanisms we implemented. We used four virtual machines (VMs) to create a CACSS cluster. One VM with 8GB of memory and 4 CPU cores was used to run MySQL, HDFS NameNode, HBase Hmaster and Tomcat with the CACSS application and allocated RAM disk space. The other three were each configured with 4GB memory and 2 CPU cores to run HDFS DataNodes and HBase Regionservers. The two graphs in **Fig. 9** illustrate respectively the total object downloading time with and without object caching enabled from CACSS of various sizes. When object caching was enabled, we saw an improvement in average download speed for all object sizes, especially for objects with sizes of 1MB and 50MB.

6   Conclusions

In this paper, we described the design and implementation of CACSS, a big data storage system, taking into account the generic principles of data storage efficiency and durability, scalability, performance and reliability. CACSS has been deployed on top of IC-Cloud infrastructure since 2012 and has served as the main storage space for several internal and external collaborative projects. CACSS delivers comprehensive features such as data access through the S3 interface (the de facto industry standard), native and user defined object metadata searching, global data de-duplication and object data caching services. The storage model we propose offers service providers a considerable advantage by combining existing technologies into a single customized big data storage system. Furthermore, CACSS performance was found to be comparable to Amazon S3 in formal tests, with similar read/write capabilities. We have seen improvement in performance with object caching enabled through preliminary experiments. However, there is still much improvement and evaluation work to be done on the newly added features such as object data de-duplication and object data caching services. These features will be addressed and their effectiveness validated in our future work.

References

1. Amazon. Amazon Simple Storage Service (S3), http://aws.amazon.com/s3/
2. Google. Google Cloud Storage Service, http://code.google.com/apis/storage/
3. AWS Case Study: SmugMug (2013)
4. http://aws.amazon.com/solutions/case-studies/elephantdrive/
5. AWS Case Study: Jungle Disk
6. Amazon, Amazon S3 - The First Trillion Objects (2012)
7. Gohring, N.: Amazon's S3 Down for Several Hours
8. Brodkin, J.: Outage hits Amazon S3 storage service (2008)
9. Li, Y., Guo, L., Guo, Y.: CACSS: Towards a Generic Cloud Storage Service. In: CLOSER 2012, pp. 27–36. SciTePress (2012)
10. Garfinkel, S.L.: An evaluation of amazon's grid computing services: EC2, S3, and SQS. Citeseer (2007)
11. Rackspace. Cloud Files, http://www.rackspace.co.uk
12. Barr, J.: (2011)
13. Wang, G., Ng, T.E.: The impact of virtualization on network performance of amazon ec2 data center. In: 2010 Proceedings of the IEEE INFOCOM. IEEE (2010)
14. Garfinkel, S.L.: An evaluation of amazon's grid computing services: EC2, S3, and SQS. in Center for. 2007. Citeseer (2007)
15. Openstack, http://openstack.org
16. Nurmi, D., et al.: The eucalyptus open-source cloud-computing system. IEEE (2009)
17. Abe, Y., Gibson, G.: pWalrus: Towards better integration of parallel file systems into cloud storage. IEEE (2010)
18. Bresnahan, J., et al.: Cumulus: an open source storage cloud for science. SC10 Poster (2010)
19. Borthakur, D.: The hadoop distributed file system: Architecture and design. Hadoop Project Website (2007)
20. HBase, A.: http://hbase.apache.org/
21. Carstoiu, D., Cernian, A., Olteanu, A.: Hadoop Hbase-0.20.2 performance evaluation. In: 2010 4th International Conference on New Trends in Information Science and Service Science, NISS (2010)

22. Khetrapal, A., Ganesh, V.: HBase and Hypertable for large scale distributed storage systems. Dept. of Computer Science, Purdue University (2006)
23. Saab, P.: Scaling memcached at Facebook. Facebook Engineering Note (2008)
24. Barroso, L.A., Dean, J., Holzle, U.: Web search for a planet: The Google cluster architecture. IEEE Micro 23(2), 22–28 (2003)
25. Chang, F., et al.: Bigtable: A distributed storage system for structured data. ACM Transactions on Computer Systems (TOCS) 26(2), 4 (2008)
26. Ongaro, D., et al.: Fast crash recovery in RAMCloud. In: Proceedings of the Twenty-Third ACM Symposium on Operating Systems Principles. ACM (2011)
27. Tianming, Y., et al.: DEBAR: A scalable high-performance de-duplication storage system for backup and archiving. In: 2010 IEEE International Symposium on Parallel & Distributed Processing, IPDPS (2010)
28. Yujuan, T., et al.: SAM: A Semantic-Aware Multi-tiered Source De-duplication Framework for Cloud Backup. In: 2010 39th International Conference on Parallel Processing, ICPP (2010)
29. Chuanyi, L., et al.: ADMAD: Application-Driven Metadata Aware De-duplication Archival Storage System. In: Fifth IEEE International Workshop on Storage Network Architecture and Parallel I/Os, SNAPI 2008 (2008)
30. Quinlan, S., Dorward, S.: Venti: A new approach to archival storage. In: Proceedings of the FAST 2002 Conference on File and Storage Technologies (2002)
31. You, L.L., Pollack, K.T., Long, D.D.: Deep Store: An archival storage system architecture. In: Proceedings of the 21st International Conference on Data Engineering, ICDE 2005. IEEE (2005)
32. Dubnicki, C., et al.: Hydrastor: A scalable secondary storage. In: Procedings of the 7th Conference on File and Storage Technologies. USENIX Association (2009)
33. Jiansheng, W., et al.: MAD2: A scalable high-throughput exact deduplication approach for network backup services. In: 2010 IEEE 26th Symposium on Mass Storage Systems and Technologies, MSST (2010)
34. Guo, Y.-K., Guo, L.: IC cloud: Enabling compositional cloud. International Journal of Automation and Computing 8(3), 269–279 (2011)
35. Sandberg, R., et al.: Design and implementation of the Sun network filesystem (1985)
36. Carns, P.H., et al.: PVFS: A parallel file system for Linux clusters. USENIX Association (2000)
37. Schwan, P.: Lustre: Building a file system for 1000-node clusters (2003)
38. Gilbert, H., Handschuh, H.: Security analysis of SHA-256 and sisters. In: Matsui, M., Zuccherato, R.J. (eds.) SAC 2003. LNCS, vol. 3006, pp. 175–193. Springer, Heidelberg (2004)
39. Apache. Hadoop MapReduce, http://hadoop.apache.org/mapreduce/
40. Borthakur, D.: Hadoop avatarnode high availability (2010)
41. Doclo, L.: Clustering Tomcat Servers with High Availability and Disaster Fallback (2011)
42. Mulesoft, Tomcat Clustering - A Step By Step Guide
43. Amazon. Route 53, http://aws.amazon.com/route53/
44. JetS3t. JetS3t, http://jets3t.s3.amazonaws.com

Towards Cost Aspects in Cloud Architectures

Uwe Hohenstein, Reto Krummenacher, Ludwig Mittermeier, and Sebastian Dippl

Siemens AG, Corporate Technology, Otto-Hahn-Ring 6, D-81730 Muenchen, Germany
{firstname.lastname}@siemens.com

Abstract. One of the important aspects of Cloud computing is certainly the pay-per-use model; users have to pay only for those resources they are actively using, on a timely basis. This model paired with principally infinite resources promises to run applications at lower costs, arguably.

This paper demonstrates by means of two case studies that applications in the cloud can cause high operational costs depending on the building blocks used. Different architectural decisions result in significantly different operational costs. Costs should thus obtain much more attention when architecting for the cloud.

Keywords: Cloud Computing, Cost-driven Architecture, Cloud Application Design, Windows Azure Platform.

1   Introduction

Cloud computing has emerged to be the current highlight in terms of IT as a service. A smart idea is in principle enough to start a new business [D.1]: no more need for large cost expenditure, no need for over-provisioning and wasting expensive resources, for not missing potential new clients. The main benefits of cloud computing, without going into technical details yet, are the elasticity and high availability of (at least theoretically infinite) hardware and software resources, the pay-as-you-go pricing model, and the self-service administration of the resources. In more economical terms, cloud computing has a very attractive benefit of turning CAPEX (capital expenses) into OPEX (operational expenses).

Still, none of these features, functional or non-functional, comes for free. A scalable architecture is essential for leveraging scalable cloud infrastructures [D.2], or in other words, simply deploying existing enterprise software into the cloud does not make the software more scalable or cloud-enabled. Cloud architecture best practices are offered by most cloud utility providers, for instance Amazon AWS [D.3] or Microsoft Azure [D.4], with illustrations of how to design for failure, how to leverage elasticity, how to decouple components and parallelize etc. These important guidelines of how to bring existing and new applications to the cloud are common and valid for all cloud infrastructure offerings, although optimal software engineering decisions might certainly depend on the particular cloud utility for which one implements the cloud-enabled application.

There is, however, one important aspect, as we will argue throughout this paper, which is (too often) forgotten, when specifying solution architectures for the cloud:

I. Ivanov et al. (Eds.): CLOSER 2012, CCIS 367, pp. 117–134, 2013.

the operational costs of running an application in the cloud. In particular from an enterprise perspective, the maintenance and operations costs are highly relevant, and they should thus have a significant impact on design decisions, as we exemplify and discuss in this paper. The total costs of running an application are comprised of various individual sources such as the charges for compute instances, storage, bandwidth or different additional services. Depending on the cost model, one or the other individual cost source will dominate the overall bill, and reducing the total cost can only be done when minimizing the use of these dominating resources, already when defining the architecture. Consequently, when architecting for the cloud, cost factors need to be taken into account, and one might consider extending the "4+1 Architectural View Model" by [D.5] with an operational cost view. While a modular design helps to reduce maintenance costs and ease evolution, the operational cost view would enable an architect to illustrate the impact of the architectural decision on the overall expenses.

The similar line of arguments was expressed by Todd Hoff on HighScalability.com: "Instead of asking for the Big O complexity of an algorithm we'll also have to ask for the Big $ (or Big Euro) notation so we can judge an algorithm by its cost against a particular cloud profile." [D.6]. It shows that while turning to cloud deployments cost-centric architectures becomes even more important, as the costs are more obviously accountable. Although, we are certainly by no means arguing that architectures should be determined by cost measures, we emphasize that discussions about architectural alternatives, about pros and cons with regard to costs have to be taken into account much more prominently when choosing the appropriate architecture for the cloud.

Existing work on cost-centric architectures is very few (cf. Section 5), and most publications and white papers rather relate to a Total Cost of Ownership (TCO) comparison between on premise and cloud deployments, not taking into account the actual architecture; for example, the Experton Group has published at business-cloud.de a TCO Calculator that helps in assessing the cost advantages of deploying in the cloud.

In [D.7], we counterwork this trend, and showcase with concrete examples how architectures impact the operational costs, once the decision to work in the cloud has been taken. This paper is a revised version of [D.7], taking into account the recent pricing models. As a technical basis for our work we are using the Windows Azure platform and the corresponding pricing models. The main reason for working with Windows Azure in the context of this paper is the comprehensive PaaS offering that ships with a complete development and deployment environment and various relevant by-products such as persistent storage, access control, or distributed cache. This has also the advantage that there are no problems with the licensing of such products, as these are part of the platform and the cost model. The latter, moreover, makes the calculation of the architecture-dependent costs much easier.

In order to clarify the baseline, we continue the paper with a short introduction to the core concepts of Windows Azure and its pricing model in Section 2. Then, we present two scenarios that are derived from real-world business cases, and based on that we will discuss and analyze the different architectural alternatives in Sections 3 and 4, respectively. In Section 5, we outline some related work with cost-centric aspects. During the practical part of our investigation, we detected some recommendations that are worth being reported on in Section 6, before the paper is concluded with Section 7.

2   Windows Azure and Its Pricing Model

In this section, we give a short introduction and overview of the core concepts of Windows Azure including the pay-per-use model. Pricing details reflect the status quo when writing this paper and will certainly change again in the future. However, regardless of the pricing details of a specific cloud computing platform, the baseline argumentation of this paper remains the same.

2.1   Core Concepts

Windows Azure provides virtual machines (VMs) that run Windows Server 2008 and are available in two forms: a Web Role hosts an IIS (Internet Information Server) and is foreseen to provide the front-ends for web applications such as ASP.NET. In contrast, a Worker Role does not possess an IIS and serves mainly as a host for backend processes. The Web Roles offer different thread modes that can be configured, e.g., to have a thread pool with delegating each request to the next thread.

Both types of roles can initiate Internet connections, however, instances of Web and Worker Roles they are not directly accessible via the Internet. All network traffic coming from outside to Web and Worker Role instances goes through a load balancer; each role can specify an endpoint configuration by which protocol (e.g., HTTP(S)) and by which port it should be accessible. Incoming traffic is routed to role instances in a round robin fashion; if there is more than one instance of a Web Role, subsequent requests will be routed by the load balancer to different instances. Therefore it is not an option to use the local file system of a Web Role for storing HTTP session data. Rather, the Azure storage mechanisms, which are table storage, queue storage and blob storage, can be used for data that needs to be processed in subsequent requests. Similarly, Azure SQL Database, a managed SQL Server in the cloud, can be used.

Azure table storage allows for storing data in a tabular manner, however, it does not enforce a fixed scheme; a row consists of a couple of properties and values, which are stored without any predefined structure. Azure queue storage allows for FIFO-style message passing between role instances. Each message can be up to 64 KB in size. Finally, Azure blob storage allows for storing binary data such as images or videos, which can be annotated with metadata. All the Azure storage services can be accessed via a RESTful interface; i.e., an HTTP protocol-based web API. This way, all programming languages with support for HTTP can use of the Azure storage capabilities, from inside the cloud or outside. Apart from that, the Windows Azure storage client library provides a more comfortable way for accessing the Azure storages.

An application built for Windows Azure runs in the context of a so-called hosted service, which defines for example a public URL prefix as well as the geographical region. Windows Azure applications are uploaded (deployed) to the public cloud environment via the Azure web-based self-management portal to a specific hosted service, either to a production deployment or a staging deployment. The production deployment is accessible via the public URL of the hosted service whereas a deployment that is uploaded to the staging area is for testing purposes and thus only accessible via a URL generated by Azure. Staging and production deployments can be swapped without service downtime.

2.2 Standard Rates

We here summarize the Azure prices as of February 2013 for the North America and Europe regions; the Asia Pacific Region is more expensive. The recent standard rates for Windows Azure can be found in *http://www.windowsazure.comen-us/pricing /details/*.

Web and Worker Roles, are charged for the number of hours they are deployed. Even if a role is used for 5 seconds only, a full hour has to be paid. As Table 1 shows, there are several instance categories, *small* (S), *medium* (M) etc., which scale in a linear manner with regard to equipments and prices. That is, a medium instance has double of CPU, disk etc. than a small instance resulting in a double price. The exception is an XS instance category.

Table 1. Prices for Compute instances

	CPU	RAM	HDD (GB)	MBps	$ / h	I/O performance
XS	Shared	768MB	20	5	0.04	Low
S	1,6GHz	1,75 GB	225	100	0.12	Moderate
M	2 x	3,5 GB	490	200	0.24	High
L	4 x	7 GB	1000	400	0.48	High
XL	8 x	14 GB	2040	800	0.96	High

For Azure table, blob and queue storages, the costs depend on bandwidth, transaction, storage consumption, and redundancy. Storage is billed based upon the average usage during a billing period. For example, if 10 GB of storage are utilized for the first half of the month and none for the second half of the month, 5 GB of storage are billed for average usage. Each GB of storage is charged with $0.07 per GB for local redundancy, and $0.095 for geographical redundancy. Storage consumption is measured at least once a day by Azure. Please note that the storage consumption takes into account the physical storage, which consists not only of raw data, but also the length of the property names, the data types, and the size of the actual data [D.8].

Moreover, any access to storage, i.e., any transaction, has to be paid: 100,000 storage transactions cost $0.01. Bulk operations, e.g., bundling several inserts in one operation, count as one transaction.

All inbound data transfers to the Azure cloud are at no charge. The outbound transfer is charged with $0.12 per outgoing GB,. It is important to note that the transferred data has some typical XML overhead according to the protocol. Data transfer is for free within the same affinity group, i.e., for VMs that run in the same data center. The affinity group can be specified in the Azure self-service portal.

The costs for Azure SQL Database, a virtualized SQL Server, are also based on a monthly consumption. One pays based on the total number of databases that existed at any point during a particular day. Up to 100 MBs are charged with $4.995 a month overall. Up to 1 GB, the overall price is $9.99. Any GB exceeding 1 GB costs $3.996. Having reached 10 GB, the prices again decrease to $1.998 per additional GB, and beyond 50 GB, a GB costs only $0.999. This means, a 10 GB is charged with $45.954: $9.99 for the first GB, and 9 * $3.996 for the additional 9 GB.

Finally, we want to mention the Azure Access Control Service for authentication, which is charged with $1.99 per 100000 transactions.

There are also some flat rates where a fixed number of VMs is paid. For instance, a 6-month commitment (*http://www.Microsoft.com/windowsazure/offers*) mostly offers a 20% off rate for resources. In case the given quotas (e.g., 750 free compute hours) are exceeded, standards rates apply for overages. Furthermore, special offers exist for MSDN subscribers, BizSpark, or MPN members. Those specific rates are out of scope for this paper.

2.3   Special Quotas and Limits

There are some quotas active that define upper thresholds. For instance, every account may run 20 concurrent small VMs (which is equal to 10 medium or 5 large ones) and possess 5 concurrent storage accounts, each having its own credentials for access. Higher numbers can be ordered, however, require negotiation with the Azure customer service. Besides this, there are a couple of technical restrictions such as the payload limit of 64 K for queues.

3   Scenario 1: Mass Data Store

This paper relies on two typical scenarios that occur quite often within Siemens. However, the scenarios were simplified in order to ease the discussion and to obfuscate the business details.

The first scenario is concerned with mass data storage. Several data providers (DPs) of given organizations provide data for a cloud-based mass data storage. The data in the cloud storage is processed by applications for analysis or other purposes; e.g., business intelligence or production process optimization. A more concrete example is a fleet management system that manages cars; each car sends data about its current state or position to a central cloud service. In this case the organizations are car fleets, the data providers are individual vehicles or fleet owners, and the collected data is processed further on to optimize fleet usage or the traffic management.

The following discussion is based upon several assumptions; most of them will be relevant for the presented cost calculations:

- There are 5 organizations with 20 DPs each for a total of 100 DPs. Each DP sends 10 data items à 1 KB per second to storage. Both the frequency of 10 items per second and the payload are assumed to be constant (varying loads are discussed later in Subsection 3.5). In summary, 1000 items are thus arriving per second (100 DPs * 10 items/s) for a total payload of 1000 KB/s.
- No data will be removed; there is an increasing amount of data in storage.
- There is a transport latency from outside the cloud to the inside and vice versa, which might of course vary depending on the overall network congestion. However, the impact on the architecture is neglectably small since we assume an asynchronous HTTP communication link between data providers and the cloud storage. Hence, the DPs are just firing without waiting for a confirmation.

Please note the main purpose of this paper is neither to present a particular application and its costs, nor to define the cheapest architecture for such. The given numbers are (realistic) assumptions taken to calculate and *compare* occurring costs in the cloud. Moreover, it is not our intention to assert a certain type of architecture; rather we want to show how architectural choices can affect costs more or less dramatically. We also recognize that changing the assumed numbers and SLAs could lead to different costs and ranking of architectures. And there are certainly further possible architectures, which are not discussed here.

3.1   The Web Role Approach

A couple of Web Roles (with threads running in it) receive data from all data providers, no matter of what organization. Threads of an appropriate number of Web Roles store data into organization-specific storages. Thus, every organization has some cloud storage of its own to keep its data – not at last due to security considerations: an organization's data must not be accessible by others. According to the incoming load, more or less Web Roles can be started, having the IIS load balancer in front of them. For the purpose of calculating costs, we fix some further system parameters:

- Small instances are taken for the Web Roles.
- We assume that each Web Role can run 10 threads without system overload. This is a reasonable number that corresponds to Microsoft's Best Practices, 2011 [D.9]. Our tests have shown that small Azure instances are already quite busy having 10 threads running.
- The Microsoft Extreme Computing Group published 2011 the results of several benchmarks for Azure. Unfortunately, the web site [D.10] is no longer available. Referring to the benchmarks, we assume that storing data from a Web Role into cloud storage is typically done in 30ms.
- Additional 40ms are assumed at the Worker Role for client authentication, authorization, and data pre-processing, including database access for getting credentials.

Summing up, this means that the processing of each incoming storage request in a Web Role has some 70ms compute latency including all storage accesses. As a consequence, one Web Role thread is able to handle about 14 requests in a second. Handling the 1000 incoming items/s (10 data items per second from 100 data providers) thus requires minimally 70 threads. According to the benchmark results in [D.10], any Azure storage solution should be able to handle a write throughput of 1000 items/s performed by 7 Web Roles with 10 threads. With the assumption that each Web Role can run 10 threads, 7 Web Roles with 10 threads each are needed to handle the requested throughput; otherwise the IIS queue of the Web Roles will fill up, letting data providers experience more and more latency. With a constant load, the IIS queues will never be able to shrink, which moreover increases the risk of losing data.

As stated previously, essential for this paper are the operational costs of architectures. The monthly costs for this first solution are as follows:

- The complete inbound traffic to the Web Role is free of charge; since July 2011.
- Seven small Web Roles à 12ct per hour cost $604.80 for 30 days.
- Table storage (no removal assumed) with a daily increase of 82.4 GB (1 GB/month à 7ct) results in further $89.40 if we consider the worst case that Azure monitors storage consumption at the end of a day: 82.4 GB for the 1st day, a total of 2*82.4 GB for the 2nd day etc. sum up to 38316 GB in a month.
- 1000 storage transactions per second lead to 2,592,000,000 per month à 1ct per 100000: $259.20.

The total costs are $953.40. A quick conclusion shows that Web Roles produce the main costs; but transactions and the storage also affect the costs.

An aspect not yet discussed is access control and security. Authentication becomes necessary when working with Web Roles, as those are able to access all storage components directly. In this architecture, authorization/authentication can be performed by the Web Role, which is both an advantage and a disadvantage: On the one hand, this provides better flexibility. But on the other hand, an additional authorization/authentication component is required that incurs further costs, either for using Azure Access Control ($1.99 for 100,000 transactions) or implementing one's own component. Anyway, the Web Roles have access to all cloud storages since they serve all organizations.

Of course, the Web Roles can also perform some pre-processing, for example, extracting data from XML input, transforming data, or condensing data.

3.2   Queues at the Front-End

In an alternative architecture, each organization obtains one dedicated cloud queue at the frontend. Data providers of each organization then put data items directly into their respective queue using the provided REST interface for the queue storage.

Since there is no longer a front-end Web Role, authorization and authentication becomes an issue: it must be ensured that a data provider is only allowed to store in the queue of its organization. In Azure, the credentials are bound to a storage account, i.e., all queue or table storages belonging to the same account share the same credentials. This implies that each organization would require an account of its own as otherwise every DP would inherently get access to all queues. The quota of five storage accounts that are granted per Azure account are just sufficient for our example; otherwise additional storage accounts would have to be explicitly requested, however, without any further expenses.

Threads in a Worker Role pick up data items from the queues and transfer them to cloud storage. The number of requested Worker Roles (threads) depends on the time for emptying queues and on the required timeliness of data in cloud storage. In fact, the queue length must be close to empty, otherwise the queue will permanently increase since the assumed load is constant. If data must be up-to-date in cloud storage within fractions of a second, more Worker Roles (threads) are required to perform the transfer. However, data provider throughput is not throttled by a too low number of

Worker Roles. There is no risk of data losses since queues are persistent, but an overflow might become critical.

We assume a queue read latency of 30ms and a typical storage write latency of 30ms (according to the Microsoft Extreme Computing Group [D.10]) for a total of 60ms. Then, one Worker Role thread is able to transfer an average of 16.67 items per second; 60 Worker Role threads distributed over 6 Worker Roles (because of the 1/10 Worker Role/thread ratio) are required to keep pace with each of the 5 queues being filled up with 200 items/s. It does not matter whether Worker Roles are assigned to specific queues or serve all queues. Scalability with regard to incoming data is limited only by queue throughput. The requested 200 items/s are easily achievable by Azure queues according to Microsoft Extreme Computing Group. If necessary, more queues could be set up, e.g., one for each data provider, which might share the same storage accounts. The number of queues and accounts does not affect the total operational costs as only the queued data and the transactions are charged but not the number.

The monthly costs for such a queue-based architecture are computed as follows:

- Incoming requests to the front-end queue are again for free.
- The background storage costs remain at $89.40.
- The storage transactions for background storage are still $259.20 as before.
- There are five newly introduced front-end queues with each queue getting in average 200 messages per second. As already mentioned, the Worker Roles will empty the queues in order to keep pace with the input stream. But even if there are 10 messages in the queue at any point in time, requiring 50KB storage (5 queues * 10 KB) over 30 days, results in the micro-costs of 0.00035ct.
- There are three kinds of inbound and outbound transactions for the queues, one to read a message, another to store, and a third one to delete the message; Azure does not offer a mean to read and delete with one operation. This means high costs of $777.60 = 3 * $259.20.
- Six Worker Roles are used each for a price of 12ct per hour for 30 days: $518.40.

Comparing the calculation with Subsection 3.1, we quadruple the transaction costs from $259.20 to now $1026.80 with the benefit of reducing 7 Worker Roles to 6 Web Roles and saving 86.40$ in a month for computation ($518.40 instead of $604.80). In addition, there are smallest amounts of costs for queue storage (0.00035ct). Hence, this architecture produces costs of $1644.60 per month and is thus about $691 more expensive than the previous one.

Technically speaking, this architecture has some advantages. First, queues allow for more flexible reactions to load changes. Queues can fill up (without causing dominating costs) to be emptied at later points in time, during low load times, if no time critical data is involved. Consequently, an interesting alternative to the proposed setting could let the queues fill up due to fewer Worker Roles, and use – if cheaper – operating hours at night to transfer the data items to the backend storage. Having storage queues filled up does not call upon the same risks as IIS queues, as storage queues are persistent. Second, the architecture can rely on Azure queue authentication as a queue belongs to only one organization, and the data providers of an organization can only fill their organization's queue. However, authentication becomes less flexible.

As another disadvantage, additional implementation effort is required to set up the Worker Roles in a multithreaded manner. In contrast, multithreading is for free in Web Roles because of configurable instantiation models. Moreover, the transfer has to be fault-tolerant due to the lack of storage-spanning transactions, deleting data in the queue and inserting it into the backend storage. And the implementation must be able to determine what data from the queue can be skipped if a crash occurs after transferring to the backend but before deleting in the queue.

A further disadvantage of this architecture is the fact that the payload of queue messages cannot exceed a 64 KB threshold in Azure. Hence, if the payload is unknown or might increase, an architectural redesign is required: one possibility is to use blobs for storing data, and to put a reference (URI) to the blob into the queue. This causes additional storage and transaction costs for blobs and an additional delay for data providers due to the blob handling.

3.3 Bulk Operations

This architecture is based upon the previous one, however, attempts to reduce the number of expensive transactions by means of bulk operations. Azure provides to this end a mean to build bulks of operations of the same kind.

At the front-end, there is no opportunity to bulk unless the data providers collect data in bulks and submit bulks to the queues. But bulk operations can be used during the internal processing: a Worker Role can fetch bulks of items from the queue, remove them in bulks, and submit bulks to the backend storage. This will in fact cause some delay in processing and lacks a little of timeliness. Moreover, some implementation overhead occurs since it is necessary to wait for complete bulks. Some fault-tolerance is again required: a Worker Role might crash while just having cached a bulk. Data is not lost in that case since queues are persistent and still contain the data.

Even if the bulk size for queues is limited to 32 at maximum, it is possible to divide the transaction costs drastically by 32. However, the queue API offers only the possibility to get data in bulks, but not to delete bulks. Consequently, the cost for getting data from the queue can be reduced from $259.20 to $8.10, but the other two transaction types stay at $259.20 each. Bulk operations are also possible for the backend storage. The table storage offers writing bulks operations of at most 100 entities and 4MB of size. This also reduces costs from $259.20 to $2.592 for queue retrieval. The total transaction costs of $529.092 (2*$259.20 + $8.10 + $2.592) remain high.

As an alternative, table storage could be used instead of queues. This offers bulk operations even for reads, writes and deletes. The challenge now is to mimic the queue behavior. One possible way is to use table storage for each organization and the data provider's id as a partition key. Hence, it is easily and efficiently possible to fetch the eldest 100 data items for a given data provider (using the timestamp in a query), to store those items in the backend storage, and to remove them. In fact, there is some implementation effort, e.g., to be sure that a bulk of 100 is available in order to avoid polling, and to coordinate the Worker Role threads, i.e., who is accessing which table. The transaction costs for the Worker Role can be divided by 100 from $777.60 to $7.776. This makes the solution with $874.78 cheaper than the one in Subsection 3.1 since $86.40 for compute instances are saved.

3.4   Direct Access to Cloud Storage

Another approach gets rid of Web or Worker Roles, in order to save costs. Data providers can store their data directly into blobs or tables; the post-processing applications then access the data provider's storage directly.

Both blob and table storages are possible in this type of architecture. However, blob storage has an important advantage over table storage: it offers fine-granular security rights. Blobs are stored in containers and the access rights of each container can be controlled individually even if the containers belong to the same account. In contrast, table stores of the same account share the same credentials. Hence, blobs are used in the following, each organization obtaining a container of its own. Note that the number of containers does not affect the operational costs.

The throughput depends on the access capabilities of blobs; the requested throughput of 200 items/s for each organization/container should be possible. Otherwise, additional accounts or containers have to be ordered.

The costs in the first month are here as follows:

- The data storage costs remain the same, and sum up to $89.40.
- The costs for storage transaction are still at $259.20.

The conclusion is quickly made. With $348.60 operational costs in the first month, this is the by far cheapest architecture – if applicable. The major benefit of this architecture is in fact the reduction of compute instances.

While financially the clear winner so far, technically this approach brings along several disadvantages. First, the backend storage is not shielded from data providers and the system fully relies on the authentication of the storage only. Furthermore, the same storage technology must be appropriate for both data providers and processing applications at the backend, but both might have different demands with regard to throughput or query functionality. If blob storage (or table storage alternatively) does not offer the requested functionality for backend applications, data will have to be transferred into an alternative cloud storage, which again requires additional Worker Role(s) and lets become the architecture similar to Subsections 3.2 or 3.3.

3.5   Load Variations

So far, we have discussed some constant load. We modify this assumption by assuming the same overall load per day, however varying over the day. For example, the load in a typical fleet management might be higher at 8-9 am and 5-6 pm.

Referring to Subsection 3.1, the IIS queues for Web Roles fill up during heavy load. The requested throughput must be handled by setting up additional Web Roles; the costs should be similar to a constant load if the data amount and transactions are the same over the whole day, i.e., there are less Web Roles at non-peak times. However, we pay a Web Role for one hour least. Not using complete hours could produce higher costs! Moreover, we have to bear in mind the time for provisioning VMs.

In Subsection 3.2, the front-end queues fill up, but no more Worker Roles are required since the queues are persistent. If there are timeliness constraints, i.e., if data must be mostly accurate in the back-end store, additional Worker Roles can reduce queues. One important question is whether the throughput of the front-end storage is enough. Well, there is still the opportunity to react on too high load with setting up more queues, which requires much effort if to be performed online.

The same holds for the architecture in 3.3: if the throughput of the front-end storage is not sufficient, higher load could be handled with more accounts.

Handling load changes by the number of Web/Worker Roles, an hourly high load is more positive than arbitrary load changes since charging is done for full hours. In this respect, Worker Roles are more advantageous, because there is a chance of having less Worker Roles: input throughput can be handled over a long period of time without corrupting the required throughput. If the payment model offers a reduced overnight rate, there will also be a chance of using Worker Roles over night at less cost.

3.6   SQL Database Instead of Table/Blob Storage

Azure SQL Database might be a good alternative to table or blob storage owing to its more powerful query mechanisms. Instead of REST, SQL Database is accessed via the usual protocol as for ADO.NET, JDBC, Hibernate etc. offering the full power of SQL. Keeping data in SQL Database is certainly reasonable if powerful evaluations are required at the backend, leveraging the full power of SQL.

In the following, we discuss the operational costs for the architecture of the previous subsection with SQL Database replacing the blob storage. In fact, each organization should obtain a own set of databases for security reasons.

The total backend storage requirement remains at a daily increase of 82.4 GB, which is 16.48 GB for each of the 5 organizations. SQL Database takes the daily peak consumption and charges for both in 1 GB steps. That is, having a peak consumption of 16.48 GB for the first day, the bill will charge 17 GB. The peaks of our scenario are thus 17 GB for the 1st day, 33 GB for the 2nd, ..., and finally   495 GB for the 30th day (30* 16.48 GB). This means a total amount of 7677 GB for the first month and an average of 255.9 GB per day. Consequently, one 150 database GB and another one with 106 GB are required, being charged with \$225.774 + \$181.818 = \$407.592 per organization in the first month. The storage costs do not differ between for Web and Business Editions.

The comparison is not precise. The table storage has some inherent storage overhead for property names etc. (cf. Subsection 2.2). Hence, a record in SQL Database is more compact than one in a table store and thus will consume much less storage. Anyway, the costs for mass storage are quite high for SQL Database. In contrast to blob/ table storage, the transactional costs are already included in the monthly fee.

It is important to note that Azure SQL Database currently has a cap of 150 GB per database. This means for larger data amounts, a sharding concept must be implemented that decides in which database to store data, how to handle an increase of data etc. Moreover, backend queries have to be distributed over the shards since no distributed queries are supported in SQL Database.

Anyway, the data will grow in future months and hence a sharding concept will become necessary soon or later unless a clean-up occurs or the database size stays below the 150 GB cap.

In fact, table storages provide a better flexibility since the structure of data does not have to be defined in advance. This point might become important if the data format changes from organization to organization or if the format changes over time.

4   Scenario 2: Data Delivery

In the second scenario, we suppose a large scale data delivery service being managed in the cloud: data is pushed into the system and is maintained in some central cloud storage. At the front end, customers expect to obtain their specific data from a cloud-based delivery service. An example could be found in logistics where post orders to a wholesale chain need to be collected, centrally managed and forwarded to individual suppliers and freight carrier services. In order to better model this scenario, we assume the backend storage to be filled once in the morning by some data provider for the purpose of a higher throughput. We again postulate some basic assumptions:

- There are 16000 clients receiving items: 0 items for 8000 clients (50%), 1 item for 3200 (20%) and 2 items for 3200 (20%), and 5 items for 1600 (10%). This sums up to 17600 items per day ((3200*1 item + 3200*2 items + 1600*5 items).
- Since each item has a payload of 50 KB, a total daily payload of 880000 KB is produced.
- Searching one item in the storage takes 300 ms even if none is found.
- 4000 clients all want to fetch their items at 8 am, 12 am, and at 5 pm; 4000 clients are equally distributed over the remaining times.
- As an SLA, clients should not wait longer than 1.5 seconds for being served.

4.1   The Web Role Approach

In the first architecture, several Web Role threads serve the clients: clients queue up in the load balancer in order to ask a Web Role for data: a Web Role thread accesses the storage to determine the data for that client and deliver the data while the client is waiting. The appropriate number of Web Roles depends on the number of clients and the given SLAs to clients.

We first focus on the three peak load times: the architecture has to serve 4000 clients at each peak time with clients of four types A to D:

A.   800 clients   accessing 1 item   (served within 300 ms)
B.   800 clients   accessing 2 items   (served within 600 ms)

C.   400 clients   accessing 5 items   (served within 1500 ms)
D.   2000 clients   accessing 0 items   (served within 300 ms)

At first, we need to calculate the number of Worker Roles that are required to satisfy the SLA of clients being served within 1.5 sec. The number of Worker Roles obviously depends on the arrival of client. The lowest number of Worker Roles is required in the following situation:

- 400 times: a client of type C arrives and is served in 1500ms; each C client requires an own thread.
- 400 times: a sequence of client types B,D,D,D (the last client of type D finishes before 1500 ms)
- 400 times: a sequence of B,D,D,A
- 80 times: a sequence of A,A,A,A,A

This optimal schedule is rather unrealistic because it usually depends on the arrival and the load balancer. Even in this best case 1280 Web Role threads (400+400+400+80) are required all together. This results in 128 Web Roles with 10 threads each.

The costs can then be calculated as follows for each peak time a day (there are three peaks a day):

- 128 Web Roles: Although the Web Roles are only required for 1.5 seconds, we have to pay for the full hour à 12ct/h, i.e., $15.36.
- Storage transactions are required for getting and deleting data. The costs are 0.08ct (4000 clients * 2 accesses * 1ct/100000).
- Outbound data transfer: 4400 items have to be delivered at each peak time for 2.64ct (4400 items * 50 KB * 12ct/GB).
- The backend storage is out of scope here.

Hence, we pay $15.39 for each of the 3 peak times, i.e., $46.17 for all peak times. In addition, one further Web Role is needed for the remaining non-peak time of 21 hours:

- The Web Role costs $2.52 (21 hours * 12ct).
- Storage transactions (2 times for get/delete): 0.08ct (4000 clients * 2 accesses * 1ct/100000).
- Outbound data transfer: 2.64ct = 4400 items * 50 KB * 12ct/GB.

The total costs are $48.72 ($46.17 (peak) + $2.55 (non-peak)) per day.

The major disadvantage lies in the fact that every client checks periodically for newly received data even if none has arrived. This produces a lot of load during peak times which in turn requires Web Roles.

4.2   Storage-Based Architecture

As a storage-based alternative, we introduce a client-specific storage: there is one account for each client in case of a table or queue store; using blob storage and client-specific containers requires only one global account for all clients, but client-specific credentials for containers. Worker Roles fetch data from the global storage and distribute the data to those client-specific storages. Clients remove their data from this storage right after pick up.

The client service time depends on the transport and access latency for storage. If one blob storage account is used for all client blobs, 4400 accesses occur at each peak time. In fact, according to [10], the available throughput is enough to fulfill the SLA that the time for being served does not exceed 1.5 sec.

The number of Worker Roles and their starting time is only important to deliver items in time before each peak time; obviously, starting Worker Roles early enough reduces the number of required Worker Roles. Furthermore, the delivery of messages into the global storage from outside is important. We here assume that data delivery has finished before any client wants to receive his data. If one Worker Role performs a "full scan" on all incoming 17600 items once a day and assigns the items to the client storages, then retrieval takes less than 88 min (5280 sec = 17600 * 300 ms). If one Worker Role is started with 10 threads, then the Worker Role must start 9 minutes before the first peak time. Afterwards, all the items are distributed.

The number of Worker Roles and threads is mostly irrelevant, since a Worker Role is paid for each hour in use according to the payment conditions. The more threads (or Worker Roles) are applied, the later processing can start, which is of few benefit only. However, a strategy to define which thread searches what becomes necessary.

Let us now calculate the overall costs for one day, assuming that client storages are filled in one step once a day, being ready for the first client.

- As explained above, the number of Worker Roles is mostly irrelevant; 1 Worker Role with 10 threads is enough to finish in one hour and costs 12ct a day.
- Additional costs arise for the client storages from the beginning to the point a client fetches items. A precise calculation is useless since even the worst case of keeping the client items the whole day is ignorable: storing 880000 KB to be delivered in the client storage for one day costs less than 7ct a month and 0.25ct per day.
- The additional outbound traffic from the backend store to the distributing Worker Role is for free, if both are located in the same data center region.
- The daily transactions (17600 gets and deletes à 1ct/10000 for the backend store, 16000 read accesses for storage in client storage) cost 0.336ct.
- The outbound data transfer from the client storage to the client costs 10.56ct (880000 KB * 12ct/GB) a day.

As a conclusion, there is an enormous cost reduction since much less Worker Roles are used than in Subsection 4.1: this type of architecture produces only 23ct per day instead of $48.

A variant of this architecture could transfer data by the Worker Role threads before each peak time: then less storage costs are consumed, but three Worker Roles are required per day. Hence, there is no benefit because of cheaper storage prices and more expensive Worker Roles. This approach might become useful if data will be delivered to the global storage several times a day.

5   Related Work

A number of researchers have investigated the economic issues around cloud computing from a consumer and provider perspective. Indeed, Armbrust et al. identify in [1] short-term billing as one of the novel features of cloud computing. And Khajeh-Hosseini [11] considers costs as one important research challenge for cloud computing. But only little research has been done in this direction.

Youseff [12] discusses three pricing models that are used by cloud service providers: with tiered pricing, different tiers each with different specifications (e.g. CPU and RAM) are provided at a different cost per unit time. A large tier machine has better equipment but also has higher costs. Per-unit pricing is based upon exact resource usage; for example $0.15 per GB per month. Finally, subscription-based pricing is common in SaaS products such as Salesforce's Enterprise Edition CRM that charges each user per month.

Walker [13] performs cost comparisons between cloud and on-premises. He states that lease-or-buy decisions have been researched in economics for more than 40 years. Walker compares the costs of a CPU hour when it is purchased as part of a server cluster, with when it is leased. Considering two scenarios – purchasing a 60000 core HPC cluster and purchasing a compute blade rack consisting of 176 cores – the result was that it is cheaper to buy than lease when CPU utilization is very high (over 90%) and electricity is cheap. The other way around, cloud computing becomes reasonable if CPU utilization is low or electricity is expensive. Walker focuses only on the cost of a CPU hour. To widen the space, further costs such as housing the infrastructure, installation and maintenance, staff, storage and networking must be taken into account as well.

Klems [14] also addresses the problem of deciding whether deploying systems in a cloud makes economic sense. He discusses some economic and technical issues that need to be considered when evaluating cloud solutions. Moreover, a framework is provided that could be used to compare the costs of using cloud computing with an in-house IT infrastructure. Unfortunately, the two presented case studies are more conceptual than concrete.

Assuncao [15] concentrates on a scenario of using a cloud to extend the capacity of locally maintained computers when their in-house resources are over-utilized. They simulated the costs of using various strategies when borrowing resources from a cloud provider, and evaluated the benefits by using performance metrics such as the Average Weighted Response Time (AWRT) [16], i.e., the average time that user job-requests take to complete. However, AWRT might not be the best metric to measure performance improvements.

Kondo [17] examines the performance trade-offs and monetary cost benefits of Amazon AWS for volunteered computing applications of different size and storage.

Palankar [18] uses the Amazon data storage service S3 for scientific intensive applications. The conclusion is that monetary costs are high because the service covers scalability, durability, and performance, which are often not required by data-intensive applications. In addition, Garfinkel [19] conducts a general cost-benefit analysis of clouds, however, without any specific application.

Deelman [20] highlights the potentials of using cloud computing as a cost-effective deployment option for data-intensive scientific applications. They simulate an astronomic application named Montage and run it on Amazon AWS. Their focus was to investigate the performance-cost tradeoffs of different internal execution plans by measuring execution times, amounts of data transferred to and from AWS, and the amount of storage used. Unfortunately, the cost calculation is not precise enough because of the assumption that the cost of running instances on AWS EC2 is calculated on a per-CPU-second basis. However, AWS charge on a per-CPU-hour basis: launching 10 instances for 1 minute would cost 10 CPU hours (not 10 CPU minutes) on AWS. They found the cost of running instances (i.e. CPU time) to be the dominant figure in the total cost of running their application. Another study [21] on Montage concludes that the high costs of data storage, data transfer and I/O in case of an I/O bound application like Montage makes AWS much less attractive than a local service.

Kossmann [22] presents a web application according to the TPC-W benchmark with a backend database and compares the costs for operating the web application on major cloud providers, using existing relational cloud databases or building a database on top of table or blob storages.

Hence, we know about two studies [20] and [22] that take roughly our direction.

6   Recommendations

We want to present some recommendations that we derived from our investigation.

While a couple of papers such as [20] have identified compute instances as the dominating cost factor, we have seen in the first scenario that transactional costs cannot be neglected. Here, bulk transactions could help, if applicable.

Indeed, compute instances are quite expensive, particularly compared to storage. Hence, one should try to minimize the number of compute instances, to allocate only instances when really needed, and to stop compute instances that are no longer needed. Strategies to adopt the number according to the recent load can help to react on varying load. But caution has to be taken since collecting performance and diagnosis data produces additional storage and transaction costs. Note also that stopped compute instances cause the same costs as running instances: an instance should be deleted to avoid running costs while still retaining the service URL.

It is also important that the costs for the staging area are the same as for the production environment. Hence, one should not forget to delete staging deployments between or after test phases.

Acquired resources should be used efficiently. For example, it is possible to run several web sites and web applications in one Web Role thanks to full IIS support. The more cores a compute instance has (determined by the instance category), the more parallel work a Web Role can handle. However, in most cases, it is better to use smaller instance categories such as XS or S: smaller instances offer a better scaling granularity while costs scale in a linear manner. In fact, there are also scenarios where a higher equipment such as 8 CPUs (XL), larger main memory, or bandwidth is reasonable, e.g., to allow multi-core programming to a larger extent.

If the load seems to be quite constant, some special offers such as a Subscription Offer (http://www.Microsoft.com/windowsazure/offers), enterprise agreements or long-term subscriptions might be a choice to save costs.

7   Conclusions

Based on Microsoft's Windows Azure platform offering, we have argued in this paper for the importance of taking operational costs into account when designing the architecture for a cloud-based offering. Given examples have shown the impact particular design decisions have on the cost of cloud applications; this is the important message of the paper. However, the paper by no means values one architecture decision over another but emphasizes the importance of considering the use and type of storage, compute instances and communication services already at early stage, in particular with respect to their impact on the operational costs.

The different architectural approaches and the resulting overall costs that at least partly diverge significantly reveal one important problem when it comes to migrating software to the cloud; the many dimensions of design decisions, and certainly the many dimensions of the pricing models. The pricing ladders not only differ between different providers in terms of charging units, special offers and free services, but already within the offers of single companies, cf. davidpallmann.blogspot.com on August 14, 2010: "The #1 hidden cost of cloud computing is simply the number of dimensions there are to the pricing model. In effect, everything in the cloud is cheap but every kind of service represents an additional level of charge. To make it worse, as new features and services are added to the platform the number of billing considerations continues to increase". In other words, there is much more to cost-effective architecture design than choosing the number and size of compute instances, or deleting stopped staging deployments when not used.

While we have supported our arguments with tangible examples and experiences we have gained from working with Windows Azure, there is further work required towards concrete guidelines and best practices in cost-effective architecture design for the cloud; also taking into account further features such as Azure AppFabric Cache, special long-term subscriptions, and other cloud offerings such as for example Amazon AWS or Google AppEngine.

References

1. Armbrust, M., Fox, A., Griffith, R., Joseph, A., Katz, R., Konwinski, A., Lee, G., Patterson, D., Rabkin, A., Stoica, I., Zaharia, M.: A View of Cloud Computing. CACM 53(4) (April 2010)
2. Hamdaqa, M., Liviogiannis, L., Tavildari, L.: A Reference Model for Devloping Cloud Applications. In: Int. Conf. on Cloud Computing and Service Science, CLOSER (2011)
3. Varia, J.: Architecting for the Cloud: Best Practices. Amazon Web Services (January 2010-2011)

134 U. Hohenstein et al.

4. Pace, E., Betts, D., Densmore, S., Dunn, R., Narumoto, M., Woloski, M.: Moving Applications to the Cloud on the Microsoft Azure™ Platform. Microsoft Press (August 2010)
5. Kruchten, P.: Architectural Blueprints – The "4+1" View Model of Software Architecture. IEEE Software 12(6) (November 1995)
6. Hoff, T.: Cloud Programming Directly Feeds Cost Allocation Back into Software Design. Blog on HighScalability.com (March 6, 2009)
7. Hohenstein, U., Krummenacher, R., Mittermeier, L., Dippl, S.: Choosing the Right Cloud Architecture - A Cost Perspective. In: Proc. on Cloud Computing and Services Science (CLOSER), Porto, Portugal (2012)
8. Calder, B.: Understanding Windows Azure Storage Billing – Bandwidth, Transactions, and Capacity, http://blogs.msdn.com/b/windowsazurestorage/archive/2010/07/09/understanding-windows-azure-storage-billing-bandwidth-transactions-and-capacity.aspx
9. Mizonov, V.: Best Practices for Maximizing Scalability and Cost Effectiveness of Queue-Based Messaging Solutions on Windows Azure, http://msdn.microsoft.com/en-us/library/windowsazure/hh697709.aspx
10. Microsoft Extreme Computing Group (2011): All Azure Benchmark Test Cases, http://azurescope.cloudapp.net/BenchmarkTestCases (web site is now offline!)
11. Khajeh-Hosseini, A., Sommerville, I., Sriram, I.: Research Challenges for Enterprise Cloud Computing. In: 1st ACM Symposium on Cloud Computing, SOCC 2010, Indianapolis (2010)
12. Youseff, L., Butrico, M., Da Silva, D.: Toward a Unified Ontology of Cloud Computing. In: Grid Computing Environments Workshop (GCE 2008), Austin, Texas, USA (November 2008)
13. Walker, E.: The Real Cost of a CPU Hour. Computer 42, 4 (2009)
14. Klems, M., Nimis, J., Tai, S.: Do Clouds Compute? A Framework for Estimating the Value of Cloud Computing. In: Weinhardt, C., Luckner, S., Stößer, J. (eds.) WEB 2008. LNBIP, vol. 22, pp. 110–123. Springer, Heidelberg (2009)
15. Assuncao, M., Costanzo, A., Buyya, R.: Evaluating the cost-benefit of using cloud computing to extend the capacity of clusters. In: HPDC 2009: Proc. of 18th ACM Int. Symposium on High Performance Distributed Computing, Munich, Germany (June 2009)
16. Grimme, C., Lepping, J., Papaspyrou, A.: Prospects of Collaboration between Compute Providers by means of Job Interchange. In: Frachtenberg, E., Schwiegelshohn, U. (eds.) JSSPP 2007. LNCS, vol. 4942, pp. 132–151. Springer, Heidelberg (2008)
17. Kondo, D., Javadi, B., Malecot, P., Cappello, F., Anderson, D.P.: Cost-benefit analysis of Cloud Computing versus desktop grids. In: Proc. of the 2009 IEEE International Symp. on Parallel&Distributed Processing (May 2009)
18. Palankar, M., Iamnitchi, A., Ripeanu, M., Garfinkel, S.: Amazon S3 for Sciene Grids: A Viable Solution? In: Data-Aware Distributed Computing Workship, DADC (2008)
19. Garfinkel, S.: Commodity Grid Computing with Amazon S3 and EC2. Login (2007)
20. Deelman, E., Singh, G., Livny, M., Berriman, B., Good, J.: The cost of doing science on the cloud: the Montage example. In: SC 2008: Proceedings of the 2008 ACM/IEEE Conference on Supercomputing, Oregon, USA (November 2008)
21. Berriman, B., Juve, G., Deelman, E., Regelson, M., Plavchan, P.: The Application of Cloud Computing to Astronomy: A Study of Cost and Performance. In: 6th IEEE Int. Conf. on e-Science
22. Kossmann, D., Kraska, T., Loesing, S.: An Evaluation of Alternative Architectures for Transaction Processing in the Cloud. ACM SIGMOD 2010 (2010)
23. Greenberg, A., Hamilton, J., Maltz, D., Patel, P.: The Cost of a Cloud: Research Problems in Data Center Networks. ACM SIGCOMM Computer Communication Review 39, 1

On-Demand Business Rule Management Framework for SaaS Application

Xiuwei Zhang[1,2,3], Keqing He[1], Jian Wang[1], Chong Wang[1], and Zheng Li[1]

[1] State Key Lab of Software Engineering, Wuhan University, Wuhan, China
[2] School of Computer, Wuhan University, Wuhan, China
[3] 94005 Troops of PLA, Jiuquan, China
xiuweizhang@163.com,
{hekeqing,jianwang,cwang,zhengli_hope}@whu.edu.cn

Abstract. SaaS (*Software as a Service*) is becoming a new direction of software industry in the new cloud computing era. SaaS applications and services must be able to react in a fast and flexible way to ever changing business situations, policies and products. In order to satisfy policy changes and other personalized requirements from different customers (or *tenants*), business rule management of SaaS needs to support multi-tenancy and online customization. This paper proposed a business rule engine based framework for managing and decoupling of business logic rule from SaaS application. It takes on-demand business rule management as an independent and online maintainable part of SaaS application, which could allow tenants to safely upgrade, delete or create rules during runtime. Finally, a practical case study in Attendance Management System (AMS) evaluates the effectiveness of the framework.

Keywords: Business Rule Engine, SaaS, Decision Table, Personalized Customization.

1   Introduction

With the emergence of Cloud Computing and maturity of Service Oriented Architecture (SOA), SaaS delivery model has gained popularity due to advantages such as lower start-up cost and reduced time to market. SaaS is the best way to adopt advanced technology and the most effective business model in the Cloud Computing era. Typically in SaaS application, configurability, multi-tenancy and scalability are the three key attributes to evaluate the maturity of SaaS application. SaaS vendor owns and takes the responsibility of maintaining a single application for multiple tenants who may have similar but also varying requirements [1]. The most ideal case for SaaS vendors is that every tenant feel comfortable using a completely standardize offering. However this ideal case usually does not happen in enterprise software application area. Normally, such one instance is used by different tenants with different personalized requirements in terms of data, process rules, and business rules (BR) [2]. In order to satisfy their maintainability of flexible business policy, we must decouple the close relationship between business data and business logic.

I. Ivanov et al. (Eds.): CLOSER 2012, CCIS 367, pp. 135–150, 2013.

Business Rule Group (BRG)[1] believes that rules are a first-class citizen of the requirements world. No matter in large enterprises or small and medium enterprises (SME), business rules change very fast and need to be adjusted timely. Software system is directly related to the business process within which it is a manifestation of some business requirements for operational control and support of decision making [3]. Nevertheless, many business rules have been bundled in program code or in database structures, so it is very hard to upgrade and expand [4]. For SaaS application, this problem becomes increasingly prominent because different tenant has different rule variation. Many tenants are running on one instance with the availability of 24*7. There may even be a situation where one tenant business rule changes may affect other tenants and even cause the entire system to change. In order to dealing with this kind of situation, the business rules of SaaS application need to be customized in a flexible way, which enables any tenants to build, execute, manage, and evolve its own rule-oriented applications. Rule engines allow the separation of business rules from the applications that use them and enable the maintenance of business logic without having to resort to code changes and software modification. Rule engine can be viewed as a sophisticated interpreter of if-then statements. It can reach a conclusion from a set of facts feed into it and trigger an appropriate action. So we can use business rule engine to separate the business logic out of the SaaS application to support online customization and multi-tenancy with the isolated rule file. Each tenant can individually configure and upgrade his own business rules. Therefore rule independency and isolation is an essential part in the development of SaaS application. In this paper, a business rule engine-based framework was proposed to help the management of business rule for SaaS application, which is convenient for tenants to change business rules on-the-fly and minimize the downtime of the application during the business rule upgrading or modification. Tenants with non-IT profession can on-line update business rule in a simple spreadsheet and deploy them with a few clicks. It makes SaaS application more robust and maintainable.

In this paper, we only focus on the business rule's online customization and multi-tenancy support. The next section identifies the related work and section 3 provides a clear and concise description of the background. Section 4 demonstrates our framework and provides explanation for our framework. Section 5 presents the implantation representing our case study and is used to exemplify the potential of our approach. Section 6 draws conclusions from our work and identifies the possibilities for future work.

2   Related Work

Business rule management of software system is not a new issue. Many researchers have done a lot in traditional applications. Initially, rule based software tools originate from work carried out in the artificial intelligence (AI) research community. Companies were faced with the need to combine domain expertise with the flexibility to

---

[1] http://www.businessrulesgroup.org/home-brg.shtml

write lots of *"if x, then y"* statements over a wide range of variables without resorting to spaghetti code [5]. Orriens [6] and Vasilecas [8] have two main views in dynamic business rule driven software system design. One of them is to design predefined executable processes and execute them by using rules in software system, where processes and execution rules are derived from business rules using transformations. Another one is discussed in work [7], where business rules and facts describing current business system state are loaded into inference engine of the software system and transformed into software system executable data analysis process according to the results of logical derivations. Computer scientists and programmers began developing rule languages and the corresponding engines that could handle the conditions and actions needed to satisfy the wide range of rules. The most successful approach for doing this has proven to be the Rete algorithm [9]. Many rule-engine tools and application development support environments was applied such as Blaze Advisor Builder, BRS RuleTrack, Business Rule Studio, Haley Technologies, ILOG Rules, Platinum Aion, etc [10].

In SaaS application, there is still lots of differences in business rule customization with traditional applications. These differences include:

— The business rule customization or configuration for SaaS applications should support multi-tenant architecture and each tenant should have their own rule customization.
— Not to affect other tenants, SaaS providers could not suspend the system when some tenants want to modify or upgrade the business rules.
— The rule customization will be executed by administrator of tenant, not by developers of SaaS provider.
— The business rule should be support Web-based online modification.
— The customization of the business rules should be simplified and friendly.

The above differences between SaaS applications and traditional software have raised many researches in this new area. Guo [11] proposed a multi-tenant supported framework to support better isolations among tenants in many aspects such as security, performance, availability, administration, etc. Zhang [12] proposed a SaaS-oriented service customization approach, which allows service vendors to publish customization policies along with services. If tenant's customization requirement is in agreement with policy after being verified, vendors will update service accordingly. This approach will inevitably burden service providers because of tenants' reasonable customization requirement increments. Gong [13] developed ECA process orchestration architecture to create flexible processes. This architecture based on both knowledge rules (separating knowledge from processes) and event-condition-actions (ECA) mechanisms to provide the highest level of flexibility. Configurability of SaaS issue was addressed in literature [14] who researched the configurability like user interface, workflow, data and access control from the different aspects of SaaS. From the customization and configuration perspective, Sun [15] explored the configuration and customization issues and challenges to SaaS vendors, clarifies the difference between configuration and customization. A competency model and framework has been developed to help SaaS vendors to plan and evaluate their capabilities and strategies for service configuration and customization. In literature [16], a flexible business process customization framework for SaaS was proposed to solve problems caused by orchestrating SaaS business process through BPEL specifications. Kapuruge [1] discussed the challenges arising from single-instance to multi-tenancy, and presented an approach of Serendip4SaaS to define business processes in SaaS applications.

To the best of our knowledge, no related work has combined the rule engine and decision table with the SaaS application for multi-tenancy support and online customization. Our work was focused on the perspective of business rule customization and configuration. In our framework, each tenant can update their personalized business rule in SaaS application by online selecting and modifying corresponding rules. Rule engine was utilized as the essential part to improve the flexibility and multi-tenancy for SaaS application, which makes business rule as an independent and maintainable part of application.

3   Background

3.1   Business Rule Engine

In business, a lot of actions are triggered by rules: "Order more ice-cream when the stock is below 100 units and temperature is above 25° C", "Approve credit card application when the credit background check is OK, past relationship with the customer is profitable, and identity is confirmed", and so on. Traditional computer programming languages make it difficult to translate this "natural language" into a software program. Business rule engine enables anybody with basic IT skills and an understanding of the business to translate statements as running computer code [17]. Business rule engine is a software system that executes one or more business rules in a runtime production environment. It will test data objects quickly in the workspace, pick out rules which meet requirement from loading rule sets, and generate an instance of rule execution.

Fig. 1 shows the basic architecture of business rule engine. Pattern matcher decides which and when rules will be implemented. The implementation sequence of rules picked from pattern matcher is arranged in agenda so that execution engine can execute the rules or other actions in order. The underlying idea of a rule engine is to externalize the business or application logic. Business rules are expressions that describe and control the processes, operations and behaviors of how an enterprise, and the applications that support it, performs. Rules assert influence over business or system behavior by recommending actions to be undertaken. A rule provides its invoker a directive on how to proceed. Further, business rule policies provide a generalized mechanism for specifying frequently changing practices, freeing system components from the burden of maintaining and evaluating evolving business and system environments [18].

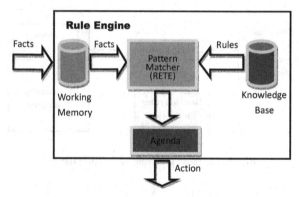

Fig. 1. The architecture of rule engine

3.2 Decision Table

Decision table is a tabular representation used to describe and analyze decision situations, where the states of a number of conditions determine the execution of a set of actions. Many variations of the decision table concept exist which look similar at first sight [8]. Decision tables are best suited for representing business rules that have multiple conditions. Adding one condition is done by simply adding one row or column. Similar to if/then rule set, the decision table is driven by the interaction of conditions and actions. The main difference is that in a decision table, the action is decided by more than one condition, and more than one action can be associated with each set of conditions. If the conditions are met, then the corresponding action or actions are performed [19]. A column in the entry portion of the table is known as a rule. Values in the condition entry columns are known as inputs and values inside the action entry portions are known as outputs. Outputs are calculated depending on the inputs and specification of the program. Fig. 2 depicts the basic principle of the decision table. It uses available information on frequency of outcome of the various cases and whether core minimization or run time minimization is the more important. A further development in programming languages will be to hand this information along with the decision table to a compiler which will then be responsible for this. Thus decision tables not only offer a clearer way of stating the logic of a program but also provide the notational means of extending the scope of automatic programming [23].

4 Rule Engine Based Framework for SaaS Application

The SaaS application is one packaged business application with Web-based user interface for multiple tenants operating on the SaaS platform. With the increase in complexity of SaaS application, business rules have become harder to express hence require additional simple and friendly way to represent. Based on the features of business rule engine, we design and implement a framework for development of SaaS application with an online business rule customization. The direct customization of

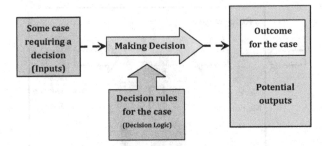

Fig. 2. The basic principle of decision table

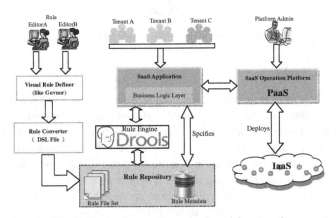

Fig. 3. The business rule engine-based framework

business rules by tenants is one of our objectives since it relieves, in many cases, the SaaS providers from doing such heavy customization tasks each time when a new tenant subscribe to the application [21]. The architecture of the proposed framework is shown in Fig. 3. The essence of this framework is to separate business rules from application, and make the business rules management as an independent and maintainable part, to support multi-tenancy. The objective of this framework is to reach a flexible and competitive scenario in which it would be easier and faster to react when demand or business changes.

4.1   Basic Units of the Framework

The biggest challenge of business rules management is tracking them down, and organizing a more effective management approach. In each case there is need for business rules management. Business rules management comprises the definition, storage, and application of the many rules used in business operations to provide organizations with greater automation, more responsiveness to change and less expensive distribution and maintenance of their business guidelines [5]. Rules management offers a solution to meet the requirements of changing business rules. The proposed framework includes the following major interrelated parts: BR definer, BR Converter, BR engine, BR repository, SaaS application and SaaS deployment system.

- **The Rule editors** can configure various business rules in terms of workflow, activity type, and business policy by using the Rule Definer tool, Tenant's business rule configured information is stored separately in tenant-specific metadata repository. Rule engine-based framework generates polymorphic service for individual tenant using tenant-specific metadata at runtime. Through the polymorphic service, tenant users feel as if they are using their own business application while service instance is shared by every tenant.
- **BR definer** acts as a Web-based tool or sub-system that helps visually manage and create new business rules, where the business policy can be changed online by tenant manager, business analysts, and software developers.
- **BR Converter** is an essential auxiliary tool of rule engine and responsible for convert the visualized rule from definer to BR engine understandable language. It also can translate the decision table to a specific executable language.
- **BR engine** is a central component which is responsible for computation and evaluation of the business rules according to the user's invocation and request. It can automatically assert the business rules for specific tenant according to the rule load metadata from repository.
- **BR repository** is a repository that stores the rule-related information and supports the flexibility of rule expression. A rule repository is a central place where managers, analysts, and software developers can define, share, and maintain the business rules of a company. This component contains two major parts: rule set and rule metadata. The former is used to store the information of business rules including decision table, "When...Then" based rule file, and DSL (Domain Specific Language) file and so on. The stored business rules in the repository are determined based on the target system's specifications. While the latter mainly includes the tenant customization and configuration information for specific tenants. Metadata is stored in the repository as management information to support multi-tenancy.
- **SaaS application** includes basic functionalities and business logic layer. We have separated the business policy out of code and take it as an independent part for upgrading and modification.
- **SaaS deployment system** includes SaaS operation platform (Platform as a service) and IaaS (Infrastructure as a Service). In SaaS operation platform, administrator will be responsible for management and deployment of SaaS application. IaaS as a basic part for SaaS deployment including hardware and storage part and so on. We will not explain more details about the SaaS deployment system because this paper focus on the relationship between Business Rule Management (BRM) and SaaS application.

4.2 Capability of the Framework

SaaS application based on this framework will be supported with the following capabilities, which also are the basic features of SaaS application.

- **Support of Business Rules Management.** Enterprises run their businesses with repeatable business processes driven by general business rules for specific situations and customers. These capabilities allow enterprises to execute business functionality using independent rule services made up of executable, declarative rules, rather than being forced to integrate the logic as code into a system.

— **Support of Online Maintenance.** Current enterprise applications require a new application maintenance paradigm that can deliver faster, easier application modification. Business rule changes are first identified by the users of the system. The fastest and safest way to empower these users is to give them the tools they need to make the application changes themselves. This can be achieved by giving them access to easy-to-use rule maintenance that allows them to maintain the policies, procedures and rules for which they are responsible.

— **Support of Multi-tenancy Customization.** As the number of tenants with subscribed SaaS application grows, specific personalized business rules are needed for most tenants. In this framework, we bind each Tenant ID with the corresponding rule files and store the metadata in repository. In order to support multi-tenancy, the most important part is the safety of specific rules with specific tenants. In this framework, the metadata of rules are used to resolve this problem.

4.3   Lifecycle of Business Rules in SaaS

In business world, some rule policies are changed periodic and others are altered disorderly depending on market competition and development. A good rules management system allows the business logic of a system to be specified external to the system itself. Rules can be changed directly by rule maintainers and editors. Many rules management system provide the whole lifecycle management from designing rules, deleting rules to editing and deployment of rules. The business rule lifecycle of SaaS including rules creation, edition, activation, deletion, etc, is illustrated in Fig. 4

— **Rules Creation.** The creation of business rules is done by rule editors. A new rule is available for editing and deleting. Only approved new rules can be deployed.
— **Rules Edition.** Rule edition is the modification of the condition part or the action part of a rule. To keep track of rule changes, only new or deployed rules can be edited. Deactivated rules must be reactivated before they can be modified.
— **Rules Deactivation and Reactivation.** A rule can be manually or automatically deactivated. For example, a rule is automatically deactivated on 1 January 2011, if its time is constrained to function between 01 January 2008 and 31 December 2010. An editor may manually deactivate a rule especially when the regulatory or policy changes. Rule editor may also reactivate a manually deactivated rule as they needed.
— **Rules Deletion.** Rules that are no longer in use in the system can be removed from the system by deletion. New rules and annotated unused rules can also be deleted.
 Rules Deployment. Rules are deployed into the repository will be reacted immediately by making a snapshot of isolation for the deployed rules in SaaS application. The deployment process of business rules includes at least the following steps [22]: (1) extract the rules in scope for the execution; (2) package the rule elements into a ruleset –a deployable artifact; (3) deploy the ruleset to the

target environment; (4) notify the engine of a new ruleset; (5) let management stack inside the rule execution environment loading the ruleset; (6) trigger the engine API to parse the ruleset; and (7) send business transactions to fire the rules.

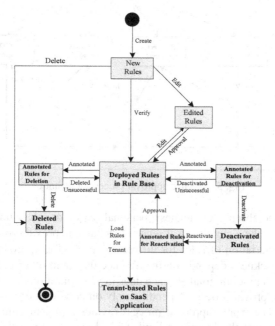

Fig. 4. Lifecycle of business rules in SaaS application (based on [5])

5   Case Study

5.1   Motivation

In order to evaluate the proposed framework, we will illustrate a business rule online customization process via an example. We take Attendance Management System (AMS) as the domain we do experiment. AMS is an easy way to keep track of attendance for enterprises, school activities, church groups, and community organizations. It has become as the necessity application for workforce performance monitoring and evaluation. The objective of this case is to develop a multi-tenancy supported AMS application with online customization. In order to show variation of business rule for specific tenant, we demonstrate a roadmap of rule policy from elicitation, presentation to implementation by the process of absence approval for sickness in AMS. The Process of Absence Approval enables employees to enter absence requests in the system. The request passes through an approval procedure in which the request is checked by employee's superiors to see if the employee's absence can be approved according to company rules. In most enterprises, the approval process for employee

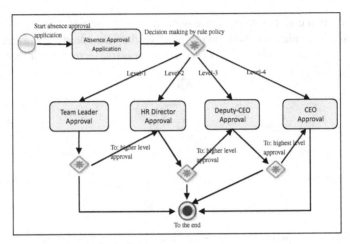

Fig. 5. Absence approval process of tenant C

who applies for the absence of sickness, personal reason or salary holiday has different rules. Here we take a simplified absence of sickness approval process in AMS as a case to show the variation of rules for different tenants. The approval process of absence policy for sickness depends on the absence days and other conditions such as total absence days in month, total absence days in year, duration time and so on.

A simplified approval process depending only on condition of absence days is depicted on Fig.5. The whole approval process divides into four situations, if the absence days not exceed the Level-1's limit. Only Level-1 approval is needed. If the absence days over Level-1 and locate in the Level-2's scope, the approval process will need both Level-1 and Level-2. Normally Level-2's approval will executed after Level-1 approval passed except for emergency situation. Level-3 and Level-4's approval have the similar approval procedure. The following italic description outline the different approval process and rule policies of three tenants A, B, C respectively.

— **Tenant A**: *Absence days for sickness less than or equal one day will be approved by team leader (Level-1). From one day to five days absence will be needed both team leader and Human Resource Department approval (Level-2). And more than five days will be permitted by Manager (Level-3).*

— **Tenant B**: *Absence days for sickness less than or equal two days will be approved by team leader (Level-1). And more than two days will approve by Human Resource Department (Level-2).*

— **Tenant C**: *Absence for sick leave less than or equal one day will be approved by team leader (Level-1). From one day to five days absence will be needed both team leader and Human Resource Department approval (Level-2). From five days to ten days absence will be approved by team leader, Human Resource Department and deputy-CEO approval (Level-3). And more than ten days need to be permitted by team leader, HR director, deputy CEO and CEO (Level-4).*

5.2   Representation of Business Rule

Different enterprises have their own rule policies for absence approval as mentioned above. Here we take Tenant C's rules as a case to demonstrate how to fill these rules into a decision table. The concrete steps are described as follows.

— Step1, Definition of the Terms

Here we draw up a list of all condition statements and actions that are mentioned above. It is clear that this example only uses absence days as the condition to determine which level of approval will be executed. The following table lists all related occurrences of these terms in the above context.

Table 1. Rule condition statement and action statement

Condition Statement	Action Statement
Absence Days	Permission level
Absence Days <=1	Team leader (L-1)
1<Absence Days<=5	HR Director(L-2)
5<Absence Days<=10	Deputy CEO(L-3)
Absence Days >10	CEO(L-4)

— Step 2, Verification of the Decision Rules

Based on the text of the regulations and conditions, the condition states and the actions, now we can proceed by defining the rules, analyzing each line in the regulation and translating it into a rule. Absence approval rule of Tenant C is also taken as an example.

- Absence days for sickness less than or equal one day will be approved by team leader.

  Rule 1: *Absence Days <=1*

  Action: Level-1 Approved (team leader)

- From one day to five days absence will need both team leader and Human Resource Director approval.

  Rule 2: *1< Absence Days <=5*

  Action: Level-1(team leader) and Level-2 (Human Resource Director) approval.

- From three days to ten days absence will be approved by team leader, Human Resource Department and deputy-CEO approval.

  Rule 3: *5< Absence Days <=10*

Action: Level-1, Level-2 and Level-3(deputy-CEO) approval.

- And more than 10 days will be permitted by team leader, HR Director, deputy-CEO and CEO.

Rule 4: *Absence Days* >=10

Action: Level-1, Level-2, Level-3 and Level-4(CEO) approval.

— **Step 3, Filling of the Decision Table**

After specifying the decision rules, it needs to fill them into the appropriate combinations in the decision table as shown in Table 2. The key point to keep in mind is that in a decision table, each row is a rule, and each column in that row is either a condition or action for that rule. "※" indicates actions in the combination will be activated, and "○" means no action will be activated by rules.

Table 2. Decision table for absence approval rule

Absence Days (ADs)	<=1	1<Ads<=5	5<Ads<=10	>10
Team Leader Approval	※	※	※	※
HR Director Approval	○	※	※	※
Deputy-CEO Approval	○	○	※	※
CEO Approval	○	○	○	※

— **Step4, Optimization of the Rule Condition**

Once a complete validation of the decision table is finished, the table could be reduced to its minimal format. The order of the conditions might influence the number of columns in the contracted table. For this case, the above condition is already the optimal one.

5.3   Implementation

In this case, we take Eclipse IDE as the development environment and java-supported rule engine Drools 5[2] as business rule engine. Drools introduce the business logic integration platform that provides a unified and integrated platform for Rule, Workflow, and Event Processing. Drools 5 is now split into four main subprojects [17]: (1) Guvnor (BRMS), a centralized repository for Drools; (2) Expert (rule engine); (3) flow (process/workflow), providing workflow or process capabilities to the Drools platform; (4) fusion (event processing/temporal reasoning), providing event processing capabilities. Drools expert is used as a rule engine and Guvnor as a visual business rule definer which allow browsing and editing the rule set. Generally,

---

[2] http://www.jboss.org/drools/

decision table is a useful way to represent conditional logic in a compact format. This format is also readily readable and editable by non technical users and will be suitable for most employees to understand. Spreadsheets may not be perfect, but popular and well-understood. So we can use them to hold the data that we supply to the business rules. Then use spreadsheets to hold the actual rules in a decision table format. Drools decision tables can utilize a spreadsheet (such as Excel, CSV) as the means to capture decision logic in a user friendly way. Because of the convenience of decision table and supportability of Drools, the decision table is adopted as business rule representation style in our application.

Fig.6 is the snapshot of the executable Drools decision table for absence approval process of Tenant C. We can update business rule in a simple spreadsheet and deploy them with a few clicks. In this decision table, the first three rows are the head information includes RuleSet, Import and Notes. RuleSet lets Drools know where the header table begins. Import lets Drools know which package these rules live in and other imported additional JavaBeans. Notes is the comment information and ignored as it means nothing to Drools. The following part is the main body of decision table. The left part of the decision table is the *"CONDITION"* cells, which makes up the *"WHEN"* part of the rule. The right part of the decision table is *"ACTION"* cells which give the *"THEN"* part of the rules. In Drools, the *"WHEN"* part of the rules define the preconditions. The *"THEN"* part defines conclusions, decision, actions, or just a new fact deduced from the knowledge base. The < *preconditions* > is also referred to as the left-hand side (LHS) of the rule, whereas the < *conclusions* > is referred to as the right-hand side (RHS). So, we can also express rules as follows:

$$\text{LHS } (< \text{rule name} >) = < \text{preconditions} >$$

$$\text{RHS } (< \textit{rule name} >) = < \textit{conclusions} >$$

The first row of decision table could be rendered like the following Drool rules language:

```
rule "absence approval"
when
em(absence_days>0&&absence_days<1);
then
Tenant.sentToApproval (Level 1);
update (em);
end
```

In order to support the online customization of business rule, it is necessary to use visual rule definer. Guvnor Editor is a user-friendly web editor which is powerful enough to modify rules. Tenants can fill in the rule name and rule description, set the priority of this rule and choose templates to define business rule in line with their requirements. The modification of decision table will need to download the decision table and modify it, then upload it with Guvnor. Otherwise, in order to keep the isolation of business rules for different tenant, we build the tenant-based security policy on the login page with different password for different tenant to prevent the violation of the rules modification. The visual rule definer of Gnuvor is shown in Fig.7.

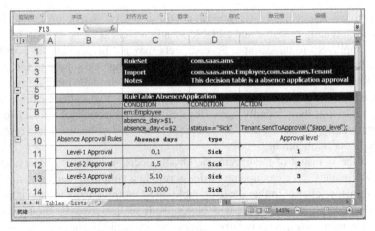

Fig. 6. Snapshot of Drools based on decision table

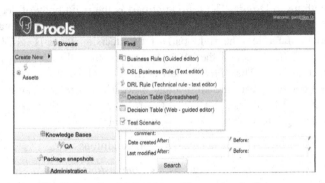

Fig. 7. Snapshot of decision table creation in Gnuvor

5.4   Prototype Application

The SaaS application of AMS prototype is developed following the proposed framework which has successfully integrated business rule engine into SaaS application. AMS is a SOA-based multi-tenant application. It allows tenant to manage their employee attendance and presence in a work setting to maximize the motivations and minimize the loss. And AMS is one of SaaS applications in Cloud Service Supermarket. Fig.8 shows a snapshot of the AMS prototype system, which is successfully deployed on the SaaS platform of Cloud Service Supermarket [20].

6   Conclusions

In this paper, we have overviewed BR engine based framework and separated three main components used for such a SaaS application development. Depending on the proposed framework, it may be possible to ensure different level of agility by an instant deployment of changes in the business policy and immediate reaction to the changes on the market or competition by changing existing business rules. These advances allow SaaS application to be more transparent, flexible and cost reduction.

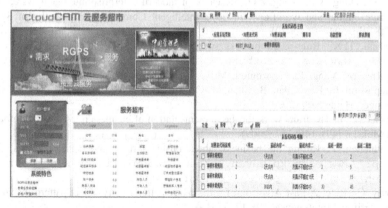

Fig. 8. Snapshots of SaaS application of AMS

Although BR engine based application has more complex development process in an initial phase, but such a system is more efficient in further maintenance and modifications for numbers of tenants with frequently changing regulations and business policy.

Although the proposed approach is convenient and effective to modify the rule file and manage the requirement changes by Rule Engine, it also brings lots of extra performance consumptions. The consumptions mainly include the following parts: the time of compiling rule files, the time of rule matching and the time of rule conflict resolution and the time for management of rule metadata.

The work presented here, is still in its earlier stage. On the one hand, business rule isolation for multi-tenant is not completely resolved by Guvnor. So there are more work still needs to be done on visual definer for specific SaaS application. On the other hand, performance evaluation work still need to be done in the future to make sure that the multi-tenant request response time is in a reasonable and tolerable ranage.

Acknowledgements. This Research Project Was Supported by the National Natural Science Foundation of China under Grant No. 60970017, No. 61202031, No. 61273216, and No.61100018, National Science & Technology Pillar Program of China under Grant No.2012BAH07B01, the Fundamental Research Funds for the Central Universities under Grant No.201121102020004, the Central Grant Funded Cloud Computing Demonstration Project of China Undertaken by Kingdee Software (China) Co., Ltd.

References

1. Kapuruge, M., Colman, A., Han, J.: Achieving multi-tenanted business processes in SaaS applications. In: Bouguettaya, A., Hauswirth, M., Liu, L. (eds.) WISE 2011. LNCS, vol. 6997, pp. 143–157. Springer, Heidelberg (2011)
2. Kwok, T., Nguyen, T.N., Lam, L.: Software as a Service with multi-tenancy support for an electronic contract management application. In: 2008 IEEE International Conference on Services Computing, pp. 179–186 (2008)
3. Wan-Kadir, W.M.N., Pericles, L.: Relating evolving business rules to software design. Journal of Systems Architecture (50), 367–382 (2003)

4. Liu, C., Dong, X.P., Yang, Z.Q.: Research of modern enterprise intelligent system based on rule engine and workflow. In: 2010 Intelligent Computing and Intelligent Systems (ICIS), pp. 594–597 (2010)
5. Gichahi, H.K.: Rule-based process support for enterprise information portal (2003), http://www.sts.tu-harburg.de/pw-and-m-theses/2003/gich03.pdf
6. Orriëns, B., Yang, J., Papazoglou, M.P.: A framework for business rule driven service compostion. In: Benatallah, B., Shan, M.-C. (eds.) TES 2003. LNCS, vol. 2819, pp. 14–27. Springer, Heidelberg (2003)
7. Vasilecas, O.: The framework for the implementation of business rules in ERP. Informacijos Mokslai (49), 146–157 (2009)
8. Vanthienen, J.: Ruling the business: about business rules and decision tables (2009), http://www.econ.kuleuven.be/tew/academic/infosys/members/vthienen/download/papers/br_dt.pdf
9. Forgy, C.: Rete: A Fast Algorithm for the many pattern/many object pattern match problem. Artificial Intelligence (19), 17–37 (1982)
10. Karami, N., Iijima, J.: A logical approach for implementing dynamic business rules. Contemporary Management Research 6(1), 29–52 (2010)
11. Guo, C.J., Sun, W., Huang, Y., et al.: A framework for native multi-tenancy application development and Management. In: The 9th IEEE International Conference on E-Commerce Technology and The 4th IEEE International Conference on Enterprise Computing, E-Commerce and E-Services, pp. 551–558 (2007)
12. Zhang K., Zhang X., Sun W., et al. A policy-driven approach for software-as-services customization. The 9th IEEE International Conference on E-Commerce Technology and The 4th IEEE International Conference on Enterprise Computing, E-Commerce and E-Services, pp.123-130 (2007)
13. Gong, Y.W., Janssen, M., Overbeek, S., et al.: Enabling flexible processes by ECA orchestration architecture. In: ICEGOV 2009 Proceedings of the 3rd International Conference on Theory and Practice of Electronic Governance, pp. 19–26 (2009)
14. Nitu.: Configurability in SaaS (software as a service) applications. In: Proceedings of the 2nd India Software Engineering Conference ISEC 2009, pp. 19–26 (2009)
15. Sun, W., Zhang, X., Guo, C.J., et al.: Software as a Service: Configuration and Customization Perspectives. In: IEEE Congress on Services, SERVICES 2008, pp. 18–25 (2008)
16. Shi, Y.L., Luan, S., Li, Q.Z., et al.: A flexible business process customization framework for SaaS. In: WASE International Conference on Information Engineering, ICIE 2009, pp. 350–353 (2009)
17. Browne, P.: JBoss Drools business rules. Packet publishing. Birmingham-Mumbai (2009)
18. Jeng, J.J., Flaxer, D., Kapoor, S.: RuleBAM: A rule-based framework for business activity Management. In: 2004 IEEE International Conference on Services Computing, pp. 262–270 (2004)
19. Vasilecas, O., Smaizys, A.: Business rule based data analysis for decision support and automation. In: International Conference on Computer Systems and Technologies, CompSysTech 2006, pp. 191–196 (2006)
20. Zhang, X.W., He, K.Q., et al.: SaaS service super-market building model and service recommendation approach. Journal on Communication 32(9A), 158–165 (2011) (in Chinese)
21. Ghaddar, A., Tamzalit, D., Assaf, A., Bitar, A.: Variability as a service: outsourcing variability management in multi-tenant SaaS spplications. In: Ralyté, J., Franch, X., Brinkkemper, S., Wrycza, S. (eds.) CAiSE 2012. LNCS, vol. 7328, pp. 175–189. Springer, Heidelberg (2012)
22. Boyer, J., Mili, H.: Agile business rule development. Springer, Heidelberg (2011)
23. King, P.J.H.: Decision tables, pp. 135–142 (1967), http://comjnl.oxfordjournals.org/content/10/2/135.full.pdf+html

Making XML Signatures Immune
to XML Signature Wrapping Attacks

Christian Mainka[1], Meiko Jensen[2], Luigi Lo Iacono[3], and Jörg Schwenk[1]

[1] Horst Görtz Institute for IT-Security, Ruhr-University Bochum, Germany
[2] Independent Centre for Privacy Protection (ULD), Kiel, Germany
[3] Institute of Media and Imaging Technology,
Cologne University of Applied Sciences, Germany
{Christian.Mainka,Meiko.Jensen,Joerg.Schwenk}@rub.de,
luigi.lo_iacono@fh-koeln.de

Abstract. The increased usage of XML in distributed systems and platforms increases the demand for robust and effective security mechanisms likewise. Recent research work discovered, however, substantial vulnerabilities in the XML Signature standard as well as in the vast majority of the available implementations. Amongst them, the so-called XML Signature Wrapping (XSW) attack belongs to the most relevant ones. With the many possible instances of the XSW attack class, it is feasible to annul security systems relying on XML Signature and to gain access to protected resources as has been successfully demonstrated lately for various Cloud services.

This work introduces a comprehensive approach to robust and effective XML Signatures for SOAP-based Web Services denoted as XSpRES. An architecture is presented, which integrates the required enhancements to ensure a fail-safe and sound signature generation and verification. Following this architecture, a hardened XML Signature library has been implemented. The obtained evaluation results show that the developed concept and library provide the targeted robustness against all kinds of known XSW attacks. Moreover, the empirical results underline that these security merits are obtained at low efficiency and performance costs as well as remain compliant with the underlying standards.

Keywords: XML Signature, XML Signature Wrapping, Web Services, SOAP, WS-Security, XSpRES, SOA, Cloud.

1 Motivation and Introduction

XML is a dominant standard for encoding documents or messages. The range of XML applications is broad. It can be roughly divided into file formats for data at rest such as Docbook, Open Office and WordML for documents or SVG for images and messages for data in transit such as SOAP, XML-RPC or ebXML. The ability of being platform-independent made XML a driving force especially in terms of systems integration. Here resides one important reason why XML is widely used in distributed system and platform contexts such as SOA and Cloud.

With the increased adoption of SOA and Cloud in sensitive application domains, the demands for security increase as well. The use of message-oriented security for

I. Ivanov et al. (Eds.): CLOSER 2012, CCIS 367, pp. 151–167, 2013.

business information based on standards such as Universal Business Language (UBL, http://ubl.xml.org/), eXtensible Business Reporting Language (XBRL, http://www.xbrl.org/) and Bank Internet Payment System (BIPS, http://www.bits.org/) is one example. Others can be found in the e-government domain where in Europe, e.g., the digital agenda explicitly includes SOA concepts as one building block for establishing ICT for public services. Based on pan-European interoperable e-signatures and e-IDs, SOA is recognized as the enabler for cross-border interoperability of e-government systems [1]. Many pilots build upon these foundations such as the e-PRIOR platform for e-procurement, which key design principles include standardized XML documents and SOAP Web Services (http://www.osor.eu/projects/openeprior).

XML Encryption [2] and XML Signature [3] are the core security standards to protect XML data. Recent research results show, however, that these upmost important security mechanisms include serious flaws. Amongst them, the so-called XML Signature Wrapping (XSW) attack is the most relevant one. As described in detail in Section 2, this attack bypasses security means based on digital signatures. Thus, from the XSW attack arises a serious security threat which is of practical relevance especially in scenarios as the ones depicted above. The impact of XSW can be seen in [4] where 11 out of 14 SAML frameworks are detected to vulnerable to this attack. Therefore, the XSW attack needs to be carefully considered and treated in these environments.

The proposed countermeasures—if effective at all—usually provide protection only in very specific settings. No comprehensive approach is available yet. This paper contributes such a holistic and integrated approach—named XML Spoofing Resistant Electronic Signature (XSpRES)—by providing an architecture and an open-source implementation of an XML Signature library that enables the standard-compliant, robust and effective protection of XML data.

Although the emphasize of the developments has been on protecting SOAP-based Web Services and the paper will remain focused on this, still the general protection strategies can be applied to other XML messages or documents to form equivalent solutions.

2   Foundations and Related Work

To lay the foundations for this work, the basics behind XML Signature Wrapping (XSW) attacks are described in the following accomplished with an analysis of the related work in terms of available countermeasures.

2.1   XML Signature

XML Signature [3] is the standard protection means for XML data. It specifies how to digitally sign XML fragments for ensuring integrity and proofing authenticity. The XML Signature element has the following (slightly simplified) structure:

```
<Signature>
  <SignedInfo>
    <CanonicalizationMethod Algorithm="..."/>
    <SignatureMethod Algorithm="..."/>
    <Reference URI="..." >
```

```
    <DigestMethod Algorithm ="..." >
      <DigestValue >...</DigestValue>
    </Reference>
  </SignedInfo>
  <SignatureValue >...</SignatureValue>
</Signature >
```

The signing process undertakes the following flow: for each document part to be signed, a `Reference` element is created and the corresponding part is canonicalized and hashed. The resulting digest is added into the `DigestValue` element and a reference to the signed message part is inserted into the `URI` attribute. Finally the `SignedInfo` element is canonicalized and signed. The result of the signing operation is placed in the `SignatureValue` element.

2.2 XML Signature Wrapping Attack

The so-called XML Signature Wrapping (XSW) attack introduced in 2005 by McIntosh and Austel [5] illustrates that the naive use of XML Signature may result in signed XML documents remaining vulnerable to undetectable modifications. Thus, with the typical usage of XML Signature an adversary may be able to alter valid documents in order to gain unauthorized access to protected resources.

In general, the attack injects unauthorized data into a signed XML document alongside with a possible reconstruction of that document so that the integrity and authenticity is still verified but untruly verified. The consequence is that the undetected modifications are treated as authorized input during any further processing steps.

To illustrate this attack, let's assume that an attacker intercepts an XML-based SOAP message. The slightly simplified structure and content of the obtained SOAP message is shown in Figure 1. The message addresses a Web Service interface for a particular Cloud service, that allows controlling the Cloud resources via such a SOAP-based API. In this example, the intercepted message has been issued by the legitimate user in order to get an overview of the available virtual machine images. The attacker needs to transform the operation in the SOAP body in order to reach the attack goals.

One possible result of a modified SOAP message based on XSW is shown in Figure 2. The original SOAP body element is moved to a newly added bogus wrapper element in the SOAP security header. Note that the moved body is still referenced by the signature using its identifier attribute `Id="body"`. The signature is still cryptographically valid, as the body element in question has not been modified (but simply relocated). Subsequently, in order to make the modified message again compliant to the XML Schema of SOAP messages, the attacker changes the identifier of the cogently placed SOAP body (in this example the `Id="attack"` is used). In this newly added and still empty SOAP body the attacker can now enter any of the operations defined by Cloud control API. In the given example, the adversary initiates a key generation process on behalf of the legitimate user being attacked.

2.3 Related Countermeasures

Since the discovery of XSW attacks by McIntosh and Austel, several countermeasures against them have been proposed and intensively discussed in the last years. In fact,

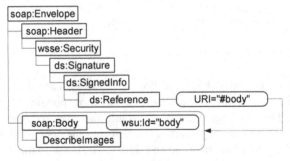

Fig. 1. Signed SOAP Message

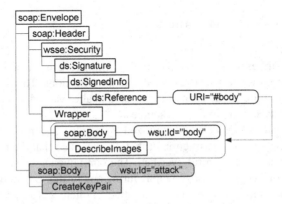

Fig. 2. XML Signature Wrapped SOAP Message

McIntosh and Austel themselves discussed in their original paper on XSW attacks what requirements a server-side security policy must contain in order to uncover the attack. The final policy included assertions such as:

- a signature must be present in the security header
- the element specified by `/soap:Envelope/ soap:Body` must be referenced from the signature
- the element matching `/soap:Envelope/soap:Header/ wsse:Security/wsu:Timestamp` must be referenced from the signature
- the signature verification key must be provided by an X.509 certificate issued by a trusted CA

In 2009 Gruschka and Lo Iacono showed with the first practical XSW attack that the proposed checks by McIntosh and Austel are not sufficient to effectively detect XSW attacks[6].

Bhargavan, Fournet and Gordon also used security policies for fending XSW attacks. They developed a formal model for policy verification [7] and derived from these results a policy adviser [8] for testing and generating security policies. They use an abstract policy language for proofing security properties and map between this proprietary language and WS-SecurityPolicy [9]. The policy adviser proposes the following security assertions:

- Mandatory elements: `wsa:To`, `wsa:Action`, `soap:Body`
- Signed elements: all mandatory, `wsa:MessageID`,
  `wsu:Timestamp`
- Recommended: use of X.509 certificates for authentication

The security requirements for an incoming message to the Amazon EC2 (http://aws.amazon.com/ec2) service are not stated as a formal security policy but in a human readable form. These requirements are:

- Mandatory elements: `wsu:Timestamp`, `soap:Body`,
  `wsse:BinarySecurityToken` containing X.509 certificate
- Signed elements: `wsu:Timestamp`, `soap:Body`

One can see that the Amazon security policy fulfills the requirement from Bhargavan et al. except for the WS-Addressing[10] requirement, which have no influence on this attack (as AWS does not honor WS-Addressing headers). But despite the fact that these requirements were formally proven, obviously such a pure policy-driven approach is not sufficient for mitigating XSW attacks. The gap between the formal policy requirement and a real-world policy checking application can still be misused for attacks. A further problem with the policy adviser approach is that strong restrictions to the security policy are made. For example a lot of elements are claimed as mandatory and the signature of the body is absolutely required which reduces the flexibility of SOAP security mechanisms. However, this is supposably not a restriction for most practical applications.

Most XSW attacks modify the structure of the original message from the legitimate sender in some way. In the example attack described in Section 2.2 a second SOAP body is inserted by the attacker while the original one is being relocated into the SOAP header. Therefore, Rahaman, Schaad and Rits introduced a method – called *inline approach* – to protect some key properties of the SOAP message structure [11]. In this system some characteristic information are collected over the SOAP message and inserted into a new element called *SOAP Account*. This element is added to the SOAP header and additionally signed by the sender. The protected properties are:

- Number of child elements of `soap:Envelope`
- Number of child elements of `soap:Header`
- Number of references in each signature
- Successor and predecessor of each signed object

If an attacker changes the structure of the message in a way that one of these properties are modified the attack can be uncovered. This is for example true for the example attack given in Section 2.2. The number of child elements of the SOAP header is changed from one to two. Thus the usage of the inline approach would have detected this attack. Nonetheless, this protection method has some disadvantages. First, the introduced SOAP Account element as well as the verification of this element is not standardized. Thus, it can for example not be claimed by a WS-SecurityPolicy [12]. Second and more importantly, this method does not generally protect from XSW attacks. If an attacker is able to modify the message structure while keeping the structure properties the inline approach can be circumvented as has been shown by Gajek, Liao and Schwenk in [13]. They improve the above discussed inline approach, but for this improved version the just mentioned disadvantages – especially the standardization issue – still remain.

The authors of [13] give in their paper some more solution ideas for fending XSW attacks. The main idea is using the verification component as a filter. In contrast to common methods where the signature verification just returns a boolean value, here the result of the transformation and canonicalization step is returned. This ensures that the following processing entities inside the Web Service framework operate truly on the message that was originally signed. One problem of this approach – as already remarked by the authors – is that the Web Service cannot operate on the SOAP envelope as a single well-formed message document but only on parts of the message which may also be divided into a forest of message trees. This problem can be solved by passing the signed elements together with its parent nodes as a spanning DOM tree to the business logic part of the Web Service. This works only, if the signature transformation does not change the content of the elements. But even this improved version is inadequate if the Web Service operates on signed as well as on unsigned parts of the SOAP message. In this case the signature component cannot operate as a filter.

Until 2009 this research work was mainly treated as theoretical, due to the rare usage of WS-Security in sensitive applications and the absence of a real-life XSW attack. In 2009 it was discovered, that Amazon's Cloud services were vulnerable to XSW attacks [6]. Using a variation of the attack example presented in Section 2.2 an attacker was able to perform arbitrary operations in the Cloud on behalf of a legitimate user. A number of related results have been published in the following, leading to the discovery of novel attack instances [14].

Along with these developments, novel defense techniques have been proposed. In [15] the authors turn toward a major characteristic of the XSW attack, which is the missing confidence of location information when using ID-based references to link the XML Signature metadata to its signed content. Since the ID attribute does not provide any details on the signed content's location in the document (and sometimes not even on its property of uniqueness), the default referencing scheme possess major challenges with respect to XSW attacks. Hence, the use of a location-aware referencing scheme is favorable. With XML Signature, this can be achieved using XPath expressions for referencing. For instance, an XPath of /soap:Envelope/soap:Header/wsse:Security/wsu:Timestamp leaves little doubt on which part of the XML document is intended to be protected by a digital signature. Furthermore, an attacker can only trick this reference in a XSW attack if he manages to trick the XPath evaluation into mapping to another XML subtree than anticipated – a way more challenging task as compared to moving an ID-equipped subtree to an arbitrary location within the XML document tree as has been used in the above example.

A critical issue with respect to XPath-based referencing is the robustness of the actual XPath expression. For instance, an XPath expression of //*[@ID="foo"] is a valid XPath expression, but is equivalent to an ID-based reference with respect to XSW attempts. As analyzed in [15], the most favorable subset of XPath when it comes to XSW robustness is the subset called *FastXPath*, which prohibits the use of several potentially vulnerable XPath properties. For instance, the use of so-called *wildcard axes* such as `descendant::` are prohibited, since they allow an attacker to move the referenced XML fragment arbitrarily within the range of that XPath location step. Analogously, the use of position indicator predicates is mandatory in FastXPath. An XPath of `/soap:Envelope[1]/soap:Body[1]` clearly selects exactly one – the first – child element of matching name, thereby fending XSW attacks that use element duplication (as e.g. used against Amazon EC2 in [6]).

In [16] the authors introduce and evaluate the possibility of hardening the XML Schema in conjunction with XML Schema validation to construct an effective protection against XSW attacks. The authors identified the following weak definitions in the SOAP Schema:

- **Element:** `xs:any` allows an element to have any kind of child elements, which are not defined by any schema. The main idea of this is to have an extensible layout, e.g. the SOAP `Header` can have any not yet defined child elements (*reserved for future use*).
- **Attribute:** `processContents="lax"` instructs the validator to only process the content if an XML Schema for it is present, otherwise just leave it out. A more drastically direction is `processContents="skip"` which causes simply no validation.
- **Attribute:** `namespace="##any"` and `namespace="##other"` allows the usage of elements from *any*, respectively from *any but its parents* namespace.

Each of these nodes allows an attacker to inject own elements, e.g. to place a XSW element. To eliminate this leakage, each instruction is removed from the hardened Schema by substituting it directly with the needed Schema parts (e.g. WS-Security). This constricts the whole document to deny any user-defined elements. It has been shown that XML Schema validation with a hardened XML Schema is capable of fending XSW attacks, but bears some pitfalls and disadvantages amongst which the increased resource consumption is the biggest obstacle.

This analysis of the related work can be concluded by noting the fact, that the XSW attack has been moved from a hypothetical to a practical security threat which needs to be urgently targeted and that there is no comprehensive approach available which provides the required protection against this attack in a standard-compliant and effective manner. This lack is targeted by XSpRES as will be introduced in the following.

3   The XSpRES Approach

As can be seen from the discussions on available countermeasures, several proposals for fending the XML Signature Wrapping attack threat exist. Unfortunately, each countermeasure has shown to become ineffective at some point for certain XSW attack variations. Hence, in order to establish a robust protection, it is necessary to combine a suitable subset of these countermeasures to come up with a holistic, integrated approach.

The long-term investigations showed that two main properties need to be preserved for signed XML data to effectively prevent XSW attacks from occurring. One is to ensure that the document structure is strictly defined and does henceforth not allow the altering of the structure by injection or reordering attempts. The other property is related to the referencing scheme which must assure that the binding between the signed parts of a document and the document structure can not be manipulated unnoticeable. Furthermore, both properties need to be constructed and implemented with the required care. As the state of the art described in Section 2.3 clearly shows is, that the simple and naive adoption of e.g. schema validation for document structure approval or XPath-based instead of ID-based referencing for an immutable binding is not sufficient for obtaining a robust protection. This is also true for a combination of these mechanisms.

As a consequence, novel mechanisms have been developed to provide adequate solutions to meet these properties. At the core of XSpRES is henceforth an enhanced referencing scheme which immutably binds the signed elements of a document with the document structure. Moreover, a scheme to strictly define the structure of a XML document or message is incorporate, alongside with according verification components. Both mechanisms are described in more detail in the following Sections 3.2 and 3.3.

Beside these crucial conceptual and technical aspects, the compliance with the relevant standards has been a high priority focus point. By achieving standard-compliance the acceptance of the developed solution can be increased, since it respects already made investments and allows for a seamless integration and migration. Moreover, it would still enable the use of the protection functions in heterogeneous environments in which it could not be deployed on every endpoint, due to restrictions of legacy systems. The architecture is therefore designed to deal with the XSW-introducing issues in the specifications and implementations by pre-processing steps. Before a standard signature is generated or verified, the XSpRES components process the XML message to ensure the discussed properties are met. The pre-processing components at the signature generation side will not make any assumption on signature verification capabilities, henceforth maintaining the standard-compliance. By this, it is e.g. feasible for a standard XML signature library to verify XSpRES-enhanced signatures, with the obvious drawback of a reduced protection level.

3.1   Architecture

An initial step for the development of a holistic defense architecture for Web Services against XSW attacks consists in the definition of a formalized model for the attack scenario. Based on the existing previous work presented in [15,17], and derived from the semi-formal *Web Services Attacker Model* described in [18], the scenario model for the XSW attack consists of three main entities: a Web Service client, a Web Service server and an external attacker [19]. The attacker is assumed to be able to access and alter XML messages exchanged between the Web Service client and the Web Service server, but is not able to interfere with the client-side or server-side implementations of the Web Services software stack directly.

Based on this abstract yet formal scenario model, the XSpRES approach derives the ability to extend the Web Service stacks at both Web Service client and Web Service server arbitrarily, as long as these extensions remain within the particular trusted domain

XSpRES Integration into WS-Framework

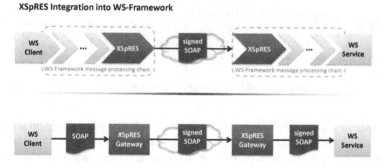

XSpRES Integration via Gateway

Fig. 3. XSpRES Architecture

and outside of the scope of the attacker. Thus, the XSpRES architecture introduces two new entities to the scenario: a client-side extension and a server-side extension (see Figure 3).

The developed architecture as shown in Figure 3 mainly consists of these extension which include the pre-processing components. There are two approaches available, in which the extensions can be integrated at the client and server side respectively. The first is a deep integration into the message processing chain of one particular Web Service framework. This would enable to make use of the provided functionality directly within the programming environment. The other approach provides the protection mechanisms as a gateway solution, which steps into the communication link at the client and the server side. Such a deployment decouples the functionality from a particular Web Service environment and can henceforth be operated with clients and services programmed in various distinct languages.

3.2 Client-Side Signature Generation Process

Though XSW attacks commonly only affect the Web Service server operations, there nevertheless exists the need to also consider the Web Service client-side to improve the overall robustness of the secured XML-based communication. The goal of the XSpRES client-side processing is to bind the XML Signature in the course of signature creation as uniquely and strongly as possible to its referring content. This is achieved by chaining a set of separate modules, which seamlessly integrate into the client-side Web Service processing flow (see Figure 4).

First, the WS-SecurityPolicy is verified to ensure the use of FastXPath expressions. Afterwards, those expressions are transformed to their prefix-free equivalent to prevent namespace injection attacks [17]. Finally, the document is signed using standard mechanisms but building on the previous processing steps. All of these components are described in more detail in the following sections.

Referencing Verification. As discussed in Section 2.3, when sticking to the FastXPath subset defined in [15], the robustness of the resulting XML Signatures against XSW is

Fig. 4. XSpRES Signature Generation Process

improved significantly. XSpRES integrates FastXPath-based referencing on the client-side for binding the XML Signature metadata more tightly to its signed contents.

The *Referencing Verification* module of the XSpRES client-side is not directly accessing the SOAP messages, but is merely used to preprocess the WS-SecurityPolicy file that defines which parts of the bypassing SOAP messages have to be signed. Commonly, the WS-SecurityPolicy document is created and provided by the Web Service server, describing its expectations with respect to signed parts in SOAP messages it is targeted with. Hence, it acts as a basis for determining the parts-to-be-signed at the client-side. However, if the XPath expressions given in the WS-SecurityPolicy file are not following the FastXPath grammar as discussed above, their effectiveness in terms of fending XSW attacks are reduced. Thus, this module's task is to preprocess all XPath expressions given in the server-provided WS-SecurityPolicy document, verifying that all of the contained XPath expressions strictly stick to the FastXPath grammar. If the WS-SecurityPolicy file fulfills this requirement, it is used in the FastXPath-based referencing module introduced previously, simply by using the FastXPath expressions from the WS-SecurityPolicy document as the reference in the XML Signatures created. Otherwise, the module throws an error and stops the client gateway.

Prefix Transformation. As pointed out in [17], the use of XPath in conjunction with XML namespaces has its issues, potentially leading to an exploitable XSW vulnerability despite the existence of a strict XPath expression for referencing. By binding the same namespace prefix to different namespace URIs at different locations within a signed SOAP message document, the server-side processing stack can be misled into a XSW attack, even when using a strict FastXPath expression.

The *Prefix Transformation* module transforms the FastXPath expressions from the server-provided WS-SecurityPolicy into an equivalent, but prefix-free variant. The FastXPath expression of /soap:Envelope[1] gets e.g. transformed into the semantically equivalent XPath expression of /*[local-name()="Envelope" and namespace-uri()="http://ns-soap"][1]. As can be seen, the problematic use of the soap: prefix is resolved into an equivalent representation holding the full namespace URI of the SOAP specification. Hence, binding the soap: prefix to another namespace URI does no longer affect the result of the transformed XPath expression, protecting against the XSW threat of namespace injection as described in [17]. In principle, it would be a valid approach to use the transformed version of the FastXPath expressions already within the WS-SecurityPolicy document itself. However, due to limited readability and considerations in respect to available tools, the XSpRES prototype sticks to the presented XPath transformation approach. This implies, that after the successful FastXPath compliance verification of each XPath expression extracted

Fig. 5. XSpRES Signature Verification Process

from the server-provided WS-SecurityPolicy, this expression is transformed into the prefix-free notation, and then used directly within the created XML Signature as XPath Filter2 referencing expression. Thereby, it can be guaranteed that a location change of a signed XML subtree within a SOAP message automatically causes an invalidation of the respective XML Signature. Even without a server-side defense mechanism, this approach provides already an effective protection against numerous XSW attack variations. However, since the server-side application logic itself might not be implemented in a way that recognizes and uses the same fixed position as input for its operations, XSW attacks remain possible even with using the prefix-free FastXPath referencing as outlined here. Thus, an additional strong server-side defense is still required in order to further reduce possible sources of errors and to decouple the verification processes from the application logic processes as much as possible.

Signature Creation. The *Signature Creation* module then creates the XML Signature for the document parts to be signed. The signature creation is in conformance with the undelying standards. To reach the targeted goal of a more unique and strict binding of the signature to its content all references are given as prefix-free FastXPath expressions.

3.3 Server-Side Signature Verification Process

In correspondence with the client-side approach, the server-side Web Service processing flow is extended using an integrated architecture of five modules that protect the server-side implementation from being compromised by an XSW attack. The goal of the XSpRES server-side processing is to extend the verification steps to include checks on the message structure and to evaluate the strict and unique binding enforced by the client-side modules (see Figure 5).

First, the incoming message is processed by the *DoS Detection* module to ensure that the XML document is of finite length. The *XML Schema Validator* module then uses a hardened XML Schema to guarantee that there are no unexpected elements contained in the message. Both, the *Referencing Verification* module and the *Prefix Transformation* module assure that the signed parts are accessed by the correct FastXPath expression and the *XML Signature Verification* module finally verifies the signature. All of these components are described in more detail in the following sections.

DoS Detection. The *DoS Detection* module is not a required component from the XSW perspective, but is a general must have protection. Such a DoS detector ensures that the XML document is of finite length and henceforth prevents the overflooding of the machine's memory—especially in the case in which a DOM based parser is used, since each element in the XML message is instantiated as an object in memory.

The XSpRES system includes a DoS detector and uses it to also check on the appearance of ID attributes. If an ID attribute occurs twice, the processing of the message on the server-side is aborted. This addition to the DoS Detector suppresses basic XSW attacks, in which the signed message part is duplicated or moved (including the ID attribute), in an very early processing stage.

XML Schema Validation. The *XML Schema Validation* module uses a hardened XML Schema to validate the incoming SOAP messages. This schema overrides the default XML Schema for SOAP messages by removing any possibility for placing arbitrary elements in the document as described in [16]. The drawback of this approach is that the schema validation of a hardened XML Schema is slower compared to the standard one, as each element must be validated. Therefore, the XSpRES implementation merges as few schemas as possible to minimize the total schema size. The considered schemas include WS-Security, WS-Utilities, XML Signature, XPathFilter2 and WS-Addressing (whereas the latter might also be negligible depending on the requirements of the underlying application scenario).

Note that the server gateway schema must be adjusted to the document structure of each to be protected Web Service, since the SOAP body element does no longer allow xs:any child elements.

Referencing Verification. The *Referencing Verification* module verifies the security policy. Therefore, it extracts the XPath expressions from a local policy file and, analogue to its client-side complement, validates if these are valid FastXPath expressions. This ensures that the horizontal and vertical position of the signed fragments is fixed.

Prefix Transformation. The *Prefix Transformation* module transforms the FastXPath expressions to their namespace-free equivalents to prevent namespace injection attacks.

In contrast to the corresponding client-side module, the received message is checked in addition. An incoming message is parsed and a lookup for a valid Timestamp element is made. Thereafter, the expressions in the XPath element children of the signature's Reference element are string-compared to those transformed FastXPath expressions from the policy file. This assures that both, the client and the server side, use the same policy.

Signature Verification. The *XML Signature Verification* module simply verifies the XML Signature in the document. As the WS-SecurityPolicy modules assures that the signed elements use the correct XPath expressions, the signed fragments are horizontally and vertically fixed, so that no known attack moved these message parts.

3.4 Backwards Compatibility and Standards Compliance

An important characteristic of the XSpRES architecture is the backward compatibility, meaning that all parts of the XSpRES architecture are able to handle communication not originating from another XSpRES-instrumented client or server. More precisely, the server-side XSpRES extension is able to process arbitrary types of XML Signatures, even if they originate from a different XML Signature creation framework than the XSpRES client-side modules. Vice versa, the XML Signatures generated by the XSpRES client-side modules remain fully compliant to the XML Signature specification, hence can also be verified by any other XML Signature verification implementation, even if it is not following the XSpRES approach.

However, obviously, the effectiveness of the XSpRES defense against the XSW attack is reduced drastically by using non-XSpRES components at either side, since this breaks the comprehensiveness of XSpRES falling back to the present state of the art.

4   Implementation and Evaluation

The implementation of each single XSpRES component is realized by only standard Java libraries. It is available as free and open source software at https://www.bsi. bund.de/SharedDocs/Downloads/DE/BSI/Downloadserver/SOA/XSpRES.html.

The client gateway acts as a simple HTTP server and signs an incoming message by using the FastXPath expressions extracted from a local policy file. These expressions are validated and transformed as described in Section 3.2. The signed message is afterwards forwarded to the server gateway.

The server gateway is based on the Apache Axis2 (http://ws.apache.org/axis2/) Web Services Framework and the XSpRES components are integrated as an Axis2 module. Thus, by this integration method, the XSpRES module can replace the signature verification of the commonly used Apache Rampart (http://axis.apache.org/axis2/java/rampart/) security module.

Figure 6 compares the signature verification of the Rampart module with all security features of the XSpRES prototype. The setup uses an AMD Athlon II X3 440 Processor with 4GB RAM.

Both, the XSpRES and the Rampart module do semantically the same: They validate the timestamp in the message header and verify the signature over the Timestamp element as well as the SOAP body element. The technical difference is that Rampart uses two ID-based references, one for the timestamp and the other for the SOAP body. XSpRES instead uses only one reference which selects both elements with the transformed FastXPath expressions from the policy file.

The measurement of the time required to verify the signature starts after the HTTP request has been received and ends just before the verified message is forwarded to the application logic. The processing time is then computed as the average of 1000 messages. The measurements have been conducted for different message sizes.

As can be seen from the visualized evaluation results given in Figure 6 both modules operate approximately equal in speed, but the Rampart module has the lack of the additional security features in relation to XSW attacks. It is also notable, that the runtime for Rampart is the same for any kind of invalid messages, whereas the XSpRES module will abort the verification process in an early stage if the message violates the schema or the policy.

A detailed runtime analysis for each XSpRES component is shown in Figure 7 for one common message size. The DoS detection takes 7ms although the StAX parser has to process the whole document. The DOM based Schema validation needs only 3ms, because the instantiation of the XMLSchemaFactory, which processes the Schema files,

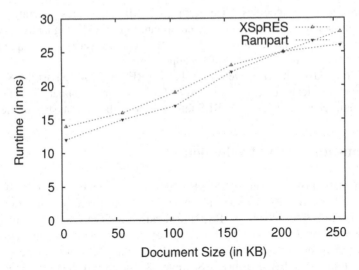

Fig. 6. Runtime comparison of XSpRES and Rampart

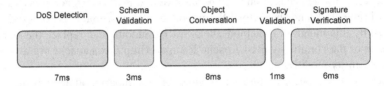

Fig. 7. Runtime analysis of XSpRES components for 200 KB message

is done once in the startup phase and thus saves 9ms per validation. The signature component can be divided into three parts: The slowest part is the conversion from the Axis2 Object Model to a Java Document Object. The policy validation is extremely fast, as it just searches for the transformed FastXPath expressions in the `Reference` element and string-compares them to those in the local policy file. The signature validation requires 6ms. In its current implementation, XSpRES uses the common DOM-based processing model. This will be replaced by a faster streaming-based signature validation [20,21] in a future work.

It must be mentioned, that the XSpRES prototype implementation is focused on security and not on efficiency in the first place. Nevertheless, Figure 6 shows that it is comparable to the Rampart security module. One reason for this is, that XSpRES is very light-weight, i.e., it is only capable of handling digital signatures. Rampart, in contrast, is much more complete in the sense of standards-compliance, including features such as encryption, username token, which impacts on the time required for signature verification. On the other hand, the processing time of the XSpRES modules can be improved significantly. By aligning the object models of the various deployed Java components, the need for the costly object conversion would be eliminated, reducing the processing time by one third.

5   Conclusions and Outlook

The use of SOA and Cloud concepts for the construction of distributed applications handling more and more sensitive data is on the rise. XML is playing an important role in such applications, since it is used for encoding data at rest as well as data in transit. The security demands coming with the processing and storage of sensitive data rely on robust and effective security technologies. Recent discoveries showed that the XML Security specifications include serious flaws and thus can currently not fulfill the required protection levels readily.

This work contributes a comprehensive approach to face these vulnerabilities providing an architecture which compiles a set of inter-linked protection mechanisms for the client-side as well as the server-side. The selection and composition of the protection means have been guided by the requirements to realize the targeted architecture in an effective, but still standard-compliant and cost efficient way. Based on this ground work, an open-source XSW protection library has been implemented, which is robust against all known instances of the XSW attack and thus provides a vehicle to generate and verify signed XML documents and messages in a fail-safe and standard-compliant manner. The seamless integration of the developed library into standard Web Services frameworks has been another requirement, enabling—amongst others—to evaluate the developments in a common SOAP setting. The obtained results emphasize that the proposed approach fulfills the targeted goals and provides an effective protection against XSW attacks at low computational extra costs and by still being standard-compliant.

XSpRES has been focussed on SOAP-based Web Services in the first place, due to the availability of practical attacks and the pressing need for more reliable and fail-safe security mechanisms. Still, the overall concept and architecture has been designed and implemented with generality in mind. Hence, the adoption of XSpRES to other domains and standards is currently undertaken. The recently reported XSW-related vulnerabilities in SAML-based identity and access management systems pose new challenges [4]. Since SAML assertions are a rather special case, it needs to be elaborated in detail, how the ideas from XSpRES can be applied. The authors of this paper also covered two interesting countermeasures to protect against XSW: (1) *See-what-is-signed* and (2) *Data-Tainting*. The first approach extracts all unsigned elements out of the XML message. As this could break the compatibility with some frameworks, e.g. because it expects a specific root element, which is removed since it is unsigned, the authors suggest to leave all ancestors of singed elements untouched. Thus, only unsigned sibling elements are removed. A problem with this approach is that the application logic may depend on some unsigned contents and cannot process the message correctly. In this case, *Data-Tainting* can be applied, which touches the problem that a common signature verification logic only returns a boolean value (valid/invalid). This techniques enforces the signature verification logic to *taint* the processed data by adding a randomly chosen attribute-value to the element. The value is then transmitted to the application logic using a separate channel. Both techniques could also be integrated into XSpRES to increase the level of security.

Beyond these improvements, further research activities are targeting the required *schema hardening* process (as briefly discussed in Section 3.3). Here, the challenge is to convert a set of specifications that are used in conjunction into a single, hardened

XML Schema description that no longer contains any schema extension points (such as e.g. xs:any or xs:anyAttribute structures). This way, there is no ambiguity in placement of critical message parts, hence preventing XSW attacks most effectively.

To some extent, this task of schema hardening can be automated. For instance, every occurrence of a schema extension point can be replaced automatically with an xs:Choice or xs:Sequence structure containing all XML schema types that may occur at these extension points. The crux is, obviously, to select the proper set of allowed specifications for each extension point. Here, a semi-automated approach, involving manual selection of specifications per extension point, then automated generation of the hardened XML Schema file, appears most promising. However, some further challenges have to be addresses, such as recursions in XML Schema structures, or alternative XML schemata for identical message parts.

Acknowledgements. This work was funded by the Federal Office for Information Security in Germany (BSI) under the contract number 882/2010. Further, M. Jensen's contribution was partially funded by the EU FP7 project FutureID under GA nr. 318424.

The authors would like to thank Holger Junker and Juraj Somorovsky for many fruitful discussions and their valuable input.

References

1. Ticau, S.A.: Security – a centrail issue of the future EU digital agenda. Service Oriented Architecture pushed to the limit in eGovernment (2010)
2. Imamura, T., Dillaway, B., Simon, E.: XML Encryption Syntax and Processing. W3C Recommendation (2002)
3. Bartel, M., Boyer, J., Fox, B., LaMacchia, B., Simon, E.: XML Signature Syntax and Processing. W3C Recommendation (2008)
4. Somorovsky, J., Mayer, A., Schwenk, J., Kampmann, M., Jensen, M.: On breaking saml: Be whoever you want to be. In: 21st USENIX Security Symposium, Bellevue, WA (August 2012)
5. McIntosh, M., Austel, P.: XML signature element wrapping attacks and countermeasures. In: SWS 2005: Proceedings of the 2005 Workshop on Secure Web Services, pp. 20–27. ACM Press, New York (2005)
6. Gruschka, N., Lo Iacono, L.: Vulnerable Cloud: SOAP Message Security Validation Revisited. In: ICWS 2009: Proceedings of the IEEE International Conference on Web Services. IEEE, Los Angeles (2009)
7. Bhargavan, K., Fournet, C., Gordon, A.D.: A semantics for Web Services authentication. Theoretical Computer Science 340(1), 102–153 (2005)
8. Bhargavan, K., Fournet, C., Gordon, A.D., O'Shea, G.: An advisor for Web Services Security policies. In: SWS 2005: Proceedings of the 2005 Workshop on Secure Web Services, pp. 1–9. ACM Press, New York (2005)
9. Kaler, C., Nadalin, A.: Web Services Security Policy Language (WS-SecurityPolicy) 1.1 (2005)
10. Gudgin, M., Hadley, M., Rogers, T.: Web Services Addressing 1.0 - SOAP Binding. W3C Recommendation (2006)
11. Rahaman, M.A., Schaad, A., Rits, M.: Towards secure SOAP message exchange in a SOA. In: SWS 2006: Proceedings of the 3rd ACM Workshop on Secure Web Services, pp. 77–84. ACM Press, New York (2006)

12. Lawrence, K., Kaler, C.: Web Services Security Policy Language (WS-SecurityPolicy) 1.2 (2007)
13. Gajek, S., Liao, L., Schwenk, J.: Breaking and fixing the inline approach. In: Proceedings of the 2007 ACM Workshop on Secure Web Services (SWS 2007), pp. 37–42. Association for Computing Machinery, Fairfax (2007)
14. Somorovsky, J., Heiderich, M., Jensen, M., Schwenk, J., Gruschka, N., Lo Iacono, L.: All your clouds are belong to us security analysis of cloud management interfaces. In: Proceedings of the ACM Cloud Computing Security Workshop, CCSW (2011)
15. Gajek, S., Jensen, M., Liao, L., Schwenk, J.: Analysis of signature wrapping attacks and countermeasures. In: ICWS, pp. 575–582 (2009)
16. Jensen, M., Meyer, C., Somorovsky, J., Schwenk, J.: On the effectiveness of xml schema validation for countering xml signature wrapping attacks. In: First International Workshop on Securing Services on the Cloud, IWSSC 2011 (2011)
17. Jensen, M., Liao, L., Schwenk, J.: The curse of namespaces in the domain of xml signature. In: SWS, pp. 29–36 (2009)
18. Jensen, M.: Analysis of Attacks and Defenses in the Context of Web Services. PhD thesis, Ruhr-University Bochum (2011)
19. Mainka, C., Jensen, M., Lo Iacono, L., Schwenk, J.: XSpRES: Robust and Efective XML Signatures forWeb Services. In: Closer 2012: 2nd International Conference on Cloud Computing and Services Science (April 2012)
20. Gruschka, N., Jensen, M., Lo Iacono, L., Luttenberger, N.: Server-side streaming processing of ws-security. IEEE T. Services Computing 4, 272–285 (2011)
21. Somorovsky, J., Jensen, M., Schwenk, J.: Streaming-based verification of xml signatures in soap messages. In: Proceedings of the 2010 6th World Congress on Services, SERVICES 2010, pp. 637–644. IEEE Computer Society, Washington, DC (2010)

Automated Non-repudiable Cloud Resource Allocation*

Kassidy Clark, Martijn Warnier, and Frances M.T. Brazier

Faculty of Technology, Policy and Management, Delft University of Technology,
Jaffalaan 5, Delft, The Netherlands
{k.p.clark,m.e.warnier,f.m.brazier}@tudelft.nl

Abstract. This paper presents an Intelligent Cloud Resource Allocation Service (ICRAS) that assists consumers with the complex task of finding the optimal configuration of Cloud resources given a consumer's specific needs. The process of selecting a CSP becomes increasingly complex as the number of Cloud Service Providers (CSP) offering similar services continues to grow. Consumers can pick and choose between CSPs based on a growing number of options, including price, Quality of Service, reputation and so forth. The advent of dynamic pricing (based on real-time availability) further increases the complexity of CSP selection. ICRAS alleviates much of this burden from the consumer by automating the processes of service discovery, evaluation, negotiation and migration. Furthermore, ICRAS monitors Service Level Agreement (SLA) compliance using non-repudiable monitoring techniques.

1 Introduction

Cloud computing [2] provides the illusion of unbounded online resources, such as cpu or storage capacity. Companies that offer these resources are referred to as Cloud Service Providers (CSP). The Cloud is sometimes also called *elastic* since customers can easily increase or decrease resource usage, such as the amount of computing power, rented from a CSP.

Similar Cloud services are offered through a number of CSPs that compete on price and service levels. Several of these CSPs also offer a whole pallet of options to their customers who can customize their own service based on metrics such as price, Quality of Service (QoS), reputation and location. Note that most of these metrics are dynamic, i.e. they change continuously. For example, some CSPs, such as Amazon Web Services spot pricing, offer dynamic pricing. This enables that the price of resources changes constantly, which reflects underlying factors, such as Cloud utilization, fluctuating energy prizes or consumer demand [3,4].

In this environment, a consumer of Cloud services faces several challenges. First, to obtain the desired initial configuration of Cloud resources, a consumer must evaluate prices and configuration options (QoS levels, location, etc.) of all available CSPs.

---

* This is an updated an extended version of the paper "An Intelligent Cloud Resource Allocation Service - Agent-based automated Cloud resource allocation using micro-agreements" [1] presented at the 2nd International Conference on Cloud Computing and Services Science (CLOSER 2012).

I. Ivanov et al. (Eds.): CLOSER 2012, CCIS 367, pp. 168–182, 2013.

The task of finding the ideal configuration is further complicated as more CSPs implement dynamic pricing. When a consumer chooses the configuration that is currently the most appropriate, a better (cheaper) configuration may become available soon thereafter. Therefore, a consumer must periodically reevaluate configurations at all available CSPs. If a consumer chooses to move from his or her current CSP to a different CSP with a more suitable configuration, the consumer is then faced with the challenge of migration. Due to inoperability of CSPs and the tendency towards vendor lock-in, changing CSPs is not a trivial task. Finally, once a consumer chooses a CSP, the consumer must continually monitor the service to detect any violations to the service agreement. Moreover, the consumer must also give evidence, for example in the from of an audit trail, that a violation has actually taken place.

To assist a consumer with these challenges, this paper introduces an Intelligent Cloud Resource Allocation Service (ICRAS). ICRAS supports the consumer throughout the lifecycle of a Cloud service. This includes, (1) discovering all available resource configurations, (2) choosing the desired configuration, (3) negotiating a service agreement with the CSP, (4) assisting in the migration of services between CSPs and (5) securely monitoring the service agreement for violations.

ICRAS aggregates information describing the available services from multiple CSPs, including current price, availability, Quality of Service guarantees, location and reputation. When a consumer requires resources, it contacts ICRAS with a description of the computing needs. ICRAS then matches the resource request to the most appropriate configuration of Cloud resources from the CSPs. ICRAS facilitates the negotiation of the necessary Service Level Agreements (SLA) with the CSPs on behalf of the consumer and assists in the migration process.

ICRAS then monitors the services during the lifetime of the SLA to ensure that there are no agreement violations. If violations are detected, corrective action can be taken. Service monitoring is performed using secure modules at both the consumer and provider. Further steps are taken to generate an audit log of service message. Using several cryptographic protocols, this audit log can guarantee integrity and non-repudiation of service messages.

The main contributions of this paper are an Intelligent Cloud Resource Allocation Service (ICRAS) that (1) maximizes the utility of the consumer, (2) supports the consumer throughout the lifecycle of a Cloud service, (3) utilizes micro agreements in order to quickly react to changes in the Cloud service market (e.g. a lower price from a competing CSP), and (4) provides monitoring of the SLA which results in an audit trail that provides non-repudiation and integrity.

The remainder of this paper is organized as follows. Section 2 introduces the core concepts used in automated negotiation and service monitoring. The ICRAS architecture is detailed in Section 3. The ICRAS protocol is explained with a use-case in Section 4. Section 5 gives an overview of an prototype implementation of the ICRAS framework in the AgentScape platform. In Section 6, other automated service negotiation architectures are compared. Finally, the implications of this research are discussed in Section 7 and the paper is concluded in Section 8.

2   Automated Negotiation and Monitoring

Negotiation is the process by which one or more parties, with possibly conflicting goals, together search for a mutually acceptable agreement [5]. The negotiation process consists of proposals, counter-proposals, trade-offs and concessions, as each party attempts to maximize its own utilities (e.g. outcomes). A common utility function for consumers in the context of Cloud computing is to reduce costs while achieving the desired resources and maintaining reasonable Quality of Service (QoS)

Much research has been done in recent years on the area of automating the negotiation process using intelligent software agents [6,7,5,8,9]. In this paper, an agent is be defined as a piece of software that is capable of autonomous action [10].

In the marketplace, agents represent the individual parties of a negotiation. Given a user's preferences and a negotiation strategy, agents are able to communicate with other agents to autonomously negotiate agreements. Furthermore, agents can learn from past social interactions and improve their response to changes in the environment or even take proactive measures when opportunity arises. The agent model supports message passing and autonomous decision making useful for automated negotiation.

2.1   Service Level Agreements

The product of a successful negotiation session is an agreement between the parties that stipulates the terms and conditions of the service. This agreement is referred to as Service Level Agreement (SLA). An SLA contains the names of the parties involved, the services to be provided and the QoS guarantees that apply. Several standards have been proposed for formalizing the negotiation and creation of the SLA document, including the Web Service Agreement (WSAG) [11] and Web Service Agreement Negotiation (WSAN) [12] specifications.

The WSAG specification describes the steps taken during SLA negotiation, as well as how SLAs are represented. The objects used in negotiation are 1) Templates, 2) (Counter-) offers and 3) Agreements. *Templates* are used by service providers to describe the services they offer, including specific configurations of price, QoS guarantees and so forth. These services are listed in the template with constraints such as `ExacltyOne` and `OneOrMore`. Upon request, a service provider sends his or her templates to a service consumer. Based on the templates, the consumer makes one or more *Offers*. An offer is an instantiated template. This occurs when a consumer chooses a specific configuration of services from a template along with their associated guarantees. If both parties accept an offer, an *Agreement* is created. The final agreement lists the parties involved, the exact services being provisioned and the specific guarantees (QoS) that apply. If the offer is not accepted, either a counter-offer is created with a new configuration or the negotiation session is terminated.

2.2   Micro Agreements

Agreements specify the terms and conditions of a service for a defined period of time. For instance, home-owners typically make a long-term agreement with the power company for a period of one year or more. The agreement typically stipulates that the home-owner may not migrate to another energy provider until the end of the period. This fixed pricing period benefits the provider two fold. First, it provides a reliable income source for the period. Second, it improves the accuracy of the usage prediction used for buying or generating electricity. Energy providers can make more accurate assumptions about energy consumption if their customers cannot suddenly move to a different provider.

The disadvantage of long-term agreements is that the customer cannot react to changes in the market, such as new providers or cheaper products. In practice, prices are constantly changing due to the constant balance of supply and demand. However, these changes are not immediately reflected in the price the customer pays, due to long-term agreements. Furthermore, due to fixed pricing, customers have no incentive to shape their demand to conform to supply. This results in lowered market efficiency.

An alternative to a long-term agreement is a micro-agreement. A micro-agreement is a short-term agreement with a period on the scale of seconds, hours or days. By keeping the period of fixed-pricing short, consumers are able to benefit from dynamic pricing, also referred to as real-time pricing. Using micro-agreements, consumers are able to shape their demand on an hourly basis, in response to changes in price. This approach increases market efficiency, lowers price and reduces the amount of unconsumed (e.g. wasted) resources. Dynamic pricing has been investigated in the area of energy markets with promising results [13].

From a technical perspective, short term agreements differ only slightly from classical agreements. No fundamental changes to the negotiation protocol are required. Protocols, including WSAN described above, already support renegotiation of existing agreements. A micro-agreement is just an agreement with a much shorter time-to-live (TTL). Additional resources are needed to handle the high frequency of agreement (re)negotiation, including hardware resources. For instance, if a single CSP has 100 customers with month-long agreements, that CSP needs resources (e.g. memory, CPU and so forth) to handle 100 agreement (re)negotiations per month. However, if agreements expire after 1 hour, this CSP must process approximately 100 agreement (re)negotiations every hour.

2.3   Service Monitoring

Monitoring is used to detect SLA violations when they occur and to identify the offending party, if possible. In some cases, no responsible party can be identified (e.g. force majeur). For instance, if a lightning strike disables the communication lines between a consumer and a provider, the consumer may incorrectly conclude that the provider has violated the SLA. Monitoring data can be used to show that the provider was not responsible for the violation.

A commonly used approach to monitoring is referred to as active monitoring. Active monitoring performs specific measurements at specified intervals. Active monitoring is used to monitor SLAs [14,15]. A service is monitored by periodically testing whether the terms of an SLA have been met by all parties. This may require measuring a single variable or a complex aggregation of variables. For instance, 'Host is reachable.' may be measured by a single request/response action. In contrast, 'Host uptime is greater than 99%.' is often measured by polling a host multiple times and calculating the average rate of success.

An important aspect of monitoring is safeguarding objectivity of monitoring results. A party to an agreement may have an incentive to manipulate the results to his or her advantage. For instance, an SLA may stipulate that a consumer receives financial compensation if a specified service is unreachable. Regardless of the actual status of the service, that consumer may want to manipulate monitoring results to make it appear unreachable and therefore collect financial compensation. To prevent this situation from occurring, a Trusted Third Party (TTP) is used to perform monitoring measurements [16,15]. A TTP is an independent party that can access all communication between the parties to the SLA. To prevent parties from manipulating the measurement results collected at their respective locations, a TTP install Trusted Monitoring Modules (TMM) at each partys location. The use of TMMs allows parties to have more equal access to the same QoS metrics. For instance, a consumer may not allow a provider to access sensitive client data directly. However, a TMM allows a TTP to access this data in a secure way. Thus, the provider has 'indirect' access to the data via the TTP and will be notified if it reveals any SLA violations. Which TMMs are required to access which QoS metrics depends on a specific SLA.

Active monitoring can be combined with an alternative monitoring technique, referred to in this paper as *passive monitoring* [17,18]. Passive monitoring uses cryptographic primitives to generate a secure audit log of all service messages. The cryptographic primitives offer integrity and non-repudiation of these messages between consumer and provider. If a conflict arises regarding SLA compliance, the audit log is analyzed to determine which party (if any) has violated the SLA.

3   ICRAS Architecture

The Intelligent Cloud Resource Allocation Service (ICRAS) requires an underlying architecture, consisting of three major components: 1) a consumer, 2) a CSP and 3) an ICRAS agent. These elements represent the three roles in the marketplace, which may contain multiple instances of each. Furthermore, this architecture provides the mechanisms and protocols that enable these parties to communicate with one another and autonomously negotiate micro-SLAs. SLAs are negotiated and created following the WSAN specification. This architecture is illustrated in Figure 1.

3.1   Consumer

Each consumer interacts directly with an ICRAS agent. A consumer specifies his or her requirements in an SLA offer. This document allows a consumer to specify 1) hard and 2) soft requirements, 3) priorities, 4) ranges of options, and 5) dependencies between requirements. For instance, a consumer requires 10 virtual servers with a combined CPU power of 20 GHz and a combined storage of 2 TB. Using the SLA notation, a consumer expresses that the CPU and storage requirements are strict, however, for a reduced price, the actual number or servers can change.

In addition to providing the initial resource requirements, a consumer is also responsible for updating these requirements. If resource requirements change, a consumer must inform an ICRAS agent of these changes. A change in requirements can occur

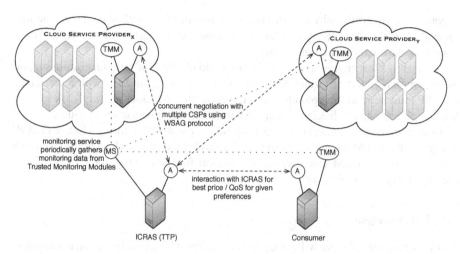

Fig. 1. ICRAS architecture with a consumer negotiating with two competing CSPs

for several reasons. First, based on current events or past experience, a consumer can predict increases or decreases in computing needs. For instance, online retailers receive more traffic leading up to the holidays. Second, a change in business needs can prompt an immediate reconfiguration of the resource requirements. For instance, a company decides to remove some legacy applications. Finally, a company's resource requirements can change due to developments in the market, such as increased competition or lower consumer demand.

To enable such changes, a consumer monitors the level of activity on his or her Cloud resources and informs the ICRAS agent if a threshold is crossed and a new configuration is necessary.

The consumer must also host a Trusted Monitoring Module (TMM) as described in Section 2.3. This module gives the ICRAS agent, acting as the de facto Trusted Third Party (TTP), access to relevant service metrics. The ICRAS agent can thus accurately assess the user experience of the service. Passive monitoring is supported by extending the TMM to include the necessary cryptographic protocols.

3.2   CSP

To enable participation in the ICRAS architecture, a CSP must offer a compatible interface that is accessed by the ICRAS agent. This interface must support two main functions: negotiation and migration. For negotiation, a CSP must generate SLA templates. For this, a CSP requires access to internal information of its Cloud. This includes real-time pricing data, Cloud utilization and system health (QoS) information, if available. On the basis of this information a CSP generates SLA templates describing the available resources. Due to the dynamic nature of CSP resource availability and pricing, these SLA templates are updated regularly.

Upon request, the SLA templates are delivered to the ICRAS agent. When the ICRAS agent makes an offer, the CSP enters a negotiation session. The strategy that drives this negotiation is determined by the CSP negotiation policy. This policy includes functions for evaluating an offer, threshold values for acceptance or rejection of an offer and rules governing the creation of counter-offers.

To support data migration to and from its Cloud, the CSP interface must support the import and export of virtual disk images. After creating an SLA with a consumer, the CSP must support the uploading and import of the consumer's virtual disk images. Likewise, these virtual disk images are exported and downloaded upon request.

To support monitoring, the CSP must also host a Trusted Monitoring Module (TMM) that gives the ICRAS agent access to relevant service metrics, such as network latency and so forth. The TMM can also include support for the cryptographic protocols required for passive monitoring.

3.3   ICRAS Agent

This paper assumes that an ICRAS agent is maintained by an independent, trusted third party (TTP). This service has no loyalty to any particular CSP and therefore can operate fully on behalf of participating consumers. The ICRAS agent has five major responsibilities: 1) discover CSP resource offerings, 2) evaluate these offerings, 3) negotiate an SLA with a CSP on behalf of a consumer, 4) monitor the provisioning of the new Cloud resources to detect SLA violations and 5) assist in migration to the new CSP.

Discovery. The process begins when an ICRAS agent receives a resource request from a consumer. The agent then queries all CSPs for one or more SLA templates describing their available resource offerings. This process is repeated at a regular interval to discover more appropriate configurations even after an SLA has been created. Depending on a consumer's preferences, he or she is notified if a new and better suitable configuration is discovered. The consumer is then given the option to renegotiate a new SLA.

Evaluation. Once received, the agent compares the CSP templates to the consumer's request. If a CSP cannot provide any of the requested resources, this CSP is removed from consideration. The remaining templates are then evaluated and ordered using the preferences of the consumer. For instance, if a consumer specifies that price is the most important attribute, the remaining templates are arranged by price. Depending on a consumer's requirements, templates from multiple CSPs can be selected for separate resource requirements. For instance, a consumer may allow processing and storage to be handled by two separate CSPs, if this meets the price and QoS needs.

Negotiation. Once the best template has been selected, the ICRAS agent contacts the responsible CSP to begin negotiations. If multiple templates from competing CSPs are considered to be acceptable, these CSPs are contacted for simultaneous negotiations. If a negotiation session results in an offer that is acceptable by both a CSP and the ICRAS agent (according to a consumer's request), this is sent to the consumer for final approval. If acceptable, the consumer contacts the CSP directly to create a micro-SLA. A micro-SLA is used so that a consumer can migrate to a new configuration or renegotiate the current configuration if the opportunity arises.

Migration. Once a consumer decides to migrate, the consumer services are migrated to the new CSP. In the most straightforward case, migration involves stopping the cloud instances at the current CSP, converting these instances (e.g. disk images) to the format used by the new CSP, transferring them to the new CSP and starting them again. The conversion process is not necessary if CSPs adopt the same industry standard, such as the Open Virtualization Format [19].

If services cannot be stopped during migration, live migration is required. Live migration of cloud instances can be possible if both CSPs are using the same virtualization layer [20]. However, the heterogeneity of current CSPs complicates the migration process.

Monitoring. The task of the ICRAS agent does not stop after an SLA has been created and a service is being used. The ICRAS agent also assumes the role of Trusted Third Party (TTP) and monitors the service to detect SLA violations by either party. Using TMMs at each party, the ICRAS agent periodically measures service performance at both the source (CSP) and end user. The ICRAS agent uses a dedicated Monitor Service (MS) to monitor the SLA for QoS violations, such as slow network response [16]. If a violation is detected, parties are notified so corrective action can be taken.

When using passive monitoring, the ICRAS agent acts as the mediator of any conflicts that occur. As mediator, the agent requests audit logs from all parties. These logs are then analyzed to determine which, if any, party has violated the SLA. The full mediation process is explained in detail in [17].

4   ICRAS Protocol

This section gives an example scenario to demonstrate the process of ICRAS mediated negotiation. This example involves two competing CSPs, a single ICRAS agent and a single consumer. Service requests, SLA templates and offers are presented in generic format rather than their official XML format.

Step 1. A consumer requires Cloud resources. A consumer specifies these needs using an SLA offer. This request is summarized in Figure 2. In this request, a consumer indicates that it needs 10 servers with CPU power between 1.5. and 3.0 GHz, at least 2 TB of storage and at least 1 GB of traffic. Furthermore, the consumer prefers the Windows OS, requires an availability of between 95 and 100 percent and a price below 1000 Euro. This resource request is sent to the CSP .

Step 2. The ICRAS agent receives the request of the consumer and queries all participating CSPs for their SLA templates.

Step 3. Each CSP receives the query and responds by sending SLA templates that describe the current resource offering to the ICRAS agent. If the templates have not yet been generated or are outdated, they are (re)generated at this point. The SLA template is generated following the WSAG specification. Example templates from two competing CSPs are shown in Figure 3. In these templates, each CSP displays the current resource offering.

Step 4. Upon receiving the templates, the ICRAS agent evaluates each template using the consumer's request. If a template cannot meet the requirements, it is immediately removed from consideration. In Figure 3, the template from CSP_x is removed because

```
                        RESOURCE REQUEST
            Num. of Servers = (10)
            CPU GHz         = (1.5 - 3.0) | CD:C1, VI:V1
            Storage  (GB)   = (2000 - *) | CD:D100, VI:V1
            Traffic (GB)    = (1 - *) | CD:D1, VI:V1
            Operating Sys.  = <Windows, Linux> | PC:YES
            Availability    = [95 - 100) | CD:C2, VI:V1
            Price (EUR)     = [0 - 1000) | CD:D2, VI:V1
```

Fig. 2. Consumer generated resource request

```
   SLA TEMPLATE CSPx                SLA TEMPLATE CSPy
Num. of Servers  = 100         Num. of Servers  = 50
CPU GHz          = 2.0         CPU GHz          = 3.0
Storage  (GB)    = 8000        Storage (GB)     = 4000
Traffic (GB)     = 1000        Traffic (GB)     = 500
Operating System = Linux       Operating System = {Windows OR Linux}
Availability (%) = 90          Availability (%) = 99
```

Fig. 3. SLA template from two competing CSPs

the availability offering is outside of the range specified by the consumer. In the case that more than one template remain after the first selection, the ICRAS agent evaluates them again to determine the most appropriate option. This evaluation is done by comparing key attributes, such as CPU or Availability.

Step 5. At this point, the ICRAS agent has selected the best matching CSP. The ICRAS agent generates an initial SLA offer, as shown in Figure 4. The ICRAS agent then contacts the selected CSP to begin negotiations. Following the WSAN specification, the negotiation consists of rounds of offers and counter-offers. If no mutually acceptable offer can be found, negotiation terminates and the ICRAS agent selects a different CSP. However, in the event that a mutually acceptable offer is found, this offer is sent on to the consumer.

Step 6. Once the consumer receives the offer, it re-evaluates the offering and, if acceptable, contacts the CSP directly to create a micro-SLA. After the SLA has been created, the service can be used.

Step 7. Upon successful creation of an SLA, the consumer migrates his or her services to the new CSP. This involves converting the virtual disk images to the format used by the new CSP and then transferring these images to the new CSP.

Step 8. Upon successful creation of an SLA, the ICRAS agent takes on the new task of monitoring the service on behalf of the consumer. Monitoring is done by periodically measuring key service metrics and storing the result. If a violation is detected (e.g. Availability is less than promised.), the consumer is notified and corrective action (e.g. fines, credits, and so forth) is taken. In addition to SLA monitoring, the ICRAS agent also periodically requests and evaluates SLA templates from all CSPs. If a new offering is more appropriate than the current one, the consumer is notified and migration can take place.

```
                    SLA OFFER
    Num. of Servers  = 10
    CPU GHz          = 3.0
    Storage  (GB)    = 3000
    Traffic (GB)     = 10
    Operating System = Windows
    Availability (%) = 99
    Price (EUR)      = 500
```

Fig. 4. ICRAS agent generated offer

5   Prototype Implementation

The ICRAS architecture is implemented using the AgentScape distributed middleware platform [21]. AgentScape is a distributed platform for mobile agents designed to be open, scalable, secure and fault-tolerant. This middleware provides mechanisms for SLA negotiation, inter-agent communication and migration. Software (Java) agents are used to represent the three major components: Consumer, ICRAS agent and CSP.

Two CSPs are chosen that fullfil the minimum standards of interoperability to support the example: Amazon Web Services[1] and CloudSigma[2]. On each of these CSPs a server instance is used to host a software agent running on AgentScape. Each agent uses their respective API to query price information and generate an SLA template describing each CSP's resource offerings.

An ICRAS agent runs on an instance of AgentScape on a local server. This agent collects templates from the agents running at each CSP. When the ICRAS agent has found the most suitable configuration, it is sent to the consumer agent, running on a separate instance of AgentScape on a separate local server. If a new CSP is chosen by the consumer, migration is assisted by the ICRAS agent. Virtual disk images are downloaded from the old CSP, converted to their target format using QEMU [22] and then uploaded to the new CSP.[3]

6   Related Works

Agent technology is being applied to the task of automated resource negotiation in many areas, including the area of Grid computing. Despite minor differences, Grid computing is an area that closely resembles Cloud computing in that both provide a paradigm of utility computing [23]. Tianfield uses agents to automate the task of resource negotiation in Grid computing [24]. As in the ICRAS architecture, agents are used to represent resource providers and brokers in a market. Agents apply a set of strategies to negotiate an agreement for resources. Agents are able to span multiple administrative domains to negotiate access to the necessary resources for a specific job. As with ICRAS, this

---

[1] http://aws.amazon.com/

[2] http://www.cloudsigma.com/

[3] Note that due to lack of standardization, a separate ad hoc solution for disk image migration is required for each unique pair of CSPs.

allows for the possibility that a single SLA includes resources from several different providers.

Sim proposes a similar architecture for automating negotiation of SLAs for Cloud resources [25]. Similar to ICRAS, this architecture supports multi-level, concurrent negotiation between multiple consumers, brokers and providers. A major difference between these two architectures and the approach used by ICRAS is the notion of time. These architectures negotiate per job, rather than per unit of time. Once an SLA is created, there is no way to dynamically respond to changes in price, utilization, and so forth. These architectures lack the benefits of micro-SLAs. There is also no impartial service to monitor the provisioning of resources according to the agreement.

Instead of agents, intelligent mapping of SLA templates is used in [26] to increase the success rate of matching Cloud service offerings to service requests. A set of public SLA templates is used as the basis of matching providers to consumers. Providers link their own template to the public template that most closely matches. The consumer then searches for a public template that matches his or her needs and contacts the related provider. To account for discrepancies between templates, users can add metadata that specifies mappings between their template and a public template. Furthermore, public templates slowly evolve to match market trends.

This approach aims to offer consumers an increased chance of finding the most appropriate resource configuration, but does not actively assist the consumer. There is no party that works on behalf of the consumer to navigate the large number of resource offerings and dynamic prices to find the most suitable CSP and negotiate an SLA. Moreover, the service migration and SLA monitoring process are left entirely to the consumer.

In contrast to the works described above, the ICRAS framework attempts to handle the entire lifecycle of a Cloud service, rather than only one or more pieces. ICRAS matching service offers to requests, such as [26] and negotiates agreements, such as [24] and [25]. In addition, ICRAS handles migration between CSPs and monitors agreements to detect possible violations.

7   Discussion

CSPs typically offer multiple interfaces to their Cloud resources, including a web interface for human access, as well as a scriptable, Application Programming Interface (API) for automated access. The API allows the consumer to purchase, launch, control and terminate Cloud resources. Furthermore, the API often gives the consumer access to pricing information. There are efforts to standardize the Cloud interface. Such efforts include the Eucalyptus [27] and OpenStack [28] open source APIs.

Another aspect that requires standardization is the data format used by clouds. CSPs use virtual disk images to encapsulate a consumer's data. These disk images use varying formats, including Amazon's AMI, Microsoft's VHD and VMWare's VMDK. If data is stored in one of these formats, there is no straightforward process to migrated to a different CSP using a different format. Each image must first be converted, following a sometimes slow and complex conversion process. While each format has its supporters, a standardized format can be used to increase the level of interoperability. The Open Virtualization Format [19] has been suggested for this purpose.

If widely adopted, these standards will make data and service migration between CSPs more straightforward. However, the main obstacle to their adoption is vendor lock-in [29]. CSPs have no incentive to make the process of service migration possible, let alone straightforward; therefore, migrating away from a CSP remains a difficult task. A consumer does not always have the option to export or download their virtual disk images from a CSP. This means, once a consumer has migrated to a particular CSP, the cost and hassle of leaving that CSP prohibits them from doing so, even if a better configuration is found at a different CSP. Note that complete state-full migration, i.e., where a snapshot of a running image is migrated and the state of the newly migrated image is updated, is still an open research question. The discussed solution would only preserve the state until the snapshot is made, so some state is lost (when the image is migrating).

Finally, wider adoption of dynamic pricing in Clouds is needed to allow users to react to changes in real market forces, including Cloud utilization. Some providers have begun offering dynamic pricing models to reflect the actual fluctuation of resource supply and demand. Dynamic pricing is beneficial to both consumers and providers of Cloud resources. Consumers can shift demand to cheaper time slots, such as evening or weekend processing, to save on costs. CSPs can take advantage of demand shifting to lower costs during peak periodes. For instance, a CSP can reduce the cost of cooling a data center at noon on a hot day by making it cheaper to use the data center at night.

Cloud computing was originally envisioned as a utility, similar to the electricity grid, where users can simply plug in to their computing needs. To enable this vision, more standardization and openness is required in the Cloud interface and data format.

The incompatibility of CSPs as discussed above greatly limits the ability to evaluate ICRAS. Preferably, an (exhaustive) evaluation would be performed to test and compare various metrics, such as migration delay, negotiation success rate and so forth. However, vendor lock-in of data formats prevents this. The scenario described in Section 5 uses two CSPs that are specifically chosen for their (limited) interoperability. However, even with these two carefully chosen CSPs, the experiment can only function in one direction. Migration is possible from CSP_1 to CSP_2 but not the other way around. CSPs must adopt open standards, as discussed above, before more extensive evaluation of ICRAS is possible.

8   Conclusions

As the Cloud continues to grow and attract users, the number of providers and Cloud resources increases. Consumers need new mechanisms to make the process of finding the most appropriate Cloud resource configuration as straightforward and automated as possible. There are many attributes that must be compared when choosing the right Cloud provider, including QoS, reputation and price.

The Intelligent Cloud Resource Allocation Service (ICRAS) gives Cloud consumers a straightforward interface to finding the most suitable Cloud resource configuration. This service compares all available offers and monitors the current price information. In addition, the service mediates the creation of micro-SLAs. Using micro-SLAs allows consumers to respond to changes in the market and renegotiated their services for lower prices or different providers. The ICRAS also monitors the service for any SLA violations.

ICRAS benefits the consumer by relieving them of the task of constantly monitoring all CSPs to find the lowest price. CSPs also benefit from ICRAS by gaining more market visibility. For instance, by participating with ICRAS, a small CSP can compete directly with larger, established CSPs, as consumers compare resource offerings independent of name recognition.

ICRAS also offers both parties the assurance that any SLA violations will be detected and reported. As an impartial party, ICRAS can monitor services without fear of bias. The passive monitoring techniques employed also generate a secure audit log that records all service messages. This log can be used to guarantee integrity and non-repudiation of these messages.

Future work will investigate the creation of complex SLAs. For instance, a consumer requires storage and compute power. One CSP offers the lowest price for storage, while another the lowest price for compute power. In this case, two separate SLAs are needed.

Additional CSP attributes will also be researched, including reputation and location. The geographical location of a CSP determines the laws that apply to the data [30].

Acknowledgements. This work is supported by the NLnet Foundation (www.nlnet.nl).

References

1. Clark, K.P., Warnier, M., Brazier, F.M.T.: An intelligent cloud resource allocation service - agent-based automated cloud resource allocation using micro-agreements. In: The Proceedings of the 2nd International Conference on Cloud Computing and Services Science, CLOSER 2012 (2012)
2. Armbrust, M., Fox, A., Griffith, R., Joseph, A., Katz, R., Konwinski, A., Lee, G., Patterson, D., Rabkin, A., Stoica, I., Zaharia, M.: A view of cloud computing. Communications of the ACM 53, 50–58 (2010)
3. Pueschel, T., Anandasivam, A., Buschek, S., Neumann, D.: Making Money With Clouds: Revenue Optimization Through Automated Policy Decisions. In: 17th European Conference on Information Systems (ECIS 2009), Verona, Italy, pp. 355–367 (2009)
4. Anandasivam, A., Premm, M.: Bid Price Control and Dynamic Pricing in Clouds. In: 17th European Conference on Information Systems (ECIS 2009), Verona, Italy, pp. 328–341 (2009)
5. Jennings, N., Faratin, P., Lomuscio, A., Parsons, S., Wooldridge, M., Sierra, C.: Automated negotiation: prospects, methods and challenges. Group Decision and Negotiation 10, 199–215 (2001)
6. Koritarov, V.: Real-world market representation with agents. IEEE Power and Energy Magazine 2, 39–46 (2004)
7. Jonker, C., Treur, J.: An Agent Architecture for Multi-Attribute Negotiation. In: International Joint Conference on Artificial Intelligence, vol. 17, pp. 1195–1201. Lawrence Erlbaum Associates LTD (2001)
8. Brazier, F., Cornelissen, F., Gustavsson, R., Jonker, C., Lindeberg, O., Polak, B., Treur, J.: A multi-agent system performing one-to-many negotiation for load balancing of electricity use. Electronic Commerce Research and Applications 1, 208–224 (2002)
9. Ouelhadj, D., Garibaldi, J., MacLaren, J., Sakellariou, R., Krishnakumar, K.: A Multi-agent Infrastructure and a Service Level Agreement Negotiation Protocol for Robust Scheduling in Grid Computing. In: Sloot, P.M.A., Hoekstra, A.G., Priol, T., Reinefeld, A., Bubak, M. (eds.) EGC 2005. LNCS, vol. 3470, pp. 651–660. Springer, Heidelberg (2005)

10. Agent Technology: Foundations, Applications, and Markets. In: Jennings, N., Wooldridge, M. (eds.) Applications of Intelligent Agents, pp. 3–28. Springer (1998)

11. Andrieux, A., Czajkowski, K., Dan, A., Keahey, K., Ludwig, H., Nakata, T., Pruyne, J., Rofrano, J., Tuecke, S., Xu, M.: Web Services Agreement Specification (WS-Agreement) GFD-R-P.107. Technical report, Global Grid Forum, Grid Resource Allocation Agreement Protocol (GRAAP) WG (2007)

12. Waldrich, O., Battre, D., Brazier, F.M.T., Clark, K.P., Oey, M.A., Papaspyrou, A., Wieder, P., Ziegler, W.: WS-Agreement Negotiation: Version 1.0 (GFD-R-P.193). Technical report, Open Grid Forum, Grid Resource Allocation Agreement Protocol (GRAAP) WG (2011)

13. Borenstein, S.: The long-run efficiency of real-time electricity pricing. The Energy Journal 26, 93–116 (2005)

14. Ludwig, H., Dan, A., Kearney, R.: Cremona: an architecture and library for creation and monitoring of WS-agreements. In: 2nd International Conference on Service Oriented Computing, pp. 65–74. ACM, New York (2004)

15. Quillinan, T.B., Clark, K.P., Warnier, M., Brazier, F.M.T., Rana, O.: Negotiation and monitoring of service level agreements. In: Wieder, P., Yahyapour, R., Ziegler, W. (eds.) Grids and Service-Oriented Architectures for Service Level Agreements. CoreGRID, pp. 167–176. Springer, New York (2010)

16. Clark, K.P., Warnier, M., Quillinan, T.B., Brazier, F.M.T.: Secure monitoring of service level agreements. In: IEEE Fifth International Conference on Availability, Reliability and Security (ARES 2010), pp. 454–461 (2010)

17. Khader, D., Padget, J., Warnier, M.: Reactive monitoring of service level agreements. In: Grids and Service-Oriented Architectures for Service Level Agreements, Core GRID, pp. 13–22. Springer (2010)

18. Clark, K., Warnier, M., Brazier, F.M.T.: Self-adaptive service monitoring. In: Bouchachia, A. (ed.) ICAIS 2011. LNCS (LNAI), vol. 6943, pp. 119–130. Springer, Heidelberg (2011)

19. Crosby, S., Doyle, R., Gering, M., Gionfriddo, M., et al.: Open virtualization format specification 1.1.0. Technical report, DSP0243, Distributed Management Task Force, Inc. (2010)

20. Clark, C., Fraser, K., Hand, S., Hansen, J.G., Jul, E., Limpach, C., Pratt, I., Warfield, A.: Live migration of virtual machines. In: Proceedings of the 2nd Conference on Symposium on Networked Systems Design & Implementation, NSDI 2005, vol. 2, pp. 273–286. USENIX Association (2005)

21. Overeinder, B., Brazier, F.: Scalable Middleware Environment for Agent-Based Internet Applications. Applied Parallel Computing. State of the Art in Scientific Computing 3732, 675–679 (2005)

22. Fabrice, B.: Qemu, a fast and portable dynamic translator. In: USENIX 2005 Annual Technical Conference, FREENIX Track, pp. 41–46 (2005)

23. Foster, I., Zhao, Y., Raicu, I., Lu, S.: Cloud computing and grid computing 360-degree compared. In: Grid Computing Environments Workshop, GCE 2008, pp. 1–10. IEEE (2008)

24. Tianfield, H.: Towards agent based grid resource management. In: IEEE International Symposium on Cluster Computing and the Grid, CCGrid 2005, vol. 1, pp. 590–597. IEEE (2005)

25. Sim, K.M.: Towards complex negotiation for cloud economy. In: Bellavista, P., Chang, R.-S., Chao, H.-C., Lin, S.-F., Sloot, P.M.A. (eds.) GPC 2010. LNCS, vol. 6104, pp. 395–406. Springer, Heidelberg (2010)

26. Breskovic, I., Maurer, M., Emeakaroha, V., Brandic, I., Altmann, J.: Towards autonomic market management in cloud computing infrastructures. In: International Conference on Cloud Computing and Services Science, CLOSER (2011)

27. Nurmi, D., Wolski, R., Grzegorczyk, C., Obertelli, G., Soman, S., Youseff, L., Zagorodnov, D.: The eucalyptus open-source cloud-computing system. In: 9th IEEE/ACM International Symposium on Cluster Computing and the Grid, CCGRID 2009, pp. 124–131. IEEE (2009)

28. OpenStack: Openstack: Open source software for building private and public clouds (2011), http://www.openstack.org
29. Weiss, A.: Computing in the clouds. NetWorker 11, 16–25 (2007)
30. Ruiter, J., Warnier, M.: 17. Computers, Privacy and Data Protection: an Element of Choice. In: Privacy Regulations for Cloud Computing, Compliance and Implementation in Theory and Practice, pp. 293–314. Springer (2011)

The IVI Cloud Computing Life Cycle

Gerard Conway[1] and Edward Curry[2]

[1] Innovation Value Institute, National University of Ireland, Maynooth, Ireland
[2] Digital Enterprise Research Institute, National University of Ireland, Galway, Ireland
gerard.conway@nuim.ie, ed.curry@deri.org

Abstract. Cloud computing has the promise of significant benefits that include reduced costs, improved service provisioning, and a move to a pay-per-use model. However, there also are many challenges to successfully delivering cloud-based services; including security, data ownership, interoperability, service maturity and return on investment. These challenges need to be understood and managed before attempting to take advantage of what the cloud has to offer. In this paper we introduce a nine-step cloud life cycle that can be used for both the migration and the ongoing management of public, cloud-based services. A consortium of organizations using an open-innovation approach developed the life cycle. This paper describes each step of the life cycle in terms of the key challenges faced, and the recommended activities, with resultant outputs, needed to overcome them.

Keywords: Cloud Computing, Project Management, Outsourcing, Life Cycle.

1 Introduction

The move to a cloud computing environment has started in earnest with the complete spectrum of businesses, from large multinationals to smaller organizations, moving their IT services to cloud computing platforms. There are many drivers for this, with reduced costs being the most commonly cited reason [1]. Cloud services may be provided in a pay-per-use model that allows companies to pay only for what they actually need, with the flexibility of increasing or reducing capacity in line with business demand. In effect, cloud computing offers the advantage of switching from a Capital Expense (CapEx) to an Operational Expense (OpEx) cost model that "charges back" the cost to the consumers of IT [8] whilst promising to deliver a reduced Total Cost of Ownership (TCO). Cloud computing also provides greater flexibility and agility as new applications and services can be deployed in less time [2].

A major driver of cloud computing is the pressure on IT departments to deliver more and enhanced services with reduced budgets, whilst responding to ever-increasing and ever-changing business requirements. Cloud computing is also seen as a way to free up IT resources to concentrate on core activities, by outsourcing non-core activities such as management of e-mail systems. An internal IT department running cloud-based services can focus its energy on services that offer core business value to the business, whilst letting the cloud service provider deal with the non-core services. While cloud computing promises significant benefits, there are many

I. Ivanov et al. (Eds.): CLOSER 2012, CCIS 367, pp. 183–199, 2013.

challenges to successfully delivering cloud-based services [3]. These challenges need to be understood and managed before attempting to take advantage of what the cloud has to offer. In this paper, a cloud life cycle approach is introduced and it is shown how such an approach can be used for both the migration and the ongoing management of public, cloud-based services.

2   Challenges with Managing Cloud Projects

Despite all of the claims made on behalf of cloud computing, it is not a panacea for all the problems faced by companies and their IT departments. Bitter experience has shown that if an IT department is struggling to deliver services, a move to cloud computing will either leave them in the same mess or potentially make if far worse. Before we delve into the key challenges to managing cloud projects, it is important to understand that cloud computing comes in four primary deployment models: public, community, private, and hybrid.

- **Public Cloud.** Public cloud infrastructure is owned by an organization selling cloud services to the general public or to a large industry group. Two examples are Amazon Web Services (AWS) and Microsoft Azure.
- **Community Cloud.** Community cloud infrastructure is shared by several organizations and supports a specific community that has a shared mission and shared goals, security requirements, policies, and compliance considerations. An example is Google Gov.
- **Private Cloud.** Private cloud infrastructure is owned or leased by a single organization and it is operated solely for that organization. Intel, Hewlett Packard (HP) and Microsoft have their own internal private clouds.
- **Hybrid Cloud.** Hybrid cloud infrastructure consists of two or more clouds (public, community, or private) that remain unique entities but are bound together by standardized or proprietary technology that enables data or application portability.

Within this work we have initially targeted the adoption challenges of migrating to a public cloud. There are a number of key challenges faced by companies that want to move to a public cloud as detailed in Table 1 [10].

In order to overcome these challenges, organizations need a systematic means of reviewing their business needs and weighing up the potential gains and opportunities against the risks, so that the transition to cloud computing is strategically planned and understood.

3   Defining the Life Cycle

In order to deliver the advantages and overcome the challenges faced by organizations that want to migrate to cloud computing, there is now a need to define a management framework for how a cloud migration project can be successfully managed. However, because the field is new and evolving, few guidelines and best practices are available To address this shortcoming, a consortium of leading organizations from industry, (including: Microsoft, Intel, SAP, Chevron, Cisco, The Boston Consulting Group,

Table 1. Chalanges of Cloud Computing Adoption

Risk Area	Description
Security [12] [13] [15]	**Physical and personnel security:** Access to physical machines and customer data may not be adequately controlled. Identity management: Access to information and computing resources may not be controlled. Application security: The applications available via the cloud, may not be secure
	Data Confidentiality: Indirect control of data leakage prevention and latent problems with security in a multi-tenant architecture
Availability / Business Continuity	The potential for downtime from either the cloud service provider or from the Internet.
Vendor/Data lock-in	Vendors use unique and proprietary user interfaces, application programming interfaces (API) and databases.
Software Licensing	Many licenses for packaged application software still restrict the physical machines on which the software can run
Lack of Standards	There is no standard open architecture defined for the cloud [4]. Each of the major cloud providers (Amazon Web Services, Salesforce's force.com, Google App Engine, and Microsoft Azure) impose architectures that are both different from each other, and from the common architectures currently used for enterprise applications.
Enterprise level: support, service maturity and functionality	Cloud computing services may not provide the levels of reliability, manageability, and support required by large enterprises. Today, many services are aimed primarily at Small and Medium Enterprises (SMEs) and at consumers, rather than large enterprises.
RoI	The expectation is that external cloud computing can reduce costs for large enterprises as well as SMEs. However, the cost advantages for large enterprises may not be as clear as for SMEs, since many large enterprises can reap the benefits of significant economies of scale in their own internal IT operations, or there is a lack of clarity on current IT consumption.
Connectivity	Cloud computing is impossible if you can't connect to the internet. A dead internet connection means no work, and in areas where internet connections are few or inherently unreliable, this could be a problem.
Compliance	How to ensure conform to local, regional and global, statutory and legal requirements.
Trust and Viability of service providers	How to assess the viability and trustworthiness of the cloud service providers.
Computing Performance	Latency Scalable Programming

Ernst & Young, and Fujitsu) the not-for-profit sector, and academia have developed and tested a life cycle for systematically managing cloud migration projects. This section outlines the design process for the cloud life cycle, how the cloud life cycle aligns with the IT-Capability Maturity Framework (IT-CMF), and why a life cycle approach was taken.

3.1   Design Medthdology

The Innovation Value Institute (IVI; http://ivi.nuim.ie) consortium uses an open innovation model of collaboration that engages academia and industry in scholarly work to amalgamate leading academic theory with the best of corporate experience – in order to advance practices for managing information technology for business value and innovation.

The development of the life cycle was undertaken using a design process with defined review stages and development activities that were based on the Design Science Research (DSR) guidelines advocated by Hevner [14]. The approach followed a similar design process used to develop a maturity model for Sustainable ICT [11] within the IT-CMF.

Within this work we have initially targetted the adoption challenges of migrating to a Public Cloud. This lead us to leverage the work by Cullen et al., 2005 [5] into the management of IT outsourcing projects using a life cycle. The Cullen life cycle is an in-depth piece of research on IT outsourcing that is backed up by many years of practical experience. We have adapted Cullen's work and applied the resulting life cycle to the problems of managing a public cloud migration and then running the cloud services on an ongoing basis. In particular, we examined the requirements of a public cloud project from both the life cycle and supply chain perspectives [17]

During the design process, researchers participated together with practitioners within research teams to research and develop the life cycle. The research team interviewed multiple cloud stakeholders to capture the views of key domain experts and to understand current practice and barriers to managing public cloud projects. The team widely consulted the relevant literature, both industrial and academic, on cloud computing. To validate the concepts and the material IVI conducted a series of workshops with three of its partners. Each partner used the IVI Cloud Life Cycle with 5 customers, where they tested and validated the material and the concepts. Each partner collated the feedback that was then jointly reviewed with IVI as a part of the workshop.

Once the life cycle was developed, it was validated within a number of organizations – with learning and feedback incorporated into subsequent versions. Cloud projects were studied within 11 organizations in order to validate the life cycle. These included organizations that had successfully delivered public cloud-based projects, and also organizations that have failed cloud projects. The research approach involved a qualitative approach to data collection. Empirical evidence was collected via semi-structured interviews with representatives of the 11 companies. From this perspective, the use of the interview was an appropriate research method, as it enabled depth, nuance and complexity in data to be captured [19].

3.2   The IT-Capability Maturity Framework

IVI has developed an IT Capability Maturity Framework (IT-CMF) that is an innovative and systematic framework, enabling CIOs/CEOs to understand and improve their organization's maturity and enable optimal business value realization from IT investments [9]. IT-CMF provides a high-level process capability maturity framework for managing the IT function within an organization to deliver greater value from IT by assessing and improving a broad range of management practices.

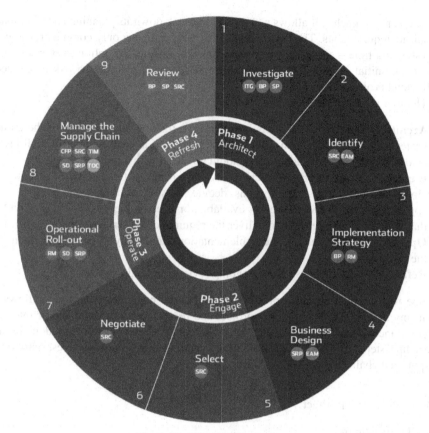

Fig. 1. The IVI Cloud Life Cycle

The framework identifies 33 critical IT processes and defines maturity models for each process. A core function of the IT-CMF is to act as an assessment tool and a management system to develop IT capabilities [6] and define the posture of the IT organization [7].

Within this work we utilize a combination of the life cycle approach and the use of IT-CMF to establish the key areas a customer must identify for it to ensure it has the required level of maturity before migrating to the cloud. The resulting cloud life cycle can be applied to both the migration and the ongoing management of public cloud services.

4   The IVI Cloud Life Cycle

The cloud life cycle is broken down into four phases that are further divided into 9 steps as illustrated in Figure 1. Each step prepares the way for the following step, so the sequence is important and must be followed for a successful outcome. The reason for such an approach is it allows a company to break down its planning and workload to suit its requirements. The basic premise is that a company only commits resources one step at a time – so, as each step is completed, there is the option to stop without losing the initial investment. This incremental approach reduces the risk associated with cloud projects.

The four stages of the cloud life cycle are:

- **Architect.** The first phase starts with the investigation and planning of the cloud project. Typically an organization will only commit a small number of high-level resources in order to decide if they should go ahead with a full-scale project.
- **Engage.** The second phase selects a service provider that can deliver the required cloud service. Many organizations decide to stop at this stage because the appropriate cloud services are not available, or because there is no cloud provider that they have confidence in to deliver the required cloud services.
- **Operate.** The third phase is the implementation and the day-to-day management of the cloud service.
- **Refresh.** The fourth phase is the ongoing review of cloud services.

In line with all well-managed projects, this structure maintains control and allows a company to stop at any step in the project and re-start when external and or internal circumstances allow, without losing the value and investment of the work done in the preceding steps. The following sections describe in detail the objectives, activities, outputs and challenges for the cloud life cycle.

4.1   Phase 1: Architect

Step 1: Investigate
This step provides an insight into and an understanding of what an organization wants to achieve by moving to the cloud, and what goals and expectations are to be met. This will be based on an analysis of the appropriate industrial segment, with insights from experts and experiences from peer organizations, together with knowledge of potential suppliers. The key challenges faced in the investigate step are:

- To satisfy new requirements within an existing or a reduced budget.
- To provide a clear cost-benefit analysis of cloud services using limited or no historical cost data.
- To clearly articulate the benefits of a move from CapEx to OpEx. This may need to consider the current CapEx investment of decommissioning existing services (depending on where the service is in its life cycle).
- Resistance by a perceived lack of financial control using the pay-as-you go model.
- The need for seed funding to investigate cloud options.

The critical capabilities used in the investigate step are IT Leadership and Governance (ITG), Strategic Planning (SP), and Business Planning (BP). The key activities and outputs of the investigate step are described in Table 2.

Table 2. Key Activities and Outputs for Step 1: Investigate

Activities	Outputs
• Determine the organization's IT objectives and its alignment with the business. • Determine what role cloud computing will play within the IT strategy. • Gather intelligence on cloud service offerings. • Validate with cloud subject matter experts.	• IT strategy for cloud computing. • Strategic intent of moving to the cloud and how it progresses the business objectives. • Intelligence document on cloud service offerings and providers. • Documented understanding of what will be achieved by comparing the strategic requirements with the available services and providers.

Within the organizations we studied it was clearly shown that having a clear vision and strategy of what can be achieved by moving to cloud computing was a distinct advantage [16]. Once the strategy and vision was clearly defined and communicated, it was a much easier task to see what services were available and what service providers could deliver. Organizations that lacked this vision experienced resistance – particularly from the user community, who were not active participants as they failed to see the strategic and financial benefits.

Step 2: Identify

Objectively assess what areas of the business are appropriate to outsource to the cloud and what impact this will have on the current delivery model. This will require an understanding of the current state, so that it can be compared to the desired future state. At a minimum, the impact on the service, people, cost, infrastructure, stakeholders and how the impact will be managed should be considered. The key challenges faced in the *identify* step are:

- To define the Enterprise Architecture. This can be particularly time-consuming if none is already in place.
- To objectively choose the appropriate service to outsource.
- To engage with both users and IT personnel who will be impacted, particularly if their job is being altered or removed.

The critical capabilities used in the identify step include Enterprise Architecture Management (EAM) and Sourcing (SRC). The key activities and outputs of the identify step are described in Table 3.

Table 3. Key Activities and Outputs for Step 2: Identify

Activities	Outputs
• Determine what services will be outsourced to the cloud, and consider impacts on the service, people, cost, infrastructure, and stakeholders. • Decide what type of cloud outsourcing model will be used, and why it is suitable. • Document the current and future states of the IT infrastructure.	• A List of services to be outsourced to the cloud, with documented understanding on impacts to service, people, cost, infrastructure, and stakeholders. • A Cloud outsourcing model, with documented justification. • Documented current and future states of the IT structure.

Choosing the correct service to outsource was influenced by the maturity of the service and the desired functionality. Organizations that successful migrated to the cloud: had a well-defined Enterprise Architecture, engaged both users and suppliers at an early stage, and recruited external expertise in areas not covered by internal resources. Organizations that attempted to correct problems with their existing services by simply moving them to the cloud, failed, as they just moved the problem to the new environment.

Step 3: Implementation Strategy

Define at a strategic level how the cloud services that are to be outsourced will be rolled out. This will document how key decisions will be made later on, by defining strategies on: staffing, communication, program roll-out, organizational rules, and risk assessment. The key challenges faced in the *implementation strategy* step are:

- To get the commitment and support to make key resources available.
- To clearly define business and technical requirements.
- To fully engage key stakeholders and users.
- To agree a formal decision–making / sign-off process with stakeholders.

The critical capabilities used in the *implementation strategy* step are Business Planning (BP) and Risk Management (RM). The key activities and outputs of the *implementation strategy* step are described in Table 4.

Table 4. Key Activities and Outputs for Step 3: Implementation Strategy

Activities	Outputs
<ul><li>Determine the roll-out approach and how the program will be managed.</li><li>Detail how the program will be staffed and reported.</li><li>Decide how cloud suppliers will be engaged, selected and managed.</li><li>Determine how risks will be assessed and managed, including data recovery and in-sourcing.</li></ul>	<ul><li>A program roll-out strategy.</li><li>A Communication strategy.</li><li>A strategy to manage staff impacted by the migration to cloud.</li><li>A Cloud risk management strategy.</li><li>A Cloud supplier management strategy.</li></ul>

One of the key findings of our research was that organizations that wanted to move to the cloud needed to fully understand the impact of the migration on the user community, and on IT support staff. Those organizations that did not understand this impact and that failed to plan accordingly either lost key resources or experienced resistance from the IT and user community – both during and after the migration.

Step 4: Business Design

Design what is to be outsourced to the cloud and what the future state will look like. This will detail the new service, how it will be managed, how it interfaces to the existing / remaining systems, and how it will be monitored and reported. To provide requirements with sufficient detail to have a meaningful conversation with suppliers so that they can be objectively compared, based on cost and quality of service. The key challenges faced in the *business design* step are:

- To provide a clear definition of the existing and desired interfaces.
- To clearly define what is negotiable / non-negotiable.
- To engage and build a relationship with the stakeholders that is based on trust.

The critical capabilities used in the business design step are Enterprise Architecture (EAM) and Service Provisioning (SRP). The key activities and outputs of the business design step are described in Table 5.

Table 5. Key Activities and Outputs for Step 4: Business Design

Activities	Outputs
• Detail the service offering you wish to tender for. • Clearly define negotiable / non-negotiable issues around contracts, service-level agreements (SLA), and pricing model	• Detailed and clear tender documents for cloud suppliers.

The research demonstrated that organizations that developed clear and concise tender documentation had improved discussions with suppliers without placing undue limitations and constraints on what could be provided. Conversely, those organizations that had poorly-defined requirements spent a lot of time in discussions with suppliers and were driven by the supplier's agenda.

4.2   Phase 2: Engage

Step 5: Select
Based on the requirements and the other criteria defined by the Architect phase this step will *select* the best supplier based on value, sustainability, and quality. The key challenges faced in the *selection* step are:

- In a lot of cases it was found that the cloud supplier provided the Contract, Service Level Agreement (SLA) and pricing as a standard offering. The challenge was to ensure all business and user requirements were still satisfied.
- To balance requirements between what functionality is available now, with what will be available in the future.
- To retain objectivity and do a thorough background check on all suppliers.
- To have a back-out / alternatives strategy if things change or go wrong.
- To retain the overall strategic intent and core requirements; that is, do not compromise to get a particular service up and running.

The critical capability used in the select step is Sourcing (SRC). The key activities and outputs of the *select* step are described in Table 6.

Table 6. Key Activities and Outputs for Step 5: Selection

Activities	Outputs
• Define the tender/bid process. • Select and staff an evaluation team. • Invite bids/tenders. • Evaluate suppliers against the defined criteria. • Shortlist the supplier(s). • Carry out due diligence.	• A tender process. • Evaluation criteria. • A shortlist of suitable suppliers with caveats. • A Due diligence report.

The organizations that were successful were characterized by:

- Only accepting solutions that had the required functionality.
- The active involvement of the user community via surveys and by validation of the proposed solution.
- Choosing suppliers that were prepared to work and resolve issues prior to the migration.

Organizations that compromised by accepting partial functionality with the promise of enhanced functionality at a later stage, or that skipped proper validation to meet deadlines, ended up with problems that led to failure of the cloud services, or were very expensive to rectify.

Step 6: Negotiate

This step is to complete the final negotiation, pick the preferred supplier, get internal approval and sign the contract(s). The key challenges faced in the *negotiate* step are:

- To maintain control and objectivity by resisting any major last-minute changes in order to achieve sign-off; in other words be prepared to walk away.
- To have clearly defined and agreed contingency plans for disaster and change scenarios.
- To understand the cloud supplier get-out clauses and to make sure there is enough time to move cloud services in-house, or to an alternative cloud supplier.

The critical capability used in the negotiate step is Sourcing (SRC). The key activities and outputs of the *negotiate* step are described in Table 7.

Table 7. Key Activities and Outputs for Step 6: Negotiate

Activities	Outputs
• Define the negotiation strategy. • Select and staff the negotiation team. • Carry out negotiations. • Select the preferred cloud supplier. • Get internal approvals and sign the contract.	• A negotiation strategy. • Results of the negotiation. • Signed final documents: Contract, SLA and Pricing document.

Our research showed significant variations in the attitude of cloud suppliers to accommodate client requirements. Some suppliers would only offer their default service offering and standard SLA, while other cloud suppliers invested significant time and effort to ensure they delivered on all major requirements. Those organizations that had invested time in the earlier steps of the life cycle, particularly the engagement of users, had a smooth sign-off with no major problems.

Problems were found with a number of organizations when they treated this final step as a rubber-stamping exercise. One example showed that although the preceding step highlighted issues around due diligence, the promise of a cost reduction resulted in a binding contract being signed. As a result, major problems occurred during implementation that lead to a contractual dispute with the supplier.

4.3   Phase 3: Operate

Step 7: Operational Roll-out

To put together a project team that will manage the transition of the agreed services to the new cloud service. This will require the transition of the service itself, the management of staff impacted, communication to all stakeholders, knowledge retention / transition, and acceptance sign-off. The key challenges faced in the *operational roll-out* step are:

- To keep to the desired timelines, particularly for dates that cannot be changed.
- To get access to appropriate case studies of previous successful roll-outs of similar services.
- To resist the temptation to compromise on quality in order to maintain the schedule.
- To get formal user and technical sign-off.

The critical capabilities used in the *operational roll-out* step are Service Provisioning (SRP), Solution Delivery (SD), and Risk Management (RM). The key activities and outputs of the *operational roll-out* step are described in Table 8.

Table 8. Key Activities and Outputs for Step 7: Operational Roll-out

Activities	Outputs
• Finalize and publish transition plans.	• A roll-out plan.
• Select and staff the transition team.	• Progress updates.
• Agree and publish acceptance criteria.	• A signed acceptance document.
• Carry out the transition.	
• Communicate progress.	
• Conduct knowledge transfer.	
• Manage staff (directly and indirectly) impacted.	

The research has shown that many of the organizations had a very smooth transition due to: good planning, the full engagement of users, and a strong partnership with the supplier. The research highlighted that using a phased approach that allowed the option to roll back to an in-house version at any stage significantly reduced the risk and exposure to the business. Organizations that experienced difficulties in the transition to cloud computing missed vital steps in their planning. Examples included: not having the system validated and tested by end users, or reducing the time required for testing to meet deadlines.

Step 8: Manage the Supply Chain

It is important to manage the new cloud service as efficiently and effectively as possible. The organization will need to adapt to the new setup, particularly at IT management level – because rather than directly managing internal resources, the requirement will be to manage the cloud supplier and in particular the supplier relationship. This will require effective monitoring and control so that issue, variations and disputes can be resolved to the satisfaction of both parties. The key challenges faced in the *manage the supply chain* step are:

- The integration of the cloud service with existing support and reporting structures.
- That IT management make a smooth transition from managing their own internal staff to managing the cloud supplier and the interfaces.
- The control, communication and coordination of internal and external changes.

The critical capabilities used in the *manage the supply chain* step include Capacity Forecasting and Planning (CFP), Sourcing (SRC), Technical Infrastructure Management (TIM), Solution Delivery (SD), Service Provisioning (SRP), and Total Cost of Ownership (TCO). The key activities and outputs are described in Table 9.

Table 9. Key Activities and Outputs for Step 8 Manage the Supply Chain

Activities	Outputs
• Manage and report at cloud service operational level. • Capture and manage issues, variations and disputes. • Manage the supplier relationship. • Change management. • Continuous improvement. • Assess and validate how the cloud service is performing.	• Day-to-day cloud service performance metrics. • Status on issues, problems, variations, and disputes. • Supplier meeting minutes. • A change management report. • Audit reports.

Building a relationship with the cloud supplier was the key to success in many of the projects we studied. Some companies have gone further and built a strategic partnership with their suppliers, which further increased their success. The research highlighted that the risk to the business can be significantly reduced if you retain the flexibility to move the service back in-house or to an alternative supplier within an agreed notice period.

Where problems arose, they were mainly around the management of the supplier. There were examples where the supplier did not deliver as per the signed agreement and in one instance the supplier went out of business, highlighting the need for adequate risk assessment and mitigation.

4.4   Phase 4: Refresh

Step 9: Review

To review the cloud service requirements based on: the cloud service itself, other changes within the business, changes within the supplier organization, or the need to change the supplier. The key challenges faced in the *review* step are:

- To prioritise and get approval to start a new cloud service project cycle.

The critical capabilities used in the review step are Strategic Planning (SP), Business Planning (BP), and Sourcing (SRC). The key activities and outputs of the *review* step are described in Table 10.

Table 10. Key Activities and Outputs for Step 9: Review

Activities	Outputs
• Gather intelligence on the relevant market segment, cloud service technology trends, and supplier offerings. • Audit cloud supplier performance and compare to alternatives. • Understand and assess how other changes in the organization impact on the existing cloud service arrangement. • Based on the above inputs, regularly reassess and review requirements. • Make and present a business case for any significant change to the current cloud service arrangement in order to get approval to start a new cycle.	• An intelligence report for next generation cloud service offerings. • Cloud supplier audit results. • A business case for any proposed changes.

Some of the organizations researched had a clear vision of the future that provided them with an understanding of how cloud service offerings could be enhanced by the use of common standards, the use of cloud brokers and a standard integrated architecture. Other organizations struggled to integrate their services due to vendor lock-in and not investing sufficient resources with the correct skills to decide what was needed for the future. In one instance it was found that cloud services were being purchased without any central control, leading to a mixture of solutions that was very difficult to integrate.

5   The Life Cycle in Action

The cloud life cycle applies proven and documented project management principles that are known by most IT and business managers. It breaks down the project into discrete manageable stages that allows the company to gather the correct information to make a decision before moving to the next stage. The life cycle ensures appropriate pre-planning so that the correct partners are chosen and that the impacts on the business are properly understood, managed, and controlled. For example it allows a company to identify the correct services to move to the cloud and to create plans for the impact on staff directly and indirectly impacted. It also provides a mechanism of building up a repository of knowledge and best practices to fill the current void created by this new use of technology, with its lack of standards and best practice.

The steps in the Cloud Life-Cycle were surveyed to determine their importance. The results from the 11 companies who participated are show in the following table.

Table 11. Survey Results: Importance of each Life Cycle stage

Architect	**Step 1. Investigate**	
	1. Determine the organisations IT objectives and its alignment with the business	4.5
	2. Determine what role cloud computing will play within the IT Strategy	4.6
	3. Gather intelligence on cloud service offerings	4.3
	4. Validate results with cloud subject matter experts and peer organisations	4.2
	Step 2. Identify	
	5. Determine what services will be outsourced to the cloud, consider impacts on the service, people, cost, infrastructure, and stakeholders.	4.7
	6. Decide what type of cloud outsourcing model will be used, and why it is suitable.	4.6
	7. Document the current and future states of the IT infrastructure.	4.8
	Step 2. Implementation Strategy	
	8. Determine the roll out approach and how the program will be managed.	4.5
	9. Detail how the program will be staffed and reported.	4.6
	10. Decide how cloud suppliers will be engaged, selected and managed.	4.4
	11. Determine how risks will be assessed and managed, including security, data recovery and in-sourcing.	4.7
	Step 3. Business Design	
	12. Detail the service offering for tender	4.4
	13. Clearly define negotiable / non-negotiable issues around: contracts, service-level agreements (SLA), and pricing model	4.5
Engage	**Step 4. Selection**	
	14. Define the tender/bid process.	4.7
	15. Select and staff an evaluation team.	4.4
	16. Invite bids/tenders.	4.4
	17. Evaluate suppliers against the defined criteria.	4.5
	18. Short list the supplier(s).	4.6
	19. Carry out due diligence.	4.6
	Step 5. Negotiate and sign-off	
	20. Define the negotiation strategy.	4.6
	21. Select and staff the negotiation team.	4.7
	22. Carry out negotiations.	4.5
	23. Select the preferred cloud supplier.	4.6
	24. Get internal approvals and sign the contact.	4.7

Table 11. (*continued*)

Operate	**Step 6. Operational roll-out**	
	25. Finalise and publish transition plans.	4.4
	26. Select and staff the transition team.	4.2
	27. Agree and publish acceptance criteria.	4.4
	28. Carry out the transition.	4.5
	29. Communicate progress.	4.6
	30. Carry out knowledge transfer.	4.4
	31. Manage staff (directly and indirectly) impacted.	4.6
	Step 7. Management	
	32. Manage and report on cloud service operations.	4.4
	33. Capture and manage issues, variations and disputes.	4.7
	34. Manage the supplier relationship.	4.5
	35. Change management.	4.6
	36. Continuous improvement.	4.6
	37. Assess and validate how the cloud service is performing.	4.5
Regenerate	**Step 8. Review**	
	38. Gather intelligence in your relevant market segment for cloud service technology trends and supplier offerings.	4.5
	39. Audit cloud supplier performance and compare to alternatives.	4.5
	40. Understand and assess how other changes in the organization impact on the existing cloud service arrangement.	4.5
	41. Make and present a business case for any significant change to the current cloud service arrangement to get approval to start a new cycle.	4.6

5.1 Case Study: Mainstream Renewable Power

Mainstream's IT organization already enjoyed a strong relationship with the business and cloud computing was considered to be an integral part of their business strategy. Using the IVI Cloud Life-Cycle highlighted the key areas where IT and the business differed in their perceptions and understanding of the benefits of the public cloud. Mainstream's business executives had a more positive view of the public cloud than their IT colleagues. The assessment results confirmed that Mainstream's cloud computing strategy already provided their initial objective of a 'single version of the truth', and that the next phase was a business-led move to the public cloud on terms agreed by all stakeholders.

'The end vision is to completely outsource using a sustainable supplier to provide resilient and secure services that are managed externally using a subscription model' John Shaw, CIO, IVI Summer conference 2011.

Previous IT strategy had delivered a secure private cloud; consequently Mainstream's executives decided to move to the public cloud. However, as cloud computing can be overhyped, it was vitally important to set realistic expectations and clarify risks. The Life Cycle assessment results delivered a strong mandate to move to the public cloud. More importantly, the assessment enabled Mainstream to convert this ambition into a complete cloud computing roadmap with supporting cost-benefit analysis.

6   Conclusions

The use of a cloud life cycle has been shown to be a very good mechanism for organizations to control and manage not only their migration but also the ongoing, day-to-day management of their public cloud environment. The research for each of the nine steps described above clearly demonstrates the value of using a cloud life cycle to control and manage the move to cloud. The cloud life cycle provides an organization with a management structure to assess the following:

- The readiness/maturity of an organization to move to the public cloud.
- How the organisation is managing the new environment on a day-to-day basis after it is migrated.
- What new services can be moved to a public cloud environment.

Acknowledgements. The work presented in this paper has been funded by Science Foundation Ireland under Grant No. SFI/08/CE/I1380 (Lion-2) and by Enterprise Ireland under Grant CC/2009/0801.

References

1. Harms, R., Yamartino, M.: The Economics of the Cloud. Microsoft (November 2010)
2. Armbrust, B., Griffith, R., Joseph, A.D., Katz, R., Konwinski, A., Lee, G., Patterson, D., et al.: A view of cloud computing. Communications of the ACM 53(4), 50–58 (2010)
3. Brooks, C.: Heroku learns the hard way from Amazon EC2 outage. SearchCloud-Computing.com (2010)
4. Buyya, R., Yeo, C.S., Venugopal, S., Broberg, J., Brandic, I.: Cloud computing and emerging IT platforms: Vision, hype, and reality for delivering computing as the 5th utility. Future Generation Computer Systems 25(6), 599–616 (2009)
5. Cullen, S., Seddon, P., Wilcox, L.: Managing Outsourcing, The Life Cycle Imperative. MIS Quarterly Executive, 229–256 (2005)
6. Curry, E., Guyon, B., Sheridan, C., Donnellan, B.: Developing an Sustainable IT Capability: Lessons From Intel's Journey. MIS Quarterly Executive 11:2, 61–74 (2012a)
7. Curry, E., Guyon, B., Sheridan, C., Donnellan, B.: Sustainable IT: Challenges, Postures, and Outcomes. IEEE Computer 45:11, 79–81 (2012)
8. Curry, E., Hasan, S., White, M., Melvin, H.: An Environmental Chargeback for Data Center and Cloud Computing Consumers. In: Huusko, J., de Meer, H., Klingert, S., Somov, A. (eds.) E2DC 2012. LNCS, vol. 7396, pp. 117–128. Springer, Heidelberg (2012)
9. Curley, M.: Managing Information Technology for Business Value: Practical Strategies for IT and Business Managers. Intel Press (2004)
10. Dillon, T., Wu, C., Chang, E.: Cloud Computing: Issues and Challenges. In: 2010 24th IEEE International Conference on Advanced Information Networking and Applications (AINA), pp. 27–33 (2010)
11. Donnellan, B., Sheridan, C., Curry, E.: A Capability Maturity Framework for Sustainable Information and Communication Technology. IEEE IT Professional 13(1), 33–40 (2011)
12. Grossman, R.L.: The Case for Cloud Computing. IT Professional 11(2), 23–27 (2009)
13. Heiser, J., Nicolett, M.: Assessing the Security Risks of Cloud Computing, Gartner (2008)

14. Hevner, A.R., March, S.T., Park, J., Ram, S.: Design Science in Information Systems Research. MIS Quarterly 28(1), 75–105 (2004)
15. Kaufman, L.M.: Data Security in the World of Cloud Computing. IEEE Security and Privacy 7(4), 61–64 (2009)
16. Li, H., Sedayao, J., Hahn-Steichen, J., Jimison, E., Spence, C., Chahal, S.: Developing an Enterprise Cloud Computing Strategy. Intel White Paper (2009)
17. Lindner, M.A., McDonald, F., Conway, G., Curry, E.: Understanding Cloud Requirements – A Supply Chain Life Cycle Approach. In: Second International Conference on Cloud Computing, GRIDs, and Virtualization (Cloud Computing 2011), pp. 20–25. IARIA, Rome (2011)
18. Mason, J.: Qualitative Researching. Sage Press, London (2002)

Performance Assessment of Web Services in the STEP Framework

Miguel L. Pardal, Joana P. Pardal, and José Alves Marques

Department of Computer Science and Engineering
Instituto Superior Técnico, Technical University of Lisbon
Av. Rovisco Pais 1, 1049-001 Lisboa, Portugal
{miguel.pardal,joana.paulo.pardal}@ist.utl.pt,
jose.marques@link.pt

Abstract. This chapter presents a performance study of the STEP Framework, an open-source application framework implemented on the Java platform that uses many popular open-source libraries, including: Hibernate, JAX-WS, and Log4J. This framework has been used for several years to teach development of distributed enterprise applications to undergrad students. This chapter also describes the performance measurements over a flight reservation web service that is included as an example in the source code distribution. It presents an assessment of the web service and shows how the performance of this specific application was studied in detail. The achieved results are put in context and compared with other technologies, highlighting the existing trade-offs.

Keywords: Web Services, Performance, Measurement.

1   Introduction

Enterprise applications have many demanding requirements [1], and some of the most important are related to *performance*. Performance analysis is a challenge [2] [3], that can be especially hard for inexperienced developers. To verify if an implementation is performing as expected, run-time data must be collected and analyzed. This data can be used to compare design and configuration alternatives. However, collecting such data in the application requires many modifications to the original source code.

The *Simple, Extensible, and for Teaching Purposes (STEP) Framework*[1] [4] is an open-source application framework. Its source code is intended to be small and simple enough to allow any developer to read and understand it thoroughly. The goal is to learn how the architectural layers are implemented in practice and to be able to change small details that are usually hidden in professional frameworks. This is especially important for students. The collected metrics allow them to better understand the existing trade-offs of alternative approaches. In fact, this framework has been used for several years in 'Software Engineering' and 'Distributed Systems' courses lectured at Instituto Superior Técnico (IST), Technical University of Lisbon, to teach Computer Science and Engineering undergrad students how to develop Web Services with enterprise-like requirements.

---

[1] http://stepframework.sourceforge.net/

I. Ivanov et al. (Eds.): CLOSER 2012, CCIS 367, pp. 200–214, 2013.
© Springer International Publishing Switzerland 2013

Before the improvements we describe here, the STEP framework did not provide means to collect run-time data for later analysis. With this work the framework was extended with monitoring and analysis tools that enable developers to collect actual performance data and to use it to study how different decisions impact the overall performance.

What follows is a brief overview of the STEP framework architecture, followed by the description of a *performance assessment study*, detailing the new added tools and the results of the conducted experiments over a flight reservation web service that is available in the distribution.

2 STEP Framework Overview

The STEP Framework is a multi-layer, Java-based, enterprise-like application framework. It can be used to develop Servlet/JSP Web Applications and Web Services.

2.1 Architecture

The STEP Framework defines a typical layered architecture [1]. The main layers are *Domain* and *Service*. There are also *Persistence*, *View*, *Presentation* and *Web Service* layers. Each layer considers different implementation concerns.

The *Domain* layer is where an object-oriented solution for the requirements is implemented. Domain objects are persisted to a database using object-relational mapping through the Hibernate[2] library and its annotations.

The *Service* layer provides access to the application's functionalities through service objects, that access the domain objects, isolating them from upper layers, and managing transactions to ensure atomic, consistent, isolated, and durable (ACID) persistence.

The *View* layer provides Data Transfer Objects (DTO) that are used as input and output for service objects and uses JAX-B[3] technology.

The *Presentation* layer is responsible for user interaction through a Web interface, implemented with servlets and Java Server Pages (JSP). It uses Stripes[4] but there are also STEP variants using Struts[5] and the Google Web Toolkit[6].

There is a *Web Services* (WS) layer that provides remote access to services, using JAX-WS[7] technology.

STEP supports *Extensions* [5][4], a mechanism for intercepting the Service and Web Service layers that simplifies the implementation of cross-cutting concerns. Extensions proved very useful for implementing the performance monitors described later in the chapter.

A STEP development branch, called SmartSTEP [6] supports WS-Policy-like automatic configuration of Extensions to provide security, reliable messaging, logging, etc; as required by parties communicating with WS.

---

[2] http://www.hibernate.org/
[3] https://jaxb.dev.java.net/
[4] http://www.stripesframework.org/
[5] http://struts.apache.org/
[6] https://developers.google.com/web-toolkit/
[7] https://jax-ws.dev.java.net/

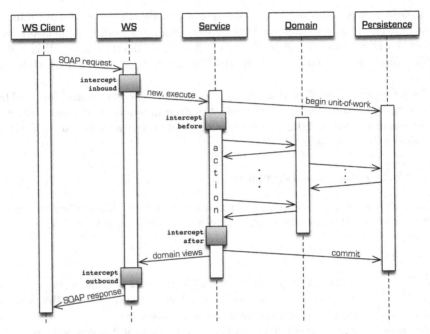

Fig. 1. Sequence diagram of a STEP Web Service invocation

2.2   Request Processing

The processing sequence of a request for a STEP Web Service is shown in Figure 1. A request begins in the client application (*WS Client*) that sends a SOAP envelope in an HTTP request to the server (*WS*). The application container at the server assigns a thread to execute the request from start to finish. The HTTP request is interpreted and dispatched to an instance of the JAX-WS servlet. The *WS* layer parses the SOAP envelope. The payload is deserialized from XML to Java objects using JAX-B.

The *Service* layer receives the view objects, starts an implicit database transaction, and invokes one or more domain objects. The *Domain* layer implements business logic using entity and relationship objects. The *Persistence* layer maps entities and relationships to database tables and vice-versa. SQL queries are generated and executed automatically by Hibernate. When the application-specific logic is complete, and if no error is reported, the *Service* layer commits the database transaction. Otherwise, the transaction is aborted and an error is returned. The resulting views (either the required results or the error message) are created and returned to the *WS* layer. The response payload is serialized from Java objects to XML. The JAX-WS servlet sends the SOAP envelope back to the client in the HTTP response. The request thread is typically returned to a thread pool, for later reuse. Several requests can be executed in parallel.

3   Performance Tools

The goal of the performance assessment tools is to breakdown the overall processing time, to identify the parts of the application that are worth improving.

Performance measurement tools can be classified as tracers and profilers [2]. A tracer [7] is a component that intercepts application code to record typed time-stamped events. Examples of tracing tools include libraries like Perf4J[8]. A profiler [8] is a program that monitors an application to determine the frequency of execution in specific code regions. A profiler can operate using sampling (application is interrupted periodically and measurements are taken), hardware counters (processor stores application performance data), or instrumentation (application source or binary code is augmented). Overall, sampling is faster but less accurate. There are several profiling tools available that combine the approaches mentioned above, like JProfiler[9] and YourKit[10]. Tracer are more lightweight than profilers because the latter require more complex interactions with applications [9]. Also, profilers are usually harder to use for server-side applications that have to handle multiple concurrent requests.

3.1 Our Approach

The performance tools for the STEP Framework follow the tracer approach. The goal was to collect run-time data, to analyze it, and to test performance improvement hypotheses. The main metric used was *request processing time* to measure (and improve) responsiveness.

The performance of Java programs is affected by application, inputs, virtual machine, garbage collector, heap size, and underlying operating system. All these factors produce random errors in measurements that are unpredictable, non-deterministic, and unbiased [10]. To quantify the random errors in measurements, the program runs had to be repeated several times. The presented values are the *mean* of the samples with a confidence interval (margin of error) computed with a confidence level of 90%, 95%, or 99%. At least 30 runs were executed for each program variation, so that the calculation of the confidence level could assume a normal distribution of the samples, according to the Central Limit Theorem [11]. Only changes in values greater than the error margin were considered statistically relevant and not the effect of random errors.

The performance analysis process encompasses all activities necessary to generate, collect, and analyze performance-related data. Figure 2 presents the data-flow diagram of our approach. Each activity is performed by a specific tool: *Domain Data Generator, Load Generator, Load Executor, Monitor, Analyzer,* and *Report Generator.*

The *Domain Data Generator* tool populates the database with realistic data, both in values and in size. The data population was realized using Groovy[11] scripts that parsed data files with domain descriptions and accessed the database to insert them.

The *Load Generator* tool produces files with serialized request objects, following templates for normal and error situations, creating loads that can be reproduced later.

The *Load Executor* tool was programmed to send requests. The script opens an object stream, reads request objects from it, and executes the operations: think (wait), search

---

[8] http://perf4j.codehaus.org/
[9] http://www.ej-technologies.com/products/
jprofiler/overview.html
[10] http://www.yourkit.com/
[11] http://groovy.codehaus.org/

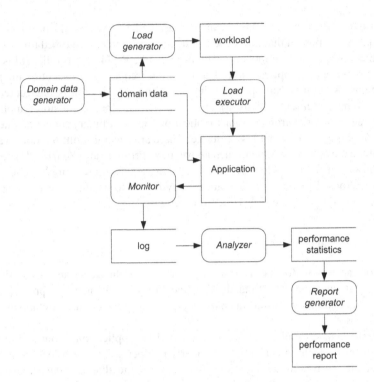

Fig. 2. Performance tool chain data flow diagram

flights, create single reservation, and create multiple reservations. The requests are sent to the specified WS endpoint. If an error is caught, the output message is logged, and the processing continues. This tool uses a thread pool of fixed size implemented with the java.util.concurrent package to run simultaneous virtual users and there is one thread for each simulated user.

The *Monitor* is the core component of performance analysis. When enabled, it collects request processing times for each architectural layer. It intercepts request processing at relevant interception points (represented in Figure 1, using grey boxes at the WS, Service and Persistence layers). Each specific interception point inserts measurement code. STEP extensions are used to intercept both the Service and the WS layers.

The *Analyzer* takes all samples of execution data resulting from multiple runs using the same settings, and computes sample statistics. A complete records file is summarized in a single row. For each numeric field, the mean, standard deviation, upper quartile, median, and lower quartile are computed. Finally, the overall statistics are computed. A similar procedure is applied to the virtual user output logs to produce error statistics from the WS client perspective that is the most relevant one for quality of service purposes.

Finally, the *Report Generator* uses the statistical data produced by the Analyzer and uses it to produce custom reports. For a more in-depth description of these tools, see our paper on the topic[12].

4 Experiments

Several experiments were conducted using the performance analysis tool chain, to identify performance problems and to propose solutions. The results are presented and discussed in this section.

4.1 Scenario System

The analyzed system was the *"Flight reservation Web Service"* (Flight WS) that is one of the example applications included in the STEP Framework source code distribution.

The initial Flight WS had only one operation: "create low price reservation". The following additional operations were developed: "search flights", "create single reservation", and "create multiple reservations". The reason for adding new operations was to allow more diverse kinds of requests using the most common data types (text, numeric, date, currency, and collections) and with different message sizes.

With the new operations it became possible to instantiate all the message archetypes defined in the JWSPerf Web Service benchmark [13], making Flight WS a typical Web Service. To a limited degree, conclusions made using Flight WS can be extrapolated to other WS with similar software architecture and user loads.

4.2 Hardware and Software Platform

The following machines and networks were used for the test runs.

Machine A with a Quad-core[12] CPU running at 2.50 GHz, 3.25 GB of usable RAM, and 1 TiB hard disk. It ran 32-bit Windows 7 (version 6.1.7600), MySQL 5.1.43, Java Developer Kit 1.6.0_18, Groovy 1.7.3, Apache Tomcat 6.0.14 and STEP 1.3.3 (includes Hibernate 3.3.2.GA, JAX-B 2.1.10, JAX-WS 2.1.7, Stripes 1.5.1).

Machine B with a Dual-core[13] CPU running at 2.53 GHz, 3 GB of RAM, and 500 GiB of hard disk storage. It ran the same software.

The machines were connected either by a 100 Mbit LAN or by a 10 Mbit LAN. The machines were configured to disable all system maintenance activities. The measurements were taken for the application's steady-state performance and not for start-up performance, since we are concerned with the running application's response times. Garbage collection and object finalization were considered as part of the steady-state server workload [14]. Unless otherwise stated, all the presented results were produced running in Machine A.

4.3 Request Time Breakdown

Table 1 presents the request processing time breakdown. Figure 3 represents the same data graphically.

---

[12] Intel Core 2 Quad CPU Q8300.
[13] Intel Core 2 Duo CPU P9500.

Table 1. Request processing time breakdown

Slice	Time (ms)	Time %
Web	2.83	0.98
Web Service	14.33	4.94
Service	203.14	70.07
Hibernate Engine	40.97	14.13
Hibernate Writes	15.52	5.35
Hibernate Reads	13.10	4.52

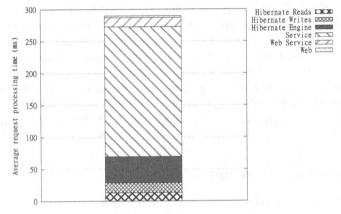

Fig. 3. Request processing time breakdown

The largest time slice is *Service* (70%) because it includes all the application-specific logic and also because it is the slice where the remaining – not specific to any layer – processing time is accounted for. The second largest slice is *Hibernates* (24%) as it manages the domain objects in the database. The *Hibernate engine* slice is significant (14%) because it includes when data is actually written to the database, at transaction commit time. The absolute value of roughly 300 milliseconds average processing time is only useful to compare with other measurements made in the same machine.

4.4   Monitor Implementation Comparison

The STEP framework performance monitor [12] had several iterations. Each was an attempt to more accurately capture the performance data.

Table 2 and Figure 4 present a comparison of the results of the same workload executed but using different monitor implementations to capture data:

– Perf4J monitor raw records (Perf4J raw);
– Perf4J monitor with aggregated records (Perf4J agg);
– Event monitor (Event);
– Layer monitor without Hibernate wrapping (Layer -Hwrap);
– Layer monitor with Hibernate wrapping (Layer).

Table 2. Request processing time percentages of different performance monitors. Each row sums to 100% of time spent.

Monitor	Web	WS	Svc	Hib Eng	Hib W	Hib R
Perf4J raw	0.71	4.26	87.00	0.00	4.58	3.45
Perf4J agg	0.79	4.51	4.59	0.00	10.86	79.25
Event	0.99	5.15	83.74	0.00	5.39	4.72
Layer -Hwrap	0.89	4.82	85.17	0.00	4.82	4.30
Layer	0.98	4.94	70.07	14.13	5.35	4.52

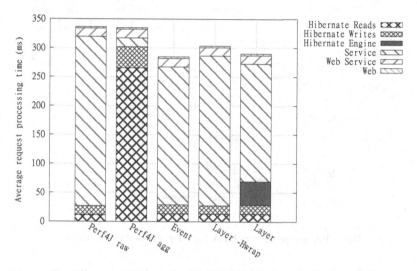

Fig. 4. Request processing breakdown of different performance monitors

The first choice for monitor was the Perf4J[14] library that uses stop-watch objects to time the execution of code blocks: on entry, the stop-watch is started; on exit, the stop-watch is stopped, timing of execution inside each layer. Perf4J delegates actual logging on the Apache Log4J library, already used by the STEP Framework. The performance events are logged in a separate log file and each stop-watch record has a start, time, tag, and (optional) message.

At first glance Perf4J was assumed to be underestimating the value of the Hibernate slice. Especially because the performance log files had (literally) thousands of lines stating that the time spent to load an object was 0 ms. These values were due to excessively fine-grained measurement of Hibernate calls. In practice, each call was too short to be accurately measured.

In the Perf4J monitor with aggregated records (*Perf4J agg*) the consecutive 0 ms records were combined and the elapsed time was computed using the time-stamps. The result of this mitigation attempt was a gross overestimation of the Hibernate slice, as confirmed by the other monitors. The mitigation failure was confirmed also by many

---

[14] http://perf4j.codehaus.org/

Table 3. Request processing breakdown for different request types, in percentages

Request	Web	WS	Service	Hib Eng	Hib W	Hib R
All	0.98	4.94	70.07	14.13	5.35	4.52
Searches	1.25	8.75	74.15	11.31	0.00	4.55
Reservations	0.71	0.83	62.69	19.37	12.17	4.23
Faults	0.83	4.60	86.73	1.96	0.00	5.89

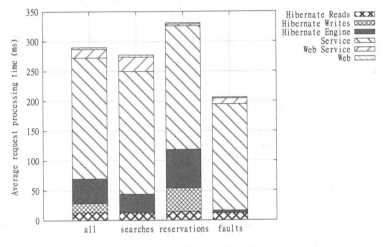

Fig. 5. Request processing breakdown for different request types

occurrences of records where the hibernate time was larger than the service time (a physical impossibility).

Since the results were not satisfactory, two new monitor approaches were implemented: *Event* and *Layer*. The Event monitor records one data record to the log for each interception point (just like Perf4J), producing a log file size proportional to the number of accessed objects, and data is written to the log file immediately after each interception. The Layer monitor keeps totals in memory and writes them to file only once per request, at the end of the request processing.

Both *Event* and *Layer* had a lower overhead when compared to *Perf4J*. However only *Layer* was capable of wrapping hibernate objects - Session, Transaction, etc - and correctly handling the nesting of calls between them. This difference is important as Layer monitor without Hibernate wrapping (*Layer -Hwrap* column) shows. It does not capture the Hibernate Engine slice, just like *Event* monitor, and a large slice of Hibernate time is lost. For this greater accuracy, the *Layer* monitor with Hibernate object wrapping was chosen as the final reference monitor that was used for all other experiments.

4.5   Request Types

In this experiment, request types are filtered and analyzed separately. Table 3 and Figure 5 present the results.

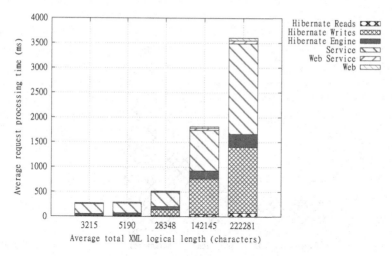

Fig. 6. Request processing breakdown for increasing SOAP size

Table 4. Request processing breakdown for increasing SOAP size, in percentages

Avg. XML len.	Web	WS	Service	Hib Eng	Hib W	Hib R
3215	0.96	5.26	73.93	14.33	0.80	4.73
5190	0.98	4.94	70.07	14.13	5.35	4.52
28348	1.53	3.93	55.69	11.78	23.57	3.51
142145	1.60	2.35	45.16	8.95	39.35	2.59
222281	1.50	1.64	50.62	7.28	36.88	2.08

Searches are read-only, reservations are read-write. Faults were mostly produced by invalid input, so no data was written. Notice how Hibernate Writes slice are empty on searches and faults. The framework handling of failed transactions is efficient because significant time savings are achieved when there is a database rollback.

4.6   Web Service Message Size

In this experiment, the SOAP message size is increased by making flight reservation requests with more passengers. Figure 6 and Table 4 present a comparison of the different workloads with increasing average XML length. The dominant slices are still Service and Hibernate. The impact of request time is very significant, above linear progression. Figure 7 shows the detail only for the Web and SOAP slices. The XML processing behavior is also increasing above linear progression.

Increasing XML size has less impact than initially predicted, providing evidence that XML parsers have been greatly optimized since the early versions where the performance degradation was more significant [13]. However, there are still practical limits for the message sizes: for messages above 150,000 characters (roughly 150 KiB assuming UTF-8 encoding) the server starts to fail with java.lang.OutOfMemoryError due to lack of Java heap space. This explains why the percentage of time spent in the service layer (c.f. 'Service' column in Table 4) actually decreases with increasing XML length.

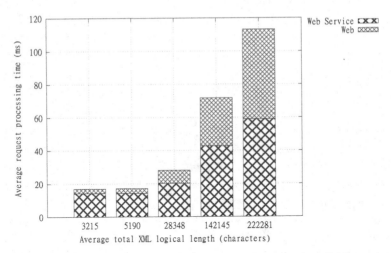

Fig. 7. Web and Web Service layers detail of request processing breakdown with increasing SOAP size

Table 5. Request processing breakdown for different cache settings, in percentages

Configuration	Web	WS	Service	Hib Eng	Hib W	Hib R
Local DB	0.98	4.94	70.07	14.13	5.35	4.52
w r-only cache	0.95	5.28	70.46	13.63	4.81	4.88
w r-w cache	0.91	5.05	65.32	13.40	4.67	10.65
100 Mbit LAN DB	0.72	4.06	65.20	16.01	8.96	5.06
w r-only cache	0.75	4.42	65.74	14.93	8.61	5.54
w r-w cache	0.68	4.19	62.33	14.76	8.16	9.88
10 Mbit LAN DB	0.28	1.88	78.50	6.83	10.64	1.88
w r-only cache	0.32	2.53	77.66	6.55	10.86	2.08
w r-w cache	0.25	1.90	77.28	6.80	10.26	3.51

4.7 Hibernate Second-Level Cache

The goal of this experiment was to measure the improvement of performance by using the out-of-the-box Hibernate second-level caching [15], EHCache (Easy Hibernate Cache). The first-level cache is turned on by default and is managed at the Hibernate Session object. Since each request has its own Session, the cache is not shared between them. The second-level cache is managed at the Session Factory object and allows sharing between sessions.

When running Tomcat and MySQL in the same machine, using the second level cache actually did *not* improve performance (c.f. first 3 rows of Table 5). The read-only cache has negligible effect (c.f. next 3 rows). The read-write cache actually decreases performance (c.f. last 3 rows).

When running Tomcat in machine A and MySQL in machine B, connected by a 100 Mbit LAN, the results were only marginally worse, despite the network communication.

Only when running Tomcat in machine A and MySQL in machine B, connected by a

Table 6. Request processing breakdown for increasing concurrent users

Users	Web	WS	Service	Hib Eng	Hib W	Hib R
1	0.98	4.94	70.07	14.13	5.35	4.52
2	1.10	4.89	70.06	14.08	4.08	5.80
4	1.21	4.04	71.09	13.58	3.97	6.11
8	2.04	4.62	65.06	17.07	5.47	5.74
16	2.75	6.07	62.55	19.56	4.80	4.26

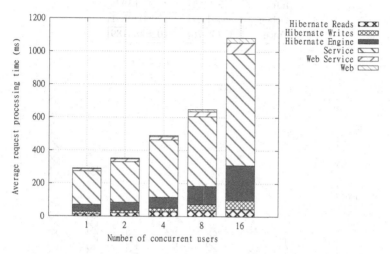

Fig. 8. Request processing breakdown for increasing concurrent users

more constricted 10 Mbit LAN, did the read-only cache prove beneficial. However, the request processing time for this configuration was approximately 3 times slower than the others.

The best solution for this application is to leave the second-level cache turned off as most caching benefits were achieved with the first-level cache.

4.8   Concurrent Users

The performance of an application in a production environment heavily depends on the number of users, making it hard to properly test the implementation in a development environment where a single user is available. In this experiment several virtual users were running at the same time. Table 6 and Figure 8 present the results.

The server scales reasonably well for the tested number of users. The request processing time stays in the same order of magnitude for a ten-fold increase in load (from 1 user to more than 10, it stays near the 1 second range).

However, there is a problem: the number of Application Exceptions stays the same (as expected in a simulated workload) but the number of System Errors steadily increases, from 0% for 1 user, to 30% for 16 users. This is caused by Hibernate optimistic cache [15] approach that throws org.hibernate.StaleObjectStateException when it detected concurrent modifications of the same objects. This happens not only for entity

Table 7. Log level average processing time and average functional log size

Log level	Time (ms)	Log size (bytes)
Off	332.52	0
Fatal	332.10	0
Error	331.69	1792
Warn	333.70	1792
Info	332.91	13978
Debug	4431.41	296059571
Trace	37430.76	2029488189

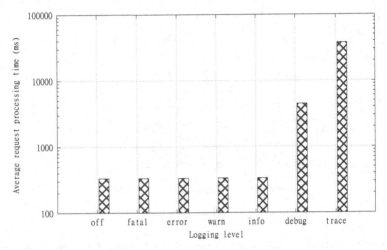

Fig. 9. Request processing times for log level settings. The y axis is in logarithmic scale.

data modifications, but also for relationship modifications. The impact of this issue is magnified because the STEP Framework cookbook[15] advocates the use of a "Domain Root" object that connects to all the main domain entities. This guideline has a measurable impact on the scalability of STEP applications and should be reconsidered in future versions.

4.9 Logging Cost

Log libraries are very important for server-side applications as a debug and diagnostics tool. The STEP Framework and the libraries it uses rely on Apache Log4J[16] to log program messages. In this experiment, the functional log level was changed from no messages ("off") up to the most detailed level ("trace"). Table 7 and Figure 9 present the results.

The cost of logging beyond "info" level is enormous, making the "debug" and "trace" levels impractical for production environments.

---

[15] Cookbooks available at http://stepframework.sourceforge.net/
[16] http://logging.apache.org/log4j/

Additional detail levels could help alleviate this problem, as well has selecting partial output only from some of the layers and not all of them, or activating them for a subset of requests (e.g. requests from a specific user).

5 Conclusions

This chapter presented the performance assessment of a representative Web Service developed using the STEP Framework. Performance monitoring is much harder than first expected. Also, assembling a tool chain to collect, process, and visualize the data is an extensive work. But the benefits of having it in place are greatly beneficial for development, especially in an open-source, academic learning environment.

The detailed description of the performance analysis process provides insight to how similar techniques can be used in other frameworks, and how to avoid some of the pitfalls, in particular, regarding monitor implementation and how measurements should always be interpreted with regard for the bias introduced by the measurement process itself.

The presented experiment findings – time slice breakdown, monitors comparison, request types, SOAP size, caching, concurrent users, and logging – are illustrative of the framework's new capabilities and of how they can be used by learning developers make more informed decisions that help give better performance to their Web Services.

Acknowledgements. Miguel L. Pardal and Joana Paulo Pardal are supported by PhD fellowships from the Portuguese Foundation for Science and Technology FCT (SFRH/BD/45289/2008 and SFRH/BD/30791/2006).

The authors wish to thank Prof. Paulo Jorge Pires Ferreira for his insightful review of an earlier manuscript.

References

1. Fowler, M., Rice, D., Foemmel, M., Hieatt, E., Mee, R., Stafford, R.: Patterns of Enterprise Application Architecture. Addison Wesley (2002)
2. Jain, R.: The Art of Computer Systems Performance Analysis - Techniques for Experimental Design, Measurement, Simulation, and Modeling. Wiley (1991)
3. Menascé, D.A., Almeida, V.A.F., Dowdy, L.W.: Performance by Design - Computer Capacity Planning by Example. Prentice Hall (2004)
4. Pardal, M., Fernandes, S., Martins, J., Pardal, J.P.: Customizing Web Services with Extensions in the STEP framework. Int'l Journal of Web Services Practices 3(1) (2008)
5. Pardal, M.: Core mechanisms for Web Services extensions. In: 3rd Int'l Conf. on Next Generation Web Services Practices (NWeSP). IEEE Computer Society (2007)
6. Leitão, J.C.C., Pardal, M.L.: Smart Web Services: systems integration using policy driven automatic configuration. In: Quintela Varajão, J.E., Cruz-Cunha, M.M., Putnik, G.D., Trigo, A. (eds.) CENTERIS 2010, Part II. CCIS, vol. 110, pp. 446–454. Springer, Heidelberg (2010)
7. Roza, M., Schroders, M., van de Wetering, H.: A high performance visual profiler for games. In: ACM SIGGRAPH Symp. on Video Games (Sandbox 2009), pp. 103–110. ACM, New York (2009)

8. Shankar, K., Lysecky, R.: Non-intrusive dynamic application profiling for multitasked applications. In: 46th Annual Design Automation Conf. (DAC), pp. 130–135. ACM, New York (2009)
9. Pearce, D.J., Webster, M., Berry, R., Kelly, P.H.J.: Profiling with AspectJ. Softw. Pract. Exper. 37, 747–777 (2007)
10. Georges, A., Buytaert, D., Eeckhout, L.: Statistically rigorous Java performance evaluation. In: 22nd Annual ACM SIGPLAN Conf. on Object-Oriented Programming Systems and Applications (OOPSLA), pp. 57–76. ACM, New York (2007)
11. Montgomery, D.C., Runger, G.C.: Applied Statistics and Probability for Engineers. Wiley (2010)
12. Pardal, M.L., Pardal, J.P., Marques, J.A.: Improving Web Services performance, one STEP at a time. In: 2nd Int'l Conf. on Cloud Computing and Services Science (CLOSER) (2012)
13. Machado, A., Ferraz, C.: JWSPerf: A performance benchmarking utility with support to multiple web services implementations. In: Int'l Conf. on Internet and Web Applications and Services (ICIW), pp. 159–159 (2006)
14. Boyer, B.: Robust Java benchmarking. IBM Developer Works (2008)
15. Bauer, C., King, G.: Java Persistence with Hibernate. Manning (2006)

CAP-Oriented Design for Cloud-Native Applications

Vasilios Andrikopoulos, Steve Strauch, Christoph Fehling, and Frank Leymann

Institute of Architecture of Application Systems (IAAS), University of Stuttgart,
Universitätsstr. 81, 70569 Stuttgart, Germany

Abstract. Brewer's conjecture, and its resulting formalization as the CAP theorem, impose serious limitations on the consistency, availability and network partitioning tolerance characteristics of distributed systems. Despite its importance however, few works explicitly consider the implications of the CAP theorem in the design of applications, especially for applications that are designed natively for the Cloud. In order to address this need, in this work we propose a CAP-oriented design methodology for Cloud-native applications. For this purpose we build and extend our previous work on Cloud architectural patterns. Finally, we show how the methodology can be used in practice to design an application solution with desired CAP properties.

1 Introduction

Cloud computing has been heralded as the realization of John McCarthy's utility computing vision, where computing is organized and offered as a public utility like electricity and water [1]. Cloud computing allows enterprises to outsource applications, systems and even their IT infrastructure to the Cloud, using one or more of the provisioned infrastructure or software services. Amazon, for example, offers Cloud solutions with usage-based costing, where interested parties can install and run their software without having to care about previously critical issues like infrastructure investment, computing power and network connectivity [2]. Salesforce.com altered radically the enterprise computing landscape by offering customizable services on the Cloud which were traditionally embedded in the IT domain of the enterprise. Cloud computing has ushered a new era of consuming and producing information and information technology by migrating the processing and storage of the information from small scale, limited purpose computing platforms like PCs, laptops and server machines to large scale, general purpose platforms offered "somewhere on the Cloud". This created the notion of *Cloud-native applications*, i.e., applications that are specifically designed and developed on top of a constellation of Cloud services, and which can fully exploit the characteristics of Cloud computing, e.g., elasticity [3].

Despite its revolutionary nature however, Cloud computing is underpinned by the same fundamental principles and laws governing large, distributed networked systems. One of the most important principles is a conjecture that Eric Brewer put forward in his keynote speech at the ACM Symposium on the Principles of Distributed Computing (PODC) in 2000 [4]. Brewer observed that there are three fundamental systemic requirements in any distributed environment that exist in a special relationship with each other: consistency (whether all parts of the system see the same data at the same time),

I. Ivanov et al. (Eds.): CLOSER 2012, CCIS 367, pp. 215–229, 2013.

availability (what percentage of time the system is up and functioning properly) and network partitioning (if the system is tolerant to network failures). His conjecture is that only two out of these three requirements can actually be satisfied at any time by a distributed system. This hypothesis was later formally proven by Seth Gilbert and Nancy Lynch of MIT [5], making it known as the CAP theorem (from the initials Consistency, Availability and network Partitioning).

By its definition, the CAP theorem is restricting the capacity of any distributed system to satisfy requirements related to the CAP properties, and as such it has a direct impact on these requirements. This impact is even bigger for Cloud-native applications where elasticity, i.e., being able to deal with shifting computational demands by scaling up or down accordingly, is one of the basic pillars of the paradigm. Elastic applications should be able to maintain similar (or better) CAP behavior independent of their scale and rely on their design to do so. Studying and analyzing therefore the effect of various architectural decisions on the behavior of the resulting application with respect to the CAP theorem becomes an important issue and is the proposed goal of this work.

More specifically, in the following we present a design methodology for Cloud-native applications which is oriented towards connecting design decisions with an estimation of the CAP behaviour of the resulting application. Furthermore, we show how the methodology can be realized as an extension of the Cloud Pattern Framework presented in [6]. Finally, we validate our proposal using a scenario running through the paper.

The rest of this work is structured as follows: Section 2 motivates the need for a CAP-oriented design methodology by means of an example. Section 3 discusses the CAP theorem in more detail and presents the proposed application design methodology. Section 4 shows how the methodology can be realized in practice, while Section 5 discusses validation. Finally, Section 6 summarizes the related work, before providing some conclusions and possible future directions in Section 7.

2   Motivation

For illustrative purposes, consider the familiar example of a simple Web shop application as depicted in Fig. 1(a). Customers browse through offered items using the Web shop user interface (*Webshop UI*). If they decide to order an item, it is packaged and sent to them by one of the stock managers in the shop using a management interface (*Management UI*). Both user interfaces access a common data store (*Stock Database*) containing the item descriptions and their availability. The complete Web shop is hosted on a local data centre, belonging to the shop owner. The Web shop, however, experiences very high workloads during specific times of the year, for example, when Christmas approaches. The shop owner therefore decides to use elastic Cloud resources to cope with such alternating workloads.

Consulting online resources, he decides to completely outsource his data store and shop interface to the Cloud, where he can use the elasticity and scalability offered by it. He decides however not to outsource the management interface and continues hosting it on premises. The new architecture of the Web shop is shown in Fig. 1(b). While the new Web shop fulfils the expectations in terms of computational resources in periods

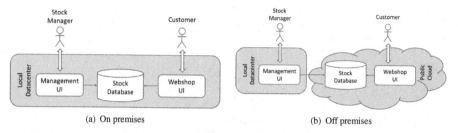

Fig. 1. Web shop example

of increased activity, the owner is very quickly faced with a new problem: fulfilling the orders depends on the link between the management interface and the data store on the Cloud. Frequent network failures in this link force the stock managers to wait before processing an order, essentially creating a bottleneck in the application. In the following sections we are going to discuss how the shop owner (or more specifically, the application designer on his behalf) would have been able to foresee this problem before actually implementing the application.

3 CAP-Oriented Design

3.1 Design Decisions and CAP Properties

Since 2000 when Brewer posed his conjecture and until today, a number of works have appeared in the literature discussing the implications of the CAP theorem in system design, see for example [7], [8], [9], [10]. These discussions however stay on the level of particular cases and best practices and do not identify or organize the underlying principles of systems design for the Cloud. For purposes of visualization, it is more appropriate to think of the CAP properties positioned along the edges of a tetrahedron, as shown in Fig. 2, with minimum values for these properties in the intersection of the axes (marked with 0 in Fig. 2). CAP properties of different systems are positioned along the axes and form triangular areas that cut through this tetrahedron.

The strict interpretation of Brewer's theorem would position any system on one of the sides of the tetrahedron. In practice however, system designers and developers trade some degree of, e.g., consistency for availability and network partitioning. Proposed solutions like the one discussed in [11], where all three properties of CAP can be satisfied (not, however, at the same time), confirm that there is actually space to outmaneuver the constraints imposed by the CAP theorem with clever design. Systems like the Amazon.com online store, for example, allow customers to buy items without ensuring their physical availability at the time of purchasing. If, e.g., a copy of the requested book is not currently available in stock then it can either be purchased transparently to the customer through a third party, or the fulfillment of the order can be delayed until it becomes available (or ultimately some kind of compensation can be offered). The reasoning here is that customers should always be served, even in case of (internal to the systems of Amazon.com) network failures and even inventory inconsistencies. The consistency of the system will actually only be eventually ensured by a set of corrective

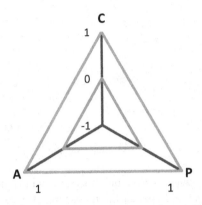

Fig. 2. The CAP Properties of a Distributed System

actions [12]. Thus, in terms of Fig. 2, it can be said that the Amazon.com store is positioned closer to the A vertex. Other systems like for example online travel agencies, trade availability for consistency and network partitioning tolerance by making sure that no two customers book the same ticket, even in the presence of network failures. In this manner they essentially position themselves closer to the C-P side of the tetrahedron.

Different system requirements therefore lead to vastly different system design solutions, and different systems (in this case Cloud-native applications) end up in different areas of the tetrahedron in Fig. 2. Identifying the key decisions and their underlying principles, and connecting them with particular CAP properties is necessary for making sure that a Cloud-native application design fits its desired characteristics. Positioning the application in the tetrahedron is however not trivial. As demonstrated in the previous section, application design usually entails a series of architectural decisions, with each one of them having potentially a different effect on the CAP properties of the application. Furthermore, particular implementation decisions like, e.g., the choice of platform for hosting an application have an indirect effect on other decisions like the way the clients will access the application. Architectural decisions are therefore in a feedback loop and their effect for the CAP properties can only be estimated by taking into account their interplay dependencies.

3.2   Application Design Methodology

The CAP-oriented Cloud-native application design methodology presented here aims to address the requirements discussed above. It comprises of 5+1 phases, illustrated in Fig. 3 and presented in the following.

Identify CAP Requirements. The first phase requires of the application developer to identify the envisioned CAP properties of the designed application. For example, in the Web shop scenario discussed in the previous section, the migrated to the Cloud system requirements effectively call for stronger consistency, with network partitioning tolerance as a secondary goal, and availability only third. Actually positioning the desired outcome as a triangle in the tetrahedron of Fig. 2 provides the application designer with a qualitative feel of the requirements that he is building towards.

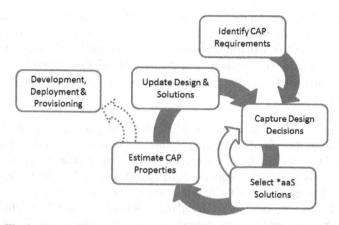

Fig. 3. The CAP-oriented Cloud-native application design methodology

Capture Design Decisions. The second phase consists of recording the various decisions made by the application designer. This involves in the case of the Web shop scenario, the decision to use a public Cloud for hosting the application, the storage model chosen etc. Capturing these decisions (and indeed facilitating the design of the application) is better performed, as we will discuss in the following section, by means of a decision support system like the one discussed in [13] (see related work section for further information).

*Select *aaS Solutions.* The third phase of the methodology complements the previous phase by translating the various abstract design decisions into concrete Software-, Platform- or Infrastructure-as-a-Service (*aaS) solutions. For the Web shop, for example, this may entail using the Amazon Web Services data storage solution. In principle, design decisions like the data storage model to be followed should "drive" the *aaS solution options. Choosing a particular solution however may influence previously taken design decisions with respect to its CAP properties. This may require a revisit of the previous phase, shown by the backward arrow in the loop of Fig. 3.

Estimate CAP Properties. During this phase, the CAP properties of the various solutions are combined in order to provide an estimate of the overall CAP properties of the designed application. It is relatively easy to assume a binary nature of the properties following the strict interpretation of the theorem. However, as discussed by Brewer himself in [14], all properties are more continuous rather than binary. Different subsystems also exhibit different properties and they contribute in different ways to the overall behavior of the system.

In order therefore to achieve an estimation of the CAP properties for the whole application, the selected *aaS solutions must be already annotated with information about their CAP properties. The annotation can be expressed as a triplet (c, a, p) with $c, a, p \in [-1, 1]$, where values closer to 1 signify a strong correlation with a property, while values close to -1 show a strong negative correlation, meaning that they affect this property of the application in a degrading manner. Estimating the properties of the system in this case can be performed by aggregating the various values for each property, and normalizing the result in the $[-1, 1]$ range. The advantage of this approach is that the result can be visualized in Fig. 2, which allows a designer to easily assess whether the designed application satisfies the requirements identified in the first phase. More sophisticated methods like log mining and stochastic methods can be used both for the actual extraction of the CAP properties of each *aaS solution and for their combination into one (c, a, p) triplet.

Update Design & Solutions. Based on whether the estimated CAP properties of the application satisfy its defined CAP requirements, the designer can choose either to proceed with the Development, Deployment and Provisioning of the actual application (not in the scope of this work), or re-enter the design cycle through the Update Design & Solutions phase. During this stage the designer attempts to identify and isolate the design decisions and *aaS solutions that produced the undesired outcome. Since changing any of them may have an impact on the overall design of the system, it is then required to re-enter the design decision/*aaS solution loop before estimating again the (new) CAP properties. This cycle may be repeated a number of times until a desired outcome is achieved.

4 Architectural Decisions and Design Patterns

In the previous section we presented a CAP-oriented design methodology for Cloud-native applications. The next step is to make this methodology concrete and demonstrate how it can be instantiated into a set of methods and tools for application design. For this purpose, in the following we focus on presenting the Cloud Pattern Framework introduced in [6], as the enabler of our methodology.

4.1 Cloud Architecture Patterns

Architectural patterns are used in many computer science domains to capture good solutions to reoccurring problems in an abstract common descriptive format, e.g., [15], [16]. A catalogue of patterns may then be used to guide application developers during the implementation. In our previous work, we abstracted the architectural principles of Cloud computing from existing Cloud applications and Cloud offerings and compiled them into a pattern catalogue [17], available also online at `http://cloudcomputingpatterns.org/`. In contrast to other pattern catalogues, we extend the use of the patterns to also describe the aspects of Cloud that are not implemented by the developer. This is necessary since Cloud applications rely heavily on runtime environments offered by Cloud providers. We describe the common concepts and behaviour of the environments in the same pattern format to ease their perception. This also allows the description of the environment in which a developer may apply Cloud architectural patterns through their interrelation to other patterns.

An overview of the resulting Cloud pattern classes is given in Fig. 4. Cloud Types & Service Models contain pattern-based descriptions of the Cloud environment. For example, there is a pattern for public Clouds (accessible by everyone), private Clouds (accessible within one company), community Clouds (accessible for a certain number

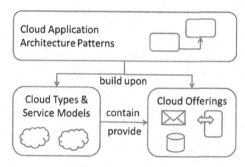

Fig. 4. Pattern Classes

Table 1. Excerpt from the Decision Recommendation Table [6]

	Public Cloud	Private Cloud	Community Cloud	Hybrid Cloud
Cloud Component Gateway	–	–	–	+
Elastic Infrastructure	+	+	+	+
Low-available Computer Node	+	∅	+	+
High-available Computer Node	∅	+	+	∅

Legend: +: strong relation −: exclusion ∅: no relation

of companies), and hybrid Clouds (a combination of at least two of the other types of Clouds) [3]. The Cloud environment that is described by this pattern class contains Cloud offerings providing computation, storage, and communication functionality. These Cloud offering patterns abstract from the concrete products of Cloud providers; for example, Amazon S3 or Windows Azure Storage are abstracted by the blob storage pattern. Architecture patterns may then be connected with these offering patterns to guide application developers when using these offerings.

4.2 Cloud Pattern Framework

To guide the application developer during the selection of applicable patterns for his concrete use case and Cloud environments, in [6] we introduced the Cloud Pattern Framework. In addition to the catalogue of patterns, a central component of the framework is a Decision and Solution Capturing component, enabled by a Decision Recommendation Table which captures the relations between the different patterns. We differentiate relations identifying the patterns to be (i) strongly related, (ii) mutually exclusive, and (ii) unrelated. Using this table (an excerpt of which is depicted in Table 1), an application developer iteratively selects patterns and receives recommendations for other patterns that may be applicable as well. Possible conflicts in the pattern selection can be identified through the evaluation of exclusion relations.

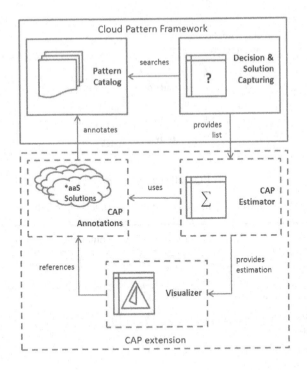

Fig. 5. CAP Extension of the Cloud Pattern Framework

For example, an application developer may start by selecting patterns that describe the Cloud environment at hand for which the application is being developed. He selects the hybrid Cloud pattern in the decision recommendation table, because the application uses different Clouds for different application components. Based on this selection, the Cloud Component Gateway pattern is recommended to the developer. This pattern describes how application components may be made accessible in different Cloud environments in case of communication restrictions and has therefore a strong relation to the hybrid Cloud pattern. Navigating through the table in a similar manner from more higher-level to more low-level patterns (e.g., type of data storage or communication mechanisms) provides the designer with a set of choices for *aaS Solutions that implement the particular pattern. Other non-functional patterns, like for example the ones we discuss in [18] can also be used for this purpose.

At this point the designer can simply choose which solution to use for the application design. The actual guidance through the recommendation table, and the recording of the various decisions that were taken is performed by the Decision & Solution Capturing module, shown in Fig. 5. The Cloud Pattern Framework therefore provides us with a set of useful building blocks (pattern catalogue, recommendation table, decision and solution capturing) for realizing the CAP-oriented application design methodology described in the previous section — as far as the decision capturing and *aaS solution selection phases of Fig. 3 are concerned. In the following we show how it can be augmented with CAP information in order to realize the Estimate CAP Properties phase.

4.3 CAP-Oriented Cloud Pattern Framework

In order to be able to estimate the CAP properties of an application in design we extend the Cloud Pattern Framework in three ways, as shown in Fig. 5 using dashed lines. More specifically, as a first step we annotate the *aaS Solutions contained in the Cloud Pattern Catalog with CAP Annotations. These annotations are triplets (c_i, a_i, p_i), where $c_i, a_i, p_i \in [-1, 1]$, in the manner discussed in Section 3.2. Currently, the triplets (c_i, a_i, p_i) are calculated by aggregating the values provided by different Cloud application developers by means of a questionnaire. The Amazon SimpleDB data storage service, for example, implementing the NoSQL Storage pattern, comes with two modes of operation: strict consistency (closer to traditional RDBMS) and eventual consistency. In the former mode, it is annotated with the triplet $(0.6, 0.25, 0.4)$, while in the latter with $(0.3, 0.75, 0.75)$. Similarly, providing a MySQL server as a Cloud offering (e.g. being deployed inside a Windows VM in Windows Azure), and implementing the Relational Datastore pattern is annotated with $(0.95, 0.4, -0.25)$ since it is only marginally tolerant to network partitioning.

The actual values of the triplets are meant to provide a qualitative feeling of how strongly positive or negative CAP behaviour is exhibited by the *aaS solution, and they can only be interpreted in relation to each other. For example, the value $c_{MySQL} = 0.95$ stands for a solution much more oriented towards consistency than, e.g., $c_{SimpleDB_{Eventual}} = 0.3$. While currently these values are only aggregations of the opinions of a limited group of Cloud developers, in the future we plan to expose them to the users of the implementation of our proposed approach, and allow for providing their own perceived values. By these means we aim to be able to provide a more up-to-date annotation set which is in a feedback loop with its consumers. In addition, we shall be also able to allow designers to add annotations for systems that do not appear in the Pattern Catalogue, provided that they are first related to an appropriate pattern.

An alternative, more objective, approach would be to categorize *aaS solutions into *property classes* with fixed values for all solutions in the class. For purposes of availability for example, class 6 systems [19], meaning that they have 99% followed by four or more decimal nines availability, could be assigned $a = 1.0$, class 5 $a = 0.9$ and so on. Defining the values for the triplets in this case is reduced to creating the classification, deciding on the fixed values for the classes, and assigning each system to a class for each property. Both of the described approaches can also be combined, allowing to better reflect the expert knowledge.

For the second part of extending the Cloud Pattern Framework we focus on the providing a CAP Estimator (Fig. 5) module. The estimator takes as input from the Decision & Solution Capturing module the list of *aaS solutions already selected by the designer. It then retrieves the appropriate CAP annotations for these solutions and calculates the overall CAP triplet for the application:

$$(c, a, p)_{estimated} = (f_{i \geq 1}(c_i), f'_{i \geq 1}(a_i), f''_{i \geq 1}(p_i)). \tag{1}$$

Different functions f, f', f'' can be applied for the $(c, a, p)_{estimated}$ resulting in different interpretations of the expected behavior of the system. For example, a pessimistic approach would be to use $f_{i \geq 1}(a_i) = min_{i \geq 1}(a_i)$, signifying that the overall availability of the system is as good as its weakest link. More sophisticated functions can be used

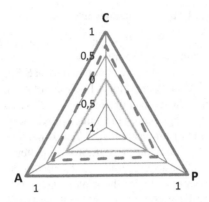

Fig. 6. Visualization of the CAP Estimation

for this purpose, with different weighting for components and network links between them, for example. For purely illustrative purposes, in this work we use the average of each of the properties, as follows:

$$(c, a, p)_{estimated} = \frac{1}{n} \sum_{i=1}^{n} (c_i, a_i, p_i). \tag{2}$$

For a Cloud application for example that comprises a MySQL server installed inside a Windows VM on Azure (implementing the Relational Datastore pattern as we saw above) with annotation $(0.9, 0.7, -0.25)$ and a Management UI as a set of JSP pages on a local JBoss server (implementing the Stateless Component pattern) annotated with the triplet $(0.5, 0.0, 0.75)$ the estimated CAP properties are

$$(c, a, p)_{MySQL_{Azure}} = \frac{1}{2}(0.9 + 0.5, 0.7 + 0.0, 0.75 - 0.25) = (0.7, 0.35, 0.25).$$

The estimated CAP properties show a system with high consistency but low availability and little tolerance in network partitioning (since it depends on the UI/Database link in order to operate correctly).

The visualization of this result is done by the Visualizer module in Fig. 5. The estimated CAP properties produced by the CAP Estimator are positioned as a triangle inside the CAP tetrahedron of Fig. 6 (extending that of Fig. 2). In the case of $(c, a, p)_{MySQL_{Azure}}$, the estimated CAP properties (illustrated by the dashed triangle) shows a clear tendency to the C vertex of the tetrahedron, denoting, as discussed above, strong consistency. The area bound by the lighter of the inner triangles in the centre of Fig. 6 denotes that one (or more) CAP properties of the application have a negative value.

Having extended the Cloud Pattern Framework to cater for the realization of the proposed CAP-oriented application design methodology, in the following we are going to validate our proposal by means of a case study. For this purpose we revisit the motivating scenario discussed in Section 2.

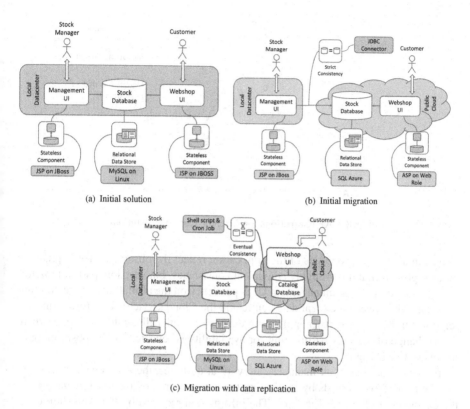

(a) Initial solution   (b) Initial migration

(c) Migration with data replication

Fig. 7. Web shop case study

5 Case Study

Returning to the motivating example, the Web shop owner starts by annotating the current architecture with pattern information to determine the current CAP behaviour as depicted in Fig. 7(a). Both user interfaces are Stateless Components (JSP pages on a JBoss server) relying on a Relational Datastore (MySQL on Linux), as external state. The links between them are synchronous and represent data base queries and, therefore, have no pattern annotated to them. From the *aaS annotations catalog, we already know that $(c, a, p)_{JSP_{JBoss}} = (0.5, 0.0, 0.75)$ and $(c, a, p)_{MySQL_{Linux}} = (0.95, 0.4, 0.25)$. Therefore:

$$(c, a, p)_{Initial} = \frac{1}{3}(2 \times 0.5 + 0.95, 2 \times 0 + 0.4, 2 \times 0.75 + 0.25) = (0.65, 0.13, 0.58).$$

In a similar manner, and for the migration to the Cloud shown in Fig. 7(b), we can see that $(c, a, p)_{Migration} = (0.68, 0.53, -0.14)$, since

$$(c, a, p)_{SQLAzure} = (0.75, 0.9, -0.5), (c, a, p)_{ASP_{WebRole}} = (0.5, 0.7, -0.3), \text{ and}$$
$$(c, a, p)_{JDBC} = (0.95, 0.5, -0.5).$$

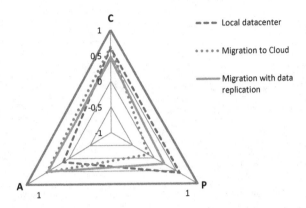

Fig. 8. CAP Estimations for different Web shop Solutions

The estimated CAP properties of the application reflect the observed ones in practice: much higher availability, roughly equivalent consistency, but very low partitioning tolerance (due to the stock management UI dependency on the availability of the communication link between the local data centre and the Cloud service). This result, and the relationship between the two application designs, is better illustrated in Fig. 8 where the exchange of network partitioning for availability is reflected by the positioning of the respective triangles.

To ensure that the stock manager can work at all times, the shop owner decides to use the best of both worlds by replicating the data required by the stock manager and the customer as shown in Fig. 7(c). The information required by the Web shop component is now contained in a separate catalogue component in the Cloud. The stock management component still contains all information about the goods and their availability. Hourly however, the data are replicated from the stock database to the catalogue database by a shell script and a cron job. This leads eventually to a consistency between the two data replicas as shown by the Eventual Consistency pattern annotated to the link. By calculating in a similar manner as above the estimated CAP properties, and for $(c, a, p)_{Script+Cron} = (-0.5, 0.5, 0.95)$, we have $(c, a, p)_{Replication} = (0.44, 0.5, 0.23)$.

This design solution therefore ensures that the availability is increased for both the stock manager and the customer and enables a system that is sufficiently partitioning tolerant by sacrificing a small amount of consistency: both the stock manager and the customer may access the information in the application, regardless of the availability of the communication link between the integrated runtime environments. The data consistency is however reduced, resulting in the possible condition that customers may order goods that are not available, because the actual product availability is only kept in the stock database. Therefore, compensation may be required in some cases, but the overall behaviour of the system is (probably) more profitable for the Web shops. Other Web shops like Amazon.com handle item availability in the same fashion. In all cases however, it is possible for the application designer to estimate the CAP properties by using the methodology and tools we discussed in the previous.

6   Related Work

Cloud application design (and engineering) is still a developing research topic, driven mostly by the industry. Solution providers like Microsoft, Amazon and IBM have offered best practices on using their solutions for developing Cloud applications, see for example [2], [20], [21]. However, these are far from systematic software engineering approaches and they do not explicitly consider CAP properties. In a similar approach to ours, the work of [22] uses design patterns in Cloud application engineering. Their focus is on Cloud transformation, i.e., migrating existing applications to the Cloud.

Patterns are commonly used to describe good solutions to re-occurring problems in a common format to organize practical knowledge and ease perception. This concept has been used originally to describe building and city architecture [23] and has since been applied to a large variety of domains, such as learning [24] or business communications [25]. Regarding software architecture and runtime infrastructure, patterns have been defined for object oriented programming [16] and messaging-based application integrations [15]. Furthermore, different pattern catalogues capture good practices for user interaction with information [26]. These patterns have also been considered during the identification of Cloud computing patterns. Many of them were transformed or applied to the area of Cloud computing.

Capturing design decisions in order to focus and verify the design process of systems is also discussed in [13], where a formal model is presented for capturing and reusing architectural decision knowledge. Furthermore, in [27], the authors present a pattern-based approach for architectural decisions. Both approaches are conceptually close to this work, but discuss service-oriented and software systems and as such they are not directly applicable to Cloud-native applications. Further investigation on how they can be reused for this purpose is however in our future goals.

7   Conclusions and Future Work

While the CAP theorem has serious implications for the design of distributed systems (and therefore also of Cloud-native applications) there are few works discussing how to design for particular CAP properties. For this purpose, in this work we presented an approach for incorporating these properties into the design of Cloud-native applications. More specifically, we introduced a CAP-oriented design methodology which connects design decisions with existing Cloud solutions and provides the means to estimate the CAP properties of an application. This methodology was then realized by using Cloud patterns in order to capture the design decisions and a set of annotations on the various *aaS solutions that realize these patterns. A visualization approach was also presented that allows for better perception of the estimated CAP properties and their impact on the application design. Finally, the proposed approach was validated by means of a case study scenario.

In the future we plan to complete the annotation of the Cloud Pattern Catalog presented in [6] so that we can empirically validate our approach using different scenarios. As part of this effort, we also plan to extend the *aaS solutions annotation procedure to as large as possible group of Cloud experts and offer tooling support for our methodology as an application in the Cloud. In addition we also plan to investigate different possible approaches in combining the CAP annotations, using for example weighted sums and other statistical methods. The proposed approach is geared towards building Cloud-native applications. The methodology discussed in Section 3, however, can be easily adapted and applied to the case of Cloud-enabled applications [28], i.e., applications that are partially or completely migrated to the Cloud. Depending on the selection of Cloud services to be used, and the envisioned topology of the migrated application, systems with radically different CAP properties could emerge. Combining this option with, for example, calculating the operational expenses of the migrated application in the Cloud, could result in a decision support system that would allow application stakeholders to figure out whether and how their application should be migrated to the Cloud.

Acknowledgements. The research leading to these results has partially received funding from the 4CaaSt project (http://www.4caast.eu/) from the European Union's Seventh Framework Programme (FP7/2007-2013) under grant agreement no. 258862.

References

1. Leymann, F., Fritsch, D.: Cloud Computing: The Next Revolution in IT. In: Proceedings of the 52th Photogrammetric Week, pp. 3–12 (2009)
2. Varia, J.: Architecting for the Cloud: Best Practices. Amazon Web Services (2010), http://media.amazonwebservices.com/AWS_Cloud_Best_Practices.pdf
3. Badger, M.L., Grance, T., Patt-Corner, R., Voas, J.M.: Cloud Computing Synopsis and Recommendations. NIST Special Publication 800-146 (2012), http://www.nist.gov/manuscript-publication-search.cfm?pub_id=911075
4. Brewer, E.A.: Towards Robust Distributed Systems. In: Proceedings of the Annual ACM Symposium on Principles of Distributed Computing, vol. 19, pp. 7–10 (2000)
5. Gilbert, S., Lynch, N.: Brewer's Conjecture and the Feasibility of Consistent, Available, Partition-Tolerant Web Services. ACM SIGACT News 33(2), 51–59 (2002)
6. Fehling, C., Leymann, F., Retter, R., Schumm, D., Schupeck, W.: An Architectural Pattern Language of Cloud-Based Applications. In: Proceedings of the Conference on Pattern Languages of Programs, PLoP (2011)
7. Hewlett-Packard Development: There is no Free Lunch With Distributed Data. HP White Paper (2005), ftp://ftp.compaq.com/pub/products/storageworks/whitepapers/5983-2544EN.pdf
8. Helland, P.: SOA and Newton's Universe. MSDN Blogs (2207), http://blogs.msdn.com/b/pathelland/archive/2007/05/20/soa-and-newton-s-universe.aspx
9. Kossmann, D.: How new is the Cloud? In: IEEE Proceedings of ICDE 2010, p. 3 (2010)
10. Mietzner, R., Fehling, C., Karastoyanova, D., Leymann, F.: Combining Horizontal and Vertical Composition of Services. In: IEEE Proceedings of SOCA 2010, pp. 1–8 (2010)
11. Pardon, G.: A CAP Solution (Proving Brewer Wrong). Personal Blog (2008), http://guysblogspot.blogspot.com/2008/09/cap-solution-proving-brewer-wrong.html
12. Vogels, W.: Eventually Consistent. Communications of the ACM 52(1), 40–44 (2009)
13. Zimmermann, O., Koehler, J., Leymann, F., Polley, R., Schuster, N.: Managing Architectural Decision Models with Dependency Relations, Integrity Constraints, and Production Rules. Journal of Systems and Software 82(8), 1249–1267 (2009)

14. Brewer, E.: CAP Twelve Years Later: How the "Rules" Have Changed. Computer 45(2), 23–29 (2012)
15. Hohpe, G., Woolf, B.: Enterprise Integration Patterns: Designing, Building, and Deploying Messaging Solutions. Addison-Wesley Longman Publishing Co., Inc., Boston (2003)
16. Gamma, E., Helm, R., Johnson, R., Vlissides, J.: Design Patterns: Elements of Reusable Object-Oriented Software. Addison-Wesley Longman (1994)
17. Fehling, C., Leymann, F., Mietzner, R., Schupeck, W.: A Collection of Patterns for Cloud Types, Cloud Service Models, and Cloud-Based Application Architectures. Technical Report (2011)
18. Strauch, S., Andrikopoulos, V., Breitenbücher, U., Kopp, O., Frank, L.: Non-Functional Data Layer Patterns for Cloud Applications. In: Proceedings of CloudCom 2012, pp. 601–605. IEEE Computer Society Press (2012)
19. Leymann, F., Roller, D.: Production Workflow: Concepts and Techniques. Prentice Hall PTR (2000)
20. Erl, T., Kurtagic, A., Wilhelmsen, H.: Designing Services for Windows Azure. MSDN Magazine (2010), http://msdn.microsoft.com/en-us/magazine/ee335719.aspx
21. Lau, C., Birsan, V.: Best Practices to Architect Applications in the IBM Cloud. IBM DeveloperWorks (2011), http://www.ibm.com/developerworks/cloud/library/cl-cloudapppractices/index.html
22. Chee, Y.M., Zhou, N., Meng, F.J., Bagheri, S., Zhong, P.: A Pattern-Based Approach to Cloud Transformation. In: IEEE Proceedings of CLOUD 2011, pp. 388–395 (2011)
23. Alexander, C., et al.: A Pattern Language. Towns, Buildings, Construction. Oxford University Press (1977)
24. Iba, T., Miyake, T., Naruse, M., Yotsumoto, N.: Learning Patterns: A Pattern Language for Active Learners. In: Conference on Pattern Languages of Programs, PLoP (2009)
25. Manns, M.L., Rising, L.: Fearless Change: Patterns for Introducing new Ideas. Addison-Wesley, Boston (2005)
26. Yahoo! Inc.: Yahoo! Design Pattern Library. Online Resource (2011), http://developer.yahoo.com/ypatterns/
27. Harrison, N.B., Avgeriou, P., Zdun, U.: Using Patterns to Capture Architectural Decisions. IEEE Software 24(4), 38–45 (2007)
28. Andrikopoulos, V., Binz, T., Leymann, F., Strauch, S.: How to Adapt Applications for the Cloud Environment. Springer Computing 95(6), 493–535 (2013), http://dx.doi.org/10.1007/s00607-012-0248-2

SLA-Oriented Security Provisioning
for Cloud Computing

Massimo Ficco and Massimiliano Rak

Dipartimento di Ingegneria Industriale e dell'Informazione,
Second University of Naples (SUN), Via Roma 29, 81031 Aversa, Italy
{massimo.ficco,massimiliano.rak}@unina2.it

Abstract. Cloud Computing represents both a technology for using distributed computing infrastructures in a more efficient way, and a business model for renting computing services and resources. It is an opportunity for customers to reduce costs and increase efficiency. Moreover, it gives to small and medium enterprises the possibility of using services and technologies that were prerogative of large ones, by paying only for the used resources and avoiding unnecessary investment. The possibility of dynamically acquire and use resources and services on the base of a pay-by-use model, implies an incredible flexibility in terms of management, which is otherwise often hard to address. In this paper, we propose an approach to to build up SLA-oriented Cloud applications, which enable a Cloud provider to offer service customized on the customer security needing. In particular, by using a Cloud-oriented API derived from the mOSAIC project, the developer can implement security features that can be offered by the Cloud provider within their Service Level Agreement. In particular, we focus on providing an intrusion tolerance service to grant an application service availability even when the host system is under attack.

Keywords: Cloud Computing, SLA, Security, Intrusion Tolerance.

1 Introduction

Cloud Computing is an emerging paradigm that allows customers to obtain easily services and resources (*e.g.*, networks, virtual machines, storage, applications), according to an on-demand and pay-by-use business model. The current Cloud providers include Quality of Service (QoS) guarantees in their Service Level Agreement (SLA) proposals [1]. An SLA is an agreement between a Cloud provider and a customer. Specifically, from Cloud consumer point of view, a SLA is a contract that grants the customer about what he/she will effectively obtain from the service. From Cloud provider point of view, SLA is a way to have a clear and formal definition of the requirements that the delivered service has to respect. In general, providers offer guarantees in terms of service availability and performance during a time period of months or a year. The provisioning contracts regulate the cost that customers have to pay for provided services and resources. On the other hand, the Cloud service provider must pay a penalty if the customer requirements are not satisfied. For example, the Cloud provider could be liable to pay a penalty for service requests that are rejected due to the unavailability of

I. Ivanov et al. (Eds.): CLOSER 2012, CCIS 367, pp. 230–244, 2013.
© Springer International Publishing Switzerland 2013

the resources. In order to support this model, the Cloud infrastructure has to continually adapt to changing of customer demands and operation conditions. For example, in order to prevent service availability violations may be required additional standby resources to handle a given number of failure, whereas to prevent performance violations may be required to scale up or move a virtual machine (VM) to another physical machine (if the current machine is overloaded). Therefore, the on-demand characteristic is one aspect that complicates the QoS provisioning and the SLA management in the Cloud Computing paradigm. In particular, a side effect of such a model is that, it is prone to cyber attacks, which aim at reducing the services availability and performance by exhausting the resources of the service's host system (including memory, processing resources, or network bandwidth) [2].

In this paper, we show how it is possible, using a Cloud-oriented API derived from the mOSAIC project [3,4], to build up a SLA-oriented Cloud application, which enables an IaaS Cloud provider to offer security services customized on customer needing. The objective is to offer, in a transparent way, a service that is able to provide the typical IaaS services (mainly VMs delivery) enriching them with ad-hoc solutions for protecting the delivered resources against a set of security attacks. The goal is to enable the Cloud customer to negotiate with the provider the level of security offered. The customer pays for the additional security service, but he/she is granted that the service is tolerant to a given set of Denial of Service (DoS) attacks (*i.e.*, continues to work even under attack) and the additional load generated is not charged.

The remainder of this paper is organized as follows: Sec. 2 presents the proposed approach. Sec. 3 presents an overview of the intrusion tolerance technologies, which represent a basis for the description of the proposed solution described in Sec. 4. Sec. 5 describes the technology we adopted in order to build up the solution, while Sec. 6 describes our Cloud application that enables the SLA negotiation and enforcement provisioning. Sec. 7 shows the final integrated solution and the offered SLA. Sec. 8 summarizes the related work and Sec. 9 concludes the paper.

2 An SLA-Oriented Security Perspective

The objective of this paper is the design and implementation of a system able to offer Intrusion Tolerance (IT) solutions *as a Service*. The key idea is that the approach of offering security solutions *as a Service* can be better achieved following an SLA-based approach: customer invokes the services always in the same way, but, due to the integration of the system together with an SLA-based application, the offered service can be enriched with security mechanisms.

In order to better illustrate the problem, Fig. 1 shows the approach we propose: the Cloud provider offers typical IaaS functionalities. In the presented example, the Cloud provider offers a set of pre-configured Web Server images, which can be acquired and configured by the customer though a well known interface. Thanks to the adoption of the mOSAIC Framework (see Sec. 5), the provider is able to offer more complex services on the top of the provided VMs. In particular, he/she offers a SLA-based application that enables the customer to negotiate, through the WS-Agreement standard description, the quality of services delivered. In our case study, we will show that the delivered VM

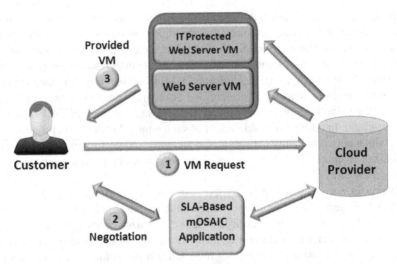

Fig. 1. Intrusion Tolerance as a Service with SLA-based approach

will be enriched, after the negotiation, with mechanisms that grant the customer against some of possible DoS attacks. As shown in Fig. 1, the customer invokes exactly the same service, but due to the SLA negotiation process, instead of the binding to an unprotected Web Server, he will receive the binding to a VM that is enriched with IT features. Service invocation does not change from final user (obtaining a standard machine or a protected one is completely transparent). Moreover, through the SLA-based application, it is possible to help the Cloud provider and customer to agree on the security granted, identifying the features that should be offered.

3   Intrusion Tolerance Techniques

Intrusion Tolerance is the ability of a system to continue providing (at most degraded) adequate service, despite the presence of deliberate attacks against the system, by both insiders and outsiders. In order to enforce the IT, several techniques can be adopted.

Replication is the technique most commonly used to perform IT. It consists to use more replicas of the same component and use specific voting algorithms, which are used to resolve any difference in the redundant responses, and to arrive at a consensus result based on the responses of perceived non-compromised components in the system. It has two complementary goals: masking of intrusions, thus tolerating them, and providing integrity of the data. Examples of algorithms are the Byzantine replication algorithms [5].

Using a *rejuvenation* approach, critical components are periodically rejuvenated to remove the effects of malicious and intelligent attackers that find ways to compromise them. An example of rejuvenation procedure could aim at loading a clean version of the application or change the cryptographic keys [6].

Redundancy is an approach different from replication, which is just one type of redundancy. Replicated components are pure replicas of each other. If the attacker has found a technique to subvert one component and all are pure replicas, it is likely that all components are likewise vulnerable. To combat this, another common technique used is 'diversity'. Diversity is the property such that the redundant components should be substantially different in one or more aspects, from hardware diversity and operating system diversity, to software implementation diversity. Therefore, through the use of diversity, the probability of a replica being compromised is independent of the occurrence of intrusion in other replicas [7].

Indirection allows designers to insert protection barriers and fault logic between client and server/components that provide the service. Since the indirection is hidden outside of the black box system, the clients see only what looks like a COTS server. There are at least four main types of indirection used by IT systems: proxies, wrappers, virtualization, and sandboxes.

Several previous techniques, commonly named proactive, aim at preventing system components being compromised. *Reactive techniques* aim at mitigating and reacting to intrusion. For example, they aim at minimizing stolen resources and disable inappropriate information flows (*e.g.*, through roll back and roll forward) to react/mitigate intrusion impact on the system. Moreover, Intrusion detection and correlation mechanisms can be used to detect intrusion and identify the specific recovery action [8,9,10]. For example, in replication, it could force the recovery of a replica that is detected or suspected of being compromised.

Reconfiguration can be proactive or reactive and can help in prevention, elimination, and tolerance. A wide variety of reconfiguration strategies are employed [11]. A challenge in devising the reconfiguration mechanisms is to protect them from being (mis)used by the attacker. It is important that the reconfiguration process be not very predictable by the attacker. Therefore, a major challenge is to make them resilient to oscillations due to transient and malicious effects that may lead to reconfigurations that drive the system to an inconsistent state.

4   An Intrusion Tolerant Solution

As case study, in this paper we adopt an Intrusion Tolerant reactive technique. The proposed IT architecture is composed of two subsystems, with distinct properties (Fig. 2). The first subsystem is the *Application VM* that hosts the application to protect, whereas the second subsystem, named *ITmOS*, is the VM that hosts the IT mechanisms. The two subsystems are connected through a secure channel isolated from other connections. The interaction of the application with the outside world is done only through the network, using a *Proxy* (based on the Squid Web proxy [12]) hosted on the ITmOS VM. A *VM Monitor* monitors the Application VM. It is a Java-based component based on Ganglia-Gmond, which is a real-time monitoring system [13]. It is used to collect system resources consumption (including CPU, memory, disk). An *Intrusion Detector* module collects data from the Proxy and alerts the *Decision Engine* component whether an anomalous behavior is observed. The Decision Engine is a centralized engine, which receives and correlates security data. It determines whether the monitored data are malicious behaviors, as well as estimates the effects on the monitored subsystem. It is responsible to identify the best reaction to take, in order to mitigate the attack effects

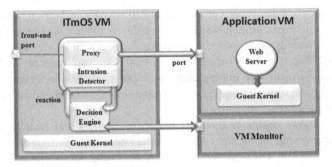

Fig. 2. Intrusion tolerant architecture

on the target application. In particular, it analyzes the received data and performs the reactions by the Proxy in response to the attack, filtering messages to the guest system as needed. The Intrusion Detector interacts with the VM Monitor through a secure communication channel.

4.1 An example of Intrusion Tolerance Approach for Denial of Service Attacks to Web Server

In our previous work [14], we present an IT approach for Denial of Service attacks to Web Server, which leverages an XML vulnerability. We focus on the Deeply-Nested XML DoS attack (X-DoS), which exhausts the computational resources of the target system, by forcing the XML parser within the server application to process numerous deeply-nested tags. In particular, the attack consists of inserting of a large number of nested XML tags in the Web messages.

Fig. 3 shows the CPU consumption depending on the number of nested XML tags and the frequency with which the malicious Web messages are injected. We perform different attack scenarios. Each scenario consists of a sequence of messages injected with a fixed frequency and a fixed number of nested tags. An attack scenario takes about 30 seconds. In particular, Fig. 3 represents the average value of CPU for the different scenarios, which are performed varying the number of tags nested to different depths (taking fixed the frequency). The experiment shows that it is sufficient to inject messages with about 35 nested tags every 100 ms, to make unavailable the Web service (*i.e.*, to exhaust the computational resources).

The implemented solution allows to trigger a specific reaction to mitigate the effects of the X-DOS attack. In particular, in order to detect the attack, an anomaly-based monitoring approach is adopted that assigns a weight to the detected anomalous events. The weight reflects the anomaly level with regard to an established profile. If this weight does not exceed a threshold estimated during a training phase, the event is discarded (*i.e.*, it is considered as a normal behavior), otherwise an alarm is triggered and a reaction is activated.

In the proposed architecture (Fig. 2), the Decision Engine correlates the events generated by both the VM Monitor hosted on the Application VM and the Intrusion Detector. As presented in [14], on the occurrence of an excessive CPU consumption, if an

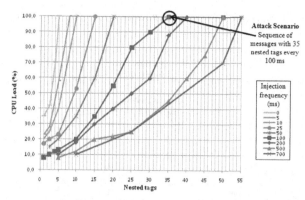

Fig. 3. CPU consumption with different message frequencies

anomalous number of nested XML tags with respect to a normal profile is monitored, a reaction in triggered. In particular, the Decision Engine alerts the Proxy, which filters each Web request that contains a number of nested tags greater than a fixed threshold. The purpose of this action is to reduce the CPU load on the Application VM, thus reducing the period in which the Web Server is unavailable.

In order to evaluate the proposed solution, a workload based on TPC Benchmark W (TPC-W) is adopted [15]. It is a transactional Web benchmark. The workload is performed in a controlled environment that simulates the activities of a business oriented transactional Web server. It simulates the execution of multiple transaction types that span a breadth of complexity. Multiple Web interactions are used to simulate the activity of a retail store, and each interaction is subjects to a response time constraint. The performance metric reported by TPC-W is the number of Web interactions processed per second (WIPS). It is used to simulated stress load and to assess the effectiveness of the proposed solution by the WIPS measurements.

An example of recovery effect is shown in Fig. 4. It represents the WIPS and CPU variations with respect to the time, during an interval time of tree minutes. The experiment consists of tree temporal windows. During the first two windows, the Decision Engine is disabled. In particular, the first 60 seconds show the values of the WIPS and the CPU load in absence of the attack. The second 60 seconds show the attack effects. We injected malicious messages with 3000 nested tags every 200 ms. During this period, the CPU load is about 100% and the number of TPC-W interactions processed is very low. Finally, during the last 60 seconds, the Decision Engine is enabled. When the Decision Engine detects the condition of a reaction (*i.e.*, the attack is in progress and the CPU consumption exceed the 90%), it alerts the Proxy, which filters all the suspicious messages. The reaction is applied until the CPU load falls below a fixed value.

5   mOSAIC: Development of Distributed Cloud Applications

mOSAIC aims at offering a simple way to develop Cloud application. The target user for the mOSAIC solution is a developer (mOSAIC User). In mOSAIC a Cloud application is modeled as a collection of components that are able to communicate each

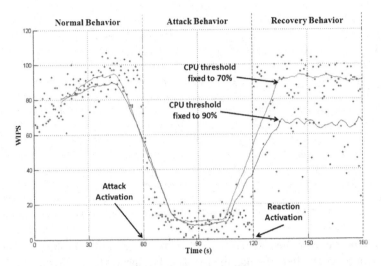

Fig. 4. WIPS evaluation during a intrusion recovery process.

other and consume Cloud resources (*i.e.*, resources offered as a service from a Cloud provider).

The mOSAIC solution is a framework composed of three independent components: *Software Platform*, *Cloud Agency* and *Semantic Engine*. The Software Platform enables the execution of application developed by using the mOSAIC API; the Cloud Agency acts as a provisioning system, brokering resources from a federation of Cloud providers; the Semantic Engine offers solution for reasoning on the resources and application needing. For the needing of this paper, we needed of concepts related to the Platform and the Cloud Agency, while the Semantic Engine will not be focused in this context. Moreover, in the following mOSAIC-based scenario, we consider that: the provider uses a set of its resources for the management of the Cloud application and hosting the mOSAIC Platform. On the top of the Platform, the provider runs its own mOSAIC Application that directly interacts with the IaaS service offered to grant added value services.

5.1   Programming with mOSAIC

A mOSAIC Application is defined as a collection of interconnected *mOSAIC Components*. Such Components may be offered by the mOSAIC Platform (*i*) as COTS (Commercial off-the Shelf) solutions, that are Commercial Off-The-Shelf components based on non-mOSAIC technologies, and adapted in order to inter-operate with the mOSAIC applications, (*ii*) as Core Components, *i.e.*, tools offered by mOSAIC Platform in order to perform predefined operations, or (*iii*) new components developed by using mOSAIC API. In last case, a component is a *Cloudlet* running in a *Cloudlet Container*. The mOSAIC Components run on dedicated VMs, named mOS (mOSAIC Operating System), which is based on a Linux distribution. The mOS is enriched with the *Platform Manager*, which enables to manage a set of VMs hosting the mOS, as a virtual cluster on which the mOSAIC Components are independently managed. It is possible to increase and decrease the number of VMs dedicated to the mOSAIC Application, which will scale in and out automatically. The mOSAIC Components can be interconnected through communication resources, queues, socket, Web services, etc. In particular, the mOSAIC Platform offers some queuing system (rabbitmq and zeroMQ) as COTS components, as well as offers some Core Components in order to help Cloud application to offer their operations as a service, like an HTTP gateway, which accepts HTTP requests and forward them on the application queues.

The Cloud application is described as a whole in a file named *Application Descriptor*, which lists all the components and the Cloud resources needed to enable their communications. A mOSAIC developer has the role of both develop new components and write the Application Descriptors. The mOSAIC API, actually based on Java and Phiton, enables the development of new components (in the form of Cloudlets), which self-scale on the described Platform and use every kind of Cloud resources, such as queues, NOSQL storage system (like KV store and columnar databases), independently from the technologies and API they adopt, through a wrapping system.

5.2   mOSAIC Offering for SLA-Based Applications

mOSAIC offers a set of features dedicated to SLA management [16] . In previous works [17,21], we proposed a case study in which we presented an application that offers security access configurations to a GRID environment in terms of SLA. The components offered in the SLA architecture should help the application developer to implement an SLA-based architecture. Figure 5 summarizes the global architecture offered in mOSAIC, showing the main modules and their respective roles:

- *SLA Negotiation*: This module contains all the Cloudlets and the components that manage the SLA documents and their formal management, *i.e.*, negotiation protocols, auditing, and so on.
- *SLA Monitoring*: This module contains all the Cloudlets and the components needed to detect the warning conditions and generates alerts about the difficulty to fulfill the agreements. It should address both resources and applications monitoring. It is connected with the Cloud Agency.
- *SLA Enforcement*: This module includes all the Cloudlets and components needed to manage the elasticity of the application, and modules that are in charge of making decisions in order to grant the respect of the acquired needed to fulfill the agreements.

In this context, we are interested mainly in the SLA Negotiation module, which offers the functionality to automatize the SLA negotiation process.

6   SLA-Based Cloud Application for IT Management

In our case study, the provider aims at developing a Cloud application that offers SLA negotiation features, following the SLA model proposed in mOSAIC, in order to offer enriched services to Cloud customers. The negotiation has the effect of enabling the adopted IT techniques. Specifically, the developed SLA-based application offers mainly two different use cases:

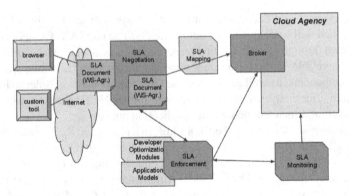

Fig. 5. Intrusion tolerant architecture

- *SLA Negotiation*: that enables a customer to negotiate a SLA, identifying the security of the services offered. Through the negotiation process, it is possible to enforce the security mechanisms described in Sec. 4.
- *VM Delivery*: that just delivers a VM to the customer. In this case, the application just forwards the request to the underlying IaaS infrastructure in order to offer the service to the Final User. Note that, depending on the SLA negotiated, the application may start several VMs for the same request done from the customer.

The SLA negotiation follows the SLA model described in Sec. 5, while the VM delivery is done forwarding the requests to the underlying IaaS provider in the case of non-protected requests, instead performing additional operation when an IT system is required.

The IaaS offers its services as usual to its own customers (the upper requests), but it is possible to offer the same services even through the newly developed mOSAIC Application. In the latter case, the requests may have or not the same format of the underlying provider. In the example, the requests are done with a very simple Restful interfaces through a JSON request attached to an HTTP POST invocation. When a request is received, it is interpreted by the mOSAIC Application that performs the local requests in order to start all the VMs needed (*i.e.*, the standard Web Server or the solution presented in Sec. 4, which includes both the Web Server and the IT Proxy connected through a dedicated virtual network).

The mOSAIC Application is fully described in Fig. 6, where all the components involved in the SLA negotiation and SLA enforcement are proposed. In particular, Fig. 6 shows the main components of the mOSAIC Application, following the architecture proposed in [4]. Our mOSAIC Application consists of four components:

- *SLAgw* that receives the WS-Agreement, stores it in the local storage (signing it in state pending), and forwards it to the decision Cloudlet;
- *SecDecision* that evaluates if the SLA is acceptable. It has the role of updating the SLA status (as an example, signing it as accepted or refused) and in case it is accepted, it forwards a request to SecConfigurer;
- *SecConfigurer* updates a KV store in which there is signed the security level agreed for each customer. In this paper, we just assume hat we offer two security level for

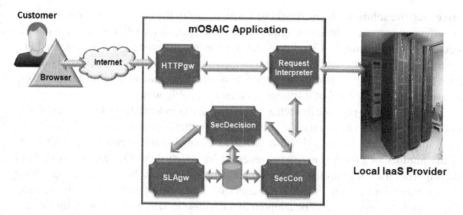

Fig. 6. SLA-based mOSAIC Application

a Web Server: unprotected and protected. However, it is possible to enrich the offer
with a lot of different solutions

– *Request Interpreter* receives the customer requests, evaluates the requests, extracting the service requested, checks the KV store in order to identify the SLA agreed,
  and then performs the request to the local IaaS provider. In case of unprotected
  request, just starts the Application VM, while in case of protected Web Servers,
  it starts both the Application VM and then the ITmOS VM, writing in the proxy
  configuration file the right configuration information. In both cases, it returns the
  IP addresses of the provided VMs.

The SLAgw is the main component dedicated to SLA management, which is offered
by the mOSAIC framework as a standalone component. SLAgw component offers a
simple way to interact with the customers in a SLA-based manner: they will negotiate
the agreement. The SLAgw sends out a message to the mOSAIC Application each time
a new agreement request take place. At the state of art, we support the asynchronous
WS-Agreement negotiation (*i.e.*, the customers agreement requests always receive a
wait reply, then it is up to the customer to query for the agreement status and to obtain
an accept or a refuse). In future work, we will support even the synchronous negotiations
and more evolved protocols. The SLAgw component does not assume decisions about
the submitted SLA, it just forwards them to a mOSAIC Application and stores the SLA
in a shared KV store.

7 Offering Intrusion Tolerance through SLA

The above proposed application enables to negotiate with the customer application the
SLA, described in WS-Agreement, in order to adapt the requests for delivering VMs
from the underlying IaaS provider. In this section, we focus on how such requests can
be described in Ws-Agreement and how to enforce the SLA in a VM request invocation.

It is important to point out that a SLA implies that the offering are *granted*, and if
not respected some penalties are applied to the peer of the agreement. Following the
above approach, we need to understand *what* the proposed IT system is able to grant.

Moreover, the solution agreed should be verifiable from the customer, in order to check the effective respect of the SLA. The adoption of SLA in the offered services has the side effect of imposing to Cloud provider to clear identify the advantages offered in a measured way. Identifying the real grants offered in the context of security is a very hard task, being at the state of art very few available solutions able to quantitatively measure the security level of a system in an incontestable way.

The approach we propose to such a problem consists in identifying the set of security threats we are able to face and try to model with quantitative parameters such threats. As an example, we can model a flooding attack as a possible threat and model it in terms of the number of flooding messages received by the system. Our SLA will be built starting from the list of all the threats we are able to face, and the offered security level will be based on the quantitative parameters we have identified to model the security threat. Such an approach can be adopted in each case in which the security threats can be modeled in terms of an attack, and it is possible to build up a quantitative model of such an attack.

For simplicity, in the following we will focus on a single attack against which our IT system work, in order to clarify the approach with a simple example. Having the proxy faces a larger set of attacks, the real SLA will be much more complex than the one proposed here. Specifically, the attack we focus, as described in Sec. 4, is an X-DoS attack. This attack founds on the simple idea that XML schema validator will be heavily CPU intensive when it has to check a (valid) XML document with a very high number of nested tags. When an attack takes place, the CPU consumption increases even if only few malicious messages are processed by the Web Server. Our solution detects the attack using the following set of information: $< MeanNumberoftags >$, $< MeanCPUUsage >$, $< TimeRange >$. The detection takes place on interval of duration time $< TimeRange >$. In such time interval we evaluate if both mean CPU consumption and mean number of tags are over fixed thresholds.

Such a model to detect the attack, that we call *SimpleThreshold*, can be model by using the following simple parameters: *CPU Threshold*, *TAG Threshold*, and *Time Range*.

Our IT model is able to grant that the Web Server is protected against a Deeply-Nested XML DoS attacks, detectable with a *SimpleThreshold* technique with parameters $< CPUThreshold >$, $< TAGThreshold >$, $< TimeRange >$. Our solution grants that if such an attack takes place, there will be no additional CPU usage on the Web Server. The user knows exactly the conditions under which its own Web Server is protected and he is able to adapt the IT Proxy parameters.

It is important to point out that, such an SLA is correct, but very hard to manage for customers, therefore, the target users are the Web Server administrator with great experience. In future work, we will offer tools that help in managing such information in a more easy way, using semantic technologies.

In order to offer the SLA in a formal way, we translate such information in a WS-Agreement template, that can be filled by users in order to negotiate the parameters. We defined a simple schema for management of our security tags, which enable to list the attacks against which the system is protected. The code represented in Listing 1.1 shows the example of guarantee terms for the Web service (that is described in an OCCI compliant way).

Listing 1.1. X-Dos Guarantee term for WS-Agreement.

```
<ws:ServiceDescriptionTerm ws:Name="WEB SERVER REQUEST"
    ws:ServiceName="SET VARIABLE">
        <Compute>
            <architecture>x86</architecture>
            <cpuCores>4</cpuCores>
                [...]
                <title>WebServer</title>
            </Compute>
    </ws:ServiceDescriptionTerm>
[...]
    <wsag:GuaranteeTerm wsag:Name="ITS" wsag:ServiceScope="WEB
        SERVER REQUEST" Obligated:"provider">
    <wsag:ServiceLevelObjectives>
        <wsag:KPITarget>
            <wsag:KPIName>XML DoS</wsag:KPIName>
            <wsag:Target>
                <itsag:Attack name="Nested TAG" />
                <itasg:Detection name="SimpleThreshold">
                    <itsag:Parameter name="CPUThreshold" value="90"
                        unit="percentage"/>
                    <itsag:Parameter name="TAGThreshold" value="20"
                        unit="number"/>
                    <itsag:Parameter name="TimeRange" value="5" unit=
                        "minutes"/>
                </itasg:Detection>
                <itsag:Reaction time="120" unit="minutes"/>
                <itsag:Description link="http://www.mosaic-Cloud.eu
                    /ITS/Attacks/NestedTag" />
            </wsag:Target>
        </wsag:KPITarget>
        </wsag:ServiceLevelObjectives>

    </wsag:GuaranteeTerm>
```

Our solution enables description of attacks, following the proposed approach just in terms of few parameters:

- *Attack* just contains the name of the attack.
- *Description* has several attributes, including the used language, the description of the attack and of the possible (supported) detection systems.
- *Detection* has an attribute that identifies the supported detection method and contains the list of parameters needed to evaluate the detection model.
- *Reaction* has an attribute, that identifies the time needed to react, which means that the system may have some side effects of the attacks for that interval of time.

Such a guarantee terms grant the customer that each attack listed as $KPIName$ and detectable with the listed detection methods will not affect the performances of the target system. It is responsibility of the IaaS provider identify the penalties to be paid in the case in which the condition is not respected.

8   Related Work

To the best of our knowledge not much work has been done in the area of configuring security requirements specified through WS-Agreement documents. Karjoth et *al.* [18] introduce the concept of Service-Oriented Assurance (SOAS). SOAS is a new paradigm that defines the security as an integral part of service-oriented architectures. It provides a framework in which the providers define their offered security assurances, as well as assess the security of their sub-services. SOAS enables discovery of sub-services with the right level of security. Moreover, SOAS adds security providing assurances (an assurance is a statement about the properties of a component or service) as part of the SLA negotiation process. Smith et *al.* [19] present a WS-Agreement approach for a fine grained security configuration mechanism to allow an optimization of the application performance based on specific security requirements. They present an approach to optimize Grid application performance by tuning service and job security settings based on customer supplied WS-Agreement specification. The WS-Agreement describes security requirements and capabilities in addition to the traditional WS-Negotiation attributes, such as computational needs, quality-of-service (QoS), and pricing. Brandic et *al.* [20] present advanced QoS methods for meta-negotiations and SLA-mappings in Grid workflows. They approach the gap between existing QoS methods and Grid workflows by proposing an architecture for Grid workflow management with components for meta-negotiations and SLA-mappings. Meta-negotiations are defined by means of a document, where each participant may express, for example, the pre-requisites to be satisfied for a negotiation, the supported negotiation protocols and document languages for the specification of SLAs. In the pre-requisites there is the element $< security >$ that specifies the authentication and authorization mechanisms that the party wants to apply before starting the negotiation. With SLA-mappings, they eliminate semantic inconsistencies between consumer's and provider's SLA template. They present an architecture for the management of meta-negotiation documents and SLA-mappings and incorporate that architecture into a Grid workflow management tool.

9   Conclusions and Future Works

In this paper, we have shown how it is possible, using a Cloud-oriented API derived from the mOSAIC project, to build up an SLA-oriented Cloud application. It enables the management of security features related to Intrusion Tolerance against XML-based Denial of Services attacks to an Infrastructure as a Service (IaaS) Cloud provider. The application that enables SLA management is built in order to receive a WS-Agreement file containing a description of the security features. We proposed a simple schema for description of the guarantees offered by the system to the customers against DoS attacks. Once the customer has obtained an agreement with the SLA management system, his requests will be transparently enriched with security features. In our case study, we support the Web Server with an Intrusion Tolerance system that grants against a defined attack type. Finally, in previous work [23], we proposed an extensible intrusion detection management framework, which can be offered to Cloud providers in order to implement distributed IDSs for detection of cyber attacks to their Clouds. In future work, we will integrate the contribute of the current paper with the implemented intrusion detection framework presented in [23].

References

1. Westphall, C.B., Lamin, F.R.: SLA Perspective in Security Management for Cloud Computing. In: Proc. of the Int. Conf. on Networking and Services, pp. 212–217 (2010)
2. Cheng, F., Meinel, C.: Intrusion Detection in the Cloud. In: Proc. of the IEEE Int. Conf. on Dependable, Autonomic and Secure Computing, pp. 729–734 (December 2009)
3. mOSAIC: Open Source API and platform for multiple Clouds (2010), http://www.mosaic-cloud.eu
4. Rak, M., Venticinque, S., Aversa, R., Di Martino, B.: User Centric Service Level Management in mOSAIC Application. In: Proc. of the Europar 2011 Workshop, pp. 106–115. IEEE CS Press (2011)
5. Kouznetsov, P., Haeberlen, A., Druschel, P.: The case for Byzantine fault detection. In: Proc. of the 2nd Workshop on Hot Topics in System Dependability, pp. 5–10 (2006)
6. Neves, N.F., Sousa, P., Verissimo, P.: Proactive resilience through architectural hybridization. In: Proc. of the ACM Symp. on Applied Computing (SAC 2006), pp. 686–690 (2006)
7. Mista, R., Bakken, D., Dyreron, C., Franz, A., Medidi, M.: Mrfusion: A programmable data fusion middleware subsystem with a tunable statistical profiling service. In: Proc. of the Int. Conference on Dependable Systems and Network (DSN 2002), pp. 273–278 (2002)
8. Ficco, M., Rak, M.: Intrusion tolerance of stealth DoS attacks to web services. In: Gritzalis, D., Furnell, S., Theoharidou, M. (eds.) SEC 2012. IFIP AICT, vol. 376, pp. 579–584. Springer, Heidelberg (2012)
9. Coppolino, L., D'Antonio, S., Esposito, M., Romano, L.: Exploiting diversity and correlation to improve the performance of intrusion detection systems. In: Proc. of the Int. Conf. on Network and Service Security, pp. 24–26 (2009)
10. Ficco, M., Romano, L.: A generic intrusion detection and diagnoser system based on complex event processing. In: Proc. of the 1st International Conference on Data Compression, Communication, and Processing (CCP 2011), pp. 285–292 (2011)
11. Heimbigner., D., Knight, J., Wolf, A.: The willow architecture: Comprehensive survivability for large-scale distributed applications. In: Proc. of the Intrusion Tolerant System Workshop, pp. 71–78 (2002)
12. Squid: an open source fully-featured HTTP/1.0 proxy (2012), http://www.squid-cache.org
13. Ganglia, a scalable distributed monitoring system for high-performance computing systems (2012), http://ganglia.sourceforge.net
14. Ficco, M., Rak, M.: Intrusion tolerant approach for denial of service attacks to web services. In: Proc. of the 1st Int. Conf. on Data Compression, Communications and Processing (CCP 2011), pp. 285–292. IEEE CS Press (2011)
15. TPC Benchmark W (TPC-W), a transactional web benchmark (2012), http://www.tpc.org/tpcw/
16. Ficco, M., Rak, M.: Intrusion tolerance in cloud applications: The mOSAIC approach. In: Proc. of the 6th International Conference on Complex, Intelligent, and Software Intensive Systems, CISIS 2012, pp. 170–176 (2012)
17. Rak, M., Liccardo, L., Aversa, R.: A SLA-based Interface for Security Management in Cloud and GRID Integrations. In: Proc. of the 7th International Conference on Information Assurance and Security (IAS). IEEE Press (2011)

18. Karjoth, G., Pfitzmann, B., Schunter, M., Waidner, M.: Service-oriented Assurance, Comprehensive Security by Explicit Assurances. In: Quality of Protection, vol. 23, pp. 13–24. Springer (2006)
19. Smith, M., Schmidt, M., Fallenbeck, N., Schridde, C., Freisleben, B.: Optimising Security Configurations with Service Level Agreements. In: Proc. of the 7th Int. Conf. on Optimization: Techniques and Applications (ICOTA 2007), pp. 367–381. IEEE Press (2007)
20. Brandic, I., Music, D., Dustdar, S., Venugopal, S., Buyya, R.: Advanced QoS methods for Grid workflows based on meta-negotiations and SLA-mappings. In: Proc. of the 3th Workshop on Workflows in Support of Large Scale Science (2008)
21. Ficco, M., Rak, M., Di Martino, B.: An intrusion detection framework for supporting SLA assessment in cloud computing. In: Proc. of the 4th Int. Conf. on Computational Aspects of Social Networks (CASoN), pp. 244–249. IEEE CS Press (November 2012)
22. Palmieri, F., Fiore, U., Castiglione, A.: Automatic security assessment for next generation wireless mobile networks. In: Mobile Information Systems, vol. 7(3), pp. 217–239. IOS Press (2011)
23. Ficco, M., Venticinque, S., Di Martino, B.: mOSAIC-Based intrusion detection framework for cloud computing. In: Meersman, R., et al. (eds.) OTM 2012, Part II. LNCS, vol. 7566, pp. 628–644. Springer, Heidelberg (2012)

Cloud Storage and Bioinformatics in a Private Cloud Deployment: Lessons for Data Intensive Research

Victor Chang[1,2], Robert John Walters[1], and Gary Wills[1]

[1] Electronics and Computer Science, University of Southampton,
Southampton SO 17 1BJ, U.K.
[2] School of Computing and Creative Technologies, Leeds Metropolitan University,
Headingley, Leeds LS6 3QS, U.K.
{vic1e09,rjw1,gbw}@ecs.soton.ac.uk,
V.I.Chang@leedsmet.ac.uk

Abstract. This paper describes service portability for a private cloud deployment, including a detailed case study about Cloud Storage and bioinformatics services developed as part of the Cloud Computing Adoption Framework (CCAF). Our Cloud Storage design and deployment is based on Storage Area Network (SAN) technologies, details of which include functionalities, technical implementation, architecture and user support. Experiments for data services (backup automation, data recovery and data migration) are performed and results confirm backup automation is completed swiftly and is reliable for data-intensive research. The data recovery result confirms that execution time is in proportion to quantity of recovered data, but the failure rate increases in an exponential manner. The data migration result confirms execution time is in proportion to disk volume of migrated data, but again the failure rate increases in an exponential manner. In addition, benefits of CCAF are illustrated using several bioinformatics examples such as tumour modelling, brain imaging, insulin molecules and simulations for medical training. Our Cloud Storage solution described here offers cost reduction, time-saving and user friendliness.

1 Introduction

Cloud Computing offers a variety of benefits including cost-saving, agility, efficiency, resource consolidation, business opportunities and Green IT [9-13, 16-18, 20, 23]. As more organisations adopt Cloud, the need for a standard, or a framework to manage both operation management and IT services is emerging. This framework needs to provide the structure necessary to ensure any Cloud implementation meets the business needs of Industry and Academia and include recommendations of best practices which can be adapted for different domains and platforms. Our framework is called the Cloud Computing Adoption Framework (CCAF). It helps organisations to achieve good Cloud design, implementation and services [11-20]. CCAF may be used from service strategy to design, development, test and user support stages. The CCAF seeks to address two problems in particular:

I. Ivanov et al. (Eds.): CLOSER 2012, CCIS 367, pp. 245–264, 2013.

- Calculating Cloud Business Performance systematically and coherently.
- Portability of services into the Cloud

This paper focuses on service portability which is the term we use to describe a recommended approach to Cloud adoption. Cloud adoption plays an important role in having a smooth transition to the Cloud environment. Beaty et al. [3] and Chang et al. [11,18,20] identify portability as an adoption challenge for organisational Cloud adoption. Although it is domain specific as there are different requirements for portability in each domain, communication between different types of clouds supplied by different vendors can be difficult to implement. Often work-arounds are needed which entail writing additional layers of APIs, or an interface or portal [2,3].

Service portability (portability in short) is illustrated using examples from Cloud Storage projects in the Healthcare industry where portability is influential in migrating existing infrastructure, platforms and applications to the Cloud and later developing new applications and services. The storage is provided using in-house private clouds, initially to provide a working IaaS infrastructure for medical databases, images and analysis in a secure and collaborative environment. These Cloud projects have been successfully delivered and provide a high level of user satisfaction and were followed up with further work to upgrade from IaaS to PaaS, which allows greater benefits, including better efficiency and better management of resources. We also present results from experiments for data services (backup automation, data recovery and data migration) which can help us to meet issues and challenges of data-intensive research. The structure of this paper is as follows. Section 2 describes the overview of Cloud Storage and Section 3 presents its deployment architecture and user support. Section 4 explains bioinformatics and its associated results. Section 5 discusses performance results for data-intensive storage. Section 6 presents topics of discussion and Section 7 sums up Conclusion and future work.

2   Healthcare Cloud Storage

Supported by NHS UK, Guy's and St Thomas NHS Trust (GSTT) and King's College London (KCL) have worked together on projects to implement Cloud Storage and deliver it as a service. The initial effort was directed to an evaluation of the technology and developed a proof of concept service. CCAF is instrumental and influential in the way Cloud Storage has been developed:

- Healthcare Cloud Storage is a PaaS system, and needed careful planning and a thorough implementation. This required integrated adoption of multiple vendors' solutions.

- Healthcare Cloud Storage is an area to experience rapid growth in user requirements and disk space consumption. Therefore, it had to be easy to use, and able to cope with increasing demand.

- Healthcare Cloud Storage is a new concept and implementation in the Health domain where private and in-house storage has been used in the past. Maintenance of data protection and security is a challenge.

Better performance in from Healthcare Cloud Storage than previous storage service is regarded as a benchmark and measurement for success by executives. Recommendations, strategy and support from CCAF provided useful good services. Healthcare Cloud Storage has used trials during its design and implementation to ensure it meets its requirement to provide a robust service.

Healthcare Cloud Storage is used by the Breast Cancer project. Breast cancer is the most common cancer in women and has a worldwide annual incidence of over 1 million cases. There are many thousands of data about patients (medical records) and tumours (detailed descriptions and images, and its relations to the patients). Data growth is rapid and the data needs to be carefully used and protected. The work involves integrating software and cloud technologies from commercial vendors including Oracle, VMWare, EMC, Iomega and HP. This is to ensure a solid infrastructure and platform is available. Researchers also use third party applications to access, view and edit tumour images from trusted locations. Security is enforced in terms of data encryption, SSL and firewalls. Ion addition to Cloud Storage, the Health Cloud platform also provides Bioinformatics services, which provide scientific visualisation and modelling of genes, proteins, DNA, tumour and brain images. Users are very supportive in this project and some of them use it daily.

2.1 Benefits from Adopting CCAF

Adopting CCAF assists with understanding of requirements, technical knowledge, use cases and issues to be aware of, before and during the project development. Healthcare Cloud Storage is implemented as a Private Cloud project and is divided into four stages summed up as follows.

Stage 1	Explore available technologies, understanding strength and weaknesses for each key technology. Capture user requirements to get into technical plans.
Stage 2	Propose a framework based on the outcomes in Stage 1 and CCAF, and carry out plans for building and validating the framework.
Stage 3	Propose and implement service oriented architecture for Cloud Storage based on CCAF. Offer services for users and research groups.
Stage 4	Continue service improvements and further integration with other services and other new requirements.

Healthcare Cloud offers a wide range of self- and automated services across secure networks. It has two different focuses. It must be easy to use and support several research groups (both synchronously and asynchronously) and be able to cope with frequent changes, updates and user activities. It must also be highly robust and stable, allowing data to be kept safe, secure and active for extended periods of time (ten years and above). Both aspects demand for the following four requirements:

- Automated backup.
- Data recovery and emergency services. Snapshots or disaster recovery are used.

- Quality of services: high availability, reliability and great usability.

- Security.

This needs the state-of-the-art design and implementation that the CCAF can offer. The CCAF positively influences the way the backup and storage are designed and deployed. CCAF also offers implementation insights such as integration, as it is a challenge to co-ordinate and to combine different research activities and repositories into a distributed storage. This leads to the use of third party applications and services to improve on the quality of services.

2.2   A Storage Area Network Made Up of Different Clusters of Network Attached Storage (NAS)

The Architecture design chosen uses two concurrent platforms. The first is based on Network Attached Storage (NAS), and the second is based on the Storage Area Network (SAN). The NAS platform provides great usability and accessibility for users. Each NAS may be allocated to a research group and operate independently. Then all the NAS can be joined up to establish a SAN. NAS supports individual backups with manual and automated options. One option is similar to the Dropbox pattern of backup enabling users to copy their files onto their allocated disk space without difficulty providing a backup facility which is easy to use and user-friendly. Such a manual service allows users to backup their resources onto a selected destination and can offer both compressed and uncompressed versions of backup as well as data encryption to enforce security.

The Storage Area Network (SAN) is a dedicated and extremely reliable backup solution offering a highly robust and stable platform. SAN can consolidate an organisational backup platform and can improve capabilities and performance of Cloud Storage. SAN allows data to be kept safe and archived for a long period of time, and is a chosen technology. A SAN can be made up of different NAS, so that each NAS can focus on a particular function.

The design of SAN focuses on SCSI, which offers dual controllers and dual networking gigabyte channels. Each SAN server is built on RAID system. RAID 10 is a good choice since it can boost the performance like RAID 0 but also has mirroring capability like RAID1. A SAN can be built to have 12TB of disk space, and a group of SAN can form a solid cluster, or a dedicated Wide Area of Network. There are written and upgraded applications in each SAN to achieve the following functions:

- Performance improvement and monitoring: This allows tracking the overall and specific performance of the SAN cluster, and also enhances group or individual performance if necessary.

- Disk management: When a pool of SAN is established, it is important to know which hard disks in the SAN serve for which servers or which user groups.

- Advanced backup: Similar functionalities to those described in the NAS, such as automation, data recovery and quality of services, are available here. The difference is more sophisticated techniques and mechanisms (use of enterprise software is optional) are required.

Some applications mainly based on PHP, MySQL and Apache have been written, to allow researchers to access the digital repository containing tumours. Users can access their Cloud Storage via browsers from trusted offices, and they need not worry about complexity, and work as if on their familiar systems. This Healthcare PaaS is a demonstration of enterprise portability. In addition, several upgrades have taken place to ensure the standard of Cloud Storage and quality of services. One example is the use of SSL certificates and the enforced authentication and authorisation of every user to improve on security. There is an automated service to backup important resources.

3   Healthcare Cloud Storage Deployment Architecture and User Support

This section describes how Cloud Storage is set up, and how its key functionality offers services and user support. Cloud Storage is a private-cloud SAN architecture made up of different NAS services, where each NAS is dedicated for one specific function. Design and Deployment is based on group requirements and their research focus.

3.1   Design and Deployment to Meet Challenges for Data Intensive Research

Design and deployment should meet challenges for data-intensive research challenges. Moore et al [25] and Bryant [4] point out that data-intensive research should meet demands for data recovery and data migration and allows a large number of data to be recovered and moved quickly and efficiently in ordinary operations and in emergency. This is suitable for Cloud Storage as the design and deployment must provide resilient, swift and effective services. Vo, Chen and Ooi [27] present their perspective on Cloud Storage and demonstrate how to perform experiments in data intensive environments, including performing read, write and transaction operations. They demonstrate their solution for data migration but there is a lack of consideration of data recovery which is important in the event of possible data loss. Abu-Libdeh, Princehouse and Weatherspoon [1] demonstrate their Cloud Storage case study which presents how "Failure Recovery" can get large-scaled data recovery and data migration completed. Although they demonstrate data migration and data recovery over months in their in-house development, they do not show the execution time for each data migration and recovery. This is an important aspect in Cloud Storage to allow each operation of large-scale data recovery and data migration to run smoothly and effectively. Design and deployment of Cloud Storage must meet demands in large-scaled backup automation, data recovery and data migration.

3.2   Selections of Technology Solutions

Selections of Technology Solutions are essential for Cloud Storage development as presented in Table 1.

Table 1. Selections of Technology Solutions

Technology selections	What is it used	Vendors involved	Focus or rationale	Benefits or impacts
Network Attached Storage (NAS)	To store data and perform automated and manual/ personal backup.	Iomega/EMC Lacie Western Digital HP	They have a different focus and set up. HP is more robust but more time-consuming to configure. The rest is distributed between RAID 0, 1 and 5.	Each specific function is assigned with each NAS. There are 5 NAS at GSTT/KCL site and 3 at Data Centre, including 2 for Archiving. Deployment Architecture is shown in Figure 1.
Infrastructure (networking and hosting solution)	Collaborator and in-house	University of London Data Centre	Some services need a more secure and reliable place. University of London Data Centre offers 24/7 services with around 500 servers in place, and is ideal for hosting solution.	Amount of work is reduced for maintenance of the entire infrastructure. It stores crucial data and used for archiving, which backup historical data and backup the most important data automatically and periodically.
Backup applications	Third party and in-house	Open Source Oracle HP Vmware Symantec In-house development	There is a mixture of in-house development and third party solution. HP software is used for high availability and reliability. The rest is to support backup in between NAS. Vmware is used for virtual storage and backup.	Some applications are good in a particular service, and it is important to identify the most suitable application for particular services.
Virtualisation	Third party	VMware VSphere and Citrix	It consolidates IaaS and PaaS in private cloud deployment.	Resources can be virtualised and saves effort such as replication.
Security	Third party and in-house	KCL/GSTT Macafee Symantec F5	Security is based on the in-house solution and vendor solution is focused on secure firewall and anti-virus.	Remote access is given to a list of approved users.

3.3   Deployment Architecture

There are two sites for hosting data, one is jointly at GSTT and KCL premises distributed in dedicated server rooms and the other is at University of London Data Centre to store and backup the most important data. Figure 1 shows the Deployment Architecture.

There are five NAS at GSTT and KCL premises and each NAS is provided for a specific function. Bioinformatics Group has the most demands. NAS 1 is used for their secure backup, and NAS 2 is used for their computational backup, which is then connected to Bioinformatics services. NAS 3 is used as an important gateway for backup and archiving and is an active service connecting with the rest. NAS 3 is shared and used by Cancer Epidemiology and BCBG Group. NAS 4 provides mirror services for different locations and offers an alternative in case of data loss. NAS 5 is initially used by Digital Cancer cluster, and helps to back up important files in NAS 3. There are two digital cancer clusters, which can back up between each other, and important data are backed up to NAS 8 for reliability and NAS 5 for local version. The reason for this is that a disaster recovery activity which took place in 2010 took two weeks full time to retrieve and recover data. Multiple backups ensure if one dataset is lost, the most recent archive (done daily) can be replaced without much time spent.

There are three NAS at the University of London Computing (Data) Centre (ULCC) where there are about 500 servers hosted for Cloud and HPC services. NAS 6 is used as a central backup database to store and archive experimental data and images. The other two advanced servers are customised to work as NAS 7 and 8 to store and archive valuable data. Performance for backup and archiving services is excellent and most data can be backed up in a short and acceptable time frame of less than one hour to back up data and images. This outcome is widely supported by users and executives. There are additional five high performance computing services based on Cloud technologies: Two are computational statistics to analyse complex data. The third one is a database to store confidential data and the fourth is on bioinformatics to help bioinformatics research. The last one is a virtualisation service that allows all data and backup to be in virtual storage format. These five services are not included in Cloud Storage for this paper.

3.4   User Support

The entire Cloud Storage Service has automated capability and is easy to use. This service has been in use without the presence of Chief Architect for six months, without major problems reported. Secondary level of user support at GSTT and KCL (such as login, networking and power restoration) has been excellent. There is a plan to obtain approval to measure user satisfaction.

4   Bioinformatics

The bioinformatics services activity started in September 2008 and was completed in February 2011. It is an in-house solution focusing on scientific visualisation and modelling aiming to understand research analysis and improve existing services. The use of Cloud offers two distinct advantages:

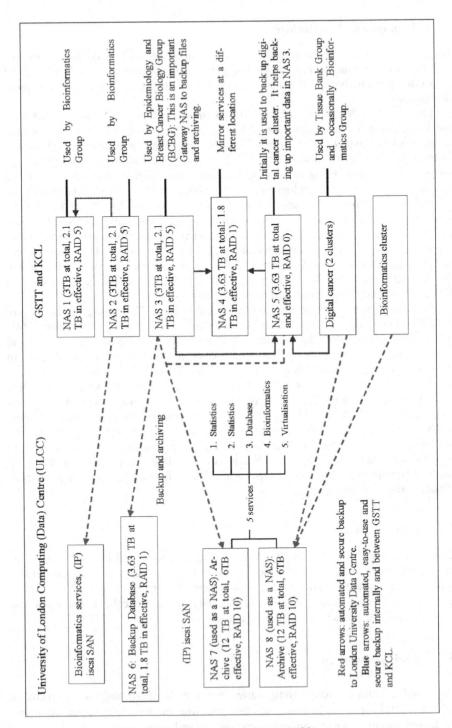

Fig. 1. Cloud Storage Deployment Architecture

(i) A PaaS for developers to simulate dynamic 3D modelling and visualisation for proteins, genes, molecules and medical imaging, where results can be instantaneous and data can be visualised, stored and shared securely.

(ii) Any complex modelling, such as growth of tumour and segmentation of brains, can be presented with the ease.

Each section is described as follows.

4.1   Tumour Modelling

Tumours develop as a result of abnormal and rapid growth of cells, and there are two types of tumours. The first type is benign tumours, which are harmless to human bodies. The second type is malignant tumours, which are malicious, should be removed and patients with them should be treated as soon as possible. Despite the fact that current technologies can take high-resolution pictures of tumours, it is extremely helpful for high performance Cloud resources to simulate the growth and formation of tumours, and this allows scientists and surgeons to diagnose possibilities of tumour growth and gain a better understanding about treatment [21]. See Figure 2 for tumour modelling.

Fig. 2. Selected figures in Tumour modelling

4.2   Medical Imaging

Medical imaging is widely adopted in Hospitals and medical institutes, and new ways to improve existing medical imaging services are regularly exploited. Bioinformatics Cloud platform allows computation and visualisation, and currently brain imaging can be used for demonstration. The aim is to study segmentation of brains, which divides the brain into ten major regions. The Cloud platform has these two functions: (i) it can highlight each region for ten different segments; and (ii) it can adjust intensity of segmentation to allow basic study of brain medicine. Figure 3 below shows selected brain imaging. Segmentation is an important aspect in brain study and it has two different functionalities. Firstly, it can highlight different areas in the cerebrum, where the different light intensity can highlight which particular areas. Secondly, segmentation can show different areas in the brain, including cerebellum, temporal lobe, mid-brain and so on. This allows medical students and instructors to understand the structure of human brain with the ease, but it also provides a platform to identity the right spot of the brain in a quick and efficient manner.

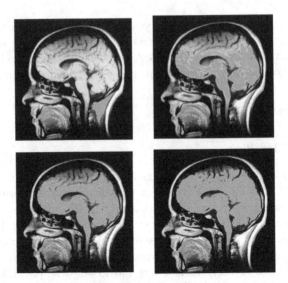

Fig. 3. Selected brain imaging

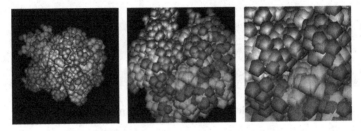

Fig. 4. Investigation of insulin molecules on Cloud

4.3   Insulin Molecules

Insulin is a hormone central to regulating carbohydrate and fat metabolism in the body, and is important for type one diabetes treatment. Insulin has a molecular structure, and the study of its structure and formation helps scientists to understand how to improve treatment. Cloud offers a platform for simulations and modelling enabling cutting-edge techniques to be used for Health Cloud for 3D Visualisation and modelling. This allows researchers to identify the areas in the molecule that they plan to study, and it allows 360 degrees rotation and zooming function, so that one particular area in the molecule can be magnified for different studies. Figure 4 shows the insulin molecule in original size and in zooms.

4.4   Simulations for Medical Training

3D simulations on Cloud are very useful for medical education and workshop, since explanations can be made easier and participants can understand better with the aid of visualisation. 3D simulations such as DNA modelling, Poyllotaxis Spirals and cleavage of embryos have been used for training, and have positive feedback and support.

5   Trials for Cloud Storage

The design and implementation of a robust Storage Area Network (SAN) requires integrations of different technologies. Only minimal modelling and simulations are needed, since the focus is on building up a service from the very beginning. Experiments provide a suitable research method, since they can identify issues such as performance, technical capabilities (such as recovery), and whether integration of technologies can deliver services. User and executive requirements are important factors for what type of experiments to be performed and measured. Thousands of files (data and records) are used for performance tests and the time to complete the same amount of jobs is recorded. Venue of test is between two sites: ULCC and GSTT/KCL and execution time is used as the benchmark. There are three data services and each service is used to perform experiments as follows:

• Backup Automation
• Data recovery
• Data migration

5.1   Backup Automation

Cloud Storage uses a number of enterprise solutions such as Iomega/EMC, Lacie, Western Digital and HP to deliver fast and reliable services including automation. The experiment performs automated backup of between 1,000 and 10,000 files, which are available in the existing system for user support. Each set of experiments is performed three times with the average time obtained. Results are shown in Figure 5.

5.2   Data Recovery

Data recovery is another important service to recover lost data due to accidents or emergency services. In the previous experience, it took two weeks to recover 5 TB of data as it required different skills and systems to retrieve data and restore good quality data back to Cloud services. Data archived as Virtual Machines or Virtual Storage speeds up recovery process. In addition, there are mirror servers so, even if a server is completely broken, data can be recovered to resume services. See Figure 6 for their execution time.

5.3   Data Migration of Single Large Files

Data migration is common amongst Clouds and is also relevant to data intensive research. When there are more organisations going for private cloud deployment, data migration between Clouds is common and may influence the service delivery [2,6,7,22]. But there is no investigation the impact of moving single large files between private clouds. Hence, the objective here is to identify the execution time for moving single large file. Each file is between 100 GB and 1 TB. Figure 7 shows the results.

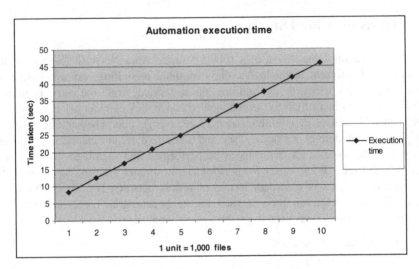

Fig. 5. Automation execution time for Cloud Storage

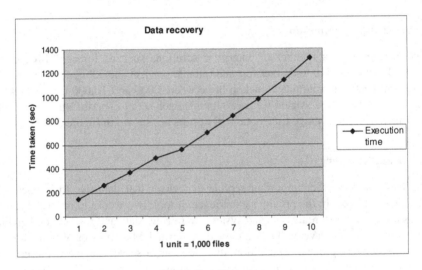

Fig. 6. Data Recovery

5.4   The Percentage of Failure Rates

The percentage of failure rates in Cloud Storage operations is important as each failure in service will result in loss of time, profit and resources. This part of experiment is to calculate the percentage of failures, where services in Section 5.1 and 5.3 are running real-time and record the number of successful and failed operations. Failed operations happen in the Cloud environments. Monitoring the failure rate is important as failures contribute to the development of risks. To reduce the impacts

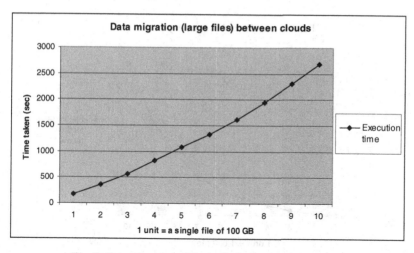

Fig. 7. Data migration of large single files between clouds

from risk (as a result of Cloud adoption), Chang et al [12,13,16,20] demonstrate that controlled risk in Cloud adoption can be monitored and presented in the form of risk-free rate, or risk-occurring rate if the focus is on the measuring the extent of failure rates. There are hundreds of successful operations versus and a number of failed operations.

5.4.1   Failure Rate in Backup Automation

Backup automation is relatively reliable and out of hundreds of thousands of operations, the failure rate is below 2%. The reason is that backup automation has been available for a significant number of years with the result that it is a mature technology

5.4.2   Failure Rate in Data Recovery

Data recovery for large-scale data in Cloud is important and the failure rate is shown in Figure 8 based on the number of successful and failed operations since 2009. The interesting result is when there is a low amount of data, the percentage of failure is low. When the amount of recovered data increases, the execution time is approximately proportional to the amount of data but the failure rate increases more quickly and the graph looks close to an exponential curve.

5.4.3   Failure Rate in Data Migration

Data migration of large files in Cloud is common and important as Storage is designed for terabytes and petabytes. The failure rate is shown in Figure 9 based on the number of successful and failed operations since 2009. Similar to Figure 8, the curve is close to an exponential one, which means when the volume of the migrated file increases, the failure rate increases significantly.

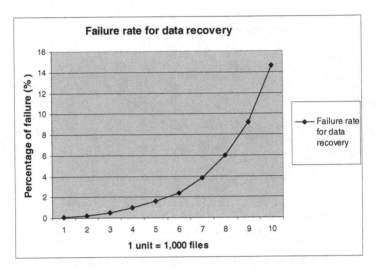

Fig. 8. Failure rate of data recovery

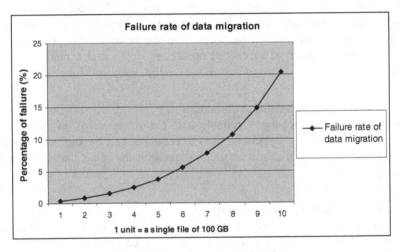

Fig. 9. Failure rate of data migration

5.5   Summary of All Experiments

Service and backup automation for Cloud storage takes the least execution time and there are several services to speed up the process of automation. Execution time is between 8 and 46 seconds backup 1,000 to 10,000 files to automatically. The second experiment is data recovery, where data archived as Virtual Machines or Virtual Storage in a well-managed platform can speed up recovery process. Data recovery takes between 135 seconds to 1,312 seconds to recover 1,000 to 10,000 of files. The third experiment focuses on data migration of large single files, which are important for data intensive research. Data migration takes between 174 seconds to 2,686 seconds to move a single file of 100 GB to 1 TB. Although Figures 3 and 4 still show a linear graph, more execution time is required to recover data and move a large single file and the percentage of unsuccessful data recovery and migration is likely to increase.

The results strongly suggest that it is quicker to move data around Clouds in many smaller files. Our results also confirm that automation in Cloud is better established than data recovery and data migration of single large files, and these two are perhaps challenges that data-intensive research need to overcome. Failure rate for these three major operations are demonstrated. Backup automation is the most reliable and stays below 2% all the times. Figure 6 is similar to Figure 5 and shows that failure rate of data migration; when the volume of the migrated file increases, so does the failure rate.

6   Discussions

There are several topics for discussions presented as follows.

6.1   Challenges for Data Intensive Research in Cloud

Cloud Storage can offer services up to petabytes of storage and beyond. The results in Section 4 confirm that large-scaled data recovery and data migration in Cloud need to improve in its technical capabilities. This is reflected in the percentage of failure rate and how the failure rate apparently increases exponentially to 14.6% as data recovery volume increases to 10,000 files. Similarly, an exponential increase is experienced to 20.4% when data migration disk increases to 1 TB per file. Our results demonstrate data recovery and data migration issues for thousands of files have to be resolved and improved prior dealing with challenges in petabytes.

6.2   User Feedback on Cloud Storage

Currently Cloud Storage has provided users the following benefits:

- Cost reduction: The service is automated and saves costs in hiring and deploying staff and deployment of a larger and more expensive project that works the same. There is no need to hire a team to look after maintenance and daily services.
- Time-saving: Cloud Storage simplifies the complex backup process and saves time in performing backups. Users find that they need not spend significant time for back up.
- User friendliness: Cloud Storage offers easy to use features and users without prior knowledge can find it simple to use.

Healthcare community has a Data Protection Policy and not all types of services are able to release data. Services that do not use patients' data or confidential information are likely to be presented.

6.3   Plug and Play Features in Cloud Storage for Data Intensive Research

There are papers explaining the importance and relevance of data intensive research, and why it is essential for Cloud development and services [22,26]. This Cloud Storage allows plugs and play, which means adding additional hard disks to existing NAS, or new NAS, can still provide services in place. This has been tested in 2010 where disk volume of NAS 7 and 8 were increased from 20 TB to 44 TB without interruptions of services. This Cloud Storage was also tested to store and protect data of up to 100 TB on another occasion. This allows any addition of hard disks and applications within 100 TB limit to provide user support and services.

Cloud Storage has been in used daily by medical researchers, and there are a few local administrators supporting a minimum level of services. The focus for this service is no longer in technical implementation but rather user satisfaction.

6.4   Relative Performance

Buyya et al [5,6,7] describe technical performance in detail. Often results are very technical and most organisations considering or implementing Clouds find those results difficult to follow [10,11,13]. Relative performance is an easier term to compare performance with, and is defined as the improvement in performance between an old service (before) and a new service (after). Latch et al. [24] also use relative performance to present their Bayesian clustering software where the key performance indicators are presented in terms of percentages of improvement. Although Latch et al. [24] still use statistical approach where some data have little impact or relevance to organisational adoption, the benefit of using relative performance approach is to bring down level of complexity and allows stake holders to understand the percentage of improvement.

A hybrid case study is relevant for organisational Cloud adoption, since data needs to be checked prior computational analysis and often this needs supporting interviews and surveys. From interviewing members of management, their views can be summed up as follows:

- They support the use of relative performance, as most of the executives are not from IT backgrounds.

- The use of key performance indicators in relative performance makes it easy for the executives to understand and follow the extents of improvement.

6.5   The Proposal for "Healthcare Platform as a Service" (Hpaas) for Research and Education

Cloud Computing offers contributions to research and development, as complex simulations can be computed and modelled with the on-demand capabilities, elasticity and scalability that Cloud can provide. Genes, molecules and medical imaging can be modelled at high speed and results can be computed and viewed in real-time. This is due to the establishment of PaaS to minimise the execution time so that 3D simulation can be running right after the code development on Cloud.

Bioinformatics services also compare the performance improvements before and after introducing Cloud as an important ROI measurement. Chang et al. [12] demonstrate that 1.2% - 7.2% time reduction for code development is achieved. Their objective is clearly met and project delivery is straightforward with progressive improvements. Different Health Cloud projects in Infrastructure, Bioinformatics, Statistics, HPC, Data Services and Security have worked together in an integrated environment to establish Health Platform as a Service (HPaas), which brings the following benefits:

- Different activities in private cloud can work together.
- The expertise in each area can be consolidated within the HPaaS.
- The outcome of one service can be the input to another.

Efficiency has improved as the Cloud saves time and resources to repeat the same processes, which can be automated. This is important in case the systems and/or services break that automated virtualised environments can quickly provision to the original setting. 3D Bioinformatics enhances the level of research and simulations can help surgeons and medical staff to make the right decisions. Chang et al. [14,17,20] also demonstrate Business Integration as a Service (BIaaS) that can further improve the process and integration of different activities in HPaaS.

7   Conclusions

This paper illustrates PaaS Portability in the form of Healthcare Cloud Storage, which is designed, deployed and serviced to GSTT and KCL under the recommendation of CCAF to ensure good Cloud design, deployment and services. Service Portability has been designed, implemented and serviced at participating organisations to provide added values such as efficiency improvement and time reduction in code development and execution time. User Groups for the system are divided into Bioinformatics Group, Databank and Cancer Epidemiology Group, BCBG Group, Tissue Bank and Senior Clinicians. The CCAF was useful and helped the Health Community to achieve good private cloud design, deployment and services while following user requirements and challenges, and executives' feedback closely.

Healthcare Cloud Storage implements a data service as an easy-to-use, automated and collaborative platform which some users use every day. It is distributed between two physical locations: University of London Data Centre and GSTT/KCL and is designed and built to align with group and research requirements. It uses a private-cloud SAN architecture made up from different NAS services.

The Deployment Architecture shows the connections between different NAS services and how they are related. These services include Bioinformatics (multiple services), joint Epidemiology and BCBG service, mirror services, two archiving services, digital cancer services and multiple backup services. Automated and secure backups take place between the two physical locations.

The first lesson from this activity is that recommendations from CCAF assist with achieving good Cloud Design. A further lesson is that using experiments when designing and implementing a Cloud-based Storage Area Network (SAN) is helpful and execution time can be used as the benchmark to determine their success. Experiments were performed in three areas: automation, data recovery and data migration.

- Automation in Cloud storage has enabled several services to speed up the process of automation. Execution time is between 8 and 46 seconds to automate backup 1,000 to 10,000 files.

- Data recovery in a well-managed platform can speed up recovery process and takes between 135 seconds to 1,312 seconds to recover 1,000 to 10,000 of files. Data migration of large single files is important for data intensive research. Data migration takes between 174 seconds to 2,686 seconds to move a single file of 100 GB to 1 TB.

- Our results also confirm that backup automation in Cloud is more mature than data recovery or data migration of single large files, and these two represent challenges that data-intensive research needs to overcome. Relative performance is between Cloud Storage and traditional storage have been presented.

Percentage failure rate is calculated for backup automation, data recovery and data migration. Backup automation failure rate stays below 2% but the failure rate increases rapidly to 14.6% for data recovery as the volume increases to 10,000 files. Similarly, a rapid increase to as much as 20% is experienced in data migration as data migration file size increases towards 1 TB. These results suggest that issues and challenges remain within data recovery and migration which will need to be resolved before systems progress to handling petabytes of storage.

Healthcare platform (HPaaS) enables different activities to work together, so that expertise in one area can be consolidated. The use of 3D simulations allows developers to compute results in real-time and data can be stored, visualised and shared securely. 3D simulations of tumour, medical imaging and insulin have also helped to improve the quality of research analysis, as well as providing better understanding in the structure and formation of these analyses. All complex life science modelling can be presented with ease, so that it not only can promote greater awareness of health and disease issue, but also improves the quality of current research and development.

References

1. Abu-Libdeh, H., Princehouse, L., Weatherspoon, H.: RACS: A Case for Cloud Storage Diversity. In: SoCC 2010 Proceedings of the 1st ACM Symposium on Cloud Computing, Indianapolis, Indiana, June 10-11 (2010)
2. Armbrust, M., Fox, A., Griffith, R., Jseph, A.D., Katz, R.H., Kownwinski, A., Lee, G., Patterson, D., Rabkin, A., Stoica, I., Zaharia, M.: Above the Clouds: A Berkeley View of Cloud computing. Technical Report, No. UCB/EECS-2009-28, UC Berkeley (February 2009)

3. Beaty, K., Kochut, A., Shaikh, H.: Desktop to Cloud Transformation Planning. In: 2009 IEEE International Symposium on Parallel and Distributed Processing, Rome, Italy, May 23-May 29 (2009)

4. Bryant, R.E.: Data-Intensive Supercomputing: The Case for DISC, Technical paper, Carnegie Mellon University (October 2007)

5. Buyya, R., Yeo, C.S., Venugopal, S., Broberg, J., Brandic, I.: Cloud computing and emerging IT platforms: Vision, hype, and reality for delivering computing as the 5th utility. Journal of Future Generation Computer Systems 25(6), 559–616 (2009)

6. Buyya, R., Ranjan, R., Calheiros, R.N.: InterCloud: Utility-Oriented Federation of Cloud Computing Environments for Scaling of Application Services. In: Hsu, C.-H., Yang, L.T., Park, J.H., Yeo, S.-S. (eds.) ICA3PP 2010, Part I. LNCS, vol. 6081, pp. 13–31. Springer, Heidelberg (2010)

7. Buyya, R., Beloglazov1, A., Abawajy, J.: Energy-Efficient Management of Data Center Resources for Cloud Computing: A Vision, Architectural Elements, and Open Challenges. In: Buyya, et al. (eds.) PDPTA 2010 - The International Conference on Parallel and Distributed Processing Techniques and Applications, Las Vegas, USA, July 12-15 (2010b)

8. Chang, V.: Cloud Storage Framework – An Integrated Technical Approach and Prototype for Breast Cancer., Poster Paper and Technical Paper, UK All Hands Meeting (December 2009)

9. Chang, V., Bacigalupo, D., Wills, G., De Roure, D.: A Categorisation of Cloud Computing Business Models. In: Chang, et al. (eds.) The 10th IEEE/ACM International Symposium on Cluster, Cloud and Grid Computing, CCGrid 2010, Melbourne, Australia, May 17-20, pp. 509–512 (2010a)

10. Chang, V., Wills, G., De Roure, D.: A Review of Cloud Business Models and Sustainability. In: Chang, et al. (eds.) The Third International Conference on Cloud Computing, IEEE Cloud 2010, Miami, Florida, USA, July 5-10 (2010b)

11. Chang, V., Li, C.S., De Roure, D., Wills, G., Walters, R., Chee, C.: The Finan-cial Clouds Review. International Journal of Cloud Applications and Computing 1(2), 41–63 (2011a) ISSN 2156-1834, eISSN 2156-1826

12. Chang, V., De Roure, D., Wills, G., Walters, R., Barry, T.: Organisational Sus-tainability Modelling for Return on Investment: Case Studies presented by a National Health Service (NHS) Trust UK. Journal of Computing and Information Technology 19(3) (2011b) (in press); ISSN Print ISSN 1330-1136 | Online ISSN 1846-3908

13. Chang, V., De Roure, D., Wills, G., Walters, R.: Case Studies and Organisational Sustainability Modelling presented by Cloud Computing Business Framework. International Journal of Web Services Research (2011c) (in press) ISSN 1545-7362

14. Chang, V., Wills, G., Walters, R.: Towards Business Integration as a Service 2.0 (BIaaS 2.0). In: Chang, et al. (eds.) IEEE International Conference on e-Business Engineering, The 3rd International Workshop on Cloud Services - Platform Accelerating e-Business, Beijing, China, October 19-21 (2011d)

15. Chang, V., Wills, G., Walters, R.: The positive impacts offered by Healthcare Cloud and 3D Bioinformatics. In: Chang, et al. (eds.) 10th e-Science All Hands Meeting 2011, York, September 26-29 (2011e)

16. Chang, V., Wills, G., Walters, R., Currie, W.: Towards a structured Cloud ROI: The University of Southampton cost-saving and user satisfaction case studies. In: Chang, et al. (eds.) Sustainable Green Computing: Practices, Methodologies and Technologies (2012a)

17. Chang, V., Walters, R., Wills, G.: Business Integration as a Service. International Journal of Cloud Applications and Computing 2(1) (2012) ISSN 2156-1834, eISSN 2156-1826

18. Chang, V., Walters, R.J., Wills, G.: Cloud Storage in a private cloud deployment: Lessons for Data Intensive research (Best student paper). In: Chang, et al. (eds.) The Second International Conference on Cloud Computing and Service Sciences (CLOSER 2012), Porto, Portugal (2012c)

19. Chang, V., Wills, G.: A University of Greenwich Case Study of Cloud Computing – Education as a Service. In: E-Logistics and E-Supply Chain Management: Applications for Evolving Business. IGI Global (2013)

20. Chang, V., Walters, R.J., Wills, G.: The development that leads to the Cloud Computing Business Framework. International Journal of Information Management (February 2013)

21. Grigoriadis, A., Chang, V., Schuitevoerder, M., Gillet, C., Tutt, A., Holmberg, L.: Cancer Cloud Computing - Towards an Integrated Technology Platform for Breast Cancer Research., Internal NHS Technical Paper (July 2009)

22. Hey, A.J.G.: The fourth paradigm: data-intensive scientific discovery. Microsoft Publication (2009) ISBN-10: 0982544200

23. Kagermann, H., Österle, H., Jordan, J.M.: IT-Driven Business Models: Global Case Studies in Transformation. John Wiley & Sons (2011)

24. Latch, E.K., Dharmarajan, G., Glaubitz, J.C., Rhodes. Jr., O.E.: Relative performance of Bayesian clustering software for inferring population substructure and individual assignment at low levels of population differentiation. Conservation Genetics 7, 295–302 (2006), doi:10.1007/s10592-005-9098-1

25. Moore, R.W., Baru, C., Marciano, R., Rajasekar, A., Wan, M.: Data-Intensive Computing. In: The Grid: Blueprint for a New Computing Infrastructure, ch. 5 (1999) ISBN 1558609334

26. Moretti, C., Bulosan, J., Thain, D., Flynn, P.J.: All-Pairs: An Abstraction for Data-Intensive Cloud Computing. In: IEEE International Symposium on Parallel and Distributed Processing, IPDPS 2008, Miami, USA, April 14-18 (2008)

27. Vo, H.T., Chen, C., Ooi, B.C.: Towards Elastic Transactional Cloud Storage with Range Query Support. Proceedings of the VLDB Endowment 3(1-2) (September 2010)

Author Index